Mass communication:
teaching and studies at universities

Mass communication: teaching and studies at universities

A world-wide survey on the role
of universities in the study of
the mass media and mass communication

May Katzen, M. A., Ph. D.
Centre for Mass Communication Research,
University of Leicester, United Kingdom

The Unesco Press   Paris 1975

Published by the Unesco Press,
7 Place de Fontenoy, 75700 Paris
Printed by Imprimeries Réunies, Lausanne

ISBN 92-3-101158-8

© Unesco 1975
Printed in Switzerland

Preface

The term 'communication revolution' has frequently been used in recent years to describe one aspect of the changing world, and it is true that accelerating technology in the post-war period has provided us with the transistor radio, electromagnetic recording—first of sound then of image, instantaneous world-wide transmission of signals through communication satellites, photo-composition and high-speed presses, computer storage and retrieval of information, to mention but a few examples. At the same time, newly independent countries have been quick to understand the importance of communication in the process of nation-building and national development, and hence to appreciate their need for trained communicators, while the more industrialized countries which for long had taken the press, the radio, the cinema and television for granted have begun to question the impact of new communication techniques on their societies, have been faced with the need to take policy decisions, and so have recognized the need for more concentrated research on the processes and effects of communication in the broader social setting.

Meanwhile, the role and purpose of universities have been subject to re-examination. The report of the International Commission on the Development of Education notes that in earlier times the patterns of higher education

> . . . doubtless responded to objective requirements for the development of knowledge. But today, this legacy must be reappraised in light of contemporary needs. Universities are more directly open to the movement of ideas than other educational institutions and more immediately required to keep up to date in the fields of scientific and technical education.
>
> *Both force of circumstance and social and intellectual criticism are subjecting universities to increasing pressure, requiring the university establishment to adapt more dynamically to the realities and needs of a rapidly changing world.*[1]

The nature of university involvement in mass communication studies has varied over time and location. Practical training in journalism within a university framework was being attempted in the United States of America before the end of the nineteenth century whereas in Europe it is almost entirely a post-war phenomenon. On the other hand, academically oriented study of the press can be traced back to the seventeenth century, notably in Germany. There has been a spectacular growth of professional training in the developing countries since the 1950s, while mass communication

---

1. *Learning to Be*, p. 9, Paris and London, Unesco and Harrap, 1972.

research, after an apparent period of stagnation, seems to be taking off with renewed vigour as researchers all over the world seek to broaden the perspectives and develop new methods for the study of the mass media. The breaking down of traditional, watertight faculty structures may well serve the advancement of this essentially interdisciplinary field of study.

At a time of renewed interest in the whole question of the role and functioning of mass communication, in the promises and possible dangers it holds out for society, it appeared appropriate to carry out a broad study of the part played by universities in this field, to examine the patterns of growth and the influences that have affected it, and to draw conclusions which may serve as guidelines for future development. Unesco invited the Centre for Mass Communication Research of the University of Leicester to undertake this study, which was entrusted to May Katzen. While the responsibility for opinions expressed remains that of the author, Unesco wishes to express its appreciation to Dr Katzen and to the Centre for Mass Communication Research for the thorough and painstaking work they have accomplished, as well as to the many respondents from all parts of the world who provided information and advice.

Contents

Introduction *9*

United States of America and Canada
        Overview *17*, United States of America *19*, Canada *56*.

Europe   Overview *69*, Austria *83*, Belgium *85*, Czechoslovakia *90*, Denmark *92*, Finland *95*, France *99*, German Democratic Republic *105*, Federal Republic of Germany *107*, Hungary *114*, Ireland *116*, Italy *117*, Netherlands *124*, Norway *128*, Poland *129*, Portugal *132*, Romania *133*, Spain *133*, Sweden *135*, Switzerland *139*, Turkey *141*, Union of Soviet Socialist Republics *142*, United Kingdom *145*, Yugoslavia *154*.

Australasia   Overview *157*, Australia *158*, New Zealand *161*.

Africa   Overview *163*, Algeria *172*, Cameroon *173*, Egypt *173*, Kenya *174*, Madagascar *175*, Nigeria *175*, Senegal *177*, South Africa *178*, Tunisia *179*, Zaire *180*, Zambia *181*.

Asia   Overview *183*, Afghanistan *188*, China *188*, Hong Kong *189*, India *191*, Indonesia *197*, Iran *199*, Iraq *200*, Israel *201*, Japan *202*, Republic of Korea *211*, Lebanon *213*, Malaysia *214*, Pakistan *215*, Philippines *216*, Singapore *222*, Thailand *223*, Republic of Viet-Nam *224*.

Latin America Overview *227*, Argentina *234*, Brazil *236*, Central America *242*, Chile *243*, Colombia *244*, Ecuador *245*, Mexico *246*, Peru *249*, Venezuela *251*.

Conclusion *253*

Appendix: a note on the survey methods employed *267*

References *271*

Introduction

This study arose as one result of the meeting of experts convened by Unesco in Montreal in June 1969, which discussed the impact of mass communication on society, the present state and organization of mass communication research, the need for research into new fields, and the need for co-operative action on the national and international levels (Unesco, 1970*a*).

The terms of reference of this study were

> to prepare a report on the role of universities all over the world in teaching and research on mass media as social institutions and mass communication as a social process.

The report was to include:
> (a) the professional training of journalists, broadcasters, producers, directors and other media practitioners;
> (b) the teaching of mass communications or special aspects of it (e.g. the press, television, radio, the cinema, etc.) in university departments or specialized institutes;
> (c) systematic appreciation and criticism of the output of any of the mass media, in university departments;
> (d) research into any of the mass media or into mass communications.

Mass media studies, as a problem area within the field of the humanities and the behavioural sciences, have come within academic range in universities only since the first decade of the twentieth century. Systematic education and investigation, however, have developed much more recently, roughly speaking after the Second World War, and more particularly in the 1960s. In many countries the field is still seen as marginal to older disciplines with fairly well demarcated fields of scope; in others it is not yet considered to be suitable for university education.

Its growth as an academic field all over the world is very uneven, and in some cases an early start has not necessarily meant a fuller development later. To some extent the growth of mass media studies in universities is linked with the development of the media themselves, and especially the extent to which they serve mass audiences, in any particular country. Thus the great interest which exists in the United States, or in Japan, comes as no surprise. However, in Great Britain for example, which has a highly developed system of mass communications with mass audiences, the systematic study of the mass media through teaching or research has barely begun to penetrate the universities.

On the other hand, the development and extension of mass communication through the mass media has often been taken as a 'modernizing' index,[1] at once the partial effect, as well as the partial cause of economic development, industrialization, urbanization, specialization, mass production and consumption, the use of modern technology, and the social and ideological transformations which accompany these processes. Many Asian and African countries are anxious to develop and extend their mass communications systems as part of wider social education plans, particularly for promoting literacy, modern agricultural methods, birth control and so on, and some countries like France hope to use mass media for schemes of cultural or social promotion. In such cases, mass media studies aimed at training communicators may be undertaken in order to promote and anticipate the growth of mass communication, or, as one Latin American writer (Fernandez, 1966) put it,

> to change, to a large extent, the contents of the messages of the press, radio and television which should stimulate the development of the Latin American nations in every respect to a far greater extent than is the case now.

Therefore, although the development of the mass media in a particular country may be a necessary condition for the existence of mass media studies in its universities, it is by no means a sufficient condition.

Almost as important in determining whether or not mass media studies are undertaken in universities is the total pattern of evolution of higher education in a particular country, determined by its whole historical past, as well as the future goals set for institutions of higher learning, of which the universities form only one part.

J. C. Butterworth, Vice-Chancellor of the University of Warwick, speaking at the Tenth Congress of the Universities of the Commonwealth in 1969 (ACU, 1969) pointed out that:

> The evolution of universities is almost wholly determined by an extremely complex interplay of local forces. I suggest that the following four considerations exert an enormous influence upon the development of a university in any particular country: first, the character of the economy, such differences as the relative size of the public and the private sector; secondly, the character of the social system, the stratification system—indeed the selection of students is, of course, primarily determined by the social system and by the pattern of schools; third, the character of the political system; and fourth, the particular characteristics of the university itself.

Other influences, too, come to mind. One is the current economic situation at any particular time, the availability of finance for education in general and the priorities which govern its use, as well as the financial state of any individual university and its own set of priorities. Another is the influence exerted by one country over another. The obvious example is the legacy of a colonial past in many of the ex-colonial areas outside Europe, where Spanish, British, French and Dutch university systems have become rooted, together with the ethos associated with them. Nor should one forget the influence of the German university system on the Netherlands, Austria and Switzerland, or the United States system on that of Japan and the Republic of Korea.

The interplay of these factors, and particularly the amount of finance available for higher education at various times, may have a crucial influence on the actual number of universities in any particular country. Quite apart from any other differences in the pattern of university education between and within countries, this factor in itself may affect the extent and range of mass media studies undertaken in its universities.

---

1. This term is used in preference to 'modernization', to indicate that it is not only the 'developing' countries which are 'underdeveloped', but that every country may be seen as more or less underdeveloped in relation to others in terms of its use of new technology, and the extent to which each country's development may be advanced in some directions and retarded in others.

Introduction

The whole intellectual and cultural tradition in a particular country may have a decisive influence in hindering or encouraging university studies in mass communication, and determining the range and scope of such studies as are undertaken. This tradition helps to create an image of what is appropriate to be studied in a university, and to what end. In most countries, firm lines of demarcation exist not only between the goals, but sometimes also between subject areas considered fitting for universities as compared with other institutions of higher learning, and there is often considerable variation between one country and another. For example, journalism became a university subject in both the United States and Germany in the early years of the twentieth century, but in each country the conception of the subject was quite different. In the United States the courses were designed to train future professional journalists; in Germany they were purely academic studies of newspapers from the point of view of contemporary history, law and politics. One important reason for the difference in orientation was that the nineteenth-century German academic tradition was strongly rooted in idealist philosophy, and one of its main goals was to encourage conceptual systems of theoretical explanation of man and society, while the American tradition was far more pragmatic and encompassed professional training as part of its activities. Then again, within the universities themselves, traditionally established boundaries have been created between subject areas, expressed in the range of separate departments and in the grouping together of departments into faculties, each of which is demarcated from others whose disciplinary field is seen as distinctly different. The pattern of these university structures may vary markedly not only from country to country, but also between universities in the same country. The decision to place, say, a journalism degree course in the Faculty of Social Science, rather than the Faculty of Law, or of Economics, may considerably affect the total content and focus of that course.

Another factor which is very important indeed in determining whether or not mass media studies are undertaken at all in a particular university is the flexibility of the regulations for curricula and degrees. Even in new, or reorganized older universities, with administrative and curricular structures specifically designed to allow new career options, and a wide range of choice in subject courses according to students' needs and preferences, traditions are soon established, and temporary expedients become frozen into rules and regulations which are difficult to change. To quote Butterworth again (ACU, 1969):

> In the developing countries the so-called new universities develop remarkably quickly, they very rapidly become mature. I know even in Britain that in a new university if you want to do anything really new you have to do it in the first five years, or the arteries harden. There is a sense, you see, in which universities are like men: young men look forward, old men look back, and middle-aged men look around.

This condition of inflexibility may make it extremely difficult to introduce new areas of studies, particularly those which are conceived to be interdisciplinary or multidisciplinary, especially when costly equipment is needed.

One reason for this rapid onset of the mentality of old age is the tremendous hold of tradition in universities. Eric Bockstael and Otto Feinstein (1970) touch on this point in *Higher Education in the European Community*:

> To adapt the university to the economic and social conditions of the contemporary world, i.e. [to] the needs of the economy and democratization, is the principle which is accepted virtually unanimously throughout Europe ... But the difficulties in putting [it] ... into practice are enormous ... and do not fail to nourish passionate discussions and conflicts between the various powers involved in higher education ... Tradition is a crushing and ambiguous force [in] ... the academic community which remains largely

closed to the outsider. Educators who, as the 'technicians of education' preside over the destiny of the university, train and recruit each other [so that] 'at the scale of successive generations, two, three centuries of history seem amazingly short; only five to six generations of teachers separate us from the colleges of the Ancient Regime, and the generation that constitutes itself today will be but renewed at the approach of the year 2000. From which stems the force of tradition and the delay of education behind the state of society.'

Teachers want to be progressive but 'they want as much, or even more, to guard traditions which have proved successful', and the influence of these two opposed tendencies, 'in turn dominated and dominating [explains] . . . the fragmentary measures, the tentative procedures, and the oscillations which for almost 200 years have marked the history of education [in France]'.

Consequently, there may be a very long and difficult road to travel, with all sorts of pitfalls to overcome, between the point when a university decides to introduce a new programme of study, and the actual realization of this intention.

Even within the same university marked differences may exist between the course and degree requirements of one administrative unit and another. This may make it extremely difficult to introduce new courses which overlap older established curricular structures, or to modify them in the light of new concepts.

Even in the United States, which has a long tradition of university-based mass media studies, and where the 'credit' system provides far greater flexibility in curricula than in many universities elsewhere, this problem may arise. In the University of Oregon, for example, a committee (University of Oregon, 1970) appointed to consider education in broadcasting there, found that undergraduate students could

> now receive a liberal arts degree through the Department of Speech with a major in broadcasting or through the School of Journalism with an emphasis in broadcasting. Several courses are cross-listed. However, degree requirements are different . . . [It] found many defects in the current broadcast programs of the School of Journalism and the Department of Speech [including] . . . duplication of course work, lack of coordination of course work offerings, artificial limits imposed upon students through various requirements, and lack of program identification for students, faculty, administrators and financing.

Similar defects were found in the photography and film areas. Although a joint Master of Fine Arts programme had been initiated between the School of Journalism and the Department of Fine Arts,

> departmental requirements have severely limited the number of students who can participate and the current graduate quota system has prevented any new applicants. This tenuous program is at the mercy of established curricular areas, forcing a lack of continuity in its potential growth.

The flexibility of regulations is only one factor which comes into play. The range and scope of university activities in mass media studies (whether in training, teaching or research, or any combination of these) is also limited or extended by how far universities already undertake work in other areas on which modern mass media studies draw for concepts and methodologies: sociology, psychology, social psychology, statistics, aesthetics, literary criticism, rhetoric, linguistics, and information theory—to name some of the newer disciplines which have proved fruitful in the past twenty-five years, apart from the older disciplines like politics, law and history. Without doubt, the development of statistically based empirical social research in the United States has decisively influenced education and research concerning mass communication there. New currents of thought, particularly in sociology and social psychology, have affected modern conceptions of the functions and effects of mass communications, and the role of the mass media in society, which have spread all over the world. This has helped to create a new conception of 'the communicator' or 'the communicologist', which is more far-reaching and subtle than older views of 'the journalist', and which is coming into general acceptance, so that subjects like 'Introduction to Communication', 'Sociology of Information' and 'Psychology of Communication' are now included in professional training courses in many countries, partly as a result of the influence of Unesco.

But in Latin America, for instance, although the need for such courses may be accepted in principle, one reason why they cannot always be introduced, or why they cannot in many instances be adequately taught, is that sociology has not until recently been part of Latin American university curricula (Labbens, 1969). It is therefore very difficult to find university teachers with the necessary behavioural-science background to teach these courses. One of the most important contributions of the Centro Internacional de Estudios Superiores de Periodismo para América Latina (CIESPAL), the Unesco-sponsored institution set up in Quito, Ecuador, to improve journalism education in Latin America, has been its annual ten-week seminars for university teachers from schools of journalism or mass comunications, which provide intensive courses in these subjects. Similarly, a short course in survey methods organized by CIESPAL in 1969 has helped to initiate research on the audiences for, and the effects of, the mass media in many countries where the course was given.

In a country where these adjacent fields have not taken root in universities to any degree, and where there is a weak tradition (or no tradition at all) of mass media studies, an immense difficulty may be constituted by the fact that its own language or languages are not internationally used, at least in these fields. This may be a particularly acute problem in newly independent countries which are deliberately trying to foster the use of indigenous languages. This is still a very real problem in Latin America, although organizations like CIESPAL and some universities like the University of São Paulo in Brazil are undertaking translations of key textbooks and other publications for the teaching of mass communication. No doubt the fact that Spanish is the language of the whole of Latin America, except Brazil, and is so similar to Brazilian Portuguese, has aided the solution of the problem in this region. But in very many areas, like India, for instance, there is no common indigenous language, but a multitude of dictinct, dissimilar ones. When a European language like English, French or German is in common use among those who enjoy advanced education, there is a strong tendency to rely heavily for information and ideas on the publications that can be easily understood. In ex-colonial areas this may mean an even greater dependence than before on an outside culture. The consequence may be to stifle mass media studies which are genuinely related to local situations and needs, and to take over concepts and methods from other countries which have no relevance to actual conditions.

Finally, it is worth stating the obvious fact that apparently fortuitous events, and the personal interests of individuals may be important influences in the scope and direction of mass media studies. For instance, it has been said that the influence of the historian Karl Bücher, who founded one of the earliest departments for the study of newspapers, at the University of Leipzig, was one reason why empirical mass communication research failed to develop in German universities until recently. Conversely, the fact that so enormously talented and inventive a sociologist as Paul Lazarsfeld became interested in radio research in the United States before the Second World War must be counted as one reason for the development of empirical mass communication research there. Similarly, the setting up of the Television Research Committee by the Home Office in Great Britain in 1962 has been a crucial factor in co-ordinating and stimulating British mass communication research since the mid-1960s. On the other hand, there are innumerable anecdotes, apocryphal or otherwise, to indicate that the personal and disciplinary hostility of rival departments, say of Journalism and Speech in American universities, have made it impossible to introduce genuinely interdisciplinary studies in mass communication.

Nevertheless, as the later sections on individual countries make clear, universities account for much of the increase in mass media studies in institutions of higher learning all over the world. And in many countries universities are the main institutions which undertake work in this field.

But there are exceptions to this generalization, particularly in professional training. In Japan, for instance, although many universities have institutes or departments of journalism or mass communications, their courses do not give would-be entrants to media professions any particular advantage in securing a position; the media organizations themselves provide the technical and professional training they think necessary once new recruits have been chosen by competitive examination. In the Union of Soviet Socialist Republics and Finland, on the other hand, universities provide professional training, as do very many United States colleges and universities, and in Brazil, for instance, a bachelor's degree is necessary to enter a wide range of media occupations, including journalism and public relations. In Canada, professional training is undertaken both by universities and by tertiary-level educational institutions (community colleges) while in many countries there are schools of professional training run by journalist associations, or by privately run specialized institutions, that may or may not demand university-level entrance requirements. In Britain, the National Union of Journalists has a special scheme for training new recruits to the newspaper industry, and university training for journalism has only just begun again after a lapse of some thirty years. Film schools tend to be distinct institutions, but again, in some countries like Britain or Italy, there is a national film school as well as film study in universities.

Furthermore, universities are by no means the only institutions to investigate problems related to the mass media. In Canada, government commissions have often studied aspects of the mass media (a recent example being Senator Davey's Commission of Enquiry) while in Sweden, the Board of Psychological Defence was for many years one of the few institutions doing research into the psychological aspects of mass communication. Then again, in some countries, like Italy, or Germany, there are many specialized institutions engaged in research which are not attached to universities. In others, like Japan, or Finland, the media organizations play a significant part in undertaking fundamental research on mass communication, to say nothing of extensive market research in areas of media impact in many other countries.

The point to be stressed here is that in many countries other institutions besides universities engage in mass media studies. Merely to describe current university-based activities without taking into account, as far as possible, the total development of training, teaching and research in mass communication in any particular country, in whatever form it may take place, is to provide a very misleading picture.

These are only some of the considerations, briefly outlined, which have arisen in attempting to describe and evaluate the part played by universities in training, teaching and research in mass communication, and to compare and contrast the development of these activities in different countries.

Other, more specific, difficulties have complicated the seemingly simple task outlined in the Unesco brief which commissioned this research project. One problem was to reach a satisfactory definition of a university. As the foregoing discussion indicated, the term 'university' has a wide and varied application from country to country, deriving from historical circumstances. Consequently, an institution considered to be a university in one country, might not necessarily be so considered in another. A comparison of the entries in compendia like the *International Handbook of Universities*, *Minerva*, *World of Learning*, *The World List of Universities* and the

Introduction

Commonwealth Universities' Handbook reveals that although there is considerable agreement about some institutions which are universities by any standard, and others which are not, there is a fairly large shadowy middle ground in between. A related problem is how to compare the degrees offered by universities in different countries. There are so many different traditions concerning the length and standard of degrees in the world, that the problem of translating them in accordance with some common standard of undergraduate and post-graduate degree (say on British or American lines) is enormous.

The other main problem of definition was what to include under mass media studies. The field shades into such areas as public opinion, market research, the sociology of leisure, mass culture, diffusion of innovations, educational technology and interpersonal communication, to name only a few.

These problems have accompanied this investigation from the first stage of locating institutions engaged in mass media studies, through the framing of letters of inquiry and questionnaire forms, to the writing of this report on the role of universities in training, teaching and research on the social aspects of the mass media and of mass communications all over the world. The investigation began in February 1970 and continued until March 1971, when the report was started. A first draft was completed and was circulated for comments among experts in various countries, and the revised version of the report was completed in February 1973. The investigation took the form of a postal survey. Letters of inquiry, supplemented by a questionnaire, were addressed to every university in the world, and to all other non-university institutions which were known to be engaged in mass media studies. Most of the inquiries were made between February and June 1970, and most of the data collected relates to conditions in 1970. A detailed statement on the methodology and its problems is to be found in the Appendix. The institutions were located, and supplementary material about their activities was derived from various secondary sources including international and national compendia related to institutions of higher learning; reports by Unesco and other bodies published at various times on education and research in journalism and mass communications; current news reports in journals; calendars, syllabuses and reports brought out by the institutions concerned, and, of course, books and articles on the social aspects of the mass media and mass communication.

In this report, reference is sometimes made to such matters as the attitude of employers and media professionals to formal training for new entrants to media occupations, the attitude of universities towards professional training, teaching and research in mass communication, and the development and financing of mass media research. Ideally, the report should also consider other important factors, such as the mass media system and the diffusion of mass communication in a country, the role and policy of the State in the development of the mass media and of education, as well as the structure and organization of the university system. It would be impossible to attempt detailed consideration of all these points within the compass of a report of this kind. Consequently, admittedly important matters such as the university system, and the development of the mass media in any country, have been largely taken for granted unless informants there specifically referred to them, or unless there was sufficient secondary source material to attempt some discussion. As far as possible some idea of the historical development of mass media studies is presented for each country, so that changes could be noted. In accordance with the Unesco brief, the main emphasis has been placed on the activities of university-based institutions, but the work of other bodies has also been included, particularly in countries where university-based activity is slight, in order to provide a context for evaluation.

The general aim of this study was to provide an over-all survey of trends and tendencies in university involvement in mass media studies. It was not intended that

Mass communication: teaching and studies at universities

this volume should be a directory or fact book containing full and precise details of the activities of every university or similar institution which is engaged in training, teaching or research in this field. Such a compendium would no doubt be valuable in its own way, but the rapid extension of mass media studies in universities in recent years, and the changes in curriculum and in research activities that are taking place would soon render such detailed description out of date. Accordingly it was decided to present the information which has been gathered together in two different ways. In the first place, a general introduction to each geographical region attempts to provide an over-all perspective on the development of mass media studies as an academic field. There are six such overviews: for the United States and Canada, Europe, Australasia, Africa, Asia and Latin America. Each overview is then followed by a detailed description of those countries in each regional area where there was sufficient evidence of university-based activities to warrant a separate entry. These country-by-country entries are arranged in alphabetical order within each region. The concluding chapter of the book presents an analysis of the survey data contained in the completed questionnaires and highlights some of the broader issues raised in earlier sections.

It is impossible to thank by name all those through whose assistance this report has been written—merely to list them would take up several pages. But I should like to express my deep gratitude to all those who filled in the long questionnaire and to record how pleasant the task of undertaking this survey has been made by the hundreds of letters I have received from people all over the world who have explained the history and present state of mass media studies in their countries and have given me their truly invaluable advice and comments. From first to last my inquiries have been met with warm cordiality, courtesy and helpfulness. I should also like to give special thanks to those informants who so kindly read the various drafts of this report, corrected errors of fact or interpretation and added new information; to J. D. Halloran and to other colleagues at the Centre for Mass Communication Research, University of Leicester and to Pierre Navaux and other members of the Mass Communication Department of Unesco (under whose sponsorship this study was launched) whose support and advice have been unfailing; and finally to the secretarial staff of the Centre for Mass Communication Research who typed, retyped and checked this manuscript with such cheerful, willing and patient efficiency.

United States of America and Canada

Overview

The development of mass media studies in the universities of the United States and Canada provides an interesting example of how two countries in the same regional area may present a very different, even a contrasting picture, in terms of the establishment and growth of a new field of academic interest.

Since the establishment of training programmes for newspaper journalism in the first decade of the twentieth century, mass media studies has been a rapidly expanding and widely proliferating field in United States universities. In no other country in the world are so many universities involved in specialized training for the whole gamut of media-based occupations—in newspapers, magazines, advertising, public relations, radio and television broadcasting and the movie industry—as well as in education, government and other fields. Academically oriented teaching about the social aspects of the mass media and mass communication has also become very widespread at undergraduate and post-graduate level since the Second World War, and takes place in a great variety of different units of varying size and complexity. Mass communication research has become a distinct, specialized field of academic investigation, and has probably attracted more funds for its prosecution than anywhere else in the world. Moreover, the distinctive research orientations developed in the United States have provided so many fruitful results that the theoretical presuppositions and the methodologies most commonly employed elsewhere derive to a greater or lesser extent from American mass media research. From all these points of view, there can be no doubt that the United States is in the forefront of the development of mass media studies as an academic field.

The Canadian picture is somewhat different. Journalism training began only after the Second World War, some forty years later than in the United States, and only in the last decade has there been a significant and rapid expansion in the wider field of mass media studies in Canadian universities. The later, and slow development of academic interest in mass communication is partly to be attributed to Canada's very proximity to the United States, partly to its differing academic traditions. Only in recent years have more than a handful of Canadian universities offered specialized integrated undergraduate teaching programmes about the mass media, and post-graduate study is even more recent. Canadian mass communication research has also had a more difficult path to tread than that in the United States. Although much important work on the mass media has been undertaken by *ad hoc* teams including academic research workers, assembled on the initiative and under the aegis of bodies such as government commissions of inquiry, the growth of permanent research units within universities has been far more limited than in the United States. However the recent upsurge of interest in the mass media in Canada, and the general recognition of their crucially important potential in forging a distinctive Canadian national consciousness based on bi-culturalism makes it very likely that mass communication studies will increase substantially in future.

Because of the very different situation of mass media studies in the universities of the United States and of Canada, the two sections that follow are different in length and in arrangement. Whereas in the Canadian section, as in those of most other countries, the specific details of current teaching and research in different universities are presented, this is not the case with the United States. Because of the long history of the subject, and the large number of institutions involved, far more material from primary and secondary sources was available from the United States than from anywhere else in the world. This fact, while it rules out the possibility of giving a detailed picture of the current activities of all, or even of the major universities involved in mass media studies, yet made it possible to trace the historical development of the field in the United States in a general and more analytical way. It also seemed fitting to do so, since the history of mass media studies in the United States forms such an important part of the history of the field in general. But there is also an additional reason that the section on the United States is differently organized and presented from all the others in this volume. Particularly since the Second World War education and research about the mass media has been widely extended all over the world and new departments and institutes have been established, frequently with the help of visiting American professors. In such cases, it has been natural to take the American version of departmental organization, field of study and methodology as a model. From many points of view this is inevitable and wise. But there is a danger that mass media studies in other countries may become overly dominated by the influence of the United States, and that the field may hence become lacking in the vitality it needs to encompass the different social and cultural situations within which the mass media operate all over the world. Thus there may be some importance in demonstrating in fair detail that the American pattern of education and research has developed over the years in response to particular, historical situations in the United States, and that it was influenced to a great degree by these sometimes accidental factors. If this background is known, administrators, educators and research workers in other countries may be in a better position to decide what to accept or reject of the American pattern in organizing their own educational systems in the mass media field, and in planning their own research priorities.

United States of America

Mass media education in the United States

Mass media education in universities and colleges in the United States presents a picture of almost bewildering diversity. Its most obvious manifestation is in the multitude of different titles for the specialized departments, schools, colleges or institutes within universities which have developed in great profusion, particularly since the Second World War—a variety of usage which is not always uniform between one institution and another. Mass media studies may take place in departments of journalism, technical journalism, agricultural journalism, broadcast journalism, mass communication(s), communication(s), communication arts and/or sciences, broadcasting, broadcast arts, radio–television, radio–television–film, television, telecommunications, visual communication(s), film, cinema, motion pictures, speech and/or drama, theatre (arts), or speech communication(s), to name only some variations. Furthermore there is little standardization of usage even in the terms most commonly used. For example, Paul V. Peterson (1970a), commenting on his 1969 survey of journalism education in United States colleges and universities, stated:

> There was some confusion in the simple questionnaire that has become a part of the . . . enrolment survey. That confusion is over a definition of what constitutes journalism. Some schools indicated that they had no major in journalism but did have one in 'communications'. In addition, there was no clarification of exactly what is taught at those schools which claim an offering in journalism.

There is considerable diversity in the kind of topics a journalism department might be expected to offer. While one journalism department might only teach courses relating to the press, another might deal also with the news gathering, processing and other informational functions of radio and television. Similarly, it is impossible to tell *a priori* whether a mass communications department focuses its attention on the press or broadcasting or both, whether it stresses the informational aspect of the mass media or treats entertainment functions as well, or whether all the individual media are regarded as components of a total social communication process.

> In some cases mass communication only means broadcasting, in others broadcasting and film, in still others broadcasting, film and journalism or (rarely) journalism exclusively. (Orlik, 1970.)

Some sociology departments are also involved in the study of mass communication (Stehr and Larson, 1972).

A correspondent who had just completed a study of mass communication education in the United States, based on a listing of journalism schools in the *Journalism Educator* reported

> a significant difference between schools offering 'journalism' and those offering 'mass communication'. The former emphasized techniques while the latter emphasized theory. Journalism majors usually take courses of a how-to-do-it nature, while the mass communication major generally takes a core of technique and theory courses plus liberal arts courses for support. I got several violent reactions to the word 'mass communication' from the

more traditional schools and some of the press—I suppose people just resist change. (De Santo, 1970.)

On the other hand, it was also felt that

> divergent viewpoints are particularly evident when one compares mass communication programs in schools of journalism and mass communication programs affiliated with schools or departments of speech or radio, television, film. (Roever, 1970.)

Similar divergences were felt to exist between the teaching of broadcasting in a journalism department as compared with a speech department:

> Broadcasting as taught within a Journalism fabric tends to be geared towards commercial newsgathering and transmission as well as the preparation of advertising. As taught within a Speech framework, more stress is placed on performance, aesthetics of production and educational broadcasting. Any good curriculum, of course, should encompass both approaches. (Orlik, 1970.)

It seems, therefore, that the diversity of terms used to describe departments and their programmes reflects a great variety of approaches and orientations (amounting almost to confusion) as between practical, professional or theoretical emphases, as well as in the extent and range of subject-matter considered appropriate within various boundaries.

These differences may be explained partly in terms of a sort of evolutionary process, which has proceeded very far in the large interdisciplinary graduate schools, and which can be seen repeating itself in various embryonic stages, particularly in smaller universities or colleges. A brief consideration of the history of mass media studies in the United States may help to explain the present situation, which is rooted in two rather different academic traditions, those of journalism and speech, which were both affected by differing pressures from potential employers on the one hand, and from the demands of their academic setting on the other. These pressures were intensified by the advent of broadcasting, and particularly of television, and by the development of mass communication research, which cut across hitherto fairly well demarcated fields.

Development of journalism education in universities and colleges

University education for journalism was probably first mooted in 1869 by General Robert E. Lee, then president of Washington College (now Washington and Lee University) in Virginia, who felt a good press would help to solve the post-Civil War reconstruction of the South (Desmond, 1949). The attempt was short-lived, however, and though several other colleges and universities made sporadic efforts to offer journalism instruction in the succeeding years of the nineteenth century 'most of these early efforts were short-lived and lacked continuity' (Siebert, 1956). Continuous, specialized, professionally oriented journalism training dates from the early twentieth century when the number of universities and colleges increased rapidly and when, under the dominance of the pragmatic philosophy it was considered appropriate to train new specialists there. A landmark in the history of journalism education occurred in 1903 when Joseph Pulitzer agreed to donate $2.5 million to establish a journalism school at Columbia University so that journalism might have the same advantages of special training as were provided for medicine, law and other professions. By the time the Columbia School of Journalism opened in 1912, journalism education had made considerable progress. In 1904, the University of Illinois began a full four-year programme and the University of Wisconsin also began courses, while in 1908 the University of Missouri opened the first journalism school as a separate entity. Over 30 universities and colleges offered courses by 1912, 455 by

United States of America and Canada

TABLE 1. Journalism education in the United States, 1948-70 (selected colleges and universities)

Year	Number of institutions surveyed	Total enrolment	Annual increase (%)	Graduate enrolment	Degrees awarded		
					B.A./B.S.	Graduate	Total
1948	73	16,619	n.s.[1]	n.s.	n.s.	n.s.	n.s.
1951	70	9,399	n.s.	n.s.	n.s.	n.s.	n.s.
1955	96	11,482	n.s.	n.s.	n.s.	n.s.	n.s.
1960	101	11,390	n.s.	1,041	n.s.	n.s.	2,740
1961	109	12,368	8.6	1,208	n.s.	n.s.	2,541
1962	96	13,137	6.2	1,258	n.s.	n.s.	2,623
1963	105	14,624	11.4	1,481	n.s.	n.s.	2,911
1964	107	15,820	8.3	1,542	2,595	438	3,033
1965	119	19,229	21.5	1,916	2,897	519	3,416
1966	118	22,339	16.2	2,360	3,186	602	3,788
1967	118	24,445	13.3	2,627	3,694	793	4,487
1968	124	27,483	12.4	2,688 (316)	4,448	872	5,320
1969	145	31,251	13.7	3,268 (357)	5,577	946	6,523
1970	162	33,106	5.9	3,692 (355)	6,524	1,077	7,601

1. n.s. = not surveyed.
2. Figures in parentheses denote Ph.Ds.
Source: Journalism Quarterly, 1960-70.

the mid-thirties and 672 by 1953 (Emery *et al.* 1965; Unesco, 1958). During the 1950s, although new journalism or communications departments were appearing among the smaller colleges in considerable numbers, the number of journalism majors remained remarkably constant (Duncan, 1961). But this stagnation in enrolment was temporary (Jones, 1968), and during the 'joyful sixties' both the number of institutions offering courses and the number of students enrolled continued to increase. In 1969, 1,148 out of 2,313 institutions of higher education offered some form of journalism education including 719 senior (four-year) colleges, of which 212 offered full major programmes, and 429 junior (two-year) colleges, of which 77 offered major courses (P. V. Peterson, 1970a, 1970b). As Table 1 indicates, enrolments increased also in the 1960s but the great rate of increase was diminishing by the end of the decade.

Journalism education has had to proceed in the face of two opposing sets of critics. The most important potential employers of journalism graduates—editors and publishers—long doubted whether there was any substitute for on-the-job training in a newspaper office, and tended to be suspicious of university graduates. On the other hand, a strong body of opinion in academic circles regarded journalism as mere 'trade-school work', and doubted that it belonged properly in a university at all. The caustic remark of Robert M. Hutchins, Chancellor of Chicago University, in 1938, that journalism schools were 'the shadiest educational ventures under respectable auspices' exemplifies this attitude.

Both these opposing attitudes still exist today, though less strongly than in earlier years. As one journalism professor explained (Van Winkle, 1970):

> In the past—let us say fifty years ago—most editors would laugh at the suggestion that they might want to employ graduates of schools or departments of journalism. In fact many editors were actually hostile to the idea that a student could learn news reporting and writing in college, and a few still are. That condition, however, has begun to change, and the change is fairly widespread. For example, the past ten years has seen an increasing number of newspapers and public relations officers and agencies sending

representatives to this campus, and to other campuses, to interview seniors in journalism as prospective employees. The representatives come from the larger and more progressive newspapers and firms; the smaller papers have shown no such aggressiveness in searching out the best graduating seniors for employment.

Nor has academic reserve been entirely dispelled, despite the great proliferation of courses, departments and schools in the United States, especially since the Second World War. The sense of pressure experienced by university journalism teachers was summed up bitterly by John C. Merrill of the University of Missouri School of Journalism (Walsh, 1968), who pointed out that practising journalists complained about professors' lack of media experience, while academicians in other disciplines complained that journalism professors did not measure up sufficiently in their degree and scholarship standards:

> Ideally, to satisfy both groups of critics, the journalism professor would be a man who has worked in the mass media for ten years, won a Pulitzer prize, acquired a doctorate and made a reputation as an outstanding researcher and teacher. In no other academic discipline is anything like this required of professors.

In the face of this cross-fire of pressures, journalism education in the United States has undergone some fundamental changes in subject-matter and in approach. In the early years, the teaching emphasis was almost entirely vocational and technical. Then, after the First World War, more academically oriented courses in press history, law and ethics began gradually to be introduced, followed by courses on current affairs, public opinion and the press as a social institution. During the inter-war period, some journalism schools and departments also began to include among the basic courses in news writing and editing, courses in related fields such as advertising, public relations and radio. Nevertheless, by the beginning of the Second World War, the overwhelming curricular emphasis was still on newspaper journalism and most departments still had comparatively small staffs (largely ex-journalists, not all of whom had postgraduate education, and a few no college degree whatever), who had to teach 'a frightening array of narrowly technical courses' (T. Peterson, 1960). But it appears that by then the main lines of the present standard undergraduate newspaper journalism curriculum had been firmly laid down (Walsh, 1968), and that after a period of very varied methods of training a fairly consistent approach to radio courses had also developed (Unesco, 1958).

The improved standards in journalism education visible by the late 1930s had come about partly as a result of the formation of the American Association of Teachers of Journalism in 1912 (renamed the Association for Education in Journalism (AEJ) in 1949) and of the American Association of Schools and Departments of Journalism (AASDJ) in 1917, which, by establishing standards for institutional membership, helped to improve the general quality of teaching. These two organizations established the periodical *Journalism Quarterly* (originally called *Journalism Bulletin*) in 1924, the recognized professional journal in the field. In 1939 the American Council on Education for Journalism (ACEJ) was founded to set and raise standards in journalism education by evaluating and accrediting sequences [1] at the request of the institution concerned, by means of a thorough on-site inspection by a group of examiners. It consisted of the AASDJ and of editors' and publishers' organizations. In 1944, another professional journalism education body, the American Society of Journalism School Administrators (ASJSA), was formed, partly in protest at what was felt to be a monopoly in journalism education by schools belong-

---

1. A sequence is a group of related courses intended to prepare the student for specialization in a particular area.

ing to the AASDJ. Both bodies, however, became co-ordinate bodies of the AEJ in 1950, and at the same time representatives of AEJ, ASJSA and AASDJ were represented on ACEJ. The ACEJ began its first accrediting programme in 1946, and issued its first accredited list of sequences in 1948 (ACEJ, 1970).

These developments, particularly those connected with the founding of the ACEJ, seem to indicate that American journalism educators had developed a considerable degree of *esprit de corps* and some unanimity on what constituted their field of study, and that they were willing to co-operate with media organizations in raising standards for the profession, particularly from the point of view of the needs of the newspaper industry.

But it was the period after the Second World War that constituted the real watershed in mass media education in the United States. Two main features of change may be distinguished. In the first place, the range of journalism education was greatly extended. Before the Second World War journalism schools had been almost entirely concerned with newspaper journalism. In the post-war period training for a number of new specialized fields assumed more and more importance. In the second place, journalism education became more research-minded. Some of the larger schools absorbed into their undergraduate curricula the results of mass media research hitherto conducted largely outside journalism schools, mainly by psychologists, social psychologists and political scientists; they began to employ more Ph. D.s schooled in quantitative behavioural-science research techniques; they began to embark on graduate programmes and to conduct research into the mass media themselves. The first change reflects the impact of changing conditions in the mass media industries on journalism education; the second reflects a new urge on the part of journalism education to gain full acceptance within the academic community. The combined operation of these two sets of changes would produce by the later 1960s some fundamental changes in attitude among mass media educators regarding the nature and functions of university-level mass media studies in the United States.

Expanding range of journalism education after the Second World War

After the end of the Second World War journalism schools
> looked beyond their newspapers to increase their offerings in radio and television, in trade and technical journalism, in public relations and . . . in some institutions advertising changed from an adjunct of the journalism curriculum into an independent curriculum with decreasing emphasis on techniques. (T. Peterson, 1960.)

These developments reflected an adjustment to the rapid expansion and swift change in the modes of mass communication in the United States particularly since the Depression. After the Second World War there was a vastly increased range of employment opportunities for college and university graduates, especially in view of the increasing drive towards professionalism in fields like radio and television broadcasting, public relations and advertising. The changing composition of the media organizations represented on the American Council on Education for Journalism is one index of the adjustment of American journalism education to new post-war conditions. In 1945, the only media organizations on the ACEJ were connected with the press—the American Newspaper Publishers Association, the American Society of Newspaper Editors, the Inland Daily Press Association, the National Newspaper Association and the Southern Newspaper Publishers Association. Since then membership has been extended to the National Association of Broadcasters (1952), the Magazine Publishers' Association (1957), the American Business Press (1965), and the Public Relations Society of America Inc. (1968). Other media organizations have been affiliated as associate members, including the International Association of

TABLE 2. Distribution of fields in journalism education in the United States, 1967 and 1970

Year	Number of schools represented	Field of journalism education								
		News editorial	Advertising	Radio-television	Public relations	Magazine	Agriculture	Community	Photo	Other
		%	%	%	%	%	%	%	%	%
1967 [1]	118	46.3	25.5	10.9	6.3	3.3	1.6	0.7	0.8	4.6 [2]
1970 [3]	57	49.5	22.3	9.7	6.8	5.8	1.0	1.0	1.0	2.9 [4]

1. *Journalism Quarterly* poll (N = 12,038 students).
2. Including students specializing in other subjects and students who were undecided.
3. ACEJ sequences (N = 103 sequences).
4. Including 2 technical journalism and 1 publishing sequence.
Sources: Journalism Quarterly; ACEJ, 1970 Accredited Programs in Journalism.

Business Communicators (1956), the International Newspaper Advertising Executives (1957), the Radio-Television News Directors' Association (1959), the National Press Photographers Association (1961), the National Conference of Editorial Writers (1962), the Associated Press Managing Editors Association (1968) and the International Newspaper Promotion Association (1969).

In 1970, the list of 103 sequences accredited in 57 schools by the ACEJ (see Table 2) consisted of 51 news editorial programmes (news and public affairs, reporting and editing), 23 advertising (advertising and advertising management), 10 radio-television (radio-television news, radio-television-film), 7 public relations, 6 magazine (professional writing), 2 technical journalism, 1 agriculture and home economics, 1 community journalism, 1 photojournalism and 1 publishing sequence. The relative distribution of these sequences roughly reflects the latest available information on the distribution of specialities chosen by third- and fourth-year undergraduate students in the annual poll conducted by *Journalism Quarterly*, which includes a large number, though not all, of the non-accredited journalism schools.

One aspect of the increased range of offerings available to journalism students was the post-war extension of pre-professional training to cover the more specialized areas of print journalism and the particular expertise associated with trade and technical publications. But probably more important in the development of new attitudes to what journalism teaching should be, was the fact that journalism departments began to be more concerned with fields which were also included in other subject areas, and which were essentially and ideally multidisciplinary or interdisciplinary in character. For example, public-relations teaching had developed mainly under the aegis of journalism since the 1920s, but was sometimes also taught in courses on public opinion or business administration. A 1964 study (Hiebert, 1965) of college and university teachers of public relations showed that 58 per cent held positions in schools of journalism or communication, 15 per cent taught in business administration departments, and 14 per cent were in several different disciplines. The study of public opinion itself, with its roots in social psychology and statistics, and its application particularly to politics and political behaviour, became a more prominent feature of the journalism curriculum after 1948, when its methods became more reliable and its results more authoritative. Advertising, too, straddles a variety of academic subject areas besides journalism, including commerce, marketing, psychology, social psychology, sociology and even design.

But, of all these extensions in the subject-matter of undergraduate curricula, probably the one with most impact on the development of mass media education in the United States was the great extension of broadcasting education after the Second World War and particularly from about 1956, with the advent of television courses.

United States of America and Canada

Development of education for broadcasting

The first radio licences in the United States were issued in the 1920s, but it was some time before radio broadcasting was seen as
> more than a special mode of transmitting at second hand the materials of other communications media . . . a mere transmission belt . . . relegated to a secondary, semi-parasitic role among the media

and emerged as a primary communication medium in its own right. *Pari passu*, for some time broadcasting was not considered fit for specialized academic instruction, but in the 1930s radio courses were introduced into the curricula of many colleges and universities as an aspect of other, already established fields. In 1938, over 300 institutions were offering at least one course in radio (Head and Martin, 1956–57).

Thus, although specialized degrees in broadcasting were first inaugurated in the early 1930s (the first master's degree at the University of Wisconsin in 1931, the first Ph. D. programmes at the universities of Wisconsin and Iowa in 1939), usually courses in radio were introduced in a piecemeal, *ad hoc* manner. In the same way that many journalism departments evolved through a member of the English department taking responsibility for the college newspaper and then starting some course work, many institutions, like Wayne State University, first started a radio club, then began running a radio station and finally introduced some courses. Pre-war activity tended to focus on the purely electronic side, or on the educational uses of radio, rather than on providing professional training for careers in radio stations and networks. Northwestern University was one of the first to develop a professionally oriented curriculum, closely aligned to the requirements of the broadcasting industry in Chicago.

By 1948, over 400 universities and colleges offered at least one course in radio, in a variety of different academic units, including schools of fine art, departments of music, or business administration, and others. But the most important source of professional training for occupations in broadcasting were journalism and speech departments which respectively catered for prospective careers in the news, and the entertainment aspects of radio (Niven, 1961).

By the late 1940s about seventy-five universities and colleges offered a degree in broadcasting. Television was becoming an important medium by that time, and television courses were added, and came to constitute an important part of broadcasting curricula by the mid-1950s.

In journalism departments, after a period of extremely varied methods of training, by 1948 a fairly consistent approach among the leading schools was being developed. Then, with the advent of television, a transitional period of curricular experimentation set in. Some schools, including some larger ones, had separate radio and television news courses; others, especially the smaller ones, combined them. But by the mid-1950s, there was general agreement that radio or television journalism must be thoroughly grounded in general techniques of journalism—news gathering, writing and editing—and a sense of news values. Because of the importance of film in television, by 1955 it was estimated that about a third of the leading schools providing training in broadcast journalism included some training in the techniques of motion-picture photography. One feature of this transition period was the difficulty experienced, particularly by smaller departments, in providing students with the very costly equipment and materials necessary for training television news reporters and producers. In some cases sheer financial necessity led to a *rapprochement* between journalism and speech departments, rooted in the realization that it was impossible for each to have separate television studios for training purposes (Unesco, 1958).

The rise of motion pictures, radio and television as mass media with a demand for trained personnel gradually involved speech and theatre departments in training students in acting, directing, producing and announcing. Speech departments developed as separate academic units in the United States after 1841 when the first was founded. By the twentieth century they dealt with several subfields including rhetoric or the art of persuasion (a branch of philosophy), theatre arts (acting, producing and allied fields concerned with drama), speech pathology and audiology. Courses in radio, and later in television performance, production and direction fitted into the general framework of theatre arts, while more general aspects of broadcasting could be treated to some extent under the theoretical perspectives of rhetoric and public address. In some cases, as at the University of Michigan in the late 1940s, broadcasting courses were introduced primarily to provide students with a fuller range of performance experiences. In other cases, speech departments responded to the increasing demands for trained personnel from the broadcasting industries. When network radio became lucrative during the late 1930s, the radio industry, like the movie industry a decade earlier, looked to the theatrical profession for producers and performers, as did the television industry in the early 1950s. Speech and theatre departments began to include courses in radio acting, announcing and production into their curricula, and later assimilated television material, 'as television was . . . run by the same people who ran the radio industry'. Even today, though most large-audience entertainment programmes are made in Hollywood, the basic structures and personnel of the radio and television industries are the same (Hirsch, 1970).

By 1958–59, 89 colleges and universities offered bachelor's degrees in radio-television, 45 provided master's degrees, and 16 doctoral degrees. By 1971–72, there were almost twice that number providing bachelor's and master's degrees (180 offering bachelor's, 87 offering master's) while 27 schools were offering a doctoral degree in broadcasting. In time 'as the uniqueness of broadcasting became apparent', the need to cater for all aspects of broadcasting in a single academic programme became increasingly evident as the disadvantages of catering for particular, narrow aspects of the field in a variety of different academic settings grew more obvious.

> If broadcasting is drama, what about news? If it is news, what about music? If it is programs, what about sales? If it is sales, what about management? If management, what about production? And so on. (Head and Martin, 1956–57.)

During the course of the 1960s, although broadcasting courses were still offered in a variety of academic settings, including speech and journalism departments, there is a striking tendency, revealed in Table 3 below, towards the formation of separate broadcast departments or to bring broadcasting under the general umbrella of mass communication. Table 3, which compares the location of bachelor's degrees in 1958–59 with 1971–72, illustrates that the tendency to form communication departments has grown rapidly, and that they are now the most important source of undergraduate degrees in broadcasting.

One of the most difficult problems facing education for broadcasting was 'the development of some kind of mutual understanding about objectives, standards and methods'. As Head and Martin commented,

> The trouble was that so many . . . courses owed their primary allegiance to educational disciplines, not primarily concerned with broadcasting that the development of common understanding has been slow.

One method of setting up common objectives, standards and methods is through accreditation. Broadcasting news sequences offered in schools or departments with a predominantly journalism orientation may receive accreditation by the ACEJ which includes representatives of the professional journalism education associations (the AEJ, AASDJ and ASJSA) as well as representatives of the National Association of Broadcasters, the professional trade association for the broadcasting industry. In 1948, following the report of a committee to study the status of radio training which found that only ten out of over 500 schools were providing adequate education, the

United States of America and Canada

TABLE 3. Types of department offering bachelor's degrees in broadcasting in United States colleges and universities in 1958/59 and 1971/72

Department	1958/59 [1]	Percentage	1971/72 [2]	Percentage
Speech-Drama-Theatre	50	53.8	51	27.9
Journalism	6	6.5	7	3.8
Broadcasting	21	22.5	47	25.7
Communications	13	14.0	77	42.1
Other	3	3.2	1	0.5
Total [3]	93	100.0	183	100.0

1. Data refer to eighty-nine institutions.
2. Data refer to 180 institutions.
3. The total number of departments is larger than the number of institutions because some offer bachelor's degrees in broadcasting in more than one department.
Sources: Harold Niven, 'Fourth Annual Survey of Colleges and Universities Offering Course Work in Radio and Television, 1958-59', *Journal of Broadcasting*, No. 3, Autumn 1959, p. 353-7; Harold Niven, *Broadcast Education 1972, Thirteenth Report: Radio-Television Programs in American Colleges and Universities 1971-1972*, Washington, D. C., National Association of Broadcasters, 1972.

University Association for Professional Radio Education (UAPRE) was founded to act as an accrediting body (Martin, 1952). But it did not obtain the necessary recognition from the American Association of Schools and Colleges, and was superseded in 1955 when the Association for Professional Broadcasting Education (APBE) was established, sponsored by the National Association of Broadcasters. The APBE has no accreditation procedures, but, by working out its membership policy with the National Commission on Accreditation, it has left itself sufficient discretion in classifying its members to maintain some standards, but has avoided charges of dictatorship which accreditation might arouse. Nevertheless, in 1968 the APBE's committee on courses and curricula issued a two-volume series of composite courses, derived from those taught by its members to provide a consensus of what is being taught in institutions emphasizing broadcast education, and to serve as guidelines for others. These outlines are very detailed, and include the objectives and level of the course, the credit given, the texts used, and an extensive discussion of the topics treated. Most of the courses dealt with are production-oriented, and directed towards radio and television. Less than one-fifth are concerned with film (APBE, 1968, 1970).

The growth of film study

The study of the cinema in United States universities and colleges exhibits some features which appear to be unique to this branch of mass communications. Academic film study has a long history. As early as 1916, a dissertation on the cinema obtained a master's degree at the University of Iowa. The University of Southern California started a course on photoplay in 1929, and began offering major sequences in cinema for the bachelor's and master's degrees in 1932 and 1935 respectively. San Francisco State College also began its programme during the 1930s. However, possibly as a result of the Second World War, only five motion-picture courses were reported in United States universities and colleges in 1945. Twenty years later, however, the number had grown to 846 offered in over 241 institutions mostly of university status. These included audio-visual courses (the use of film for informational purposes, for the development of skills, and for increasing motivation for learning), film-production courses (writing, directing, producing, editing, composing and acting for motion pictures), courses on the history and aesthetics of the cinema (to develop students' awareness and critical judgement of film) and communication courses (on the social and psychological aspects of film as a medium of mass communication) (Kuiper *et al.*, 1966). Despite the expansion in film studies between 1945 and 1966, since then, as Thomas Fensch (1970) wrote in *Films on the Campus*:

> There has been an explosion in film interest on the nation's campuses that will not only continue, but increase, in the coming months and years . . . 'Create a Film Revolution', the National Student Association urges, and throughout the country students have responded . . . They have dramatically changed film instruction and film making on college and university campuses everywhere . . .
>
> It is a phenomenon not easily paralleled in the history of American higher education. Film-studies programs have proliferated at an amoeba-like rate . . . In the past, when a new department or area of study was needed on a campus [the administration formed] committees to study curricula and begin courses. Textbooks were compared and chosen by faculty members and degree requirements were established by executive fiat. In the past few years, however, the impetus for film study has come from students. They have *demanded* to be able to major in film making. *They* have forced university officials to hire professors . . . And when deans claim that there is no room in the . . . budget to buy cameras, students have bought their own.

Not only have many new full-time professors been hired who have received their training as commercial film workers or have graduated from one of the larger universities where film is taught, but, as John B. Kuiper (1972) observed:

> What has happened frequently is that professors in many disciplines have been given the opportunity to teach a new course on film.

The extent of the growth in film study may be illustrated by some statistics quoted by Fensch.

> Applications to the film program at the University of Southern California have doubled in the last five years; the film enrolment at the University of California at Los Angeles has more than doubled to over 450 students in the last four years. Boston University's film program had 125 students in 1965, 250 in 1967. Northwestern University has doubled its enrolment in film every year for the past three. The University of Iowa had 40 students in 1964; it now has nearly 100. Similar examples can be found at many other schools.

The *American Film Institute's Guide to College Film Courses* for 1970 includes 233 universities and colleges where film courses are taught, including 68 schools where a major sequence, at undergraduate or post-graduate level or both, is offered. This publication notes that budget allocations for film programmes in colleges and universities have seen an average increase of 301 per cent over the last five years—another indication of the growth of film study in higher education (Greensfelder, 1970).

Fensch attributes the current vogue for film to two factors. First, film provides a cheap,[1] quick medium for expressing student creativity, which can be quickly processed and judged, and which allows the student film-maker to work with others,

---

1. Cheap only in relation to commercial motion-picture production. Dr Kuiper (1972) writes: 'Even at a primary level student film making has proven to be relatively expensive and I find it difficult to agree with Fensch here . . . of course my reaction is tempered by knowledge of the present economic problems which beset American universities.'

rather than in solitude, unlike other modes like writing or painting. Second, there is a new, enthusiastic and knowledgeable student audience for movies of all kinds.

> There is a language of film now that did not exist earlier, and it is to the credit of astute college students that they have helped to develop and sustain it.

The study of film has become firmly rooted in United States colleges and universities as the number of degree programmes offered at bachelor's, master's and doctoral levels in 1970 shows.

In a survey of types of degree offered in film in sixty-eight United States colleges and universities offering film majors in 1970, a total of 62 bachelor's degrees (41 B.A.s, 10 B.F.A.s, 11 B.Sc.s), 47 master's degrees (29 M.A.s, 13 M.F.A.s, 5 M.S.s) and 10 doctoral degrees (10 Ph.D.s) were offered (Greensfelder, 1970).

Many institutions offer more than one type of bachelor's or master's degree. Some schools offer only undergraduate or only post-graduate degrees, others offer degrees from bachelor's through master's, to doctoral degrees. But, although the intervening years have seen great expansion in film courses, the statements made in 1966 by the Curriculum Committee of the University Film Association (Kuiper *et al.*, 1966), that 'there is no unanimity of opinion in educational circles concerning the proper justification for such courses' probably still has some force. There are still many colleges and universities where film is not yet fully accepted as a valid academic field of study, and where rigidities in academic structure impede its full development.

The range of departments in which film majors are offered is very wide. This fact partly reflects, and is partly responsible for, the variety of orientations towards film—professional training for the motion-picture industry, self-expression, film history, criticism and aesthetics—and the cinema as a medium of mass communication. All or some of these aspects may, of course, be considered in conjunction, as well as separately. Thus, there are a large number of specialized departments of film, cinema or cinematography which give degrees in film or some equivalent title (which accounted for about 40 per cent of all film degrees offered by United States colleges and universities in 1970). But major sequences in film also occur in departments of broadcasting, communication, mass communication, speech and/or theatre, fine arts (Greensfelder, 1970), as well as many other *milieux* including schools of education or engineering, and audio-visual centres—places where there are strong production units (Woodliff, 1971).

The location of courses (rather than major sequences) is even more varied. When the primary interest is in the language of film, in film aesthetics and history, courses may be taught in departments of English, art, humanities, education, even religion. Sometimes courses are given in more than one department and in such cases, interdepartmental rivalries may prevent the integration of a full-scale major sequence. In some colleges and universities, particularly in the smaller four-year liberal-arts colleges, courses in film-making and in the history and aesthetics of the cinema are being offered on an extra-curricular basis by interested faculty members.

In some ways, therefore, it seems that though formal academic study of the cinema is advancing rapidly, it is still lagging behind the extent of student interest in the field. One reason may be that, as P. B. Orlik (1970) of Central Michigan University opined,

> there is virtually no communication between the profession and the academic study of film, though some slight overtures are reportedly now being made. The professional directors, cinematographers and like craft unions are among the tightest in the country, allowing little entry from outside, and the Motion Picture Academy offers little more than Oscars.

Consequently, it would appear that professional associations among film educators have not developed to the same extent as in journalism or broadcasting education.

Dr Orlik continues:
> There is no counterpart to AEJ or APBE for film since (1) there is no industry willing to co-operate, (2) film study is so divergent from school to school and may be in Departments of Art, Journalism, Speech, Radio-Television, even Sociology, (3) film teachers may be members of the Speech Association of America, the APBE, AEJ or other organisations which give them some sort of professional home base, but none of which are geared to the needs of film education or study.

Nevertheless, it is true that several professional organizations cater for the needs of university film teachers. The most important of these are the Society of Cinema Studies (SCS) (formerly the Society of Cinematologists) and the University Film Association (UFA) (formerly the University Film Producers Association). Both these organizations publish a journal. The American Film Institute's Education Department also undertakes organizing work. A new organization, the National Association of Media Educators, was founded in 1971 (Young, 1971).

All in all, there seems reason to believe that film study will develop as an increasingly specialized field in its own right, as well as being integrated into programmes which treat other media of mass communication, especially television. At the same time, the cinema, as has been suggested above, already is and probably will continue to be treated essentially in a multidisciplinary or interdisciplinary manner.

Development of new administrative structures

To sum up, in the post-war period what had once been minor subfields developed into major subdivisions of interest which could no longer be easily accommodated within old-established administrative units. This was the case especially in the teaching of television broadcasting in departments of journalism and speech. For journalism departments, television involved the study of a new audio-visual medium which often presented fundamentally different problems from those of the traditional print media. For speech departments, too, the study of broadcasting involved a fundamental reorientation from individuals and small groups to mass audiences. Both journalism and speech departments appear, in the main, to have made similar adjustments to the problems imposed by coping with a new technology in the context of the simultaneous burgeoning of other important subfields (public relations, public opinion and advertising in the case of journalism, modern rhetoric, theatre arts, speech pathology and audiology in the case of speech). In both types of department there has been the development of more specialized teaching, resulting in more specialized administrative units, ranging from divisions within a department or school to the creation of separate departments.

In the early stages of these developments the result was often an administrative muddle and even from the point of view of pure administrative convenience a need arose to group together some, or all, of these different fields into one new overarching administrative unit.

As Theodore Peterson pointed out in 1963, in the later fifties and early sixties
> a number of college presidents and faculty committees . . . wished to tidy things up by grouping a number of administrative units under a single administrator. Speech, theater arts, journalism, advertising, broadcasting, the university's radio and TV facilities and its printing plant, the student newspaper, the public information office, the alumni publication—they all deal in communications, don't they? Well, why not lump them all into a single administrative unit?
>
> There is no good reason against it . . . so long as the objective is simply administrative expediency and so long as it is clearly recognized that the

> result will be adhesive rather than cohesive. Such units have little in common educationally, and some have almost antagonistic aims. Put them together, and the result is a little like the early empires that adhered. . .by external force; it is not at all like the later nation states that are cohesive . . . held together from within by some common ideology, by common aspirations.
>
> Some . . . have used the term 'communications' to bring more compatible units together. Instead of wrenching the term 'journalism' to cover advertising and broadcasting, say, we have put journalism, advertising and broadcasting under shelter of an umbrella we call communications. Since those areas have a great deal in common that arrangement makes infinitely better sense than the first one; but it is still essentially an administrative convenience, and it leaves unresolved the implications for curriculum and approach.

But integration has not been confined to the administrative level. Particularly in the 1960s, mass media education in the United States has been characterized by the growing appearance of multidisciplinary and even interdisciplinary studies. The extent of co-operation between various departments varies greatly according to the particular situation in any college or university. It may be affected to some degree by many factors ranging from the attitude of the State legislature to mass media education, the financial situation of the particular institution of higher learning and its financial priorities, and even the personal relationships existing at any particular time between different heads of department, including the degree to which 'academic empire building' is taking place.[1]

Consequently, there are innumerable variations in the pattern of adjustment. At the one end of the scale are the schools of communication,

> each significantly different from the other. The School of Communication at the University of Washington is basically oriented to journalism, while the School of Communication at Ohio University is primarily speech based. The Annenberg School of Communication at the University of Pennsylvania is oriented to journalism, creative writing, and the performing arts. Michigan State University has an actual College of Communication Arts which has combined journalism, speech and communication departments under a single administrative umbrella. Each of these universities, and very many more, met its own administrative, curricular and disciplinary needs, and each developed its own strengths and weaknesses. (University of Oregon, 1970.)

At the other end of the scale are those varaitions which stop short of integration. In broadcasting, for instance, they may range from the duplication of courses dealing with similar subject-matter in both the departments of journalism and of speech, the cross-listing of some courses for students attached to each department (but not necessarily with the same requirements or regulations in each case), the appointment of a broadcasting co-ordinator to deal with curricular problems arising between the two departments, or even a committee to co-ordinate matters.

A response from the Dean of the Social Sciences Division of the College of Liberal Arts at the University of Minnesota (Webb, 1970), indicates the kinds of issues involved, and the solutions attempted:

> This College has two large and longstanding departments with concerns in Mass Communication. Both have turned out hundreds of professionals

---

1. Several letters have been received which suggest that in some universities and colleges, rivalries or antagonism between journalism and speech departments have led to both simultaneously offering similar courses in news writing and journalism and in the theory and practice of broadcasting, to their own students.

over the decades. The School of Journalism and Mass Communication is one of the largest and most well-known in the country and offers a wide range of courses leading to undergraduate and graduate degrees. The Department of Speech Communication and Theatre Arts is also very large. Both are concerned with the mass media and in recent years have converged somewhat in their aims and interests, especially with regard to curricula dealing with broadcasting. The convergence of interests led to considerable difficulties as to the proper development of the departments. A liaison committee was formed to coordinate development and, as Dean of Social Sciences Division, I am Chairman . . . The general result of improved liaison has been close cooperation between the two groups. This has done much to increase the 'academic power' of both departments. The allocation of resources in a large university such as this (we have close to 50,000 students) is a matter of complex discussion, and the existence of the committee is viewed by both departments as a means of improving the flow of resources as well as the curricula available to students.

Because of the existence of old, well-established academic patterns of administration and teaching, given expression in the regulations which lay down patterns of study for particular degrees, and which can be changed by the Senate only after often very long discussions and negotiations, it has sometimes been easier to introduce multidisciplinary or interdisciplinary patterns at graduate level, where degree regulations are often more flexible and where more experimentation is allowed than at undergraduate level. At the University of North Carolina at Chapel Hill, for example, as the Chairman of the Department of Radio, Television and Motion Pictures explained (Wallace, 1971),

> a major change in instructional approach was undertaken some six or seven years ago, when the School of Journalism received approval for a doctor of philosophy degree in mass communication research. This is a very flexible degree in which many different departments may share, including my own. The joining of various departments and disciplines to offer advanced programs as well as undergraduate studies is more noticeable now than it was some years ago.

Development of new orientations to mass media studies

It seems that occasionally, the grouping together of previously separate units under one over-all administrative structure was the first step which afterwards prompted the search for a means of providing intellectual coherence, as well as administrative convenience, in thus linking them together. This search for the educational, as distinguished from the merely administrative implications of the term 'communications' has affected departments and schools rooted in journalism as well as speech. In short, to some extent at any rate, it was necessary to provide a theoretical *raison d'être* for what might originally have been the mere manipulation of formal entities.

The fact that mass media education in the United States, unlike that in some other countries, has been so decisively concentrated in academic institutions would probably in any case have eventually stimulated a need for more intellectually acceptable content, especially once journalism education had met the demands of the mass media industries, and was in a better position to adjust to the pressures of an academic setting.

As Theodore Peterson forcefully put it in 1960:

> One danger . . . is that journalism educators who do not really comprehend the nature of the transformation in journalism education will seek the trappings without the substance. We are in some danger of becoming

gimmick artists. One such gimmick is the term 'communications'. One danger is that we will use the term for reasons of status, just as undertakers have become morticians and trash-haulers have become sanitary engineers. Communications is more than journalism writ large, and no dreary little journalism trade school is going to work a wondrous improvement by changing its designation from journalism to communications. The change must rest on a reorientation of faculty thinking, on a reorientation of the instructional program and on a distinctive approach to the subject matter of the courses.

In the 1960s, some journalism educators were becoming increasingly concerned about their relationship with the universities; with, as one journalism professor baldly put it (T. Peterson *et al.*, 1963),

> the relationship between the journalism education business and the higher education business ... Could the study of journalism mean much more not only to the student but to the university which provides it if the traditional patterns of instruction were sharply altered ? ... Our whole future ... is riding on the relationship of journalism education to the institution of higher education ... As the pressure of members and budgets increases, the inspection of each of the components of higher education will become closer and more rigorous. Changes will be made, and the discipline of journalism study cannot assume that it will be able to generate all these changes by itself, and in its own good time ... There are college administrators these days who seriously question the defensibility of continuing journalism education at all in the light of budget pressures.

Not surprisingly, the president of the AEJ in his 1970 address made the same point, that 'university budgets are being tightened in these tense times' and that 'we must prove our need to society by serving society's needs' (Ames, 1970).

A decade earlier, in a presidential address to the AEJ, Charles T. Duncan (1961) pointed out that enrolment in journalism departments was not keeping pace with the rise in student numbers elsewhere in universities, and that journalism might not be able to attract the best students. Although the lag in journalism enrolments disappeared during the later 1960s, a more powerful and enduring reason for anxiety became evident: the fear that it was becoming increasingly impossible for mass media education, in post-war conditions, to ever be able to cope satisfactorily with the narrow—and expensive—demands of the mass media industries. One reason that professional training in journalism, and later in broadcasting, developed in academic institutions in the United States is probably partly connected with the vastness of the country and the great proliferation of relatively small mass media enterprises, especially after the 1920s, at a time when new technologies were adopted relatively slowly. These enterprises gradually came to realize that it was cheaper and more convenient for preliminary training, at any rate, to be conducted outside media organizations, and that the facilities provided by universities and colleges could well be used to this end. This situation has become ever more difficult to maintain in circumstances where technological innovation becomes more widespread and rapidly adopted in all the media industries.

Thus the impetus towards a more integrated and academic approach in mass media education has been provided partly by the uneasy feeling, voiced in both journalism and broadcasting education circles, that training in techniques has not, and perhaps cannot, keep pace with rapid technological change in all the mass media, and that universities would be better advised to provide the kind of general teaching which will enable the student to cope with new situations. P. S. Underwood, Assistant Director of the School of Journalism at Ohio State University, expressed this view most tellingly in 1970:

> In my view, the most important immediate problem for journalism educators is adjusting their educational programs to the fantastic technological developments that are taking place today in communications. I'm afraid too many of us are teaching from the viewpoint of a professional world that is disappearing. Very few, if any, of us have any clear idea of what the journalistic profession is going to be like ten years from now. Will we have newspapers as we have always known them? If you talk to the scientists, it is obvious this is a serious question. If so, should we be bothering to teach students something about typography? What will the editing process be like if electronic machinery takes over completely?
>
> We are in the midst of a technological revolution in communication machinery. What effect will this have on the journalistic profession, and what should we be doing about it now? This is, in my opinion, the major question we all face at this particular time.

Some prominent journalism educators have long been urging that there should be a new orientation in teaching.

> We should look at journalism education more from the standpoint of the long-term interests of the student than from the day to day requirements of industry, and more from the standpoint of the purposes of higher education than from the character of demand in the current market . . . Likewise, we should be more concerned with offering courses that will measure up to the intellectual standards of a great university, and a lot less concerned with training students to satisfy the conventional requirements of this or that beginner's job in industry. (Jensen, 1963.)

Many educators feel that a more general teaching approach, avoiding narrow specialized training in techniques, is desirable because

> the number and variety of different communication media, channels, techniques, tools and jobs is so great, and their specific operations so intricate, that it would be hopeless to cover more than a few,

and that

> as a practical matter, persons move about freely in the communication complex and specialists often do not practise what they were particularly trained for. This flexibility of personnel in communication careers is one of the attractions of such careers. (Carter, 1963.)

Kenneth W. Hirsch (1970) points to the 'outpouring of technical innovations in electronic communication . . . soon to be commonly used and accepted' including facsimile newspapers, direct popular votes by closed circuit television, picture telephones, hologram 3–D movies, television records, and a great many different channels for special audience television programmes through cable television systems. He also draws attention to the consequences for professional education of the enormous potential growth and distribution of amateur movies, the increased participation of individuals in vocational interests through speciality-audience programmes made available by cable television, which may affect social interaction based on place of residence, and the widespread use of video equipment for surveillance.

> These innovations promise great opportunity for profit. The institutions of radio, television and film will undergo—are already undergoing—a great transformation [yet none of] the leading schools programs . . . shows adequate treatment of the changes that are forthcoming.

He considers that academic programmes concentrate too much on performance and production and are geared to prepare students for careers in broadcasting stations and networks,

> areas in which few people actually get jobs; there are undoubtedly many more people . . . in peripheral areas of broadcasting and film than . . . in radio

and television stations and networks dealing with production ... The curricula continue to attempt to supply industry personnel needs which have, however, largely disappeared ... In the process many other occupations which might benefit from such prospective employees are overlooked.

He recommended a new thrust towards preparation for careers in instructional/educational broadcasting. This is a field which already provides

a substantial area of professional employment ... there are hundreds of radio and television stations—and closed circuit—all employing graduates of the mass media studies programmes. A goodly portion of students who are taught production and programming do [already] enter the field in these areas

as Charles Woodliff (1971) of Western Michigan University pointed out. But CATV will almost certainly further increase the demand for students trained in instructional or educational broadcasting. In this respect—in being able to take advantage of employment in education—broadcasting students may perhaps have the edge over students of journalism, and students trained in communication or mass communication may be in the best position of all to move freely among present-day media-oriented occupations (including advertising, public communication and opinion research), and entirely new fields that technological innovations may create. The precise implications may not always be immediately apparent, and may take some time to be implemented. But the impact of the need for new approaches seems apparent, in some institutions at least.

To sum up, it has been shown that the rapid growth of mass communication in the United States, particularly after the Second World War, led to the proliferation of new subject areas connected with training students for occupations in the mass media. This in turn produced new academic structures within universities and colleges, which, by bringing together apparently heterogeneous elements, prompted a need for some kind of intellectual cohesion to bind these units together. At the same time rapid technological changes in the mass media, and the even more rapid and fundamental changes forecast for the future, created a situation of great fluidity within and across the various media industries and institutions, as well as a combination of increasingly specialized skills which rapidly become obsolete with technological innovation. This situation has made it appear that the once-primary justification of teaching 'skills' courses in an academic environment, namely the ability to provide the student with the expensive professional training that was too costly and too time-consuming for the press, broadcasting and other media industries to provide themselves, was becoming less valid with time. Consequently, it has been argued, both these trends have operated in recent years to stimulate a more academic approach away from skills and techniques to more general and theoretical approaches.

Development of graduate education

Previous sections have explored the interplay of various factors which have helped stimulate a more academic orientation, especially in the larger schools and departments concerned with mass media education in the United States in the 1960s. One of the most important factors, so far mentioned only in passing, is the great extension of graduate education [1] since the Second World War, and the 'feedback' effect which developments in post-graduate work have had on pre-professional training and undergraduate teaching.

1. The extension of graduate education in mass media studies is in keeping with the general trend in the United States for graduate education to expand rapidly since the Second World War. According to statistics issued by the United States Department of Health, Education and Welfare, there were 132,000 students enrolled in graduate programmes in 1958–59, over 798,000 in 1969, and the number is expected to reach 1,300,000 by 1979 (Hegener, 1970).

Although, to some extent, graduate education has served to provide advanced professional training (as, for example, in the programmes offered at the Columbia Graduate School of Journalism, the School of Public Communication at Boston University, and the Medill School of Journalism at Northwestern University, all of which are outstanding examples of schools with a professedly professional orientation), an important, if not the main impetus for providing graduate courses in mass media studies after the Second World War, was the need to provide more faculty members to staff the greatly increased number of departments and to teach the ever-larger number of students in colleges and universities.

During the inter-war period university and college journalism departments were staffed largely by ex-professionals. In the post-war period, although media experience was, and is still, considered an important qualification in hiring a new faculty member, the fluid and expansive condition of the mass media industries makes it difficult to obtain sufficient numbers of this type of potential teacher—at any rate of the quality thought necessary under post-war circumstances.

David Boroff, who made an intensive study of over twenty-five journalism schools on behalf of the Ford Foundation in 1963 reported that:

> The melancholy fact is that, with the exception of perhaps eight or nine strong schools, journalism education is sunk in a morass of demoralization, low standards and self-contempt. It inhabits the poverty sector of academia. And this at a time when communications—not only nationally but internationally—have reached a new pitch of urgency and complexity. The first strike against the journalism schools is the faculty ... Many are refugees from the city room because they couldn't really make the grade. Cut off from the mainstream of journalism yet not really part of the academic community, they often become insulated and unworldly.

Clifford Weigle, a journalism professor himself, alleged that 'our faculties have been dominated by a hodgepodge of inadequately talented, underpaid, ex-journalists of one sort or another'.

Both Boroff and Weigle felt that the way to improve journalism education was to increase the salaries of university and college professors of journalism so that top-flight professionals could be attracted to it (Walsh, 1968).

Although it is doubtful whether university salaries could ever have been raised to a point where they could be competitive with the highest paid in the media industries, there is some indication that, in fact, colleges and universities on the whole, used financial incentives to attract full-time [1] faculty members with Ph. D.s.

A 1964 study of AEJ members (Maclean et al., 1965) showed that 206 members (about two-fifths of the total membership) belonged to what the authors called the 'communication research group'. Over half this group had Ph.D.s, and a quarter of them (about fifty in all) had Ph.D.s in communication, mass communication or mass communication research. This group was relatively younger than the others, and had relatively less experience in the media, yet more of its members earned incomes of $12.100 or over than any other group.

This finding reinforces the already-observed tendency that a higher degree, and more and more, a doctorate, is becoming necessary, perhaps not to enter mass media teaching in the larger colleges and universities, but almost certainly to rise to the highest levels in that field.

As Theodore Peterson observed in 1960:

> Until World War II the journalism teacher with a Ph.D. was a comparative rarity. Journalism administrators themselves doubted that, all things consid-

---

1. At the part-time level, there was apparently an increased employment of top-flight professionals in journalism schools (Jones, 1968).

ered, a doctorate was of much earthly use . . . A few brave souls did get their Ph.D.'s of course. Nine of them were teaching journalism in 1927. Twelve years later, the number had grown to 35, or about 14% of the teachers in accredited schools.

By 1964, the aforementioned AEJ membership study found that of 637 respondents (65 per cent of the total membership), 92 per cent had a bachelor's, 84 per cent a master's and 30 per cent a doctor's degree. The authors noted that the percentages increased somewhat in the case of academic respondents teaching in academic institutions.

Although this trend is clearly visible, it should be noted that the percentage of Ph.D.s in journalism schools is much lower than the 82 per cent found in the late fifties by Lazarsfeld and Thielens (1958) in a study of college teachers of social science courses. Nor is this a trend which has been fully accepted by all departments of journalism. Journalism educators, until fairly recently, were deeply divided as to the relative merits of a Ph.D. degree as against professional experience gained by several years' experience of working in the media. Nevertheless, with the increasing tendency of journalism education to be extended into graduate work—to provide more skilled pre-professional instruction as well as to train future teachers of journalism for high schools, junior colleges, and above all, for colleges and universities—it is likely that this trend will continue.

Graduate education in journalism, of course, long pre-dates the Second World War. The University of Missouri, for example, awarded its first M.A. degree in 1921, and its first Ph.D. in 1934. In 1935, the Pulitzer School at Columbia went from an undergraduate to a master's degree programme, and in 1938, Northwestern University's Medill School of Journalism began to offer a full five-year professional programme. Nevertheless, before the Second World War, only a handful of schools offered the master's degree, and just one, the University of Missouri, offered the doctorate although some provided a minor in journalism for doctoral candidates who majored in history or political science. During the late forties and through the fifties, master's degrees in journalism multiplied; by 1960 a majority of the ACEJ-accredited schools were offering them. But the most significant feature of the post-war period was the increase in doctoral programmes in mass communications, which combined journalism with work in behavioural science. This new degree was initiated by Iowa State University in 1944, and by 1964 similar programmes were being offered also by Illinois, Stanford, Wisconsin, Syracuse, Michigan State, Southern Illinois and North Carolina. Only three universities—Missouri, Northwestern and Minnesota—provided a Ph.D. in journalism. By 1970, fourteen of the fifty-seven accredited schools were giving Ph.D. programmes and the degree was also being offered by many non-accredited schools (ACEJ, 1970; Emery *et al.*, 1965).

Table 4 illustrates the changes in graduate education in journalism between 1960 and 1970.

Several interesting points emerge from this table. Graduate enrolment in journalism schools has increased more rapidly than total enrolment, and there has been an increase in the number of schools with graduate programmes. More significantly, the average number of graduate students per graduate school has doubled, and has increased even more in the ten schools with the largest graduate enrolments. But these 'top ten' now have a smaller percentage of total graduate enrolments than they did ten years ago.

The data available for graduate education in broadcasting is not stricly comparable with that in journalism, being derived from different sources. But Table 5 indicates how much education in broadcasting has been extended in the sixties. Between 1958/59 and 1971/72 the number of schools offering bachelor's degrees and those offering master's degrees has roughly doubled, while the number of students enrolled in undergraduate and master's programmes has increased fourfold. The increase in schools offering

TABLE 4. Development of graduate education in journalism in the United States, 1960/70

	1960	1970	Increase (%)
Total number of journalism schools (*Journalism Quarterly* survey)	101	162	60
Total enrolment	11,390	33,106	190
Graduate enrolment	1,041	3,692	255
Graduate enrolment as percentage of total enrolment	9	11	22
Number of schools with graduate enrolments	43	74	72
Number of enrolments in schools with graduate enrolments	7,646	24,403	219
Graduate enrolment as percentage of total enrolment in schools with graduate enrolments	14	15	7
Average number of graduate students per graduate school	24	49	104
Average number of graduate students in ten schools with highest graduate enrolment	65	147	126
Graduate students in ten schools with highest graduate enrolment, as percentage of total graduate enrolment	62	40	(35)

Source: *Journalism Quarterly*, Autumn 1960 and Winter 1970.

TABLE 5. Development of graduate education in broadcasting in the United States, 1958/59 to 1971/72

	1958/59	1971/72
Number of schools offering bachelor's degrees	89	180
Number of schools offering master's degrees	45	87
Number of schools offering doctoral degrees	16	27
Number of undergraduate majors	2,763	11,995
Number of master's students	391	1,895
Number of Ph. D. Students	109	259
Total enrolment	3,263	14,149
Graduate enrolment	500	2,154
Graduate enrolment as percentage of total enrolment	15.3	15.3
Total number of students in schools with graduate programmes	...	10,574
Total number of students in schools with graduate programmes as percentage of total enrolment	...	74.7

Sources: Harold Niven, 'Fourth Annual Survey of Colleges and Universities . . .', op. cit., Harold Niven, *Broadcast Education 1972 . . .*, op. cit.

doctoral programmes has been slightly less, as has the number of doctoral enrolments, but the proportion of graduate to total enrolments has remained remarkably constant. In 1971/72, three-quarters of all students enrolled in broadcasting courses were studying in schools with graduate programmes. Table 6 indicates that the tendency to place broadcasting courses in separate departments of communications or broadcasting is as evident in graduate education as in undergraduate programmes.

The pattern of graduate education in mass media studies and related fields in the United States in 1970 has been summarized as follows (Hegener, 1971); of the 232 universities surveyed, all of them were found to offer graduate programmes in one or

TABLE 6. Types of department offering broadcasting degrees in the United States in 1971/72 (180 schools with 183 departments)

Department	Bachelor's	Master's	Doctorate
Communications	77 (42.1%)	37 (41.1%)	10 (33.3%)
Broadcasting	47 (25.7%)	27 (30.0%)	11 (36.7%)
Speech-Drama-Theatre	51 (27.9%)	24 (26.7%)	7 (23.3%)
Journalism	7 (3.8%)	2 (2.2%)	2 (6.7%)
Other	1 (0.5%)	0 (0.0%)	0 (0.0%)
Total	183	90	30

Sources: Harold Niven, *Broadcast Education 1972...*, op. cit.

more communication field, broken down as follows: 134 (57.8 per cent) offered graduate programmes in rhetoric and public address, 132 (56.9 per cent) in journalism, 130 (56.0 per cent) in communication, 91 (39.2 per cent) in radio, television and film, and 80 (34.4 per cent) in communication theory.

Ninety-four of these universities—somewhat under half those offering graduate programmes in mass media studies or related fields—offered one graduate programme only. In forty-six cases this was journalism, in twenty-two communication, and in twenty-one rhetoric and public address, while only three offered a programme in radio-television-film, and two in communication theory, without at the same time offering a graduate programme in another field. Of the 138 universities which taught two or more graduate programmes in these areas, 56 (about 40 per cent) gave graduate programmes in four out of the five subfields, and 28 in all five.

An analysis was made to determine which two fields tended to cluster together most frequently. It was found that the two subfields which correlated best were rhetoric and communication theory, both being concerned with intrapersonal and interpersonal communication, small-group communication, as well as general problems of persuasion and opinion change. Next came radio-television-film and communication, radio-television-film and communication theory, and radio-television-film and rhetoric. Interestingly enough, journalism and radio-television-film tend to correlate less than any other pair. These results seem to add weight to the contention, developed above, that especially at post-graduate level, the study of radio-television and film has tended to be offered along with other fields of mass media studies and especially to be associated with theoretical perspectives. Journalism studies, on the other hand, do not have the same broad perspectives and tend to remain functionally independent of theory and other media. Unfortunately, the detailed pattern of cross-listing of courses between different graduate programmes in each university, which would add more substantive evidence to this contention, is not available.

It is difficult to give a meaningful yet concise description of the multitude of different graduate degree courses in mass media studies in United States universities. They vary along many different dimensions including the size, standing and age of the graduate section, the interests, particularly the research interests, of the faculty, and the extent to which other institutions in the same geographical area have already specialized in a particular field, which may lead other institutions about to embark on graduate work to decide to teach different concentrations. All these factors, among many others, help to determine the field and orientation of the graduate work in any particular institution.

It appears that graduate work has been extended less in advertising and public relations than in journalism, broadcasting, mass communications and communications generally. Within these major fields, a fair number of highly specialized subfields have developed, and are likely to increase in future, either through providing one or more courses for credit, or through creating a new area of concentration consisting of a group of related courses, or by offering a new degree in a particular specialized field. It would be impossible to give anything like a full range of examples to illustrate these developments but one might mention communication research and international communications which are being taken up by an increasing number of universities, as well as others such as urban problems, minority-group communication (including fields like the Black press) and highly technical fields like biomedical communications, mental-health communication, or informational communication. The orientation and focus in graduate education varies enormously from university to university, and sometimes even between two departments in the same university.

Bearing in mind this diversity and the fact that any particular department may offer either one degree only, one degree with different specialized options, or many different degrees, generally speaking the master's degree involves a number of courses of advanced-level standard, in sequences which may or may not be rigidly structured, leading to advanced specialization in a particular field. It is often multidisciplinary or interdisciplinary in approach, and is, generally speaking, more flexible than the bachelor's degree. A very common pattern is to have a number of core courses, which all students are required to take, with a series of options available according to the student's own choice. It sometimes, though not always, has a thesis requirement. It usually, though not invariably, involves some training in research methods (very largely implying the use of quantitative statistical tools and training in the use of experiment, content analysis and surveys) and most often some review of the results obtained in mass communication research. It usually involves two years of study after the bachelor's degree.

The master's degree is becoming the terminal degree in training advanced specialists for the higher echelons of the media industries; for fields like government departments and agencies where 'professional communicators' may be used in social advertising programmes such as pollution control, public health, mental health, agricultural extension and so on; for specialists in educational technology; and for high-school and college teachers of journalism and broadcasting. It still remains the terminal degree for entering the lowest levels of senior college and university teaching, in smaller and poorer institutions.

The doctoral degree is even more flexible than the master's and usually involves taking some advanced courses of study, combined with the writing of a doctoral dissertation, of publishable standard.[1] It is rapidly becoming the required degree for promotion to the higher levels of university teaching generally, and for entry into some branches of mass media education, such as communication theory, a field which is becoming more widespread particularly in larger academic institutions.

---

1. Donald L. Shaw (ed.), *Journalism Abstracts, M. A., M. S. and Ph. D. Theses in Journalism and Mass Communication*, published by the Association for Education in Journalism. Vol. 7 (1969) and Vol. 8 (1970) and earlier volumes in the series provide information on theses accepted for graduate degrees in journalism schools. Kenneth R. Sparks, *A Bibliography of Doctoral Dissertations in Television and Radio*, 2nd ed., New York, N. Y., School of Journalism, Newhouse Communications Center, Syracuse University, lists over 900 Ph. D. dissertation titles related to broadcasting arranged into twelve categories, presented between 1925 and 1970.

But the doctoral degree is above all the required qualification for specialized research in mass communications, especially behavioural-science research, which requires specialized training in research methods. The growth of doctoral programmes in mass communication has therefore developed concomitantly with the growth of mass communication research based in mass media education departments (which will be discussed in the following section), and has led to the creation of a growing number of trained mass communication research specialists.

One of the most significant aspects of the extension of mass media education to the graduate level in the United States is that it has brought teaching and pre-professional training into a much closer relationship with mass communication research. Mass communication research was at first conducted by political scientists, historians, psychologists, social psychologists, sociologists and others who were not based in academic departments engaged in training students for occupations in the mass media. But once such departments began to offer graduate work, particularly at doctoral level, they had to conform to the generally accepted academic standards laid down in universities that students should make some new contribution to knowledge. As Wilbur Schramm (1959) put it,

> communication research has made a bridge between the professional or trade activities of [journalism] schools and the ancient and intellectual strengths of the university.

A parallel development linked with the great extension of mass media education into the graduate field is the extent to which teaching staff in colleges and universities have become more research-minded, and at the same time more inclined to do research similar to that conducted in the behavioural sciences. From one point of view, this seems to be another indication that departments concerned with mass media education have become increasingly integrated into their academic setting, subject to similar pressures as other members of the academic community ('publish or perish' is a well-known United States academic syndrome) and striving for the same goals: the increase of knowledge and service to society.

For example, the Association for Education in Journalism has a number of divisions with separate memberships, including the research division, founded in 1955. It was at first the subject of some criticism, even hostility, by more traditionally minded members, but is now one of the largest and most active in the AEJ. It has recently begun to work with other divisions in an attempt to stimulate and build up strong research programmes among all divisions. The leadership of the AEJ has recently begun to stress the importance of the research function, and of its influence on teaching. In 1968 the address of Ralph Nafziger, the executive secretary, ended on the note that

> In recent years there has been a rising degree of acceptance ... of AEJ by the mass media and an equal wave of recognition of journalism education in academic circles in response to a continuing rise in levels of instruction and in the development of high standards for research in journalism and mass communications ... A considerable number of our schools and departments have maintained a balance between their professional training programs, largely on a fourth or fifth year basis, and their research activities. Professional training programs, fed and enriched more and more by investigative studies, have continued to improve, and new approaches to research have become much better known and more diversified ... Surely there is nothing incompatible between a professional training program largely on an undergraduate level and a development of mass communication as a discipline located mainly in graduate schools. They supplement each other. Graduate programs above the level of professional master's programs are designed especially for the development of teachers and researchers ... In this way we are

keeping step with the times and with similar developments that have already occurred in all of the social sciences and in most of the professional training programs in institutions of high learning. (Nafziger, 1969.)

W. E. Ames of the University of Washington, AEJ president in 1970, went further and stressed that journalism schools should concentrate on societal needs 'both in our training and our educating roles' and that research in this area was of paramount importance.

> How can we as college professors avoid the responsibility of producing the research, analysis, criticism and theory necessary to permit the dissecting of the communication function within our society? . . . We must gain the understanding necessary to preserve and bring to higher levels of functioning that vital process of communication upon which a free society depends—and while we're at it, let's check that self-evident truth. (Ames, 1970.)

In spite of the evidently strong thrust towards research, and towards academic as well as professional goals, it would be mistaken to imagine that journalism educators are not still deeply divided as to the functions they should perform and the kind of orientation that their teaching should take. Although there is no longer so sharp a cleavage between the 'green eye shade' (practical) and the 'chi-square' (behavioural-science research) protagonists, the aims of university journalism teachers, and their approach to their subject are still diverse.

The findings of the 1964 attitude study of AEJ members would probably still hold today. AEJ members clustered into two large groups, each accounting for about 40 per cent of the total members surveyed. One group, labelled the Communication Research Group, was strongly in favour of more research and theory in journalism education, though not necessarily only of the quantitatively based type. This group was, on average, younger than the rest, had more Ph. D.s in it, and more of its membership was to be found in big universities. The other large group, labelled the Defenders of Journalism Schools, was far more oriented towards the needs of the media industries, especially the newspaper industry, both in training and in research. The three other groups, each of which had less than 10 per cent of the total number of members surveyed, consisted of those who strongly favoured a liberal arts background (rather than practical training or behavioural science courses) as the best type of teaching, those who strongly supported the teaching of techniques in journalism schools, and those who were strongly antagonistic to communication research and theory (Maclean et al., 1965). Even at present, in universities where the necessity for research is accepted, there is still serious division on what kind of research should be conducted.

Of course, the ultimate test of the extent to which research has found a lasting place in journalism schools, is the extent to which research and research findings become integrated into teaching, ultimately at the undergraduate level. R. O. Nafziger (1970) summed up the tendencies in this direction as follows:

> The curricula in the schools have changed throughout the years in keeping with the changes in research and the interests of the faculties. For example, much more research in all aspects of mass communications is in progress today than was true a few decades ago. Moreover, the tendency for applied and basic research findings to find their way or to be incorporated into undergraduate as well as graduate courses is clearly evident, although the extent of this tendency among all schools probably is not great. It could and likely should be further developed.

In conclusion, it seems clear that mass media education in the United States has been undergoing some great changes, especially in the last twenty years. These have brought about a variety of approaches, as a result of various adjustments to pressures arising from rapid technological change in the mass media industries, as well as from the pressures within the academic environment of the universities. Consequently there is still a great diversity in the types of education offered and in the institutional framework in which that education is given and, it would seem, some degree of confusion in aims.

Although it is ten years since he uttered them, the warnings of Theodore Peterson (1960) still appear to be relevant to the future of mass media education in the United States:

> There is a danger that our individual schools will do what seems fashionable, not what they can do best, given their staffs, resources and special circumstances. I can see no reason that a three-man department which is doing an excellent job of preparing undergraduates for newspaper work should feel compelled to become a school of communications . . . that a school of journalism in a small college in an isolated part of the country should feel compelled to create an institute for the study of the foreign press . . . that a school with facilities for only sound undergraduate instruction should feel compelled to launch an elaborate graduate program . . . that every school or department should feel compelled to have a research institute, however small. Our schools could far better exploit their special strengths and overcome their weaknesses.

Mass communication research in the United States

More academic research into the social aspects of the mass media and mass communication has been undertaken in the United States than in any other country, even in the last two decades when academic interest in the mass media has grown rapidly all over the world. Moreover, the type of research done in the United States has been more influential than any other in determining the field of investigation and the methods employed. This is not to deny that there are other, very different approaches to mass media, but it is still undoubtedly true that the mainstream of mass communication research stems from traditions established in the United States, and adopted to a greater or lesser extent all over the world.

Definitions of the field

The term 'mass communication research' has come to have a rather specific connotation in the United States, and by extension, in other countries too. As a starting-point one may cite the definition given in *Introduction to Mass Communications*, by Emery et al. (1965), the textbook most commonly used in introductory courses in American journalism schools.

The authors state:

> a broad definition of research is simply 'careful investigation' . . . and would include almost any kind of study (literary, biographical or historical) . . . Mass communications research has taken on a somewhat more specialized meaning, however . . . It is usually considered as behavioural research—the study of human beings (rather than inanimate objects) . . . a branch of the behavioural sciences such as psychology, sociology and anthropology . . . It is also interdisciplinary research . . . It borrows the tools and knowledge of various other fields . . . which will help in the understanding of mass communications problems. It does not confine itself to any particular point of view or theory or subject matter. It may borrow from linguistics, general semantics, philosophy, economics or any other discipline which might help communications effectiveness. It is *scientific research*, since it uses scientific methodology . . . Its methods must be objective (as opposed to subjective)

and systematic... Although most mass communications research is done on specific problems the goal—as in any scientific field—is to formulate general principles and theories which can bring about more effective communication.

Being scientific, it is, of course, *quantitative* research... It is generally *primary* research rather than secondary. That is, the mass communications researcher customarily gathers new and original information rather than relying on printed source material...

And of course, the subject matter of communications research is communication. More specifically, it is concerned with *mass* communications, the communications behaviour of large numbers of people, particularly those who make up the *audiences* for the different media. But other groups can be studied, too, of course—newspaper reporters, news sources, magazine editors, or public relations men... [Thus] it also includes the study of the communicators, their media and the content of their messages.

This is not the only definition that might be legitimately applied. It leaves out other kinds of research done in the field of journalism and mass communications (e.g. historical, literary, biographical, legal, economic, international aspects...) It also includes some topics which might be claimed by other disciplines. It is, however, a reasonably comprehensive definition of the specialized type of mass communications research which has grown up recently.

This definition has been quoted at length not because it would necessarily be accepted without question by most American mass communication researchers,[1] but because it brings out some salient points of view that have held sway in the United States until fairly recently. This definition highlights the strongly empirical tradition in media research, its dependence on quantitative methodology, and its concomitantly strong preference for short-run, highly specific studies, rather than long-term studies concerned with historical processes. Interestingly, it focuses on the audience as the most important part of the subject-matter of the field. The communicators, their media and the content of their messages are seen as a secondary consideration, perhaps because their relation to the audience is taken as given. This is in line with the goal of theory-making which is stated to be 'to bring about more effective communication'. Such a formulation leaves closed the question of 'effective for what end', which would include considerations about what should be communicated and who should have access to the media of public communication, as well as what is implied by 'effectiveness' in any case. In short, this definition puts the researcher in a stance of alignment with two important power groups—media organizations and government—who both see the audience as being 'out there', and seek better ways of knowing about it so as to communicate more effectively with it. As Otto Larsen (1964) pointed out, much mass

1. Merely to cite one example, one may compare the tone and content of this definition with that of Morris Janowitz (1968):
> Urbanization, industrialization, and modernization have created the societal conditions for the development of mass communications. In turn, these processes of social change produce societies that are highly dependent on mass communications. Mass communications comprise the institutions and techniques by which specialized social groups employ technological devices (press, radio, films, etc.) to disseminate symbolic content to large heterogeneous and widely dispersed audiences. In other words, mass communications perform essential functions for a society that uses complex technology to control the environment. These functions include the transmission of a society's heritage from one generation to another, the collection of information for the surveillance of the environment, and the correlation of the various parts of the society in response to changes in the environment. Social science research on mass communications seeks an objective understanding of the institutions that fashion mass communications and the consequences of communication and mass persuasion for human society.

communication research, also, 'has tended to view persons as "targets" of communications impact rather than as part of a total communication process'.

In this sense, this definition encapsulates a good deal of the history of mass media research in the United States, at least since the 1930s. In many important ways, some of the characteristic features of this research are the result of the circumstances of its development, many of which still operate strongly today.

A comprehensive history of mass communications research in the United States has yet to be written, although it has been touched on in interesting and suggestive ways by many active researchers, in surveying the development of their own fields of interest. The full accomplishment of this task would be an important contribution to the sociology of knowledge, by relating changes in perspective, in theoretical presuppositions (stated or implicit), and in the kind of problems tackled, to changing social preoccupations and priorities, to changes in the theory and methodology of the social sciences generally, as well as to the history of the mass media themselves.

Development of research into the mass media

One of the most striking features in the development of mass communications research is that it has developed a highly sophisticated methodology, but that, as most commentators agree, its theoretical development has lagged behind. This may apply to empirically based social science in general, but in media research the gap between theory and methodology seems also to be linked with two main currents in its history. First, much of the finance on which it has depended has been forthcoming to solve immediate problems arising in the media industries and in public policy. Second, it has interested academic researchers from different disciplines who have drawn on many different theories and models at different levels of abstraction. The influence of these two trends will be discussed in more detail below.

Academic interest in the mass media in the United States dates back to work done on newspapers from the 1890s onward, almost entirely devoted to historical, legal and ethical aspects of the press, and using mainly historical methods. This tradition, which became strongly rooted in journalism schools, was applied to radio and motion pictures, and was joined by aesthetic explorations of media content from the point of view of literary or art criticism and rhetoric. It remains an important part of the total output of mass media research, in journals like *Journalism Quarterly, Television Quarterly* and numerous journals devoted to film criticism. It is characteristically undertaken by the individual researcher, partly because it is relatively inexpensive to undertake in comparison with other types of research. It is largely concerned with media content, and critical analyses and interpretations of content form the bases of deductions about the social values carried by the media, and their social significance.

But the type of mass communications research described by Emery, Ault and Agee saw its birth only in the 1920s and 1930s. It was given an enormous fillip during the Second World War, and achieved its 'take-off point' as an acceptable and well-populated field of interest only in the 1950s, as the discussions centring around Bernard Berelson's famous 'obituary notice' of 1959, *The State of Communications Research* indicate (Dexter and White, 1964).

Why did mass communication research in its present form develop in the 1920s and 1930s? The reasons seem to be connected with the fact that a number of factors were present together at that time, and operated concurrently to make it possible.

One of the founding fathers of mass communication research, Paul Lazarsfeld (1963), points to three main concerns which prompted research into the mass media in the 1920s and early 1930s. One was the concern with the adverse effects on children of the products of the growing movie industry, which were tested, and purportedly proved, by laboratory experiments. Another was the suspicion that the United States had been persuaded to enter the First World War by allied propaganda which was investigated by examining its content. Lastly, the advent of commercial radio resulted in fierce competition for advertising between newspapers and radio on the basis of their ability to prove that each had access to a larger body of consumers. This rapidly led to great refinement in statistical techniques for counting audience members and identifying their main characteristics by age, sex, education, income, social class and so on. As Merton (1968) points out, these categories 'happen to correspond to the chief statuses in the social structure' so that 'the procedures evolved for audience measurement' also had intrinsic academic interest.

The 1930s saw the full development of urbanization, and mass consumption occurred with concomitantly eager competition for lucrative mass markets, so that market research gradually became a customary instrument in production and marketing. At the same time, during the New Deal, the federal government began to use and refine survey techniques, and the scope of censuses was extended. Public-opinion polling also began in the 1930s. These were developments outside the universities which made available both the necessary basic data for research (although even by the mid-1930s, the most elementary quantitative data about newspapers were still lacking) (Schramm, 1957), and increasingly refined techniques of assembling and using them.

Alongside this, developments inside American universities during the 1930s paved the way for providing the necessary training for research workers. In sociology, Lazarsfeld (1962) points out that the characteristically American version of graduate education, the guided thesis, appeared only in the 1920s, to replace the erstwhile European practice of students choosing their own topic and pursuing it alone until they were ready for the final oral examination. This new method, pioneered in sociology by the 'Chicago school', made available an educated pool of research labour, which could gain its apprenticeship training in empirical research techniques while contributing to aspects of ongoing field research in a teaching department.

Also at this time, empirical sociological research was developing, particularly in Chicago, and pressures were put on university administrations to adjust their institutional structures to accommodate it, and thus make possible the university research institute which has become a characteristic form of organization in large-scale university-based mass communication research. Indeed, Lazarsfeld considers the research institute to be crucially important in the successful operation of empirical sociological research; both he and Merton explain the possibility, even the necessity, of the development of methodological precision as arising from the need to organize and standardize the operations of a large research team.

Finally, the coincidence that during the 1930s many European intellectuals emigrated to the United States, is probably as significant in the development of American social science as in American physical science. Although detailed research would be needed to establish the point, it seems probable that their uprooted situation encouraged many of these *émigrés* to break new ground in new fields of inquiry that might otherwise have been ignored in academic research, and to bring fresh insights to bear on them (Fleming and Bailyn, 1969; Lazarsfeld, 1969). The outstanding example is, of course, Lazarsfeld himself, who has done more than any other single individual to create and shape American mass communication research.

In spite of all these developments in the 1920s and 1930s, however, it was only after the Second World War that mass communication research, like empirical sociology,
> acquired prestige, a home in universities, financial support, textbooks, or enough devotees to form . . . a critical mass: the number of people sufficient to maintain each other's interest by providing a reciprocal reference group. (Lazarsfeld, 1962.) [1]

1. The point is made, referring to empirical sociology, but it applies to any new field developing a separate identity of its own.

It was, in fact, the Second World War that provided the opportunity, the testing ground, and the forcing bed for mass communication research. Then propaganda studies, already begun in the late 1920s as an aftermath of the First World War, became a matter of high priority to the United States Government. Like the physical scientists, behavioural scientists, especially experts in psychology, public opinion and attitude research, were co-opted into existing for new government departments (Lyons, 1969). The war brought social scientists into contact with new population groups and with other academics, and war needs forced them to refine methodologies. To take one example, content analysis: Harold Lasswell, the pioneer in this field through his work in 1927 on First World War propaganda, was put in charge of the War Communications Research Group at the Library of Congress, which was engaged in studying enemy propaganda. Other social scientists were studying news and broadcasts from many countries in other agencies.

> A kind of ongoing seminar [developed], methodological memoranda were circulated and discussed (in fact for a long time these were the chief texts) and out of it came the sophisticated method described in Lasswell and Leites' *The Language of Politics* (1949) and summarized in Berelson's *Content Analysis as a Tool of Audience Research*. (Schramm, 1957.)

Similarly, in public-opinion research, the methodological work done by Samuel Stouffer in the army's Research Branch, culminated, among many other studies, in *Measurement and Prediction* (1950). It is worth stressing, in view of the future pattern of mass communication research, that the work undertaken during the Second World War, like that done earlier for commercial purposes, was practically oriented, and that the information gained

> had to be used not in formulating and refining theories of human behaviour but in solving the problems at hand. (Lyons, 1969.)

Finally, another result of wartime activity was that teams of researchers were formed, some of whom continued to work together afterwards, as in the case of the team under Rensis Likert and Angus Campbell, many of whom moved from the Department of Agriculture to the Survey Research Center at the University of Michigan after the war. Carl Hovland is an outstanding example of a psychologist who moved into mass communication research during the war, and continued it at Yale afterwards.

In various ways therefore, the Second World War paved the way for the establishment of the many institutes and centres attached to American universities which are wholly or partly devoted to mass media research. In the 1950s, more and more American universities began offering the Ph.D. in mass communication research emphasizing quantitative research techniques. This enabled graduate students to participate in large research projects and to receive research training at the same time, in the manner pioneered by the Bureau for Applied Social Research at Columbia University (Fiddle, 1948; Lazarsfeld, 1962). These trained graduates became an important constituent of that reciprocal reference group which is so crucial in the development of a new field of research interest. For example, by 1955 there were sufficient numbers of them in journalism schools for a communication research division of the Association for Education in Journalism (AEJ) to be founded. The activities of this division and its offshoots have helped to stimulate quantitative mass communication research in journalism schools especially since the mid-1960s.

More and more of the larger American universities concerned with graduate education in mass media studies now conduct mass communication research, and a growing number of separate, formally constituted research centres have been created since the 1950s, and especially during the 1960s, with their own, separate research budgets. (It may be noted in parentheses that these institutions are mostly unable to carry on a requisite scale of operations on the finance allocated to them by their parent university and to a greater or lesser extent they must depend on limited grants allocated for specific research projects by non-university bodies—media organizations, foundations and government agencies.) There are now some fifty-five research centres attached to American universities which are partly or wholly concerned with mass media research. They include such well-known bodies as the Institute of Communications Research at the University of Illinois, Urbana, the Bureau of Applied Social Research at Columbia University, the Bureau of Media and Public Opinion Research at Indiana University, the Center for International Studies at the Massachusetts Institute of Technology (MIT) which has a separate division for international communication research, the International Communication Institute, and the research programme of the Department of Communication at Michigan State University, the Communication Research Division of the University of Minnesota, the Institute for Communication Research at Stanford University, the Center for Communication Research at the University of Texas, the Communication Research Center at the University of Washington, the Mass Communications Research Center at the University of Wisconsin, the Center for the Advanced Study of Communication at the University of Iowa, as well as many others. These centres conduct service studies for media organizations, or more commonly, 'pure' research funded by government agencies, by foundation grants, by the media, by the university, or by some combination of these. Their operation would be impossible without the participation of graduate students and full-time researchers at all levels of seniority and experience who commonly conduct the research programmes in conjunction with members of the teaching staff concerned with mass media education.

Finance for mass media research

The mention of funding leads us to one of the crucial factors in mass communication research, the availability of finance. This factor may affect the total pattern of research in several ways. Quantitative research has demonstrated its ability to provide clear answers to practical problems, and even to clarify cloudy issues by reducing them to clear formulae [1] (sometimes at the risk of over-simplification, by abstracting from complex issues a few variables which can be tested operationally, and then assuming that the research design which investigates these has given a final answer to a complicated matter in real life). Since quantification has enormous prestige, in any case, because of its successful use in the physical sciences, there may be great pressures on research workers to submit research proposals to fund-giving organizations which can be easily 'operationalized' and to leave to one side problems which may have greater theoretical importance or wider social significance. This may lead to an unfortunate split between empirical research, and theoretical, or critical analysis, which may not be able to attract the necessary funds to be able to

> start questioning some of the basic assumptions [about the relationship between social institutions and societal needs] do the necessary research to test these assumptions and provide society with the series of essays disciplined with data which will enable society to operate from a base of understanding. (Ames, 1970.)

It is also possible, because so much past and present mass communication research has consisted of unconnected service studies for media industries, or investigations on behalf of government agencies, that this, in itself, has helped to inhibit the development of theory in the mass connunication research field, without which criticism of the operation of media industries, even when supported by data, is likely to amount to little more than moral exhortation.

An investigation of the potential or actual availability of finance for various types

---

1. Lazarsfeld (1962) considers this to be a most important function of methodology as such, which, at its best, may even lead beyond to new theoretical insights.

of mass media research would give some indication of the actual priorities, expressed in concrete terms, which particular groups or agencies hold in relation to the mass media. Thus research commissioned by media industries is one indication of their immediate marketing needs as well as their more long-term interests. Research commissioned or paid for by State agencies may indicate the focus of immediate issues of military, economic or other aspects of public policy, and may also reveal how effective public concern about the media may be at any particular time.

There is not sufficient information available to present a methodical analysis of these factors. Nevertheless some details about the financing of mass communication research may reveal to what extent academic research reflects, and serves the needs of media industries, the State, or the public at large.

The close connexion between both the day-to-day and the more long-term interests of media organizations and trends in mass communication research is a well-known phenomenon. A good deal of research has been prompted and paid for by interested media organizations mainly because they wish to obtain more sophisticated knowledge about audiences than circulation and ratings figures can provide. From one point of view, this research can be seen as a means of providing indispensable feedback information that would otherwise be fragmentary, or even impossible to get or to measure. Sometimes this research is not published. But when it is it may provide an essential bedrock of information which can be applied to academically oriented research.

Service research for the media industries remains an important aspect of the output of many schools and departments of journalism and mass communication in the United States. In 1969 these departments, or the specialized research institutes attached to them, at UCLA, Columbia, Creighton, Florida, Idaho, Indiana, Iowa, Louisiana State, Minnesota, Missouri, Northwestern, Ohio State, South Dakota State, Syracuse and Washington Universities indicated that their research included service research, and in some cases was almost exclusively devoted to it (Blum, 1969).

Leslie Moeller (1968) argues that the changing structure of media industries will inevitably make the results of pure research into mass communication ever more important to them.

He notes
> the trend in mass communications toward bigness . . . toward mixed-media conglomerates (. . . bringing several media, and segments of the knowledge industry under one mass media tent) the push for diversification, all of which increasingly calls for intensive planning and for the technical specialized know-how which produces a technostructure

and points out that smaller industrial units will be affected if larger ones take on these characteristics. He goes on:
> The mass media are changing, and will change even more, in directions which will assure that they will more and more read the results of research which can be described as 'science based'. It is important to note . . . that *Editor and Publisher* is now quite regularly presenting a summary of such research results [and that] the largest US newspaper-oriented association ANPA sponsors the science based Editorial Research Reports [prepared] at the Massachusetts Institute of Technology which has no journalism program.

In this regard, it is interesting to note that one of the most comprehensive bibliographies of mass communications research (Danielson and Wilhoit, 1967) which lists 2,284 articles published in 48 American journals between 1944 and 1964, was funded by a three-year grant from the Educational Committee of the Magazine Publishers' Association. The authors first planned to include only articles which specifically mentioned magazines but
> a little reflection and experience, however, soon reconfirmed the obvious—that all mass media are inter-related and that a finding involving

television may be of great interest to someone working in the magazine or the newspaper industry. Gradually, therefore, the bibliography became more and more inclusive. At the end, the only instruction given to bibliographers was to ask this question . . . 'Would an intelligent, receptive magazine executive find this article to be of value in his work?'

The close connexion between media organizations and academic researchers is in many ways advantageous to research. It provides the necessary finance for work which might otherwise be too costly to undertake. Even when service studies alone are undertaken, they provide useful training in research methods as well as the data which can serve to underpin pure research. They may also indirectly finance other, academically oriented, research being undertaken concurrently in the same institution. In fact, many large media organizations are interested in financing pure research and do so, and some researchers feel that the media should provide more funds for this purpose. As important as finance is the friendly contact which commissioned research may create between academics and media personnel, without which important work, particularly on communicators and communication organizations would be impossible to undertake.

Nevertheless, many commentators have pointed out the real potential dangers which may arise from too close a connexion between media organizations and academic researchers. One danger is that valuable results remain the private property of the sponsor and are not published at all, or not in the form intended by the researcher. Another, more insidious danger, is that the immediate needs of media organizations will press too heavily on the orientation taken by mass communication research, so that the search for and use of sophisticated methodology which will produce foolproof, immediately usable findings of a simplistic kind, will outweigh the need to ask and answer questions which are difficult to 'operationalize' through quantitative techniques of experiment, survey and content analysis.

The other main interested party in mass communication research in the United States is the government and its various agencies. Here again, a great deal of research has been initiated and sponsored by the government's immediate need for knowledge on certain issues of moment. One need only refer to the interest in propaganda during and after the Second World War, when studies by leading academics like Lasswell and Hovland and their associates were financed by the War Department, the Treasury and other government agencies, with very fruitful results for the development of knowledge about the field in general. The relationship between media research, governmental preoccupations, and wider societal concerns associated with the mass media in the United States would repay future detailed investigation. It is clearly related to a more general phenomenon, the tendency, during and since the Second World War, for government to rely increasingly on academic investigation and advice in matters of applied science, including social science. And, as the State takes on an increasing range of functions, so the range of its interests in pure science must grow.

Several examples of research areas in which much work is being done, and which are connected, directly or indirectly, with government needs, spring to mind. One is the prospects and regulation of cable television. Another is educational television. Clearly the future of satellite communication is also relevant here, and according to one informant (Wiebe, 1970) interest in satellites has been important in stimulating the growing interest in international communications. But the growth of this research area is also rooted in the Cold War, the post-war shift from isolation to international involvement, and the cross-cultural implications of American aid to underdeveloped areas and to United States foreign policy generally (Markham, 1970).

At present, many research programmes depend on government funding. In 1969, for example, the Department of Communication at Michigan State University stated that its research support was 'drawn heavily from government, including the Department of Defense and the Agency for International Development', while the University of Missouri's School of Journalism stated that it undertook 'basic communication researches for state agencies (e.g. Public Library, Public Health Service)'. In 1969, the Institute for Communication Research at Stanford University derived about 56 per cent of its budget from government contracts and grants, compared with 12 per cent from the university and 30 per cent from foundations. The Center for Communication Research at the University of Texas also secured part of its budget from governmental and military sources and the Department of Agricultural Journalism at the University of Wisconsin also secured funds additional to those allocated to it by the university from the government (Blum, 1969).

Not only can money be obtained from government agencies for research on projects which would be difficult to finance from university funds or foundation grants, but government-sponsored research may initiate work by individuals or teams from many different institutions, academic or otherwise, and co-ordinate it, if need be, with the speed and efficiency of a military operation.

An example of the wide range of studies commissioned by one agency alone is the research programme involving twenty-three projects on the impact of televised violence on children's behaviour, attitudes and development. It was initiated in 1970 following the report of the National Commission on the Causes and Prevention of Violence (1969) which emphasized the need for research. The $1 million dollar research programme was co-ordinated by the National Institute of Mental Health (NIMH), part of the Department of Health, Education and Welfare (HEW) and was the special responsibility of the Surgeon-General's Scientific Advisory Committee on Television and Social Behaviour, a body formed at the request of the Senate Subcommittee on Communications. Eighteen of the twenty-three projects (totalling $897,000) were allocated to researchers at fourteen universities. Reports were submitted within six months to a year of allocation, so that the committee could prepare an over-all report to the Surgeon-General by late 1971. The projects involved a wide spectrum of subjects (preschool children to university students) and research techniques (polygraph records, experiments, filmed responses, direct observation in family settings, survey questionnaires and content analyses). The areas investigated were also widely ranging, including analyses of viewing behaviour, especially of children in family settings, their involvement with programmes, their social interaction in the viewing situation, their perception and understanding of televised violent content, the relative effects of fantasy and realism in shaping aggressive attitudes and behaviour, the immediate effects of viewing on attitudes and values, for example in relation to the legitimation of violence, and detailed analyses of the content and programming of American television (*HEW News*, 1970; United States, 1972). It is most unlikely that a research programme of such dimensions could be mounted by individual researchers on their own initiative.

On the other hand, the need to satisfy the public that something is being done about a problem, and the need to deliver results quickly, may end in large funds being spent on producing a set of scattered, unco-ordinated research reports which do not tackle the problem within a common framework of questions and theoretical perspectives. Consequently, at best, interesting new data is produced, but no advantage is gained from mounting a large research operation rather than the normal individual initiatives of academic researchers. Because the research has not been structured in the first place, the results will not build up into a coherent whole which gives meaningful answers to the problem at hand. This was unfortunately the case in a series of studies on educational television commissioned in the early 1960s, under Title VII of the National Defense of Education Act of 1958 (Kitross, 1967). In these circumstances the devotion of public money for academic research may backfire, and the initial naïve assumption that research can give quick and easy answers to complicated social problems may be replaced by the equally simplistic notion that all academic research is a waste of money.

To turn to the present pattern of finance in United States mass media research, the data collected in this survey, though incomplete, allows some tentative conclusions to be drawn. In all, 81 university-based institutions submitted detailed titles of their ongoing research. Of these 268 projects, 99 were financed by individual researchers or their publishers, or did not specify their source of funds. Of the remaining 169 projects all listed only one source of funds except for 6 which listed two. The part played by external sources of finance in university-based mass media research in 1969–70 can be broken down into government- and non-government-financed projects. Thirty-two of the 169 projects (18.9 per cent) were financed by the federal government and 7 (4.1 per cent) by state/municipal governments. Non-government financing accounted for 45 projects (26.6 per cent) financed by foundations, associations or other universities and 85 (50.3 per cent) by the researcher's university or department.

To sum up, only half the projects listed were funded by the researcher's own department or his university. One-quarter derived their support either from foundations (including the Ford and Carnegie Foundations, the National Science Foundation, the Brookings Institution, the Twentieth Century Fund, and the National Endowment for the Humanities), from professional associations (including the Corporation for Public Broadcasting, the National Association of Broadcasters, the Association for Education in Journalism and other educational bodies), or from universities apart from the one to which the researcher belonged. A little less than one-quarter of the projects were supported mainly by various federal agencies (the Department of Health, Education and Welfare, the U.S. Office of Information, the Group Psychology Branch of the Office of Naval Research, the Office of Educational Opportunity, the Office of Education, the National Bureau of Roads, the Departments of Public Health and of Agriculture, the U.S. Forestry Service and the National Aerospace Administration). However, it should be noted that the proportion of mass communication research projects financed by federal-government bodies is probably much larger than the above figures suggest, since federal funds may be channelled indirectly through foundations such as the National Science Foundation. Interestingly, no projects commissioned by media industries such as individual newspapers were listed by respondents, presumably because such information was confidential.

The pattern of media research therefore seems partly attributable to the amount of money made available to answer urgent or potentially urgent questions of concern to media industries, government, or sufficiently influential, or merely vocal sections of the public. These questions may be ill-informed, or they may spring from ill-founded assumptions about the relation of mass media to sociological, psychological or political processes. Also, the preoccupations underlying the willingness to devote private or public funds to university-based research are likely to be sporadic, erratic, and not necessarily related to each other in any scientifically systematic way. It may happen, of course, that research, in laying bare the difficulties that arise when the wrong questions are asked, may stimulate a series of studies in which a particular problem is systematically investigated. This occurred, for example, in the series of persuasion studies undertaken by the research teams at Columbia and at Yale. But normally it is not so, and it is unlikely to be so in unconnected, single, service studies for media industries. Consequently, if a sizeable proportion of mass communication research in universities consists of single studies with narrow focus, this may partly account for the oft-noted tendency of American research to amass 'aggregates of discrete tidbits of information' and to concentrate on establishing the existence of 'relations which occur empirically', rather than those which 'subsist logically' (Merton, 1968).

It need not be emphasized that heavy reliance on outside funds, particularly those supplied by media industries and government, is not a phenomenon unique to the United States, but occurs wherever mass communication research is conducted on any scale. But because of the wealth of the United States, its media industries and its government agencies probably have more funds available to use for research, if they wish, than anywhere else. Moreover, since American media research has been so influential all over the world, it is possible that the intellectual situation of American mass media research will recur to some extent everywhere. Indeed, a fair amount of mass media research undertaken in other countries, particularly in the Third World, is initiated by visiting American professors, sometimes with the aid of funds from the United States. This increases the probability of American research methods being exported overseas, often without due consideration for different social and economic systems and day-to-day conditions in different countries. It is unfortunately still true that some American researchers, and those whom they have influenced elsewhere,

> merely assume that if only The Method i.e. the correct statistical methodology is used, such studies as result—scattered from Elmira to Zagreb to Shanghai—will add up finally to a full-fledged organised science. (Mills, 1959.)

Present and future trends

It is clearly impossible in a work of this kind to review the changes in substantive content of American mass communication research over the years. Useful surveys are contained in Klapper (1960), Schramm (1962), White (1964), De Fleur (1966), Tannenbaum and Greenberg (1968) and Kline and Tichenor (1972). In general terms, it is clear that in the course of time the accumulation of empirical research findings have led to the formulation of more complex and sophisticated hypotheses to explain the operation of mass media. Until about the mid-1950s most American mass communication research was underpinned by the implicit assumption that mass media messages had a direct, persuasive impact on the passive audience members who received them. Whether the disciplinary orientation was political, sociological or psychological, and whether the techniques used were content analysis, survey questionnaire, interview or laboratory experiment, it tended to be assumed that the audience consisted of a collection of individuals who could be more or less easily 'brainwashed' by powerful mass media to modify their behaviour through the manipulation of their opinions and attitudes. In the later fifties and early sixties simple effects hypotheses were superseded by the interposition of mediating factors, intervening variables between content and audience, related to aspects of the individual's own psychological make-up and social needs and his group membership. Sociological and social-psychological research on opinion leadership in information diffusion, on cognitive dissonance and on uses and gratifications have transformed the earlier, simple, one-directional flow from content to audience into a far more complex, convoluted model of the communication process, focused primarily on the audience's manipulation of mass media content to serve its own needs, rather than the manipulation of audience reactions by mass media. These research areas tend to stress the informational aspects of mass communication and the elements of rational choice involved in mass media use. Even in highly structured laboratory experiments to test the effects of media content particularly on children, earlier hypotheses of direct imitation have been replaced by more complex psychological mechanisms such as identification or catharsis, the concept of attitude has become far more complex, and it is not always assumed that attitude changes automatically imply changes in behaviour. There is also a growing body of research on the social role of mass communication, its function in legitimating certain values, or as a screening mechanism which defines the social situation for the audience, or as a feedback mechanism between various subsystems in a total social system tending towards homeostasis. Such postulates have directed renewed attention to the role of the communicator in the mass communication process, especially the news process. Earlier gatekeeper models which emphasized the power of a single individual to affect the total news flow, have given way to more elaborate hypotheses

TABLE 7. Distribution of ongoing research projects in United States universities in 1969/70, by medium studied

Medium	Number of projects	Percentage of total	Medium	Number of projects	Percentage of total
Multi-media projects			*Single-media projects*		
Mass media generally	128	48.9	Newspapers	35	13.4
Radio and television	11	4.2	Television	28	10.7
Newspapers and periodicals	10	3.8	Radio	11	4.2
Radio, television and printed media	4	1.5	Cinema	10	3.8
			Other	10	3.8
Other multi-media projects	15	5.7	TOTAL (all projects)	262	100.0

involving the effect of multiple gatekeepers and their professional news values in shaping content, and, more recently, the role of organizational structures within media industries and of reference groups in bringing these values into being. This type of research emphasizes the dependence of mass communicated content on communication organizations and, implicitly or explicitly, on their systematic relationship with other social groups and the structure of society as a whole.

The development of these approaches has resulted in research being increasingly focused on mass communication as a total process, rather than on its particular characteristics and operation in relation to any single medium. The data received in connexion with this survey revealed that some two-thirds of the projects under way in 1969/70 were concerned with the mass media generally, or with two or more media considered together, as Table 7 demonstrates.

This survey also tried to gauge the future thrusts of American research. Respondents were asked to fill in a grid (as in Table 8) with the main media listed along the vertical axis, and various types of research along the horizontal, in respect of research planned to start in 1970/71. Any particular topic might result in several squares being filled in. For example, the effects of televised violence on children would result in the squares television—content, television—audiences, television—effects being marked. The sum total of the responses for each medium by research area were summed and percentages derived, so that a sort of demographic map of the pattern and range of intended research might be revealed. It can be seen that the most popular field for our respondents at any rate was the mass media generally, followed by television, newspapers and radio. The study of periodicals and of the cinema did not attract much interest. The original grid also contained books and advertising as possible research topics, but the responses were so small (fifty and six respectively) that it would be highly misleading to draw any conclusions from them, and they have been omitted from the table.

Our respondents indicated a concentration of interest on the study of effects, an area which has also attracted significant interest in all other mass media except the cinema. One may conclude therefore that as far as our respondents are concerned, effects research is still the strongest strand over-all in American mass media research. The study of audiences also evoked much interest, particularly in regard to periodicals, radio and television, and content research was also a popular field, especially in relation to the study of individual media. These areas have always dominated American mass media research, and are likely to continue to do so. Other traditionally popular areas, revealed in Table 8, are newspaper and cinema history and aesthetic study of the

United States of America and Canada

TABLE 8. Percentage contribution of various research areas to study of each medium in research planned in the United States after 1970

Research areas	Mass Media generally	News-papers	Magazines, journals, comics	Radio	Television	Cinema
History and development of	5.7	16.4	8.8	6.8	7.3	14.5
Legal and governmental regulation of	3.5	5.2	7.7	11.7	10.4	4.3
Censorship—formal and informal	3.5	7.0	5.5	5.4	3.8	2.9
Economics of	2.2	3.8	2.2	2.4	1.9	4.3
Instructional role/use of	5.9	5.2	7.7	9.3	16.9	8.7
Institutions and personnel in	3.5	5.2	1.1	4.4	3.1	0.0
Content of	7.6	11.3	20.9	11.7	10.4	13.0
Audiences for	8.6	8.5	15.4	14.1	11.9	4.3
Attitudinal, behavioural and informational effects of	15.7	10.8	16.5	11.2	10.8	4.3
Political role of	7.8	6.6	2.2	6.8	8.5	2.9
Social consequences of	7.6	7.0	6.6	6.3	6.5	4.3
Introduction and diffusion of Art and aesthetics of	1.6	1.4	4.4	4.4	2.3	27.5
Mass communication between different countries through	4.6	1.9	1.1	2.9	3.9	1.4
Research techniques in	12.2	1.9	0.0	2.0	1.9	1.4
Other	10.0	7.9	0.0	0.5	0.4	5.8
	100.0	100.1	100.1	99.9	100.0	99.9
	N=370	N=213	N=91	N=205	N=260	N=67

cinema. It is interesting to note that the regulation of radio and television broadcasting has also attracted a significant amount of interest, perhaps because of the activities of the Federal Communications Commission. An important strand in forthcoming television research will be focused on its instructional role and uses, an area which has aroused much public interest, and where funds for research have been made available by various grant-giving bodies. Finally, attention may be drawn to the high proportion of responses in the category of research techniques in mass media generally, which indicates a continued interest in methodology among American mass communication researchers.

It would be dangerous to generalize too far on the basis of responses to one survey taken at a particular time. But it is interesting to draw attention to some areas which obtained very few responses: the political role of mass communication, media regulation and censorship, the study of media institutions and personnel, and the economic aspects of mass media. All these areas are connected in some way with questions of power and control, and with the constraints on mass communication that derive from the situation and operation of media institutions within the total social structure. It would seem that only when these areas are given as much attention as other aspects of mass communication research that a comprehensive, scientifically critical and empirically based account of mass media as social institutions and mass communication as a social process can be constructed. It seems likely, since questions of power and control have raised so much controversy in American social science generally in recent years, that some repercussions may be expected soon in the field of mass communication research.

If there is one country in the world where training, teaching and research in the social aspects of mass media and mass communication have become fully accepted as a valid field for university study, that country *par excellence* is the United States. As the foregoing sections have demonstrated, the field has a long and interesting history, and over the course of time there have been significant changes in content and orientation which have been accompanied by structural adjustments in American universities to accommodate them. Consequently, education and research in various aspects of mass communication have become fully established as an integral part of the spectrum of academic activities in a large number of universities. In the United States education and research about the mass media and mass communication is a strong and growing field which has given a distinctive stamp to contemporary study of the mass media all over the world. The American contribution to mass media studies has been overwhelmingly important in the last four decades; its present variety, richness and originality promises that future contributions will be equally significant.

Canada

In 1969 T. J. Scanlon of Carleton University, Ottawa, observed that attempting to encompass developments in Canadian journalism education of the previous five years was

> like trying to trace the course of a quiet stream, which, as a result of a cloudburst, has suddenly become a raging river and flooded its banks.

Between 1945 and 1965, only three institutions offered mass media teaching, Carleton University in Ottawa, the University of Western Ontario in London, Ontario, and Ryerson Institute of Technology, a tertiary-level institution in Toronto. All three had established journalism departments immediately after the Second World War, because many ex-servicemen wished to have professional training in journalism, and the Canadian Government was loth to finance the university education it had promised them in the journalism schools of the United States (Unesco, 1958).

In 1965, the first university-level course in mass communications was begun at Loyola College in Montreal. Other universities followed suit, offering courses, and programmes in a few instances, at undergraduate, and, less often, at post-graduate level. In 1971 the Association of Universities and Colleges of Canada stated (AUCC, 1971):

> Communications studies are becoming more important in many Canadian universities [and] . . . a new emphasis is developing with communications courses being offered by several different departments (often together under an interdisciplinary umbrella) slanted to a theory of communications more than professional usage in journalism and [school] teaching. The new approach tries to make possible a critical understanding of how the media of mass communication serve and reflect society.

This assessment is perhaps a little overstated, but there is, nevertheless, a new trend towards the study of communications in Canadian universities. Since the inauguration of the undergraduate major in Communication Arts at Loyola College in 1965, the University of Windsor began a three-year Communication Arts major in 1969, and the University of Toronto started its undergraduate sequence in communication in 1970.

Laval University's course in journalism and information, begun in 1968, is strongly oriented towards mass communication; and the professional journalism degree courses at Carleton and Western Ontario universities are shifting in this direction. At postgraduate level, the University of Saskatchewan (Regina) already offers a master's programme, the Université de Montréal was preparing to do so in 1972, and the University of Western Ontario is also on the point of extending its post-graduate work in this field. Many diploma courses in mass media studies are provided in Canadian universities, and since the late 1960s communication courses have begun to appear among offerings for degrees in sociology, fine arts, business administration and education.

Commenting on the increased interest in mass communication since 1965, J. E. O'Brien, S. J., Chairman of the Communication Arts Department at Loyola College wrote (O'Brien, 1970, 1971):

> Several factors might account for this—excitement about EXPO ['67] and the new experiments in perception, the dawning awareness about the all-pervasive influence of mass media in Canada, the 'sudden discovery' of McLuhan, the opening of Junior Colleges (a two-year span between high school and university), the obvious interest of students and, perhaps not least, the opening and almost immediate success of the department at Loyola.

Nevertheless, the over-all impression of present Canadian university-level studies on the social aspects of mass media and mass communication, as the detailed exposition will make clear, is that while very many courses are offered (at least one in almost every Canadian university), in most cases teaching is unspecialized, scattered among different departments as part of other disciplines, and tends to be somewhat inchoate and unorganized.

The Telecommission, a federal group appointed by the Department of Communications, recently conducted an eighteen-month inquiry into present and future prospects of telecommunications in Canada. Its *Multidisciplinary Manpower Study* included a survey of Canadian universities, to determine how far they could meet the need for policy-making executives with a multidisciplinary background (Telecommission, 1971). It revealed

> a very limited emphasis on communication as a distinct discipline. The majority of respondents [covering all Canadian graduate schools] reported no graduate program in communications. There are, however, a number of courses being offered in other faculties which relate to communications . . .
>
> Responses to the question on dissertation topics showed a similar lack of emphasis on communications. There appears to be a general appreciation however that this is an area of great potential . . .

Canadian mass media research has been relatively recent, and much of it has been done for various Royal Commissions, such as those on Bilingualism and Biculturalism (set up in 1963) or on Publications (the O'Leary Commission appointed in 1961), and for various other boards, committees, agencies and other government bodies. The briefing of some of these bodies has been very extensive and has often included some investigation into the mass media from various points of view, particularly the Special Senate Committee on Mass Media under the chairmanship of the Hon. Keith Davey. Some of this research has been undertaken with the assistance of academic staff of Canadian universities and other institutions of higher learning, but it has sometimes been limited in its availability and distribution.

Informants in Canada have attributed the relatively undeveloped state of Canadian academic mass media studies to a variety of factors. One important reason seems to be that, as one correspondent (Selby, 1970) observed,

> Canadian studies in the media have been neglected or overshadowed because of our contiguity to the United States.

Another (Gordon, 1970) went further and explained:

> Most of our faculty people are trained in the U.S. . . . virtually all of our journals, books, ephemera and programming comes from the U.S. We depend upon American equipment (with built-in assumptions) and find, alas, that any work done in Canada by Canadians only merits serious attention when it is approved and taken up by some U.S. institutions . . . Also, almost all the business firms (and agencies, equipment makers, programme packagers, writers, etc.) associated with communications take the U.S. style as their standard. Despite regulations governing Canadian content we don't manage much beyond the form rather than the substance sought.[1]

Furthermore, university-level mass media teaching appears to have been affected, and possibly somewhat inhibited, by the growth of communication courses in community colleges and other tertiary-level vocational institutions, particularly in the last decade. Many college departments are very well equipped, and employ media professionals to teach courses on production. They reach very high standards in practical work, but the feeling has been expressed that they are not always a genuine substitute for more academically oriented teaching that tends to take place in university-based departments.

The third factor which appears to be at work in creating and sustaining the pattern of mass media studies in Canada is the relative scarcity of available resources—financial and intellectual—for the development of specialized university-level courses. For example, in Nova Scotia (Hancock, 1970):

> In 1962 a school of journalism was mutually organised in Halifax by three of our Nova Scotia universities. The school had grown so rapidly in three years that, ironically, it brought the program face to face with a financial problem which ultimately resulted in the suspension of classes in communications. Consequently, we now have no degree training in communications in any of the universities in this region.

Financial problems have come to the fore again recently in some instances. For example, one correspondent explained (Mamet, 1971):

> The present high unemployment situation in Canada with many University graduates including a goodly number of PhD's unable to find positions, has directed attention to the whole matter of higher education and the powers that be are questioning the possible reduction of operations and a complete reorientation of the higher educational system. There seems to be greater interest now in the Community College concept which in a sense will further reduce the possibility of funds for the University.

The responses to the Telecommission survey indicated that the introduction of multidisciplinary communications programmes in the social sciences and humanities was hampered by shortage of qualified staff and financial resources. Existing graduate programmes were mostly felt to be limited by shortages of academic staff, graduate financial assistance and research equipment and training facilities (Telecommission, 1971).

All these factors, operating in combination with the traditionally suspicious attitudes towards new fields that sometimes obtain in older, well-established disciplines, have encouraged that sprinkling of mass media courses in different departments that is characteristic of many Canadian universities. Consequently many Canadian students who wish to pursue studies in mass communication, particularly at postgraduate level, go to universities in the United States.

---

1. See also evidence of T. L. McPhail, Department of Sociology and Communication Arts, Loyola College, in: The Senate of Canada, *Proceedings of the Special Senate Committee on Mass Media*, the Hon. Keith Davey, Chairman, No. 26, Thursday, March 5, 1970, p. 22.

Nevertheless, several factors have combined to foster the present and anticipated future growth of mass media studies in Canadian universities. The Telecommission reported a growing belief that telecommunications were a vital and informing link between the many regions and the two cultures of Canada.

Finally, one might add that the Telecommission's survey, by focusing attention on the extent of graduate work in communications, its present inadequacies, and its future prospects, may in itself stimulate more systematic teaching in mass media studies, particularly in view of its conclusion that 'there is a fairly urgent need for multidiscipline trained graduates [in communications]'.

Against this general background, a more detailed discussion of mass media studies in Canadian universities can now be given, starting with the activities of those universities which have departments of journalism.

Universities with journalism programmes

There are two old, well-established journalism programmes in Canada, both in the province of Ontario.

Carleton University in Ottawa was the first Canadian University to establish a full-time formal course of professional training in journalism in 1945, closely modelled on the schools of journalism in the United States, and especially the Columbia Graduate School of Journalism. The impetus was provided by the fact that a number of ex-servicemen wanted to study journalism, and since the newly created Carleton College (as it was then) had been considering starting a course, it was considered appropriate to place it there. The original instructors were professional journalists (a policy which still continues) and the course was oriented towards print journalism, consisting of press history and law, and practical training in basic skills like reporting and editing, within a framework of social science and humanities courses. Related fields like typography, layout, news photgraphy, public relations and radio journalism were also treated. At present the emphasis is

> shifting ... from the ... conventional techniques of journalism to include such courses as The Modern Environment: an inter-disciplinary course ranging from the nature of the modern community to the philosophic questions raised by the study of the culture of science, [although the programme still includes] courses on the fundamentals of reporting, editing and newspaper production. (AUCC, 1971.)

In 1970 the Journalism Department of Carleton University had nine permanent academic staff, eight special and sessional lecturers and seminar leaders, and five field-work supervisors who were working media professionals. It offers a four-year full-time honours programme leading to a Bachelor of Journalism degree, and a one-year postgraduate diploma course open to holders of a bachelor's degree. The undergraduate course emphasizes liberal scholarship and basic skills. The emphasis is on print journalism but there is opportunity for specialization in radio and television, public relations, film, and other fields. About seventy students a year qualify, and about 75 per cent of past graduates have become working journalists. Graduate students do advanced work in specialized fields, and carry out directed research leading to a thesis.

The Carleton University Senate has approved in principle the construction of a new Media Centre, to be completed by 1973, which will make it possible to increase the television content of Carleton's journalism course.

Members of the department engage in research. Recent publications included work on the effects of colour in mass communications, including television, and the impact of television news.

The Journalism Department in the Faculty of Social Science at the University of Western Ontario, London, Ontario, was also established at the end of the Second World War, in the Faculty of Arts and Science. Courses began in September 1946, and the first students graduated in 1948. Like Carleton College, the University of Western Ontario modelled its course on those in United States journalism schools. In 1951, the three-year course became a four-year Honours Bachelor of Arts degree. A one-year post-graduate course, leading to a Diploma in Journalism, open to graduates in fields other than journalism was set up in 1954.

The present honours degree programme comprises twenty-three and a half courses; seven and a half are journalism courses and sixteen are in the liberal arts and sciences. The emphasis is towards journalism within a mass communication context, rather than instruction in the principles and techniques of newspaper journalism alone. The course includes a public-relations option.

The programme is structured so that

> a student may . . . take half of his arts and sciences courses in a single field such as Political Science, English, History, Economics. This opportunity to concentrate in a second field has made it possible for many Honours Journalism graduates to continue to postgraduate study in those fields, even to the Ph. D. level. On the other hand a journalism student may sample widely among the dozens of fields of study offered in the University. (Wild, 1970.)

The post-graduate diploma course consists of the journalism courses offered in the honours programme, or their equivalent, and additional seminars and projects.

Apart from its professionally oriented honours and post-graduate diploma courses in journalism, the Journalism Department also offers a survey course on mass communication (emphasizing the structure of the mass media, their relationship to the social, economic, political and cultural environment, elements of mass communication theory and critical analyses of media coverage of important issues). This course may be taken by students registered in other programmes, who do not intend to become journalists. It is hoped to expand it to a core of four offerings.

The Sociology Department in the Faculty of Social Science at the University of Western Ontario, has, since 1966, offered a senior undergraduate course on the sociology of communication (called Communication and Social Character), which deals with communication and opinion research methodology, the symbolic content of media messages, symbolic transmission within groups, the mass media as institutions, the effects of mass media on behaviour, socialization and opinion-formation, neo-formalism in mass communication analysis, and contemporary Canadian concerns with respect to mass media. In 1970 a master's course on sociology of communication was introduced. The University of Western Ontario is preparing to establish a Social Science Communications Research Centre which will have facilities for research into television effects and will be fully equipped with television viewing rooms, control rooms, etc. (Singer, 1970).

Laval University in Quebec has offered a programme in journalism and information in the Arts Faculty at bachelor's-degree level since 1968. It was the first French-language university in Canada to do so. Its emphasis is theoretical rather than practical. There is

> an attempt to make the students understand the problems of communications, the problems of the mass media, the challenges that are facing them, the shortcomings and an analysis of what they are doing etcetera . . . We . . . feel . . . that practical training can be done more quickly in . . . a television studio or a newspaper office than . . . at university . . . and . . . you may be training people to do the wrong things in any case.
>
> Practice in the mass media is changing so rapidly and it varies so widely also from enterprise to enterprise and from group to group that really you

might be training somebody to do something that they will have to unlearn ... when they get out. (Sloan, 1969.)

Enrolment, amounting to 100 in 1970, was the largest for any journalism course outside Ontario. The twenty course offerings include communication, history of collective communication, sources of information, the law and communication, editorial *genres*, stylistics, public opinion, comparative study of treatment of information, ethics, the publication of a newspaper, knowledge of news, information in French-Canadian society, public relations and publicity, government information, modern theories of communication, media enterprises, contemporary foreign press, group newspapers and the provincial press, radio and television news.

The full journalism training programme begun in 1962 at the University of King's College, Nova Scotia, was abandoned in 1966. Now the university offers scattered communication courses in its extension service to any students who wish to attend.

Dalhousie University, in Halifax, which is affiliated with the University of King's College, offers a diploma in journalism.

Since 1966, Mount St Vincent University, in Halifax, Nova Scotia, has offered a part-time summer course in journalism, leading to a certificate after three years, in collaboration with Pennsylvania State University.

Communication programmes

Several Canadian universities now offer courses in communications at bachelor's- or master's-degree level.

The first communication-oriented university department in Canada was the Department of Communication Arts established in 1965 at Loyola College, Montreal. It has grown rapidly and attracted students 'from India, Yugoslavia, the United States and most provinces of Canada'.

The Chairman wrote (O'Brien, 1970, 1971):

> We are not interested in preparing students directly for positions in media. Rather we stress theory and practice with great emphasis on creativity throughout. Some of our graduates have gone to universities in the United States, Canada and Europe, others are working in media, media professions, education, personnel work, management etc. [The Department] bases its work in communication theory and research, cinema, radio and television on a solid foundation in the liberal arts, [and intends] to develop in students a scholarly and creative approach to mass media.

There are two programmes. A four-year major course in communication arts for the Bachelor of Arts degree was inaugurated in 1965. It was to become a three-year course, with a minimum of seven full courses in the Communication Arts department in the 1971/72 academic year. In 1967 a one-year post-graduate diploma course in communication arts was introduced.

Both programmes deal with the media generally, especially radio, television and the cinema, also with advertising. They cover historical, ethical, organizational and aesthetic aspects; educational uses of mass media; social and psychological studies; research methods; mass media as cultural forms; and photography as a visual language. Instruction in media skills is also provided. Loyola College runs a European Summer Institute in Communication Arts in the major Western European centres, for both programmes. There are ten full-time academic staff and two part-time media professionals in the Communication Arts department. Its research includes recent publications on history and aesthetics of cinema and television, and educational uses of mass media.

The Regina Campus of the University of Saskatchewan has offered a two-year M.A. programme in communications since 1967 in the Faculty of Graduate Studies. The programme includes, but is not limited to, mass communications. In July 1970, the Chairman of the Administrative Committee of the M.A. programme explained (Smythe, 1970):

> As we have defined our interests they range over the full span of man as a message and symbol using animal. Studies centred in Fine Arts, in Computer Science, in Biology, and in Social Sciences, are equally expected here. This is possible because we do not have any faculty hired specifically to teach 'Communications'.

There is no specific budget for mass media research, but four members of staff are at present engaged in research.

Some undergraduate teaching on mass media is offered in the Divisions of Fine Arts and of Social Sciences. In the Division of Fine Arts, the Department of Visual Arts has offered film study as one subject in the Bachelor of Fine Arts degree since 1968. Students may take as many as twelve classes in film (covering history, aesthetics and practical film-making) under a directed study programme of individual instruction.

The University of Windsor at Windsor, Ontario, established its Department of Communication Arts in 1969. In 1970 it had three full-time staff. In 1969, a first-year introductory survey course was offered, three second-year classes were started in 1970, and third-year classes began in 1971. The department hopes to offer a fourth-year honours programme as soon as possible and to increase its academic staff. Its orientation is not towards professional training but towards a critical understanding of the media. So far its major concern is to build up its undergraduate teaching programme, but it hopes to sponsor and encourage mass media research as soon as it is feasible, especially in regard to Canadian and Canadian-American problems.

The University of Toronto, Ontario, has a Centre for Culture and Technology, directed by Marshall McLuhan. It is an interdisciplinary centre for graduate work.

In 1970, the University of Toronto began a new undergraduate programme, its 'New Program', whereby, instead of choosing major subjects for a bachelor's degree, students are encouraged to organize a programme which has its own organic unity. Many courses are interdisciplinary, and sequences of these, called 'faculty studies', are being developed in the Faculty of Arts and Science. Communications is the newest sequence to be organized, and the description states that (AUCC, 1971):

> Implications of electronic communications will occupy only a secondary role ... the focus ... will be on the efforts of humans to communicate with each other in the realms of logic, art, gesture and propaganda. The ultimate goal ... will be to analyse the contemporary problem of alienation and communication failure.

In 1971/72, the University of Toronto is offering an undergraduate degree in cinema.

Saint Paul University in Ottawa has an Institute of Social Communications, which offers a curriculum leading to a Diploma of University Studies in Communication. Some of its courses may also be taken for degree purposes by students registered in other faculties of both the University of Saint Paul and the University of Ottawa. The institute is only two years old, and at present is most under-staffed, the only full-time teacher being the Director. Its regular academic programme has been very popular (140 students being enrolled for all courses in 1970) as has its summer session. An interesting feature of the institute is that it is completely bilingual, and has attracted an almost perfect balance of French- and English-speaking students, including some from the United States.

At present it offers an undergraduate diploma of one to two years in social communications. Its courses cover the media generally from historical, economic, legal and ethical points of view; the structure of media institutions; educational uses of media;

sociological studies of the media; practices and techniques in radio, television and cinema; the aesthetics of cinema, historical and pastoral perspectives, and philosophy of social communication.

At the University of Montreal, as Jean Cloutier (1970) explained, there was no central body teaching communication in 1970. There are communication courses in several departments, especially in the Sociology and the Political Sciences departments and the Institute of Psychology. The Department of Extension offers teaching in public relations leading to a certificate equivalent to one year's full-time study, and will offer a similar course in journalism in 1971.

The Audio Visual Centre gives courses in the arts of communication; photography, audio-visuals, graphics, multi-media, cinema and television, which are taken by students mostly in the Faculty of Educational Sciences and in adult education. The Faculty of Educational Sciences offers a bachelor's degree with a speciality in audio-visual media, as well as a master's and doctoral degree in that area.

But the University of Montreal had decided to extend its mass communication teaching in 1971. The Dean of the Faculty of Philosophy explained (Belanger, 1970) that that faculty had been asked by the university to set up a programme in communications which would eventually lead to the creation of a department for training and research in this field. At the same it is intended to combine the efforts of staff in various departments who are interested in communications problems and have been doing research in this field, so that, with the addition of personnel specifically trained in communications research, it should be possible to offer doctoral training in communications research from the very beginning. Also a review of isolated courses taught in several departments is being undertaken, and new ones planned, so that all of these combined will be offered as a minor subject in communications for various degree programmes.

Universities with scattered mass media courses

The information supplied in Table 9 illustrates the extent to which mass media studies are included in various programmes in a number of Canadian universities.

Tertiary-level institutions

The picture of the scope and extent of mass media studies in Canada would be incomplete without brief reference to the vocationally oriented training for media occupations offered by Canadian community colleges (colleges of applied arts and technology, institutes of technology, *collèges d'enseignement général et professionnel* and similar institutions). Table 10 summarizes the activities of those colleges which supplied detailed information to this survey in 1970. The table shows that apart from Ryerson Polytechnical Institute, which has two separate Departments of Journalism and Radio and Television Arts founded in 1948 and 1952 respectively, almost all the departments or sections dealing with mass media studies started their activities after the mid-1960s. The three main areas dealt with are newspaper journalism, broadcasting and advertising.

The most recently available information on the teaching activities of these institutions is shown in Table 11. It will be seen that the majority of colleges offering mass media programmes are in Ontario, which has more than all the other regions combined. The increase in mass media programmes, even between 1970–71 and 1971–72,

TABLE 9. Scattered media courses in Canadian universities

University	Faculty, department or programme	Course offerings
Alberta, Edmonton	Psychology	Social psychology and creativity
	Sociology	Public opinion and mass communication
	English	Creative writing
	Drama	Film and television
	Art	Film
Brock, St Catherines	Drama	Three mass media courses, concentrating on the cinema
Calgary	Communications media	Produces broadcast material and provides some training
	Drama	Three courses in film and television
	Sociology	Socio-psychological effects of media
	Education	Instructional media and technology
George Williams, Montreal	Fine arts	Five film courses and two courses in drawing and graphics for media
	Educational technology	Communication methods
McGill, Montreal	English, Anthropology, Sociology and Political science,	Single courses on communication, mass communication, public opinion
	Speech pathology	Bachelor's degree in communication
McMaster, Hamilton	English	Single course on Art of the Film
New Brunswick, Fredericton	English	Occasional courses in mass media
Simon Fraser, Burnaby	Education	Four media courses
	General education programme	Courses in the arts, including film
Waterloo	Arts	General course on origins and evolution of media
	Fine arts	Fifteen courses on film
	Political science	Mass media and law; public opinion
	Sociology	Language and culture; communication
	Psychology	Three courses partly concerned with communication
	English	One or two courses on media
	Electrical engineering	Eleven courses in communication theory and systems, information theory and transmission
Waterloo Lutheran	English	Single course on film
York, Downsville	Fine Arts	Courses in film and film production

also emerges from a study of this table. It will be seen that the number of colleges offering programmes in communications increased from eighteen to twenty in these two years, the number offering journalism programmes increased from fourteen to nineteen, and the number offering programmes in radio and television arts increased from thirteen to sixteen. There is also a slight indication that the tendency exists to extend the length of the courses to three years.

United States of America and Canada

College	Department and date of foundation	Mass media teaching staff	Qualification[1]	Main teaching orientation
Ontario				
Cambrian College, North Bay	Communication Arts (1969)	12 full-time, 6 part-time	Two-year Diploma of Applied Arts (14)	Newspapers, radio, television, advertising.
			Three-year Diploma of Applied Arts (0)	
Centennial College, Scarborough	Division of Applied Arts (Communications programme)		Three-year major in journalism, creative writing, radio-television writing	Writing skills for journalism, advertising, broadcast script-writing, broadcast production
Conestoga College, Kitchener	Communication Arts (Radio-television) (1967)	4 full-time, 3 part-time	Three-year Diploma	Radio-television
	Journalism (1967)	2 full-time	Three-year Diploma	Journalism
	Film (1967)	2 full-time, 1 part-time	Three-year Diploma	Film production
Durham College, Oshawa	Applied Arts Division (1968)	5 full-time, 1 part-time	Two-year Diploma in Communication Arts, Advertising Option, Public Relations Option, Graphic Communications Option (22)	Print, broadcasting, cinema, advertising and media generally
			Advanced Certificate in Communication Arts (one additional year)	Print, broadcasting, cinema, advertising and media generally
Georgian College, Barrie	Communication Arts (1970)	1 full-time	One-year Certificate in Media Procedures	Print, broadcasting, cinema, advertising
			Two-year Diploma in Communication Arts	Print, broadcasting, cinema, advertising
Mohawk College, Hamilton	Communication Arts (1967)	4 full-time, 7 part-time	Three-year Diploma of Applied Arts (25)	Newspapers, radio, television, advertising, public relations

1. Figures in parentheses (where given) indicate graduations in 1970.

TABLE 10. (continued)

College	Department and date of foundation	Mass media teaching staff	Qualification [1]	Main teaching orientation
Ryerson Polytechnical	Journalism (1948)	6 full-time, 4 part-time	Three-year Diploma in Journalism (36)	Newspaper journalism
	Radio and Television Arts (1952)	8 full-time, 5 part-time	Three-year Diploma in Television Arts (52)	Broadcasting, media generally
Sir Sandford Fleming College, Peterborough	Audiovisual (1969)	1 full-time, 1 part-time	Diploma in Audio-visual Techniques	(Details not available)
Alberta				
Northern Alberta Institute of Technology, Edmonton	Radio and Television Arts (1966)	4 full-time, 2 part-time	Two-year Diploma in Radio and Television Arts (15)	Radio, television
Southern Alberta Institute of Technology, Calgari	Communication Arts, Journalism Section (1967)	4 full-time, 3 part-time	Two-year Diploma in Applied Arts (Journalism) (4 full-time, 8 part-time)	Print media, Book publishing, advertising, some broadcasting
	Television, Stage and Radio Arts Section (1967)	4 full-time	Two-year Broadcaster Certificate (6)	Radio, television, cinema
British Columbia				
British Columbia Institute of Technology Burnaby	Broadcast Communications (1964)	6 full-time	Two-year National Diploma of Technology-Broadcast Communications (30)	Radio and television broadcasting, news writing and news gathering, advertising
Vancouver City College, Vancouver	Technical (Journalism Section) (1965)	1 full-time, 5 part-time	One-year Certificate (15) Two-year Diploma (5)	Print media, broadcasting, advertising

[1] Figures in parentheses (where given) indicate graduations in 1970.

United States of America and Canada

When this survey was undertaken in 1970, most of the staff of community colleges involved in mass media studies were not undertaking research into the media. However, some mass communication research was reported. The Journalism Section of the Communication Arts Department at the Southern Alberta Institute of Technology runs a continuing cost analysis of Alberta weekly newspapers, and a nine-month market survey of these weeklies was planned. Extraordinary expenses are met by the Alberta Weekly Newspapers Association. One member of the Department of Business at the Northern Alberta Institute of Technology was investigating the economic effects of cable television on radio and television broadcasting. A member of the Communication Arts Department at Mohawk College of Applied Arts and Technology in Ontario had recently done research on the press and on media monopolies. Further research was planned into the regulation and censorship of newspapers, radio and television; television content; and practices and techniques in radio.

TABLE 11. Location and duration of programmes (in years) in communications, journalism and radio and television arts in community colleges in Canada, 1970-71 and 1971-72

Region and college	Communications		Journalism		Radio and television arts	
	1970-71	1971-72	1970-71	1971-72	1970-71	1971-72
Alberta						
Northern Alberta Institute of Technology	–	–	–	–	2	2
Southern Alberta Institute of Technology	–	–	2	2	2	2
Lethbridge Junior College	–	–	2	2	2	2
Mount Royal Junior College	2	2	2	2	2	2
British Columbia						
British Columbia Institute of Technology	–	–	–	–	2	2
Cariboo	–	–	–	1	–	–
Vancouver City College	2	2	2	2	–	–
Manitoba						
Red River Community College	2	2	–	–	–	–
Ontario						
Algonquin College of Applied Arts and Technology	–	–	1[1]	1[1]	–	–
Cambrian (North Bay) College of Applied Arts and Technology	2; 3	3	2; 3	3	2; 3	2; 3
Cambrian (Sault Ste Marie) College of Applied Arts and Technology	–	2; 3	–	2; 3	–	–
Centennial College of Applied Arts and Technology	3	3	3	3	–	–

TABLE 11 *(continued)*

Region and college	Communications		Journalism		Radio and télévision arts	
	1970–71	1971–72	1970–71	1971–72	1970–71	1971–72
Conostoga College of Applied Arts and Technology	–	3	3	3	3	3
Confederation College of Applied Arts and Technology	–	–	–	–	2	2; 3
Durham College of Applied Arts and Technology	2	2; 3	–	–	–	–
Fanshawe College of Applied Arts and Technology	3	2	3	3	3	3
Georgian College of Applied Arts and Technology	2	2	–	1	1	1
Humber College of Applied Arts and Technology	3	3	3	3	–	3
Lambton College of Applied Arts and Technology	–	2	–	–	–	2
Loyalist College of Applied Arts and Technology	2; 3	2; 3	–	2; 3	–	2; 3
Mohawk College of Applied Arts and Technology	2	3	–	–	–	–
Niagara-Welland College of Applied Arts and Technology	2	–	2	2; 3	2	2; 3
Ryerson Polytechnical Institute	–	–	3	3	3	3
St Clair College of Applied Arts and Technology	3	3	3	3 [2]	–	–
St Lawrence-Kingston College of Applied Arts and Technology	2	3 [3]	–	–	–	–
Seneca College of Applied Arts and Technology	2	2	–	–	–	–
Sheridan-Oakville College of Applied Arts and Technology	–	2	2	2	–	–

Québec

Region and college	Communications		Journalism		Radio and télévision arts	
	1970–71	1971–72	1970–71	1971–72	1970–71	1971–72
Collège d'Enseignement général et professionel de Jonquiere	3	3	–	3	–	3
Collège d'Enseignement général et professionel de Limoilou	3	–	–	–	–	–
Collège d'Enseignement général et professionel de St Hyacinthe	–	–	–	–	3	–
Institut de Technologie Maritime de Québec	1 [4]	1 [4]	–	–	–	–

1. Copywriting.
2. Offered as a communication course.
3. Commerce.
4. Radio Communications.

Source: Canada Department of Manpower and Immigration, *Community College Career Outlook* 70-71, Ottawa, 1970; *Community College Career Outlook* 71–72, Ottawa, 1971.

Europe

Overview

It is extremely difficult to make meaningful generalizations about the past development and present state of training, teaching and research in European universities. This is not surprising considering the variety and range of patterns of higher education, of university structures, and of academic traditions in some thirty European countries; their differing historical experiences and social, economic and political circumstances; the differences between one country and another in regard to the development of any particular mass medium, the audiences it serves, the purposes for which it may be used, as well as the sheer extent of the total network of mass communication in any particular country. A few examples may serve to illustrate the diversity which Europe presents in regard to university-based mass media studies, as they have developed over the last half-century or so.

Cyprus, Gibraltar, Luxembourg and Monaco have no universities, while the universities of Albania, Greece, Iceland and Malta were undertaking no systematic training, teaching or research in the mass media when this survey was undertaken in 1970, and, as far as could be ascertained have never done so. In Germany, the continuous history of academically oriented teaching and research on newspapers began during the First World War. Press studies were widely extended in the inter-war period, diminished during the Second World War, and revived again afterwards. But German universities have only recently, and to a slight extent, included practical training in their curricula. In the Soviet Union, on the other hand, university training in journalism started in 1923, and continued, in various forms and on a comparatively small scale, through the Second World War. Since 1946 there has been an enormous expansion of Soviet university-based journalism studies combining training, academic teaching and research, so that today with six faculties of journalism, and eighteen departments, universities are more extensively involved in mass media studies than anywhere else in Europe. In Great Britain, again, London University ran a systematic course of professional journalism training for some years between the two world wars; that lapsed, and only in 1970 was the field taken up again at Cardiff University. Meanwhile, although four specialized university centres for mass communication research were established in the 1960s, teaching about the mass media has not become a regular part of university education to any significant degree. Finland presents another picture: there, one institution (the present University of Tampere) has a continuous tradition of mass media education and research going back to 1925, but it achieved full university status only in 1966. Its journalism course was at first academically oriented, but since 1960 professional training has been combined with academic teaching and research along American lines. In Finland some teaching and research takes place in a few other universities, but less extensively. Different examples could be added, but enough has been said to indicate that the general European picture is one of great variety.

Nevertheless, it may be possible to venture on some broad tentative generalizations to bring out certain contrasts and similarities between different countries in Europe, and between Europe and other regions.

Professional training

In the first place, as far as professional training for mass media occupations is concerned, a broad contrast may be drawn between training for occupations in the cinema, and training for the press and radio and television broadcasting. Very rarely do universities provide professional training for film directors, producers, scriptwriters, cameramen and so on. Such training is characteristically provided by separate film schools, or by film departments attached to other institutions of higher education (academies, colleges and the like) which may be of university level, but do not have university status. This situation is in contrast with the United States where, as has been shown, universities play a significant role in imparting the techniques of film-making for future entrants to the movie industry.

The situation regarding professional training for journalism is more complex. Broadly speaking, in eastern Europe universities have played an important part in the provision of specialized skills to would-be entrants to journalistic occupations in the press, radio and television. In the Soviet Union, for example, universities have provided professionally oriented courses in various forms since the early 1920s, while Czechoslovakia, the German Democratic Republic, Poland and Yugoslavia started university-based professional journalism training after the end of the Second World War. In these countries training is combined with academic teaching and research in a manner somewhat analogous to the pattern of activities in many American universities, in separate faculties of journalism or in journalism departments often set within faculties of philology, though the pattern of administrative structures varies from country to country and sometimes between universities in the same country.

On the whole in western European countries university courses in journalism have tended to be academically rather than professionally oriented. Where specialized training for entrants to media occupations has been thought necessary, it has generally been organized by the industry itself (as in the case of the many in-service training schemes provided by broadcasting organizations, or the special courses run by journalist associations and other professional bodies) or it has been located in tertiary-level institutions. Before 1960 only a handful of western European universities offered regular courses of professional training for journalism (one of the first to do so was the Free University of Brussels in 1945). But during the 1960s many more have begun to offer training courses, although university preparation is still not the main, or even a major avenue for entering journalism in western Europe. Nevertheless, in Austria, Belgium, Finland, France, Federal Republic of Germany, Italy, Spain, Switzerland and the United Kingdom there is at least one university whose courses are intended above all for future journalists. During the last ten or twelve years there has been a noticeable tendency to gear such courses to radio and television, public relations and advertising as well as the press, and to set them within the general context of mass communication and the social sciences. The increase in university-based professional journalism education, and the changes in scope and emphasis, partly reflect wider changes in thinking about the aims and function of education which have led to reforms in the structure and content of university systems in many European countries. They also have been affected by the growing realization that since rapid technological changes in media industries must render highly specific training obsolete rather quickly, the preparation of 'generalists' instead of 'specialists' may be the best way to anticipate such developments. Finally, in this connexion, one should mention the influence of Unesco, through its conferences, and particularly in establishing a special regional centre (the Centre International d'Enseignement Supérieur de Journalisme) in conjunction with the University of Strasbourg. This centre provides a locus for advanced-level discussion of the problems of higher education for journalism by those concerned, and has helped to raise standards in journalism education in Europe and the Near and Middle East and Africa since its inception in 1956.

A recent innovation in Europe is the institution of subgraduate diploma courses in the techniques of information in France, Italy and Sweden. These courses are designed to produce middle-level communicators for a variety of occupations in which knowledge of mass media skills will be used—in government information departments, industry, adult education and so on. The provision of such courses indicates a new realization of the growing importance of mass communication in modern life, and a willingness on the part of universities to provide basic general training to meet current and future needs for a wide range of media-based occupations.

Academic teaching and research

It is above all in academically oriented teaching and in research that the universities of Europe have played their most important and characteristic role in the development of mass media studies. Even in these spheres, however, there are great differences from country to country. In Austria, Federal Republic of Germany and Switzerland, for example, mass communication research is legally recognized as a distinct field of study in which separate degrees may be offered by universities. The characteristic form of organization is a university chair through which academic teaching is provided, to which is attached a research institute. A similar pattern exists in the Netherlands, but there mass communication is not legally recognized for full degree purposes. In all these countries, historical and political aspects of journalism is being joined by sociological studies of the mass media as social institutions.

In France, much greater integration of teaching and research has been provided by the incorporation of often previously independent units into the French university structure as pluridisciplinary units for teaching and research, which increasingly are being permitted to grant first-, second- and third-level degrees. There is considerable variety in the teaching and research emphasis in mass media studies among the various universities involved in this field, from studies in journalism and mass communication to psychological, sociological and cultural studies of film, literature and mass culture. In Italy, in addition to specialized units for teaching and research at many Italian universities, including journalism, advertising and public relations, as well as sociocultural studies, especially of film and spectacle, an increasing number of Italian universities have been permitted since the early 1960s to offer a variety of courses on various aspects of the mass media and mass communication for a wide range of bachelor's-level degrees in the general field of the humanities and the social sciences. In Great Britain too, there has been a considerable increase in university involvement in mass media studies, especially in research. But the specialized units for mass media research are barely involved in academic teaching. Teaching about the mass media is by and large provided, in fragmentary fashion, by departments of drama, education, sociology, or political science, as part of their own disciplinary perspectives. The only exception is in film studies, where some specialized teaching takes place mainly on the history and aesthetics of the cinema. In Sweden, again, there are few specialized units in universities for mass media studies. But there has been considerable expansion, particularly in research about the mass media, and to a lesser extent in teaching, especially related to the informational aspects of mass communication in society, in which sociology and political science departments in various Swedish universities have been largely involved.

It is clear therefore, that there are manifold differences from country to country in the extent to which mass media studies have become incorporated in the activities of universities over the past fifty years or so, and in the approaches taken towards the field. In order to make some over-all assessment of the present situation in regard to university-based mass media studies in Europe two different but complementary perspectives may be used. One is to describe how, and to what extent the different media of mass communication—the press, cinema, radio and television—came into the range of academic interest in Europe at different times. Another is to delineate the main methods and the most characteristic orientations which have been used in mass media research and teaching. These two approaches in combination will provide some indication of how the present variety of interests and approaches in various parts of Europe came to develop.

From press studies to mass communication research

Broadly speaking, in most European countries, the first medium to receive detailed systematic study was the press. It was in Germany that study of the press was more fully developed than perhaps in any other European country. The field was regarded as a distinct branch of learning—newspaper science *(Zeitungswissenschaft)*—which became incorporated into the activities of many German universities in the inter-war period. Some features of the academic study of the press in Germany may therefore be briefly discussed to illustrate certain dominant trends in this field in Europe.

In Germany, as indeed in most western European countries until recently, technical and vocational training was not considered an appropriate function for universities. The study of the press in German universities was therefore not connected with professional training, but was an entirely academic subject, linked with the disciplines to which German scholarship had made such outstanding contributions in the nineteenth century—history, political economy and law.

Several reasons may be advanced to explain why the study of newspapers became a recognized teaching subject in German universities immediately after the First World War, and why, after the foundation of the first Institute of Newspaper Science at Leipzig University in 1916, as many as twelve similar institutes had been established by 1933. One reason is the long-standing tradition of scholarly interest in newspapers in German universities. Lectures on journalism were given at Leipzig University in 1672, and a doctoral thesis on the press was presented there in 1690. There were lectures on newspapers at Halle University in 1700, and August von Schlözer, a well-known editor of his time, gave lectures and seminars on the press at Göttingen University between 1775 and 1805. There was a long and lively tradition of political journalism in Germany 'where newspapers developed particularly early and in very abundant forms, doubtless in conjunction with the politically complicated federalistic structure' (Noelle-Neumann, 1971). There was also a long tradition of university professors with an academic interest in the press, who were also well-known editors, stretching from von Schlözer through to Karl Bücher, editor of the *Frankfurter Zeitung*, Professor of National Economy and founder of the first Institute of Newspaper Science at Leipzig University in 1916, and other founders and directors of important university institutes in the 1920s: Aloys Meister at Münster (1920), Karl d'Ester at Munich (1924), Martin Mohr at Berlin (1925) and Emil Dovifat, also at Berlin (1928) (Noelle-Neumann and Schulz, 1971). One might also mention the relative flexibility of the administrative structure of German universities, which enabled new areas to be incorporated, alongside established disciplines in separate research institutes attached to university chairs, closely associated with research seminars for advanced students (Clark, 1968).

During the twenties, there was considerable expansion of newspaper study in German universities: by the mid-twenties, sixteen universities were providing study programmes in this field. The first courses were envisaged mainly as a branch of contemporary political history, as at the University of Münster for example where, until the thirties interest was focused on the historical development of the newspaper and an abundance of material was accumulated. But with the rise of new media, especially radio, and later television, they too began to be studied alongside newpapers, using the same perspectives that had been applied to the press. This led to a changed conception of the scope of the field, and the names applied to it changed accordingly. The original designations used—*Zeitungskolleg* (newspaper course), *Zeitungskunde* (newspaper study), *Zeitungswissenschaft* (newspaper science)—became inappropriate with the rise of radio. In 1926, Karl Jaeger, Bücher's assistant at the Leipzig institute, wrote a work entitled *Von der Zeitungskunde zur Publizistischen Wissenschaft* (From Newspaper Study to the Science of Journalism) whence the term '*Publizistik*', the most usual designation for the field after 1945. The word derives from *publicirn* (to publish, from the Latin root *publicare*), first used in a German text in 1472. It has strong associations with politics: by association with late Roman usage the publicist is concerned with public affairs, especially public law, and declares his political convictions through the publication of his views (Noelle-Neumann and Schulz, 1971). The field of *Publizistik* is public communication, especially in conjunction with propaganda and public opinion, press history, the ethics of journalism, press law and freedom and control of the press.

The 'characteristic content of publizistik included a marked historical component and a strong emphasis on the role of the publicist in the formation of political convictions and his role as opinion leader in economic disputes' (Noelle-Neumann, 1971). These features are linked with aspects of German historical experience: the early, abundant development of newspapers; the use of periodicals, reviews and newspapers by outstanding, influential and highly respected figures, as a public forum to spread ideas and mould public opinion from the seventeenth century onwards and the strongly political character of the German press, as well as the deliberate, systematic use of mass media for propaganda during the First World War, in the rise to power of the Nazi party, and in the Second World War. The methods employed were descriptive and analytical—biographical studies of outstanding publicists in Germany and abroad; histories of the development of printing technology, of particular forms of the newspaper and periodical press and of the political influence of the press; analyses of stylistic devices such as emphasis, repetition and other rhetorical forms and their effectiveness in terms of aesthetics and mass psychology; economic studies of press enterprises; studies of press laws and the legal framework within which the press operated. The characteristic orientation of *Publizistik*, as of *Zeitungswissenschaft*, was theoretical, historical and normative. The normative aspect was emphasized by Emil Dovifat, a leading German scholar in the field from the 1920s to the 1960s. He stressed the active purposive character of the communication process, which, far from being an anonymous force working through faceless communicators to influence the disembodied attitudes of a passive audience, was rather the deliberate, intentional moulding, by one man, through public means, of not only the attitudes but, more important, the public actions of many men. The communication process therefore involved moral attributes like intention and will, which were mediated through public norms. Hence Dovifat's stress on the intellectual and especially on the personal moral intentions of the publicist, and his insistence that *publizistik* could not, and should not be value-free. It must assess and judge the intentions and moral values of the publicist in terms of public responsibility in the use and misuse of the media of public communication for good or bad ends, for democracy or dictatorship (Harting, 1971).

The German conception of press studies was taken up in many European countries, especially those where mass media studies were started before the 1950s. There are traces of its influence in the institutes for press science or press research in Austria, Belgium, Finland, France, the Netherlands, Norway and Switzerland (as well as in the Republic of Korea and Japan). In these countries the press was accepted as an academic field in its own right, and historical, political and legal perspectives were employed in its study and extended to other mass media. But the press remained the central core of mass media studies in this mode.

The great lacuna in this type of mass communication research—theoretical, descriptive, analytical—was its lack of emphasis on empirical methods. Although Max Weber and Ferdinand Tönnies 'spent a great part of their working lives in drafting and processing public opinion surveys and analysing statistical surveys' and Weber even proposed to make a survey of the press in 1910, empirical mass communication research has only developed in the Federal Republic of Germany since the Second World War, largely under the influence of American mass communication research. Elizabeth Noelle-Neumann attributes the lack of an empirical research tradition in the Federal Republic to a variety of factors. Its development was hampered by the fact that German universities concentrated on abstract philosophical and historical studies: scholars were not interested in questions of method, and their questionnaires were primitive, so that the data accumulated could not be satisfactorily analysed. Moreover, German academic traditions made it difficult to organize a large number of researchers in neighbouring disciplines. Also, there was lacking that continuity and consecutiveness in the studies undertaken which might have helped to establish a methodology of research. She also attributes the lack of interest in empirical press research in German universities partly to the influence of Karl Bücher who not only felt that the press had a tendency to lower cultural standards, and was a dangerous manipulative force on public opinion, but also rejected the possibility of systematic studies because, as he said: 'How can we calculate how many people read newspapers regularly if we do not even know how many families read a single issue together?' As has been seen, the rise of new mass media in the twenties and thirties

> caused researchers even in the thirties, to consider how they might place their research on a more solid foundation. But this trend was brought to a halt in 1933,

and was resumed only after the Second World War (Noelle-Neumann and Hauser, 1970).

It is tempting to argue that the very definition of the field, whether of *Zeitungswissenschaft* or *Publizistik*, in itself impeded its full extension from the press to other media, and especially to mass communication viewed as a single, total whole. *Publizistik* tended to emphasize the role of the individual publicist using the media deliberately for certain ends, and thus tended to take the audience for granted, or to treat it as a collection of unique individuals. But forms of mass communication like advertising, radio and television operate in less direct and more anonymous ways, and it is often difficult, even impossible to attribute intention, responsibility and direct causation in tracing the processes of their operation. It is possible to argue that without reliable, empirical methods of research, detailed knowledge of the size and composition of the audiences for mass media, as well as of the social and psychological effects of particular types of mass communication is more or less ruled out.

After the Second World War, there was a new drive among German scholars to extend the field to encompass mass communication as a whole, with corresponding changes of designation. In the Federal Republic of Germany terms which include communication or mass media have become increasingly used, such as *Kommunikationswissenschaft* (communications science), *Kommunikationsforschung* (communications research) or *Massmedienforschung* (mass media research), or *Mediakunde*, *Medienpedagogik* which are used in teacher training. In the German Democratic Republic the term '*journalistik*' is used to describe the separate faculty at Leipzig University.

But, as Professor Kurt Kosyk of the University of Bochum observed in a letter of 26 October 1971,

> the change of name and the enlargement of the subject—which today means not only the media but also the communicator and the recipient as well as the process of communication in society—has not been very easy in Germany. The financial basis in my opinion is still much too small to fulfil what has been pointed out by the new concept.

In spite of the long history of specialized mass communication study and research, there is still some difficulty in obtaining general recognition of the fact that,

> the subject ... demands the integration of knowledge accumulated in several specialized fields from the aspect of journalism, of public communication in general. The social psychologist is concerned with the socio-psychological problem [of the mass media] the politologist with its role in the political process, the historian with the history of the press, the student of business management with the economic aspect, and the [jurist] with press legislation—each of them in addition to other subjects and only from time to time. But public communication cannot be scientifically studied in this way. It calls for continuous and integrative research—and hence for more staff too. The seven chairs of public communication in the Federal Republic, isolated and scantily equipped, are not enough if progress is to be achieved in a branch of learning that requires large-scale, empirical research. (Noelle-Neumann and Hauser, 1970.)

But in spite of these difficulties, there is no doubt that in recent years the scope of the field has been extended to all the mass media and to mass communication in general, and that research and study is conducted from the point of view of a variety of orientations. There is still a strong strand of mass media research based on historical studies of the press, of which the main centre is the University of Bochum. But this type of research is less dominant than it used to be. Today, as Professor Noelle-Neumann wrote in a letter of 21 September 1971:

> the field is dominated by the tension between empirically oriented communications research [as at Mainz or Munich] and the doctrine (of a Marxist character) of the political economy of the mass media (as at the Free University of Berlin and at Münster).

Interestingly enough, this same tension is reported to exist in Japan, where mass communication research has been strongly influenced first by German, and then by American conceptions.

A similar expansion of the range of the field from historical, political and legal studies of the press to the study of mass communication from a variety of viewpoints, including sociological and social-psychological investigations of audiences and communicators, has taken place in other European countries too. In Austria, for example, in the early sixties, the Institute at Vienna University shifted its research emphasis from press history to mass communication in general, and began to concentrate on empirical methods of social research and statistics. In Finland, the Department of Journalism at the University of Tampere changed its name to the Department of Mass Communication, and turned from press studies to empirically based research on the role of the mass media in society. In Belgium, by the mid-sixties, the field was known as communication science *(communicatie wetenschap)* and was regarded as an autonomous body of knowledge. Here, as in the Federal Republic of Germany, a variety of orientations were already being used in its study: the University of Ghent concentrated on press history and law, the Free University of Brussels on the sociology of the mass media and especially of news, and the University of Louvain on empirical mass communication research and methodology.

Cultural studies and film research

The rise of the cinema as an important mass medium stimulated a great deal of research and discussion in and out of universities in many European countries, especially from the 1930s to the 1950s, although its roots may be traced to the early years of the twentieth century. Whereas the primary orientation of press studies was political, research on the cinema tended to stem from psychological, sociological and cultural perspectives.

From the later nineteenth century onwards the effects of industrialization, political democracy and more widespread education evoked much discussion and speculation, both hopeful and pessimistic, in many European countries, especially Britain, France and Germany. In Britain, for example, during the 1930s through the 1950s many literary and cultural critics, following in the tradition of John Stuart Mill and Matthew Arnold, engaged in analyses, critiques and criticisms of contemporary culture, especially the relationship of élite culture and popular, mass culture, and the impoverishment of cultural norms in modern, urban, technologically advanced Western societies. In general, the tone of this debate tended to be nostalgic and cautionary, although the potentially beneficent effects of modern technology and universal literacy in raising material, cultural and moral standards (if rightly used) also formed an important focus of attention. On the whole, literary examples drawn from popular fiction, magazines, the popular press and advertisements were used to illustrate these writings, but their range covered the quality of modern life in general, from architecture to fashion.

During the heyday of the cinema as a mass medium of entertainment a great deal of interest was aroused concerning the cultural status of film, largely drawing on ideas current in the general debate on mass society and mass culture. Consequently in almost every European country, especially Belgium, Czechoslovakia, Denmark, France, Germany, Italy, the Netherlands, Norway, Poland, Sweden, the Union of Soviet Socialist Republics, the United Kingdom and Yugoslavia, a considerable amount of empirical research work was undertaken, mainly by psychologists, sociologists and educationists, centring round the educational possibilities of the cinema, and exploring the validity of fears that widespread cinemagoing was having, or might have, a harmful effect on the physical, mental and moral health of its audiences, especially children and young people. It is interesting to note that many of the concerns of this research, as well as the methods used in these investigations, were later transferred to research on television, as an entertainment medium, especially in relation to public concern about the supposed effect of violent television content in stimulating or exacerbating juvenile delinquency.

In addition to this large body of 'effects' research about the cinema, the development of the film as an important and wholly distinctive art form produced a body of film theory concerned with the language of film and its special processes, and the history and aesthetic criticism of films, comparable to similar work on other art forms like music, literature and graphic art. Here again, it is impossible to single out the work produced in any one country by professional film-makers, film critics and academics, although interest in theory and education about film was and is particularly strong in Belgium, France, Italy, the U.S.S.R., the United Kingdom and other countries.

The two main strands in theory and research on film (cultural-aesthetic and sociological-psychological) were brought together in the filmology movement which originated from the writings of Gilbert Cohen-Séat in the 1940s and 1950s. He proposed a philosophy of the cinema which distinguished between the filmic phenomenon, the way in which the film creates its own world through a system of visual and verbal images, and the cinematographic phenomenon constituted by the effect on the spectator of the film medium, and the sociology of the cinema. A special Institute for Filmology was created at the Sorbonne, and the movement spread all over Europe, being especially strong in Belgium, France and Italy. Although the Sorbonne institute closed down in 1961, filmology has influenced the study of the mass media as entertainment ('spectacle' or show). It remains an important branch of mass media education and research, especially in Italy.

One outgrowth of the filmology movement in France was the development of structuralism which transferred the idea of the image in the language of film to all the products of the mass media, and thence to contemporary culture in general. Structuralism uses methods derived from linguistics and structural anthropology to 'decode' the total system of images current in contemporary life, as well as subsystems constituted by newspaper reports or articles, advertisements, films, styles of fashion, architecture and so on, or by single examples of these *genres*, in order to derive the essential pattern of the characteristic emphases and omissions in the vision of life given to those who live in modern, technologically based societies. Its analysis of the significance of these symbolic structures has been influenced by Marxism, Freudianism and existentialism (Burgelin, 1968). Today the main centre for structural studies is the Centre d'Études de Communications de Masse at the École Pratique des Hautes Études in Paris. But structuralism has influenced studies of mass media content in relation to contemporary culture, not only in France, but in Britain and other countries.

Development of broadcasting research

Historically speaking, the last mass medium to be incorporated into the framework of mass media studies was broadcasting. As we have seen, attempts were made to assimilate radio broadcasting as a medium of information within the general perspectives of press research from the mid-thirties, but without great success. Social scientific research on broadcasting remained a relatively neglected field in and out of academic circles in most European countries until about ten years ago, even though radio had become a mass medium by the early thirties, and television was well-established by about the mid-fifties in most countries. But, as in the United States, it seems fair to say that it is the growth of research interest in television which has not only stimulated the general field of mass media studies in Europe, but has also enlarged the framework of thinking about the media to encompass mass communication as a total social process.

Two main factors appear to be responsible for the development of social scientific research on television. One is the growth of interest in more sophisticated and socially relevant research on the part of some broadcasting organizations, partly stimulated by the growth of competition in monopolistic or virtually monopolistic situations. The other is the growth of public awareness of the importance of television as a mass medium, which has often been accompanied by waves of public concern about the effects of television viewing on young people. These factors have not only aroused academic interest in television research; they have also helped to make funds available for that research to be done.

To illustrate the influence of these factors one may briefly refer to developments in Scandinavia and in Britain.

In the Scandinavian countries there was little academic interest in broadcasting research before the early 1960s. In Denmark, for instance, an investigation by the Danish Research Secretariat in 1970 found that very little had been done in this field apart from sporadic audience surveys sponsored by Danish Radio, including a survey of listeners' mail undertaken in 1929, a systematic survey of the radio public for Danish Radio in 1950 (the first in Scandinavia) and similar work, largely by commercial organizations, in 1960, 1964, 1968, 1969 and 1970.

In Sweden, as a survey of mass communication research before 1968 by Kjell Nowak (1968) revealed, concerted research had been largely concerned with measuring audience size and was very much consumption-oriented.

More academic work on mass communication had been done than in Denmark, but mostly by isolated research workers, doing one-shot studies, concentrated on attitude change, reactions to mass communicated information, public-opinion formation and content analysis. In Nowak's opinion, there had been

> very few attempts to study the media as organizations in Swedish society... there is no systematic knowledge about the roles, functions, attitudes and behaviour of professional mass media communicators in Sweden; there had been little work on the importance of personal influence or on the diffusion of innovations or on methods and theories of message analysis (Nowak, 1968).

The weakness of academic research before the early 1960s was matched by the indifference of the media organizations. As K. Nordenstreng (1971a) observed:

> The national broadcasting companies were over-confident and passive in their operational approach. Unlike commercial broadcasting, no audience research has been needed in order to guarantee the income of the company; the citizens automatically continue to pay their licence fees. The behaviour of the audience has been considered rather irrelevant since the companies have been largely convinced that their message—mostly conservative and elitist [in] character—is appropriately received. By and large ... broadcasting activity has been perceived with few burning scholarly problems and a minimum of societal concerns.

> But a passive conception of broadcasting, accompanied by a scarcity of research is no longer the tone of Scandinavian communications. During the past ten years—after the breakthrough of television—there has been a rapidly growing awareness of the social implications of electronic communications. Along with a new active broadcasting mentality—aimed at versatile and stimulating programming—scientific research into the process of broadcasting as well as communications in general is becoming a significant and influential institution in Scandinavia. The emergence of research is mostly due to the broadcasting organisations themselves; the universities perhaps have had some social scientists interested in communications problems, but these academicians have been able to accomplish little without grants from broadcasting.

The two countries in which the broadcasting organizations themselves have taken a leading role in initiating research are Sweden and Finland. Sveriges Radio and Yleisradio both established separate research departments in the 1960s, and both have recognized that (in the words of Olof Rydbeck, the then director of Sveriges Radio, in 1969):

> unbiased, cross-disciplinary and high quality research into the mass media ... is a necessary condition for enabling the broadcasting media to exploit their long-term positive potential to the full and to defend themselves against the pressures from opinions which enlist allegedly negative effects with the aim of circumscribing broadcasting's freedom of action.

The research department of Sveriges Radio (SR/PUB) has taken a particularly active role in research into mass communication, partly because there was no specialized university centre for mass communication research in Sweden, although both the

Department of Political Science at Gothenburg University and the Economic Research Unit of the Stockholm School of Economics conducted some mass media research. SR/PUB has conducted empirical research at various levels in order to provide the means for making decisions on general broadcasting policy, programme planning, and production of programmes. Its activities have ranged from research on the role of broadcasting in society, detailed studies of the audience (including its size, habits, knowledge, preferences and reactions to programmes) and studies of the impact of particular programmes and the effectiveness of different programme formats. In Finland the Section for Long Range Planning of Yleisradio is 'a kind of working arm of the central management' and is thus concerned not only with providing the means for taking decisions about Finnish broadcasting policy, but also with doing research on the goals of policy. Its activities were more closely linked with academic research because of the long-standing commitment of the University of Tampere to mass communication research. At first a group of experts, consisting of university professors and representatives of Yleisradio decided on the research to be undertaken, which was financed by Yleisradio and conducted by academic researchers. More recently however the section has drawn up its research programme itself and has either commissioned academic researchers or commercial organizations to conduct it, or has used its own research staff to do so (Nordenstreng, 1971a).

The result of these initiatives by the broadcasting organizations in Sweden and Finland has been a great expansion of research in all aspects of mass communication in both these countries. Furthermore, since 1969 the broadcasting organizations of Denmark, Finland, Norway and Sweden have established a joint committee to achieve permanent research co-operation, by exchanging information and experiences and to establish common projects. One such project has been a comparative analysis of audience reactions to a simultaneous Nordvision programme, another is an investigation of the way in which the four broadcasting organizations treat news material. These projects have been undertaken partly by academic researchers in the four countries concerned, and the second in particular included not only direct study of communicators, contents and audiences but also comparative studies of the press.

Another aspect of closer co-operation between the four broadcasting organizations is the proposal to establish a Nordic documentation centre for mass communication research on the joint initiative of Sveriges Radio and the Swedish Newspaper Publishers' Association, to store, abstract and retrieve mass communication research documentation produced in the Nordic countries.

All this has led to valuable cross-fertilization of methods and concepts of research between research workers in different Scandinavian countries. The Scandinavian countries present a unique example of how broadcasting organizations have co-operated with academic researchers in encouraging and initiating research, and how such research has come to be focused on the wider problems of the role and functions of mass communication and the mass media in society.

The development of research into broadcasting and its extension to the wider field of mass communication as a social process followed a somewhat different course in Great Britain. Before the 1960s, very little empirical social scientific research had been undertaken on broadcasting. The BBC itself collected information about radio audiences through its Listener Research Department, established in 1936 (the precursor of the present Audience Research Department) and later about television audiences. By 1939, the department had worked out the corner-stones of its activities, a continuous daily sample survey (using aided recall) to establish audience size and composition, and weekly surveys of listener panels, to test reactions—procedures which were extended in more sophisticated and methodologically tighter form to television audiences after 1948. In 1952 a special projects section was formed to undertake non-routine inquiries on topics like comprehensibility of broadcast material, prior level of knowledge of target audiences on matters to be dealt with in forthcoming programmes and more general inquiries on listening and viewing patterns, audience tastes and so on (Emmett, 1966). Similar audience research activities were undertaken on behalf of commercial television when it was inaugurated in 1955.

Although the BBC Audience Research Department has amassed valuable information about audience size, composition and preferences, and has built up a highly sophisticated methodology to ensure the reliability of this information, its work was deliberately restricted to purely service activities. Since 'sociologists and social psychologists who had worked or seemed willing to work in mass communication could almost be counted on one hand' (TVRC, 1966) by the early 1960s, and there was no specialized academic centre for mass communication research, very little research had taken place in Britain on the social aspects of either broadcasting, or the mass media in general.

However, during the early sixties, as a result of rising expressions of public concern over juvenile delinquency and fears that the introduction of commercial television would increase its prevalence, the Home Secretary called a conference representing religious, educational and other interests which led to the offer by the Independent Television Authority (ITA), the body set up to control commercial television, 'to finance research into the impact of television on society with particular reference to its effect on young people'. After discussions with the ITA and the BBC, the Home Secretary called a conference of experts in psychology, sociology, social studies and statistics in May 1962. It recommended that the research should not be primarily concerned with the direct study of the effect of television on delinquency but 'should deal with the part that television plays or could play, in relation to other influences in communicating knowledge and fostering attitudes'. It also recommended that a committee be set up to consider the whole problem, to initiate and co-ordinate research, and to administer the funds made available by the ITA, amounting to £250,000 over five years. The Vice-Chancellor of the University of Leicester was appointed Chairman of the sixteen-member committee. It first met in July 1963, with a sociologist on the academic staff of Leicester University acting as its secretary.

The terms of reference of the Television Research Committee (TVRC) were:
> to initiate and co-ordinate research into the part which television plays or could play, in relation to other influences, as a medium of communication and in fostering attitudes, with particular reference to the development of young people's moral concepts and attitudes and the processes of perception through which they are influenced by television and other media of communication.

The Television Research Committee found itself faced with the task of defining its objectives and working out a research strategy. There was little on which it could build, in terms of past British research on broadcasting or the other mass media. Unlike on the Continent, there was no specialized centre for press research. Although there was a growing body of knowledge about various aspects of the contemporary press and its history (built up partly by the investigations of the Press Commissions of 1948 and 1961), it had been conducted mostly in a random and unsystematic fashion. Research on the cinema had received more impetus. Many investigations took place, sometimes in connexion with official commissions of inquiry, on the size and composition of cinema audiences, the time spent at the cinema by children of different ages, backgrounds and education, their motivations, attitudes and reactions to films, and above all the effects of cinemagoing on children's eyesight, sleep patterns, mental health, reading habits, tastes, school achievement and so on. Much work had also been done in universities and organizations like the British Film Institute to explore the possibilities of using film for teaching purposes, and to disseminate understanding of the language of film. But though far more work had been undertaken on the cinema (some of which provided the model for some early television research) it could not be said that a coherent, systematic research tradition had been created. As far as broadcasting research was concerned, some pioneering studies had been undertaken by the early 1960s on the impact of broadcasting in society. Foremost among them were a far-reaching investigation of television's effects on children's tastes and values, financed by the Nuffield Foundation, undertaken by a research team at the Department of Social Psychology in the London School of Economics, and studies of the impact of television on elections, and on the comprehensibility of broadcast material at the University of Leeds, financed by a fellowship created by Granada Television in 1957. But here again, the field was in its infancy, and there was hardly a consistent tradition on which to build.

The Television Research Committee discovered that there was a shortage of trained social scientists whose research interests were relevant to even the widest interpretation of its terms of reference: it was able to support only one of the research proposals presented to it. It therefore decided

> to proceed slowly, clarifying by its own studies both the significance of the terms of reference and its own ultimate objectives, identifying the problem areas amenable to social scientific research, assessing the social relevance of the specific questions that could be formulated within these areas, seeing what methods, skills and resources were available . . . to answer these questions, and then finally establishing its research priorities.

Rather than dissipating its funds on single, unconnected studies, it proceeded to construct long-term strategies of research which would enable investigations to take place in a concerted, systematic and co-ordinated fashion. It therefore published a series of working papers, and organized a series of seminars on problems related to the mass media, gradually developing

> a broader, less conventional, more adventurous approach [and recommending] investigations along a wider front than one normally found in mass communication research [including] the influence of different forms of presentation of news, current affairs and political issues . . . [the values embedded] in media content . . . omissions as well as commissions [of media coverage of issues], questions of trivialization and over-familiarization and the possibility that the media were working against instead of in support of an active 'participatory' democracy. (TVRC, 1966.)

In thus taking an active and creative part in broadening and deepening the conception of the whole field of mass communication research, to include all facets of the mass media as social institutions and mass communication as a social process, the Television Research Committee probably has a unique record, since most *ad hoc* bodies of this kind usually see their function in purely administrative terms, and tend to take a static, passive view of their terms of reference. In this sense, its activities have left a permanent imprint on British mass communication research, and the investigations sponsored by it at the universities of Leicester, Leeds, Birmingham, Aberdeen and the London School of Economics have also influenced research workers in other countries.

But an equally important legacy of its constructive approach is that mass communication research has become institutionalized within the British university system. Under its aegis permanent specialized units for mass media research in British universities were encouraged to develop. It established the Centre for Mass Communication Research at Leicester University to act as its institutional base in 1966, and has helped to create similar units, each with its own special interests, at the universities of Birmingham and Leeds and the London School of Economics. The existence of these specialized university units for mass communication research has helped to funnel more funds from different sources into the field. Consequently, continuous cumulative research on a broad front, rather than single isolated *ad hoc* studies on different aspects of various media, has become more evident in the later sixties in Britain.

To sum up, then, in Europe a rich variety of approaches and traditions over the past half-century have contributed to create considerable diversity of orientations from country to country, even between universities in the same country. Nevertheless, over the past ten years or so, there has been a distinct tendency in those countries where mass media studies have made most progress for research on each medium to be undertaken increasingly within a framework of mass communication as a whole and for mass communication to be seen as a social process operating through the mass media as social institutions.

Although European universities are less involved than those of the United States in education and research on the mass media and mass communication, there is no doubt that generally speaking the field is increasingly accepted as one which merits academic involvement. The proof of this assertion may be found in the increasing number of specialized courses dealing with the mass media in academic curricula, and of specialized centres for various forms of mass communication research attached to universities, particularly during the 1960s.

As correspondents from various European countries have indicated, the field is still beset with difficulties. It is still struggling to establish its own distinct body of knowledge and expertise, against the tendency to fragmentation and incoherence which stems from the fact that it is a field of interest, though in a secondary way, to well-established disciplines with their own distinctive orientations. Even in the Federal Republic of Germany, with half a century of specialized mass media studies in universities, this difficulty exists, and all the more so in countries like Denmark or Great Britain, where specialization has come lately, or is not yet apparent. One result of this situation is that finance for mass media research, particularly for long-term critical research rather than for short-term highly specific studies, is difficult to come by, so that the compartmentalized, fragmentary nature of the field is thereby perpetuated. Another aspect of this situation is the relative isolation of teachers and research workers interested in the mass media, and their ignorance of the current activities of their colleagues in other countries.

However, there is reason to believe that these difficulties are becoming less oppressive. To the extent that the mass media are becoming recognized as an important aspect of modern societies so will the need grow for focused interdisciplinary teaching and research at university level which will help break down compartmentalization and encourage the provision of larger funds for research. In Europe, perhaps more than in any other region of the world, élitist views of culture have helped shape the structure and content of education in general and more particularly of university education. Universities have enshrined and reflected traditional values of high culture and have in their turn provided generally accepted canons of judgement for scholarship and culture. One important reason for the relatively difficult passage which mass media studies have had to undergo in the process of being recognized as an acceptable academic field is that the mass media have been primarily regarded as purveyors of cheap mass entertainment which threatened to erode and vitiate cultural standards. However, since the Second World War, and especially in the last decade, there have been striking changes in attitudes towards the scope and function of education, including university education, and parallel changes in generally accepted definitions of culture. One indication of these changes was provided by a recent intergovernmental conference at Helsinki on cultural policies in Europe, which included ministers of culture and other ministers concerned with culture (Unesco, 1972). The conference 'unanimously rejected the idea of an elitist culture' and 'several delegations stressed the importance of mass communication media for cultural dissemination and artistic creation'. Many recommendations dealt directly or indirectly with mass communication. *Inter alia*, governments were urged to formulate policies to take account of the potentialities of electronic communications for providing education, information and leisure to larger, more diverse national and international audiences; to encourage research on the production and reception of cultural programmes, the analysis of audio-visual languages, and new ways of encouraging audience participation; to encourage educational institutions to incorporate aesthetic and socio-economic education about mass media in their curricula; to set up research institutions to investigate different sectors of the public and their attitudes to the new cultural forms fostered by mass media, and in the light of their findings to train organizers of cultural activities capable of reconciling traditional forms of art and culture with these new forms. The fact that a governmental meeting on cultural policy at ministerial level has thus recognized the importance of the media in cultural life and has strongly emphasized the need for teaching and research on mass communication indicates how far public opinion, and influential opinion at that, is now prepared to take the mass media seriously. If the recommendations of this meeting are implemented, education and research in mass media studies are likely to increase in many European countries.

As the field becomes extended, and the number of full-time teachers and research workers committed to mass media studies grows, so will the number of professional societies increase to provide a locus for contact and discussion. There are already a number of such societies, especially in the Federal Republic of Germany, and the International Association for Mass Communication Research, through its conferences, provides a means for European teachers and research workers to meet one another and their counterparts from other countries.

Finally, the recent setting up of a number of regional centres for the collection, abstraction and dissemination of information about mass communication research (including three at present in Europe: one in Strasbourg for French-language material, another in Leicester for English-language material and the Nordic centre for Scandinavian material) will help to create further intellectual contact between those interested in this field. In this context the very variety of orientations and perspectives towards the mass media that have been developed in Europe may well stimulate further vigorous growth in the field in the future, and prevent it from becoming too narrow and stereotyped.

Austria

Systematic study of the mass media has a comparatively recent history in Austria compared to many other parts of Europe. Before the Second World War, the Society for Knowledge of the Press organized courses for prospective editors, but they ceased with the arrival of German troops in 1938. Nevertheless, these courses were the precursor to the formation of the Institute for Newspaper Science *(Zeitungswissenschaft)* at the University of Vienna in 1942. Not until 1968 was a second institute for the systematic study of mass communication established, at Salzburg University (Unesco, 1958). These two universities alone conduct systematic specialized teaching and research on mass media, although other universities have recently begun to include mass media courses among the curricula of other disciplines.

Austria is fairly unusual in that although there have been sporadic attempts to establish professional schools for journalism outside the universities, they have not survived, probably because neither the press nor the professional organizations felt a real need for them. On the other hand, in Austria, as in the Federal Republic of Germany, the academic study of mass communications is now a designated separate field of study in universities (Noelle-Neumann and Hauser, 1970) unlike in many other countries.

The Institut für Zeitungswissenschaft der Universität Wien (Institute for Newspaper Science at Vienna University) was founded in 1942. There was no university chair in the subject at Vienna University between 1945 and 1969, but it was re-established in March 1969, when the institute's name was changed to Institut für Publizistik (mass communication research). The changed title reflected a changing orientation, as Professor Paupie, the Director, explained (Paupie, 1970):

> In the early sixties the Institut für Publizistik then still called Institut für Zeitungswissenschaft [newspaper science] began to shift its emphasis from a primarily historically oriented discipline, concentrating mainly on the media of the press, to the new electronic media and experimental communications.
>
> Next to the introduction of new courses, such as Public Relations, Media Analysis, Opinion Research, etc., the department began systematically to investigate the methodology of communication and its implications, as it had been recently developed in the Anglo-American academic world. This included, for example, finding new methods in the field of empirical social research, as well as observing the field of statistics. Over the last [few] years it has been felt that the large scale of sociological communicative effects of mass media have been somewhat neglected in our country. Therefore we feel that now more attention will be paid to the context, form and effects of the media message.

The Vienna institute has two full-time academic staff and ten part-time media professionals engaged in teaching, and four full-time academic staff on research appointments.

The four-year teaching programme leads to a Doctor of Philosophy degree awarded in the Faculty of Arts. Seventeen students graduated in 1968 and twelve in 1969. The course covers mass media generally, and newspapers, radio and television in particular, with some attention paid to advertising and the cinema. Aspects dealt with include the history, regulation, economics, professional ethics and structure and operation of media institutions in these media; the educational role of mass media; sociological and psychological aspects of mass communication, and research methods. Some practical instruction in techniques is also given. The course is aimed at intending media professionals.

The major research activity of the Vienna institute has been a handbook on the history of the Austrian press, of which two volumes have so far appeared. Other recent projects have covered such subjects as education and television, case studies of the Austrian press, and a study of the scientific and theoretical aspects of empirical research in communications.

The University of Salzburg founded a Chair in Mass Communication Research and Communication Theory in 1967, and an institute, the Institut für Publizistik und Kommunikationstheorie, in 1968. It has seven full-time academic staff, and two part-time professionals teaching mass communication. Its four-year course, leading to a Doctor of Philosophy degree, covers newspapers, radio, television and the cinema.

The institute's programme is designed 'not to produce journalists but rather to set students on the way to becoming experts in various branches of communication'. Accordingly its curriculum covers the methods, basic concepts and theories of mass communication; the description and analysis of media systems and media in the social and governmental spheres; and legal, formal and practical outlines of media and interpersonal communication.

In 1970, the director explained (Noelle-Neumann and Hauser, 1970):

> In view of the modest reserves which the Austrian government and private patrons can make available for non-applied academic research, the Salzburg Institut für Publizistik und Kommunikationstheorie has concentrated on three main areas of study that can be financed relatively 'cheaply'. They are:
> (a) the search for possibilities of establishing theoretical and methodological links between such extremes as the humanities and the social science approach to communication, or the normative and value-free approaches of research;
> (b) communicator research and
> (c) content analysis.
>
> Projects of this kind can be carried out in a relatively short time by small groups working on a modest budget.

As far as teaching outside the specialized institutes at Vienna and Salzburg universities is concerned, the Institute for Theatre at the University of Vienna included several lectures on film, the theatre as a mass medium, television, dramatic theory and criticism of the spoken word in radio, and introduction to scope of mass communication research, in its courses in 1970.

The University of Graz had a series of eight seminars on mass communication for the first time in 1970, in the Faculty of Law and Political Science. They were so successful that they were to be extended in 1971.

The Institute for Psychology at the University of Innsbruck has not so far been much concerned with social psychology, including mass communication, nor with mass media research. But in 1970 a new lecturer was appointed in journalism, with many years' practical experience; consequently this field is now likely to be developed.

As far as tertiary institutions are concerned, the Advanced Training and Research Institute for the Graphic Arts in Vienna which trains photographers, designers, reproduction technicians and executives, and managers of printing plants, has a department which deals exclusively with book and newspaper publishing.

Finally, brief mention should be made of the International Institute for Music, Dance and Theatre in the Audio-Visual Media (IMDT), founded in 1969 in Vienna as part of Unesco's regular programme. The foundation of this institute is connected with the work of the International Music Council—a Unesco-sponsored organization in Paris. The IMDT has a department for basic training, a department for workshops and production (in which television techniques are used as an integral instrument of the aesthetic structure of the work, and not merely as a recording medium), and a research department.

Belgium

Although Belgium is a fairly small country, the situation with regard to training, teaching and research in mass communication is rather complicated since, because of the division between French- and Flemish-speaking elements, and between Catholics and non-Catholics, there is a proliferation of educational and research institutions at various levels, to cater for these different sections of the population. This situation, although it has led to a considerable amount of activity in Belgian mass media studies, has also had certain disadvantages. In a report presented to the Sixth World Congress of Sociology in 1966, Professor Guido Van Parijs (1969) commented on the extent to which the oppositions between State and non-Catholic *(libre)* universities, and between French- and Flemish-medium universities had created barriers between different university research centres and between individual research workers, which prevented any fruitful exchange of views or any collaboration between those working in the same discipline. Although political changes since then, and the establishment of separate French and Flemish sections in most universities may have removed some of these difficulties, no doubt some vestiges still remain.

In view of these barriers, it is perhaps all the more remarkable that there was a basic similarity of approach, even in 1966, between all the university institutions involved in mass media studies, which transcended differences of emphasis from one to the next.[1] This basic similarity was evidenced by the fact that in Belgium mass communication was not considered to be part of sociology, psychology, or any other discipline, but was

> the object of an autonomous science (the science of mass media) which is slowly organising itself while keeping multiple points of contact with history, political science, sociology, psychology, linguistics etc.

Furthermore, as far as teaching was concerned, although the different university institutions laid different degrees of stress on practical training, in all cases they went beyond the limits of professional journalism training in the strict sense of the word (Van Parijs, 1969).

In 1966, in Professor Van Parijs's view, Belgian empirical mass media research was essentially concerned with the press, and less often with the other mass media, partly because the press was for so long the main medium of information, partly because of its greater accessibility for study. Five years later, one is struck by how far other media are investigated, especially television and film. Education about film and television is also more widespread than in many other countries. Another interesting aspect of Belgian mass media studies is the extent to which criticism of the arts (art, literature and music) is considered to be an integral part of journalism training, and is also the subject of research. This is probably related to Belgium's artistic heritage, a live heritage today, which is reflected in columns devoted to criticism of the arts in the main Belgian newspapers.

Specialized mass media teaching dates back to the period immediately after the First World War, as a result of the need felt by the General Association of the Belgian Press, to provide training for Belgian journalists. This resulted in the formation of the Institute for Journalists in 1922, which became legally independent of, though still effectively controlled by, the General Association of the Belgian Press in 1937. A separate section for Flemish-speaking students, with its own staff, was set up in 1934.

University-level education on mass communication in Belgium began immediately after the Second World War. In 1945, a Section of Journalism (the present Section of Journalism and Social Communication) was established at the Free University of Brussels. In 1946, the Catholic University of Louvain introduced courses on the press into its *licence* in political and social science. They constituted a subsection of journal-

---

1. In 1966, the University of Ghent was oriented towards press history from a political-science base, and the legal aspects of communication techniques. The Free University of Brussels was working towards a conceptual framework and the sociology of events *(la sociologie événementielle)*. The University of Louvain was particularly interested in moral and ethical aspects and in the conditions of objectivity of information, in methodological problems and in questions of public relations.

ism, the forerunner of the present Department of Social Communication in the Institute of Political and Social Sciences in the Faculty of Economic, Social and Political Sciences, founded in 1966. At each university there is a completely separate French- and Flemish-speaking division, with separate and slightly different courses. In 1962, the University of Ghent founded a Seminar of the Press and Mass Communication Media in the Faculty of Law, which was soon after legally allowed to grant qualifications in mass media studies. Teaching is conducted only in Dutch (IAMCR, 1968; INBEL, 1970; Unesco, 1958).

Teaching and research in Belgian universities

The Free University of Brussels (Université Libre de Bruxelles) began a teaching programme leading to a *licence* for intending professional journalists in 1945. It was apparently the first university in Europe to offer a complete training course for journalists. The curriculum was revised in 1962, to include more extensive work in film and television. Later, a post-graduate qualification, *docteur* in journalism and social communication, was introduced, which takes at least three years to obtain. It was first granted in 1971. In the 1967/68 academic year, a separate Flemish-language section was organized modelled on the French-speaking one.

There were two full-time staff and six part-time media professionals engaged in teaching in 1970. The course for the *licence* in journalism and social communication covers the mass media generally, and newspapers, magazines, radio, television and the cinema in particular. Students, in addition to courses in sociology, psychology, political economy, law, historical criticism and logic or philosophy, take core courses in public law, psychological contact and interviewing, contemporary political doctrines, history and structure of the mass media, law of mass media, sociology of mass media, and practical training in print journalism. Optional courses include theory and practice of public relations, the structure and execution of programmes in radio-television broadcasting, the structure and representation of dramatic works, and cinematographic art.

Mass media research is conducted by the Centre d'Étude des Techniques de Diffusion Collective, originally an independent research institution, but part of the Institute of Sociology of the Free University of Brussels since 1968. This centre has a long interest in the sociology of mass media, in studies of mass media content and in mass communication theory. Recent publications include among others works on the audience for broadcasting, the political role of the media, communication theory, public opinion, the youth press in France and Belgium, and comprehension of information in radio and television.

In 1959, the Institute of Sociology (the Solvay Institute) attached to the Free University of Brussels founded the Séminaire du Film et du Cinéma which has

> worked since . . . through study groups on Belgian cinema, the sociology of film, filmology—visual information, perceptual and other aspects, and a group on film and education, which is by far the most active and important. The Solvay Institute, because of its courses, meetings and publications, is one of the most influential of European centres for research into the educational and cultural implications of films. (Maddison, 1969.)

In 1970 the Katholieke Universiteit te Leuven had eight full-time staff engaged in mass media teaching and research, and five part-time media professionals engaged in teaching. Instruction is provided at the bachelor's, master's and doctoral level for a qualification in political and social sciences, and for a special one-year diploma in audiovisual media.

Until about 1963, the teaching focused largely on general communication science, professional ethics, propaganda and sociological studies. The curriculum for the degree-level courses has since been expanded to include the print media, broadcasting and the cinema. Some work is also done on advertising. Teaching includes the history, regulation and ethics of each medium; the structure and operation of media institutions; sociological and psychological studies of the main media; research methods; and the aesthetics of broadcasting and the cinema. There is also course work on general communication science, communication by images, use of language in communications, public opinion and propaganda, public relations, and means and forms of communication. Teaching for the audio-visual diploma focuses on radio, television and the cinema, and is not as comprehensive.

Mass media research at the Katholieke Universiteit te Leuven is undertaken by the Centrum voor Communicatie Wetenschap (Cecowe). The range of research of this centre, once almost entirely devoted to newspapers, has been greatly extended especially since 1963 when its staff was increased. In 1966, Professor Van Parijs noted that work at Louvain had been much influenced by American empirical mass communication research, especially in its methodological aspects.

In 1970 Cecowe was conducting eight research projects, including an analysis of the 1958 election campaign within a general theory of propaganda and a structural analysis of meaning in film and time-spatial aspects in the language of film.

The Department of Social Communication at the Université Catholique de Louvain offers teaching for the *licence*, the *graduat* and the *doctorat* in social communication and is also a communication research institution. In 1972 it comprised twenty teachers and researchers. A certain number of its taught courses are preparatory to the general study of social communication. These compulsory courses include law, ethics, social psychology of mass media, research methods, theories of communication process, and science of public opinion and propaganda. Optional courses allow specialized study of specific media to take place in relation to the history, psycho-sociology, technique and language of each medium. Other optional courses allow on the one hand the extended study of social communication in general, and include semiology, philosophy and theology of communication, and on the other give preparation for certain areas such as advertising, leisure, public relations, cultural promotion and communication in developing countries.

The research of the Department of Social Communication is undertaken in a pluridisciplinary manner, and investigates social communication and its various concrete modalities from the point of view of philosophy, psychology, sociology, theology, linguistics, semiology, etc. In the past few years, its main publications have included studies on Jacques Feyder, artisan of the cinema, human existence and social communication, anonymous communication, the State and the press, television and teaching, the structures of filmic experience, and radio, television and political power.

The department holds research seminars on semiotics, empirical research methods and content analysis An interfaculty seminar deals with various problems in social communication; for example, in 1972/73 social communication in the university *milieu* (Bachy, 1973).

In September 1962, the University of Ghent was empowered to award the diploma of *licencié en science de la presse et de la communication* in the section of Political and Social Sciences of the Faculty of Law. The *licence* involves four years of study and may be followed by the *doctorat*. The language of instruction is Flemish. Teaching for the *licence* comprises background study in politics, economics, banking, contemporary Belgian history, and the history of science, and several compulsory courses on mass communication. Options, involving more advanced study, include: the written press in Belgium and abroad, the psychology of communication, techniques and practical exercises in audio-visual communication, the sociology of communication, copyright, comparative study of press law, and socio-economic consequences of scientific and technical evolution.

As far as research is concerned, the University of Ghent has been influenced by German theories of *Zeitungswissenschaft* and *Publizistik*, and its research has centred on press history from the point of view of political science, and legal aspects of mass media.

There is as yet no specialized department dealing with mass communication as such at the University of Liège, but it trains researchers in education in its Department of Educational Research (Laboratoire de Pédagogie expérimentale) in the Institute of Psychology and Educational Sciences, and these courses include a study of methods used in mass media research. The department has done research on mass media, especially in regard to legibility, visibility and intelligibility. A technique of analysing visual language has been created and is being tested, the relations between sound and image have been studied, and attempts have been made to measure the comprehensibility of televised instructional programmes.

Tertiary-level institutions

A considerable amount of vocational training combined with academic teaching takes place at advanced-level institutions, which do not have university status.

The Institute for Journalism in Brussels gives a two-year evening course of lectures and practical work in French and Flemish leading to a certificate. The Institut des Hautes Études des Communications Sociales or IHECS (Institute for Advanced Studies in Social Communication) in Ramegnies-Chin, Tournai, is a Catholic institution which provides a four-year training course in French for careers in the press and information, public relations and publicity, and adult education and leisure.

Four advanced-level institutions in Brussels provide training in audio-visual media in French. INSAS (Institut National Supérieur des Arts du Spectacle et Techniques de Diffusion) offers a wide range of courses, lasting between two and four years and combining specialized theoretical and practical instruction with general education for occupations in radio, television and the cinema. IAD (Institut des Arts de Diffuison) a Catholic institution, provides for similar occupations. InRaci (Institut de Radio-Électricité et de Cinématographie) aims at producing specialized technicians for the electronic media. Finally, the National Advanced School of Architecture and the Visual Arts has a section of animated cinematography (Section de Cinématographie Expérimentale d'Animation) which may also be applied to films about art, documentaries, and publicity films.

Two schools in Brussels, RITCS (Hoger Rijkstechnisch Instituut voor Toneel en Cultuurspreiding) the Flemish-speaking counterpart of INSAS, and Na.Ra.F.I. (Radio- en Filmtechnisch Instituut) the Flemish-speaking section of InRaci, provide training in the Flemish language for occupations in the audio-visual media.

The Advertising School (Stedelijke Publiciteitsschool) of Antwerp, an evening school founded in 1955, prepares students for careers in advertising, marketing, public relations and so on, through a three-year syllabus leading to the Graduate in Advertising degree, a tertiary-level qualification. Similar courses in French are provided by the Institut Supérieur de Marketing et de Publicité in Brussels, which also gives a course on publicity techniques at Liège.

Other non-university bodies

The Institut Belge d'Information et de Documentation (INBEL) in Brussels provides in-service training for information officers from all over the world, mainly from underdeveloped areas. It brings out a periodical, *Interstages*, ten times a year, as well as other occasional publications.

The Institut des Émissions Françaises de la Radio-Télévision Belge (The Institute of French Transmissions of Belgian Radio-Television) has two research sections. The Audience Research Department (Service de l'Enquête Permanente sur les Programmes) undertakes continuous audience research, especially for news programmes. The results are not made public but are distributed to French-speaking Belgian universities. The Bureau of Studies (Bureau d'Études) deals with the mass media generally, and publishes a revue, *Cahiers RTB-Études de Radio Télévision*, at irregular intervals.

Czechoslovakia

The idea of specialized, formal training for journalists in Czechoslovakia dates back to 1910 when the matter was first considered. In 1928, a Section of Journalism was established at the Independent School of Political Science, Prague. After the Second World War a Faculty of Journalism was formed in the newly created Higher School of Political and Social Science in Prague, and when this became the Higher School of Economics, journalism was transferred to the universities, and sections of journalism were established in the Philological Faculty of Charles University, Prague, and in the Arts School of Comenius University, Bratislava (Unesco, 1958).

The Journalism Department at Charles University, Prague, was raised to the level of a faculty in 1960, and is now the Faculty of Culture and Journalism. Journalism remains a separate section within the Faculty of Philosophy at Comenius University, Bratislava. At both universities the undergraduate course in journalism may be taken full-time, and lasts five years. The course includes general subjects like philosophy, history, political economy, international relations, language and literature, as well as specialized courses on press history, law, theory and principles of journalism, and practical work on journalism techniques in print media, radio and television. Postgraduate work is also provided for.

As far as professional training for journalism outside universities is concerned, the Czech Press Agency (CTK) runs an international school of journalism and press agency techniques in Prague.

The Academy of the Performing Arts (AMU) in Prague has a Faculty of Film and Television, where creative personnel in these media receive training, in full-time courses lasting four years in the case of film and television editing, and production, and five years in the case of film and television play-writing, direction, camera and documentary creation. All the courses include study of theory, history and aesthetics.

As far as academic university teaching is concerned, the mass media are dealt with as part of the lecture courses in sociology and pedagogy offered in the School of Philosophy and the Pedagogical Faculty of Charles University.

Research into the mass media and mass communications takes place in specialized research institutes connected with, or separate from the universities, and in the research departments of the broadcasting organizations.

The Institute for the Theory and History of Information Media in Prague was created in 1965. It is administratively attached to the Faculty of Journalism at Charles University and its budget is administered by the faculty. Its research field includes mass communication theory, theory of information, audio-visual journalism, typography, publishing, history of Czech and world journalism, and sociology and psychology of mass media. It has compiled a retrospective bibliography of the Czech press, and lists of journalism theses presented in Austria, Czechoslovakia, the German Democratic Republic, the Federal Republic of Germany and Poland.

The Institute for Culture Research in Prague also undertakes research connected with the mass media.

The Research Institute of Education in Prague has a department which carries out research into audio-visual aids, educational television, and the use of radio and film in schools.

The Institute for Mass Media Research attached to the Research Institute of Culture and Public Opinion in Bratislava was founded in 1955. It is a purely theoretic enterprise for co-ordinating theory and research into mass media in Slovakia. It conducts no teaching though it co-operates with the Chair of Journalism at Comenius University in Bratislava.

It has two departments, the Department of Content Analysis of Mass Media, and the Department of Sociology of Mass Media. Its research projects and programmes are all directly financed by the Ministry of Culture of the Slovak Socialist Republic. Recent publications by members of the Institute for Mass Media Research have focused on adult education through mass media; the social and political role of journalism; the effects of mass media, especially television; content analyses of the Slovak daily press and detailed research on components such as intelligibility, headlining and word usage in the press; and a number of bibliographies on mass media and mass communication research.

The Department of Sociology of Mass Media is preparing final reports on two research projects, one on the extent of knowledge of the inhabitants of Slovakia, another on the effects of television. It is also carrying out socio-psychological research on the effects of mass communication media in small groups, and is preparing a long-term project on the relation between television and children. Finally, an atlas of readers of the press is being constructed, and work on an encyclopaedia of journalism is proceeding.

Both Czechoslovak Radio and Czechoslovak Television have active research departments. The Research Department of Czechoslovak Radio in Prague started systematic research in 1966, and operates either through a permanent network of questioners all over the Czechoslovak Socialist Republic or in collaboration with a similar research department of Czechoslovak Radio in Slovakia covering both national republics separately. Research is conducted through selective sample surveys and covers the entire population over 15 years of age as well as specific groups of listeners. It has three main tasks. It conducts systematic research into listening conditions, listening habits and the use of radio as part of leisure activities. It also does broad research into sound-radio activities, especially specific creations for radio, the culture of the language used and their relationship with television, and the history of broadcasting.

The head of the research department of Czechoslovak Television in Prague explained that the main department had four sections, that of audience research, theoretical studies, documentation and library. The audience-research section was for many years mainly engaged in standard daily inquiries into audience size and audience reaction to single programmes. This was found to be unsatisfactory in many ways, and the section is experimenting with other techniques. In addition special surveys were undertaken. The theoretical section is the newest, and is still in the process of settling its aims and means. Its interests range from lexical publications and handbooks for specialized activities in television, to comparative studies of Czech and foreign television programmes.

Denmark

Teaching and research [1] into the mass media and mass communication in universities in Denmark 'were started very recently and ... consequently the results so far are very sparse and scanty'. This was the opinion of the Danish Research Secretariat which was undertaking a survey in 1970 of research on the mass media in Denmark. The survey showed that almost no research had been done before the late 1960s, apart from sporadic audience surveys for Danish radio.

The over-all picture of mass media studies in Denmark is that first, there has recently been an increased interest in mass communication research (perhaps partly stimulated by the inquiry of the Danish Research Secretariat) in many directions—linguistic, historical, economic, psychological and sociological—not, as yet, matched by a corresponding increase in teaching. Characteristically, this research consists of one or more projects taking place concurrently in several different institutional structures in the same educational institution. In other words, mass media is not so much seen as an integrated study in its own right, but is rather studied from the point of view of other disciplines.

Professional training in journalism takes place at the Danish School of Journalism at Aarhus. The school was founded in 1946 as part of the University of Aarhus in cooperation with the Danish press associations and financed by contributions from press organizations and the government. Journalists who had completed at least one year of apprenticeship, attended a three-month course at the school, underwent a further year's apprenticeship and ended their training with another three months at the school.

In 1970 the Danish parliament passed a new law making the school an institute of higher learning in its own right.

This meant a complete change in the training structure for Danish journalists. The new law came into effect in September 1971. Now journalists are trained for four years, spending thirty months of that time at the school, the other eighteen months being spent with newspapers.

The study programme, which is subject to revisions, at present foresees a preparatory course of six months followed by an examination. Of the 110 students admitted to the preparatory course, only 75 may be allowed to continue, according to the law. These 75 follow special courses for one year, centred around a points system. During

---

1. A review of past trends and present activities in Danish mass communication research is to be found in *Statens Humanistiske og Samfundsvidenskabelige Forskningsråds Symposium, 10 og 11 maj 1971, på Den Internationale Højskole i Helsingør om Massekommunikationsforskning*, [Copenhagen], [1971], 131 p. (Mimeo.).

that year the student must gain twelve points in various disciplines, three points being the highest possible in any one discipline.

When the student has spent at least eighteen months at the school, including the preparatory period, and gained his twelve points he joins a newspaper for eighteen months. He then returns to the school to specialize in fields of his own choice and to write his final thesis.

The School of Journalism is unique among the Danish institutions of higher learning in that it is part of the Prime Minister's office rather than of the Ministry of Education. This goes back to a tradition whereby the Prime Minister is minister for the press.

For administrative and other purposes the law of 1970 divided the organization of the school into two, but they are physically the same.

The Institut for Presseforskning (Institute for Press Research) is responsible for research and contacts with other institutions of higher learning, mostly the University of Aarhus. The institute has five departments, the heads of which are responsible both for their research programmes and for teaching within their fields at the school. The institute has a very small research staff of its own and most of its work is carried out in close co-operation with the senior lecturers of the school who may of course also start their own research projects.

In 1970 the Institute of Political Science at the University of Aarhus was planning to begin teaching on mass communications in 1971. At that time, two members of the institute's staff were engaged on two six-month projects, both totally financed by the Danish State Radio, and it was planning other projects in the field of radio and television.

In January 1971, the Psychological Institute at Aarhus University was planning to undertake research on the short-time retention and long-term reaction to television news content, while the Institute for Linguistics was undertaking a linguistic analysis of the language of newspapers.

The study of film has recently been started at Copenhagen University, at the Institute of Theatre Science, where the teaching of mass communication in relation to society has been started very recently. Since about 1960, sociological studies of the mass media have been offered irregularly, as part of the curriculum for students pursuing the Master of Science degree in sociology at the Sociological Institute at the University of Copenhagen.

Some of the academic staff had recently done research on mass communication, including a comprehensive study of mass communication research in Denmark up to 1967, but no research was being undertaken on the mass media in 1970, nor was any planned for the immediate future. In addition, research projects concerned with aspects of the mass media have been carried out at Copenhagen University by the Institute for Economic History, the Psychological Laboratory, the Institute of Nordic Literature, and the Institute for Sociology.

At the time of the Unesco survey, Odense University, a new university founded in 1964, had not yet undertaken any systematic teaching or research in mass communications. However, the Rector wrote in July 1970 that

> the university is at present contemplating the practical (mainly financial) problems involved in associating the subjects of film aesthetics and film history with subjects already taught. The 'Filmfonden' (under the Ministry of Culture) takes an active interest in the matter, but a definite solution is not yet within sight.

Other institutions, which, though not strictly speaking universities, are of university level, are also engaging in studies on the mass media. The Copenhagen School of Economics and Business Administration (Handelshøjskolen, København) in its Institute of Marketing Communication provides teaching and engages in research on marketing communication. Teaching started in 1955, and a systematic course has been given since 1959. The course for both degrees includes teaching on advertising practices and techniques in the mass media generally and in the newspaper and periodical press, and marketing communication strategy and technique in the media generally.

The Institute for Organization Sociology and the Sociology of Work at the Copenhagen School of Economics has two research projects under way on mass communication, one on the production of culture, and the internal organization of institutions concerned with the formulation of culture, and another on the Danish Advanced Technical School.

The Royal Danish School of Educational Studies (Danmarks Laererhøjskole) through its Institute of Development Psychology, has recently begun to offer teaching about children and the mass media to students pursuing the undergraduate degree in education and educational psychology. Some research is also being undertaken by the institute.

The Danish Library School has four research projects on mass media: on recent books read; a long-term survey on the development of children's reading habits; readers' and library needs; research on communication of events in the daily press.

The Danish Film Academy (Den Danske Filmskole) founded in 1966 to provide technical and artistic training in film production, offers a two-year course in sound, direction and camera work.

Finally, mass media studies have been, or are being, undertaken by some non-educational bodies in Denmark.

The Institute for Peace and Conflict Research previously conducted an investigation into international news, comparing news media of North America with those of Europe, but has no research on the mass media under way at present.

Since 1970, two members on the staff of Danish Radio have been concerned with research, and are at present engaged on a Scandinavian project dealing with the selection, presentation and to some degree, audience reactions to news broadcasts in television in Denmark, Finland, Norway and Sweden, including a comparison between the ways of broadcasting news (through radio and television) in all four countries for the week 22–29 March 1970. The study, planned and executed co-operatively by the Scandinavian broadcasting organizations, is focused on the analysis both of the content of news and of the communicators involved. The Danish part of this project is being undertaken in collaboration with the School of Journalism at Aarhus, and the Institute of Political Science at Aarhus University. This and other studies are additional to audience surveys (for example, ratings), which are being undertaken for Danish Radio by non-academic organizations.

Finland

Finland [1] has a long history of teaching on journalism in academic institutions—the longest in Scandinavia.

Journalism education began on an informal basis in the mid-1920s when short courses were organized by the Finnish Association of Journalists, followed, after 1945, by the Association of Magazine Editors, to provide further education for practising journalists who belonged to these organizations. Meanwhile academic institutions had also started to provide journalism courses: the School of Social Studies in Helsinki introduced courses in journalism in 1925, and the University of Helsinki began to offer subsidiary courses in elementary journalism in the mid-1950s. In 1943 the School of Social Studies got a permanent lecturer in journalism, and in 1949 a professorship was established (corresponding to the German *Zeitungswissenschaft*), the first chair in journalism in Scandinavia. Thenceforth students of the School of Social Studies could combine journalism with other courses for degree purposes.

In 1960, the School of Social Sciences (which gave instruction in Finnish) moved from Helsinki to Tampere. At the same time its chair was transformed into a chair of journalism and mass communication along American lines. In 1966 the school became a full university, the University of Tampere (IAMCR, 1968; Unesco, 1958).

Professional training

At present, Tampere University is the only academic centre for journalism training in Finland. It also provides formally separate academic journalism education in the Faculty of Social Sciences (see below). Instruction for a two-year, practically oriented course in journalism designed mainly to train personnel for the daily press, is taught in an undergraduate-level college, connected with Tampere University, which provides vocational training in various fields. The vocational journalism course is taught by four lecturers. About 100 students were registered in 1969. The language of instruction is Finnish.

Professional training for journalism in Swedish has been provided since 1962 by a tertiary-level institution, the Swedish School of Social Studies (Svenska Social- och Kommunalhøgskolan) in Helsinki. The three-year vocational course produces over twenty journalists each year for Finland's Swedish-language press. In addition to these public institutions for journalism training, a large private publishing house in Finland, Sanoma Oy, established its own school of journalism in 1967 which gained State approval in 1969. The school's fifteen-month 'year' has been passed by about twenty journalists on each course. In 1971, it began systematic pre-professional training for picture editors and news photographers. Since 1969 it has also provided follow-up courses for its own 250 journalist employees.

No Finnish institution provides full-time follow-up training for journalists. This constitutes a problem because only one in five of Finland's 2,500 working journalists have received a basic training in journalism, although many have received academic

---

1. I am indebted to Kaarle Nordenstreng, University of Tampere, for details on mass media studies in Finland. Unless otherwise stated, information on Finland is derived from personal communication with Professor Nordenstreng or from questionnaire responses.

degrees. Since 1924, short follow-up courses have been organized by the trade unions and the Finnish Cultural Foundation, but the government is now considering the problem of making better provision for further training of working journalists.

Film and television professionals are trained at the Finnish Institute of Industrial Arts in Helsinki whose Department of Camera Art provides a special four-year course. About ten students graduate each year.

Teaching

Teaching and research on mass communications takes place at several academic institutions in Finland, both at university, and at tertiary level.

The most extensive education on the social aspects of the mass media and of mass communications is given at the University of Tampere. In addition to the two-year professional course in journalism, mentioned above, the Faculty of Social Sciences of Tampere University also offers the possibility of taking journalism and mass communications, or radio and television, for degree purposes. At the first level (the candidate's degree in social science, leading to the title of master), involving a period of study lasting four to five years, students must take one major subject, and two or three subsidiary subjects. Journalism and mass communications, or radio and television, or both, may be taken as major subjects, usually in combination with sociology, political science, international politics and economics. The major subject is taken at three successive levels of difficulty *(approbatur, cum laude approbatur* and *laudatur)* and the subsidiary subject at the first two of these. The first level includes a basic, introductory course in the mass media as social institutions and mass communication as a social process. To proceed to the second level it is necessary, among other requirements, to have had three months' practical employment in a media organization or in an institution engaged in research, and further experience is required to take the third level. Both second and third levels involve a common core of reading, and options, which are very extensive indeed at the final stage. To successfully complete the major course, it is necessary to write a thesis.

Students wishing to undertake further study or research may proceed to the licentiate (master's) and then to the doctorate degree. About twenty to thirty students a year obtain the licentiate's, and fewer than one a year, the doctorate. The teaching is provided by two professors, two docents, three lecturers, three assistants and a number of visiting specialists.

The regulations of the Faculty of Social Sciences for 1971 state that the instruction offered in the major course in journalism and mass communications aims

> to give the student as clear a picture as possible of the mass media as social institutions, together with a knowledge of research technique and adequate technical skill in practical mass communication work to qualify for activity in the daily press, radio or television.

The main emphasis regarding general knowledge about mass communication lies in the relations between mass communication and the rest of contemporary Finnish society. The policy statement for the study of mass communication issued by the Institute of Journalism and Mass Communication at Tampere University in 1971 states that

> in teaching, the splitting of the mass communication field into parts according to the technical media (like press, radio, TV, cinema etc.) should be avoided, and instead attention must be centered around the socio-politico-economical forces governing the production and consumption of mass communication.

Most students who graduate in journalism and mass communication find employment in the media, and some in public-relations work, staff journals, advertising, organization activity and communications research.

Teaching on journalism began to be offered in 1966 at the University of Helsinki, through the departments of Sociology and Political Science in the Faculty of Social and Political Science, and teaching on mass communications was started in 1968. In response to this survey, the spokesman for the university observed: 'Because there are not enough teachers in mass communication, only one assistant professor, one lecturer and one assistant', students can take mass communications only at the grade of *approbatur* and *cum laude approbatur*, not *laudatur*. To do this final grade they have to transfer to the University of Tampere, although they may study some aspects of the subject at a higher level at Helsinki University, in the departments of Sociology, Politics and Social Psychology. 'It is possible and desirable that later on the [*laudatur* grade] will be added to the present lower examinations.'

Mass communications teaching covers

> the activity and the instruments of mass communication as a social phenomenon . . . the social and social psychological foundations of mass communication and . . . its effects in political life, in the structure of society and in human behaviour. The principal point in teaching is . . . the theoretical foundations and scientific analysis. Practical exercises of journalistic expressions are nevertheless necessary to understand the conditions of mass communication.

These practical exercises, with alternatives of the press or radio and television, take place during the *approbatur* grade. They do not aim at making professional reporters for the press or electric media. They are considered useful for all active members of society and for the future scientist. At the grade of *cum laude approbatur*, all students take a course in communication research methods and may choose between general mass communication research and press research.

In spite of its relatively short existence, 500 to 600 students have been registered for the mass communication courses. They have come from all faculties, but mainly from the Faculty of Social and Political Science, and from the Faculty of Philosophy.

The Institute of Sociology at the University of Turku gave regular courses on human communication with special reference to the press in the first half of the 1960s, but these have been discontinued. However, the institute conducts some mass media research.

At the Swedish School of Economics (Svenska Handelshögskolan) in Helsinki (Lodman, 1970), mass communication is 'an integrated part of the teaching in Marketing of all levels', while at the Turku School of Economics, Turun,

> Teaching of mass communications is given in connection with the teaching of marketing. It includes the theory of mass communication, research methodology, and mass media . . . Particular emphasis is given to the study and research of advertising. Research in mass media is concentrated on advertising and public relations. (Halme, 1970.)

The Department of Marketing at the Vaasa School of Economics has, since 1969, included teaching on the mass media for the degrees of Bachelor of Economics and Master of Arts in Economics. One full-time and four part-time staff provide this teaching, which centres on advertising (including techniques) but also deals with sociological and psychological studies of the mass media and research methods.

Research

Mass communication research takes place both in the universities, particularly the University of Tampere, and in other educational institutions. In addition the Finnish broadcasting organization, Yleisradio, not only does research itself but also commissions a great deal of academic research.

The Institute of Journalism and Mass Communication at the University of Tampere has the longest tradition. Its research fields have been content analysis and readership analysis and it has done work on themes connected with journalism technique. Recently this hitherto press-oriented institute has started a specialized section on electronic media (radio, television and film).

Besides its Institute of Journalism and Mass Communication the University of Tampere has been active in communication research through its Research Institute, a centre for carrying out projects commissioned from outside and for giving training in research to social science students. Less permanent research activity has taken place at the institutes of education in the universities of Tampere and Jyväskylä and Turku. In the view of Kaarle Nordenstreng (Nordenstreng, 1971a), until very recently the Head of Research of Yleisradio and now the Head of the Department of Journalism and Mass Communication at Tampere University:

> Unlike Swedish broadcasting research, Finnish research got from the very beginning a stimulating contribution from the academic communication research: this was largely due to the activity shown by the University of Tampere which has got both a research institute for social studies and an institute for journalism and mass communications for the training of journalists and communication researchers.

Studies carried out at Tampere University have covered size and composition of radio and television audiences, surveys of audience reaction and comprehension, uses and gratification studies, and content analyses of programmes. Research undertaken in other universities has included audience-reaction studies and media-consumption patterns. A major project carried out co-operatively by various universities and Yleisradio is a psychological and sociological survey of the effects of the introduction of television in Finnish Lapland.

Yleisradio has taken a very active interest in research, and has defined its research interests very broadly. As Professor Nordenstreng points out (Nordenstreng, 1971a) instead of conducting its research, as most broadcasting organizations do, to serve practical programming, and thus concentrating

> on the *means* of communication, the Finnish approach has concentrated on the *goals* of communication, and research has been carried out primarily for clarifying and planning the objectives of programming, i.e. for formulating the programme policy.

The origins of this policy of long-range planning date back to the beginning of 1965 (Yleisradio, 1967) when

> plenty of questions relating to programme policy as well as economic, technical and organizational problems associated with them had accumulated and demanded a prompt but at the same time well weighed solution based on a general view of the situation.

The working group assembled to consider these problems felt that broadcasting should not merely reflect, in a passive way, social life and conditions, but should rather be a live and active factor in the community, offering it 'a changing vision of the world based on correct information and facts', not by implanting any particular view of life but by 'offering building materials for personal opinions'.

In this framework of social and policy orientation, the research commissioned by Yleisradio was first decided on by a group of experts consisting of 'professors in sociological, psychological, educational and communications research at various Finnish universities' and representatives of Yleisradio; the universities undertook the research, and the broadcasting organization provided the funds. To ensure continuity and to achieve a closer integration of research and long-range or daily planning, a new special section for Long-Range Planning (LRP) was formed

> to provide information for decision-making, based on scientific research, extensive expert knowledge and careful development prognoses, and to coordinate and tentatively shape long-range component plans and investment proposals drawn up for the various sections.

Accordingly the LRP section was to include both the function of a research department and that of a planning unit, closely integrated.

Since 1968, the LRP section itself has decided what research needs to be done, and has used the universities to help to implement its programme. In many cases, the research is actually done by the LRP section's own researchers—in 1970 it had a staff of two senior social science researchers (who were permanent members of the LRP team) and three other researchers, as well as other administrative and computation staff. Although the amount annually spent by Yleisradio on research ($90,000 in 1969, under 0.3 per cent of its total budget) is less than many other broadcasting organizations, a great deal of research is generated by it. This is partly because since the formation of the LRP section, Yleisradio has become less interested in pure data gathering (for instance it has ceased doing expensive continuous audience-rating surveys), and more interested in theoretically oriented research which will help it decide what its goals should be, and therefore in more 'fundamental' or 'academic' research than most audience research departments (Nordenstreng, 1971a).

France

France has a long and lively tradition of interest in many facets of mass media, particularly the press and film, and many different institutions have grown up over the years to further activities in training, teaching and research related to mass communication. Several distinct strands in French mass media studies may be distinguished. One is the empirical study of the French and foreign press, characteristic of the Institut Français de Presse, which has inspired comparative journalism studies in many countries, and has been extended to all the mass media. The mass media are seen from the angle of political science, as essential sources of information for the public. This type of work may be contrasted with another mode of mass media study, developed by Gilbert Cohen-Séat in the later 1940s, which was concerned with the unique properties of film, with the disturbances caused by filmic perception on the spectator's psychological and physiological mechanisms of perception, and with the language of film images. Its viewpoint was psychological and social-psychological. It was the subject of a special centre at the Sorbonne, which closed down in 1961, and spread throughout the world in the later 1940s and early 1950s. It still remains a significant part of mass media studies in Italy. A third mode is structuralism, which is concerned with all the mass media, as creators of contemporary culture, and particularly with the values embodied in media images—verbal and visual. It aims to use the methods of semiology, the analysis of systems of signs, to derive the structure of individual media messages, and thus ultimately the symbolic structure of the total system constituted by all media content, so that the role and effects of mass media in modern technological societies may be assessed. It developed in the later 1950s and early 1960s, and its most important centre is the Centre d'Etudes de Communications de Masse in Paris, although it has spread to other countries too, especially in association with studies of mass culture (Burgelin, 1968; Maddison, 1969).

Many other institutions besides the universities have participated in mass media studies in France. But with the gradual reorganization of the French university system that culminated in the new pattern of universities established since 1968, the universities have taken on new functions, and new units have been created to associate previously separated activities and institutions, particularly in pluridisciplinary studies. Under the new system, several institutions of long standing have been incorporated into the new universities, and some new ones have been created, while provision has also been made for links to be established between universities and some institutions outside the university system which are involved in mass media studies.

University institutes of technology have been established in many of the French universities, and eight of these offer courses in 'careers of information'. Most of them, however, are concerned with training documentalists and public-relations officers; only those of Bordeaux III and Tours provide training for the mass media. Degree-level mass media studies take place at the universities of Paris I, Paris II, Paris III, Paris IV, Bordeaux III and Strasbourg III.

Professional training

Journalism

The only university-based training in journalism which is recognized by the French journalism profession is that provided by the University of Bordeaux III and the Centre Universitaire d'Enseignement en Journalisme, at the University of Strasbourg III, which awards a professional diploma as well as academic degrees. Holders of this diploma are allowed to have an apprenticeship period of only one year, instead of the normal three years, when they enter employment. Teaching is oriented towards the press, radio and television and includes their history, regulation, censorship and organization, and the ethics of journalism.

The oldest surviving school of journalism is the École Supérieure de Journalisme (Advanced School of Journalism) at Lille, founded in 1924 under the auspices of the Catholic Faculties of Lille, which now gives a three-year professional course in journalism, concentrating on newspaper journalism.

After the Second World War, the journalism profession felt the need to set up a school to cater for the large number of would-be journalists. Thus an independent professional school was set up in Paris in 1946, the Centre de Formation des Journalistes or CFJ (Centre of Training for Journalists). In 1970, the CFJ was providing a three-year diploma course in journalism in print media and broadcasting, dealing with their history and organization all over the world, the economics and regulation of these media in France, press ethics and journalism techniques. The CFJ, in collaboration with the École Supérieure de Journalisme at Lille, established a separate centre, the Centre de Perfectionnement des Journalistes et de Cadres de Presse (CPJ), in Paris in 1969 for the further training of professional journalists and press personnel. There is also a private Higher School of Journalism in Paris which receives French and foreign students.

Public relations training

CELSA, the Centre d'Études Littéraires et Scientifiques Appliquées at the University of Paris IV has a Section of Information and Public Relations, including social relations, publicity (advertising) and public relations. The centre gives general professional training at the level of the second cycle and specialized training at the third cycle. The training is provided by professionals, and it includes a twelve-month *stage* (training period) in a media enterprise.

The university institutes of technology at Paris V, Nancy and Strasbourg have a public-relations option in their *carrières de l'information* sections, and provide two-year subgraduate vocational training in this field.

Public-relations training is also given at the Institute of Economics and of European Co-operation (IECE), at the Institute of Public Relations, and at the College of Moral Sciences—all private establishments in Paris.

Training for film and television

In 1970, when this survey was conducted, professional training for directors, producers and other creative personnel in the film and television industries was provided by State and private tertiary-level educational institutions, rather than by universities, and by the ORTF (Office de Radiodiffusion-Télévision Française), the French broadcasting organization.

The Institute of Advanced Cinematographic Studies (Institut des Hautes Études Cinématographiques IDHEC) in Paris, is a film school under the supervision of the Centre National de la Cinématographie, a branch of the Ministry of Cultural Affairs set up to supervise, control and if necessary to subsidize the French film industry. It provides training for creative personnel for the cinema and television, and is the major institution in this field in France. It was in the midst of reorganization, and in moving to new quarters in 1970, so precise up-to-date details of its teaching could not be ascertained. IDHEC was founded in 1944, and gives a two-year diploma course of instruction (followed by a compulsory period of practical training for French students), for would-be directors, producers, cameramen, sound, montage and animation specialists in the cinema and television. Twenty-seven students were admitted in 1970/71, including six foreign students. The first year's courses are introductory ones and taken by all students, and students specialize in their chosen branch of study in the second.

The Conservatoire National d'Art Dramatique in Paris, a school for actors, though mainly concerned with theatre, does give courses related to radio and television. Provision has been made for the establishment of closer links between it and the University of Paris III, where new departments of cinematographic studies, and of techniques of expression and communication have been created.

The Conservatoire National Supérieur de Musique in Paris, gives a course in connexion with the ORTF, on teaching of music applied to the audio-visual field.

The Advanced School of Television (École Supérieure de Télévision) was established at Yerres, near Paris, in 1969. It is a private establishment which offers training in various careers in television—journalism, production, direction, scriptwriting, montage, camera work and so on.

Other institutions which provide training for radio and television are the Studio-École Radio-TV (Studio School for Radio and Television) at Maisons Laffitte, the École Supérieure de TV (Advanced School of Television) at Choiseul, and the Centre de Formation de l'ORTF (the ORTF Training Centre) at Montrouge.

Academic teaching and research on mass media in French universities

Journalism and mass communications

Two French universities conduct teaching and research on journalism and mass communications, the University of Paris II and the University of Strasbourg III.

Under the new organization of French universities, the Institut Français de Presse (the French Institute of the Press) has been fully incorporated into the University of Paris II. This institute is a descendant of the Institute of Press Science of the University of Paris, the first institution established for systematic academic study of the press in France, which published a series of outstanding reports on the French and the foreign press entitled *Cahiers de la Presse* just before the Second World War. It closed down during the war, to be succeeded by the Centre d'Études Scientifiques de la Presse (Centre for Scientific Studies of the Press) in 1945, which in turn was superseded by the Institut Français de Presse founded in 1951. In 1957, it became an institute attached to the Sorbonne, and devoted itself to research. In 1966, however, it was empowered to prepare students for the *doctorat* in the law and economics of mass communication granted by the Faculty of Law of the University of Paris, as well as for the *doctorat* in the history and social psychology of mass communication in the Faculty of Letters and Human Sciences. It now gives preparation for the *licence* in sciences of information (a four-year course) for a *doctorat* in sciences of information (two years' study after the licence, culminating in a thesis) and also gives a diploma for two years' study. It is a pluridisciplinary institute for teaching, research and documentation whose field includes the press, radio and television, and related spheres like public relations, advertising, press agencies, information services, public-opinion polling and the study of public opinion. Its research has included comparative studies of press content all over the world, and in this field, as in others, it has had an important influence on empirical mass communication research in France and in other countries.

In the past, it has been closely associated with the Institut d'Études Politiques (Institute of Political Studies), since both bodies were administered by the National Foundation of Political Sciences, and it was largely responsible for the mass media studies undertaken by the Institut d'Études Politiques. Special provision has been made for closer co-operation between the Institut d'Études Politiques and the University of Paris II.

The University of Strasbourg III is concerned with journalism in two ways. It provides teaching for the *licence en journalism*, the *maîtrise de journalisme* and for the *doctorat de 3e cycle*. Teaching for the licence deals with the press, radio and television, and the mass media generally, and covers their history, regulation and economics, and media organizations in Western and Eastern countries. The ethics of journalism and practical techniques are also included in the course. For the *maîtrise*, teaching concentrates on sociological and psychological studies especially of the press and broadcasting, in Western and Eastern countries, and research methods, including an introduction to modern mathematics and to the treatment of news by computer science.

The University of Strasbourg III is also the seat of the International Centre for Advanced Training in Journalism (Centre International d'Enseignement Supérieur de Journalisme or CIESJ) which was set up in 1956, in response to a suggestion of Unesco, to provide training for teaching staff, offer refresher courses for teachers of journalism as well as for practising journalists and to undertake studies in teaching methods and mass communication techniques. It was the first such regional training centre set up with assistance from Unesco, whose sphere of action included Europe, Africa and the Near and Middle East. From its inception, it has interpreted its role as pertaining to all the mass media. It organizes short courses which are attended by experts from its regional area, to compare the teaching methods in journalism training all over the world, and to discuss other matters of importance to journalism.

The CIESJ also conducts research into mass communication, the results of some of which are published in its quarterly review, *Journalisme*. Its most recent research project is on the impact of mass media on social and economic development in developing countries, undertaken in co-operation with CIESPAL (its counterpart for Latin America).

A documentation centre for the collection, abstraction and dissemination of information about mass communication research has been established at Strasbourg which will act as a regional centre for mass communication research material in the French language, and will co-operate with similar centres now established in Ecuador, Scandinavia, Singapore, the United Kingdom and the United States to establish an international network of information in this field.

Techniques of expression and communication

The University of Bordeaux III includes among its specialities the study of literature, and techniques of expression and communication. In 1970, when this survey was undertaken, the Unité Pluridisciplinaire de Techniques d'Expression et de Communication or UPTEC, (Pluridisciplinary Unit of Techniques of Expression and Communication) provided instruction for the *maîtrise*, in a four-year course including journalism, cinema, radio, television, bibliography, theatre, documentation and public relations. The course was oriented towards literary criticism, sociology, economics, linguistics and the sociology of literature. At that time, it was also providing post-graduate seminars, and supervising student theses, presented under more traditional disciplines like sociology, psychology and literature, since it had not yet received permission to grant the *doctorat* degree.

When this survey was conducted, the Institut de Littérature et de Techniques Artistiques de Masse or ILTAM (Institute of Literature and the Mass Media) was in process of being integrated into the structure of the University of Bordeaux III. It was founded in 1965, and since 1967 it has been a research body associated with the Centre National de la Recherche Scientifique. It comprises three research units, each with its own particular activity. In 1970, the Centre de Sociologie des Faits Littéraires (Centre for the Sociology of Literary Production) was undertaking research into books and reading in developing countries (in collaboration with Unesco), book distribution, historical literary sociology, the social psychology of the reader, the sociology of literature, and the sociologies of African literature. The Centre for the Mass-Produced Book is studying reading habits among the salaried classes. The Study Group on the Vocabulary of the Creative Arts is producing an international dictionary of literary terms commissioned by the International Association for Comparative Literature and conducts research into the lexicology of literary criticism and art criticism.

After this survey was conducted a new Department of Techniques of Expression and of Communication, and a new Department of Cinematographic Studies were created at the University of Paris III. Provision has been made for co-operation between this university and non-university institutions, such as the Centre Audio-Visuel and the Centre de Télé-Enseignement.

Finally, some mass media teaching is included as part of other offerings. Thus at Paris I there is a Centre for the Study of the Economics of the Press within the Department of Economics, while courses on the cinema are included in the Arts and Letters Departments of Grenoble III and Paris VIII.

Non-university institutions

The work of a few non-university institutions may now be briefly alluded to, although there are many more than these connected with mass media studies in France.

The leading centre for structuralism in France is the Centre d'Études de Communications de Masse (CECMAS) established within the École Pratique des Hautes Études in Paris in 1960. It is concerned particularly with the analysis of the content of the press, and of films, and with theoretical and practical problems of education in the light of the diffusion of mass culture. It views its work as embracing the whole field of mass culture and thus having a wider scope than mass communications.

CECMAS is a centre generally oriented to research and is attached to the National Centre for Scientific Research. It does not provide systematic teaching for degree purposes, but there is a fortnightly working seminar each year from November to June, which has no fixed programme, but where certain researchers give papers on their work in progress. Its work is linked with the research teaching and training conducted in the École Pratique des Hautes Études.

Some idea of the tone and the scope of the work of CECMAS may be gauged from the statement which always appears on the back cover of its journal *Communications*:

> Large circulation Press, Radio, Television, Cinema, Advertising, Songs and Popular Novels: through all these massive channels, the astounding development of which characterises the modern world, the man of the technological civilisation is building up a new culture. What are its contents? Its languages? Its functions? Its values? Its effects? How does it define itself in relation to traditional bodies of knowledge, in relation to other cultures? On this subject, situated at the very crossroads of great current events and of sociological science, the review *Communications* publishes the work, the reflections and the questions of the researchers of . . . [CECMAS] and of specialists all over the world.

The over-all approach of the research done at CECMAS is sociological, but not exclusively so, and the methods used derive from social psychology, psycho-analysis, ethnology, economics, demography, and in particular structural linguistics. In its work undertaken between 1960 and 1969, four main problem areas may be distinguished: the relationship between 'global society' and mass communications (including analyses of mass culture, television and educational television); the effects attributable to mass communications within the total context of the individual's primary and secondary group membership (including study of the effects of filmed and televised violence on children); the uses and gratifications of media consumption, and the systems of symbols projected by mass media (including audience breakdowns by age, sex, education, group membership, etc. undertaken to establish a typology of media use according to statistical models tested by structural analysis); and social aspects of media content, derived by structural analysis (including studies of the image—cinema, press and advertising illustrations—written discourse, message forms (rhetoric) and the structure of narratives). Some research at CECMAS is also concerned with crises and the adaptation of societal structures to them.

The ORTF (Office de Radiodiffusion-Télévision Française), the French broadcasting organization, apart from the conventional type of audience and programme research similar to that undertaken by other broadcasting organizations, also devotes part of its efforts to study the implications and effects of television as a new audio-visual art, as well as a conveyor of information and of values. It has produced a large number of experimental films, which are transmitted in the ordinary way in order to study these processes in natural communication settings.

German Democratic Republic

Journalism training

The University of Leipzig has perhaps the oldest tradition of academic interest in journalism of any in the world. In 1672, lectures on journalism were given at this university, and the earliest modern developments in research and teaching also occurred here, with the setting up of the first institute for the study of newspapers in 1916, under Karl Bücher, and the foundation of the first separate chair in journalism in 1926. Immediately after the Second World War, the institute was renamed the Institut für Publizistik und Zeitungswissenschaft (Institute for Journalism and Newspaper Study) and in 1954 it was raised to the level of an independent Faculty of Journalism (Fakultät für Journalistik). Since 1968, it has been titled the Journalism Section (Sektion Journalistik). The Karl Marx University of Leipzig is the only university in the German Democratic Republic where advanced specialized study of journalism takes place.

The aim of the four-year full-time course is to combine a theoretical understanding, grounded in the principles of Marxism-Leninism, with a high degree of practical skill, and a knowledge of the conduct of journalism based on the necessary qualities of good character. The orientation of the course is to produce a trained individual who is first and foremost a journalist *per se*, and only secondarily a newspaper, radio or television journalist. The course aims at providing a basic orientation in journalism followed by additional specialization in the student's chosen field (print media, radio or television). To enter the course, students must have completed their secondary-school education and have done one year's voluntary work on the editorial staff of a press, radio or television enterprise. The essential core of the training consists in the completion of sixty compulsory exercises at regular intervals throughout the four-year period, starting with simple exercises in writing reports and essays, and continuing with increasingly difficult assignments. In the final year students' articles must be accepted and published in the relevant printed or audio-visual medium. Students work through these exercises individually and in groups, and the exercises integrate the substance of various content areas which provide the basic material for the exercises. These basic content areas are: (a) Marxism-Leninism; (b) a general preparatory area including politics, military politics, the Soviet Union today, the building of the German Democratic Republic and similar subjects, realized through lectures, seminars, colloquia and above all excursions; and (c) the theory and practice of journalism, ranging from the details of different aspects of journalistic work in each medium to the general consideration of journalism as a consensus building institution in society. This area includes such aspects as the ideological aspects of journalism in socialist countries and elsewhere; the foundation of journalistic styles in the different media; the principles of journalistic work methods in the press, radio and television; journalistic psychology in relation to the audience and in relation to the psychological requirements of journalistic work and the journalistic creative process; and the management and planning of socialist journalism. These subjects form the content of the first three basic years. In the fourth year, students specialize in a particular medium (print, radio or television) and content area (foreign politics, political economy, cultural politics and so on). The curriculum also includes a series of related subject areas (German and Soviet literature, history, psychology, cultural theory); special training in speech education, obligatory for radio and television specialists; and training in Russian and in another foreign language

(English, French or Spanish). Training takes place through lectures, seminars, colloquia and excursions, and above all through the series of compulsory exercises. Students evaluate each other's work individually and collectively, and are evaluated by the faculty members. A feature of the organization of the course is the formation of small groups of four to six students who are attended to from beginning to end by a mentor, who is himself a working journalist, who advises and supervises the group.

Outside the Karl Marx University, journalism training is also conducted by the Technical School run by the Union of German Journalists; in journalism classes conducted for functionaries of the Party and the Mass Organizations in Party High Schools; and in various other organizations. The Union of German Journalists also runs a Solidarity School, founded in 1964, for journalists from developing countries.

Film training

The University of Halle-Wittenburg has a school of cinematography which trains directors, producers and other professional personnel for the film industry. There is also a tertiary-level institute in Potsdam Babelsberg, the Deutsche Hochschule für Filmkunst (German Advanced School for Cinematography), for the training of film practitioners.

Research

The Journalism Section of Karl Marx University at Leipzig conducts a wide range of research. Its main research areas include history of journalism, sociology of journalism, sociology of the press, organization of editorial work, methodology of journalism, press illustration, stylistics, literary criticism, psychological problems of the influence of the press, cultural questions in journalism, Marxist theory of the press, the press in Western countries and in Africa, and others.

Outside the university setting, research is also conducted by research departments of the radio and the television organizations, which are run by the State Committee for Radio and the State Committee for Television respectively. Another body, the Zentralinstitut für Jugend Forschung (Central Institute for Youth Research), in Leipzig, specializes in multidisciplinary research into matters concerning youth. Several of its studies have been concerned with youth and mass media, such as the effects of certain films on young people, media-using habits of youth, the acceptance of messages carried by media, and mass media and attitude change.

Federal Republic of Germany

The historical role played by German universities in the development of mass communication studies and their influence, not only in Europe but in other regions, has already been discussed at length in the introduction to this chapter. This section will therefore concentrate on the situation in the Federal Republic today.[1]

After the Second World War, although only five of the older institutions survived, new ones were established, and a growing tendency revealed itself to widen the field to include all the mass media, not only the press, and to see mass communication as an integrated whole. Furthermore, there was a tendency, more marked in some institutions than in others, perhaps, to turn from historically oriented research to research

> based on theory ... using the empirical methods ... customary in the fields of sociology and anthropology etc. [and to place] greater emphasis on the study and solution of current problems of communication [partly influenced by] the ideas and achievements that have come from research in the United States.

Teaching and research in universities

Specialized institutes

There are now six university institutes for the study of mass communications in the Federal Republic of Germany and one section for journalism and communication, where mass communications may be studied as a major or a minor subject. The most convenient way of considering their activities is to treat them in the order of their foundation.

The University of Münster established a lectureship in journalism in 1919, following a successful series of lectures on the press at the suggestion of Aloys Meister, the historian. In 1920, Meister established a Seminar for History of the Press and Newspaper Archives, as the 'polito-historical' department of the History School, to co-ordinate lectures in journalism. At the same time a Political Science Section of the Seminar (or school) of Economic and Social Sciences was formed, which held colloquia on practical aspects of journalism.

In 1948 the lectureship in journalism became a Chair in Communication Research and Recent History, and films and radio were consistently studied, as well as the press. Münster was one of the first universities in the Federal Republic to give systematic attention to these new mass media.

In 1970, the institute consisted of three full-time staff, teaching mass media courses, and three part-time professionals. There were three full-time academic staff on research appointments in a separate research department established in 1965. The curriculum of the institute comprises the history of newspapers, magazines, radio, television, the cinema and advertising; the history, regulation, censorship, economics and organizational aspects of the media generally; as well as mass communication theory, sociological and psychological studies of the media, and research methodology.

---

1. Unless otherwise stated, citations derive from statements prepared by directors of the research institutes and other institutions assembled in Noelle-Neumann and Hauser (1970).

The main fields of research of the Münster institute are the history of the mass media, the history of journalism, the evolution of communication behaviour in social systems, communication media in developing countries, and research methodology.

The Institute for Political and Communication Sciences at the University of Nuremberg (Erlangen-Nürnberg) is the successor to the Institute for Newspaper Studies (*Zeitungskunde*) which was founded in 1923 and renamed the Institute of Journalism or Newspaper Science (*Zeitungswissenschaft*) in 1948. When Nuremberg School of Economics and Social Sciences was fused with Erlangen University, the Bavarian Ministry of Culture and Education 'came only half-way towards meeting the Faculty's request for a chair of public communication research' and combined it with political science in the new chair established in 1961.

During the early sixties, only students of economics and business administration could take communication research as a minor subject, but students studying for the sociology degree or the trade-school teacher's degree could not, and no ruling had been issued about political science students. Now, however, students in any field may choose politics and communication research as a minor field, and the institute's courses may be taken by undergraduates in the Faculty of Economics and Social Science and the Faculty of Arts.

The institute defines its main fields of study as ' problems of mass communication in complex social system; analysis of the communication process and its subsystems (newspapers, editorial staff, radio and television corporations)'.

More specifically, it sees the communication system as slotting into the political system, and investigates problems related to their interrelatedness. As the Director, Professor Ronneberger, put it:

> We in Nuremberg want to find out . . . the possibility of a change in political attitudes resulting from the reading of newspapers, the hierarchic structures of newspapers and broadcasting corporations, the links between local newspapers and dominant structures in the municipalities, regional newspapers and the density of communication, the controlling functions of the media, and the worth of current talk about the press fulfilling a public task etc. . . .
> Communication research and politics are increasingly becoming the central problems of our society; it probably was never otherwise.

Recently concluded and current projects in 1970 revolved round two main themes: the relationship between the mass communication system and the political system, at municipal, state *(Land)* and federal level; and mass media as large-scale industrial enterprises for the production of information.

The Social Science Research Centre (Sozialwissenschaftliches Forschungszentrum) of Erlangen-Nürnberg University is engaged in a series of research projects on socialization and communication, with financial help from the Deutsche Forschungsgemeinschaft.

The Institut für Zeitungswissenschaft (Institute of Newspaper Science) in the Faculty of Philosphy I at the University of Munich was established in 1924, the first director being Karl D'Ester, who held the position until 1954. At first, the only degree awarded was the Dr.Phil.; the master's qualification was first granted in 1967.

The Munich institute's orientation is towards the integrated study of social communication, including interpersonal and mass communication. Its courses cover the historical development of newspapers, journals, radio and television, including the history of newspapers in the world; media censorship; legal regulation of newspapers; ethics of journalism; media institutions, especially in the press and advertising, and in radio broadcasting in Britain; practices and techniques in the press, broadcasting, the cinema and advertising; the educational role of newspapers, and film; the aesthetics of film; mass communication through broadcasting, including Radio Free Europe, international broadcasting, and broadcasting in Czechoslovakia. Sociological and psychological studies of the mass media are a feature of the curriculum. Research methods, and the theory of social communication, are also dealt with.

The institute's main research fields are social communication from the anthropological and sociological viewpoints; communication research with emphasis on mass culture and communication policy; theory of journalism (newspapers as 'topical forums' of society).

The present Institut für Publizistik of the Free University of Berlin was originally founded in 1928 as the Institut für Zeitungswissenschaft of the University of Berlin, and was reconstituted in October 1948 with the founding of the Free University in West Berlin.

There is one endowed chair in mass communication research in the Philosophical Faculty of the Free University of Berlin, held by the Director, and there are two other professors, and nine other academic members of staff, assistants and lecturers. Recently the institute applied for another endowed chair, in communication research, and more assistant professorships because of its large enrolment, amounting to over 500 in 1969/70.

The institute provides teaching for the M.A. and Dr.phil. degrees. Undergraduates are encouraged to major in a specialized field, 'be it physics or Arabic studies, architecture or law', with public communication as a minor field, since

> in the age of world wide communication there is a greater need for experts in the most widely differing fields than there was in the days of the all-round journalist . . . Neither journalism in its widest sense, nor advertising and public relations work, will in future be able to dispense with specialists capable of assessing and forming opinions on the material they pass on.

After their first degree, students can take a doctorate in communication research, with the solid basis of thorough knowledge of their major field to build on.

The Institut für Publizistik of the Free University of Berlin undertakes general empirical communication research, with special reference to the German Democratic Republic and the eastern European states.

The Institut für Publizistik in the Faculty of Economic and Social Sciences at the University of Göttingen was established in 1962, although it has its origins in a lectureship in public-communication research established at the college of Social Sciences in Wilhelmshaven-Rütersiel in 1953, and the Institute of Public Communication Research founded in the Faculty of Economic and Social Sciences which is now incorporated in the University of Göttingen. It has two full-time staff teaching students who take public communication as a major or minor subject for the Diploma in Social Sciences, or the M.A. degree in the Department of Philosophy. Its programme deals with mass media generally, especially the newspaper and periodical press, including history, regulation and censorship, institutions, practices and techniques, aesthetics, sociological studies and research methods. At Göttingen University,

> In the Faculty of Economic and Social Sciences, *Publizistik* is counted among the social sciences [with] sociology and politics, economic and social psychology, economic and social history. There are no obstacles to studying *Publizistik* within the Faculty of Economic and Social Sciences together with one or more of its other disciplines, for example, economics, business administration, statistics and econometr[ics], economic pedagogy.
>
> Historic fields of [communication media] . . . have their place [in the course] as well as problems which are considered urgent at the present time. Students in Göttingen may survey the development, present status and . . . changes in public communication.
>
> Examination regulations—e.g. for a diploma in social economics—require intensive work on many political, social and economic problems.

Thus the field of *Publizistik* must, now and in future, offer only a well-considered selection instead of an unlimited range of subjects for lectures, seminars, and colloquia. Except for a lectureship for the study of radio and television, no enlargement of the field is intended. Practitioners are only asked to give lectures or reports as part of established seminars, but not to give whole courses.

The Institut für Publizistik of the University of Mainz is the latest specialized institute to be established in the Federal Republic of Germany. It was founded in 1966 following the setting up of a Chair in Public Communication Research in the Faculty of Law and Economics in 1964. Students in the Faculty of Arts and the Faculty of Law and Economics may take *Publizistik* as a major or a minor field for the degrees of Dr.phil., M.A., Dr.jur., Dr.rer.pol., and the undergraduate Diploma in Sociology. In 1970, there were 200 students registered with the institute, including forty taking public communication as a major subject. There were four academic staff, including the Director.

The teaching emphasis is on methodology of communication research (including readership, audience and public-opinion research) and on practical instruction in writing and editing through group work, exercises and seminars, with critical analysis on the style and content of material from the press, radio and television. Courses deal with history of the mass media, sociology and psychology of mass communication, organization of the media, and press law in joint lectures with law professors, as well as press economics with economists of the faculty. The proportion of courses of an academic and theoretical nature to courses of a more practical orientation is 2:1.

The main fields of interest of the Institut für Publizistik at the University of Mainz are the development and application of methods of empirical social research to mass communication problems. The institute works in close collaboration with the Institut für Demoskopie, Allensbach, which has been conducting surveys in the Federal Republic since about 1947, about a third of which relate to the mass media. They include panel studies of one to two thousand people to test the effects of mass media, studies of press statistics, and content analysis of telecasts and dailies.

Since the University of the Ruhr, at Bochum, was founded in 1965, there have been lectureships in mass communication research there. There is a Sektion für Publizistik und Kommunikation (Section for Mass Communication) within the framework of the Institute for Education. Since July 1971, mass communication may be chosen as the main subject for the M.A. and Dr.phil. degrees. Previously it could only be taken as a minor field. There were about 165 students registered in 1971. The academic staff consisted of the Head and four lecturers and assistants.

This institute is the most important centre of historical press research in the Federal Republic today. Its main fields of interest are social history of the press in the nineteenth century; Federal Republic press reports about the German Democratic Republic; the effects of the mass media on youth.

Other universities

Teaching and research in mass communications is conducted also in several other universities of the Federal Republic, within the framework of social science, history, political science, education and agriculture.

The Research Institute for Sociology at the University of Cologne has a division for mass communication, founded in 1963. The division has five full-time staff, one engaged in teaching on the mass media, and four on research appointments. Teaching, for the Diploma in Sociology, covers history, censorship, regulation, economics, and the educational role especially of newspapers, radio, and television in the Federal Republic of Germany, with comparative work on other western European countries, some developing countries and the United States. Sociological studies and research methods used in the Federal Republic of Germany and the United States are also considered, as well as the history and sociology of magazines, the aesthetics of media and the history of the cinema in the Federal Republic of Germany.

The institute undertakes empirical research on mass communication. Its central interest is the structural-functional analysis of mass communication processes. It is concerned with the history and the present and the future structure and functions of the mass media; the content of the mass media and its uses and effects.

The University of Cologne also has a Department of the History of Journalism attached to the Historical Seminar. No details of its teaching or research programme have been obtainable.

At the University of Frankfurt, the Seminar for Sociology began offering mass communication teaching for its Diploma in Sociology in 1970, including the history, economics, organizational structure, aesthetics and sociological aspects of the media generally, especially the cinema.

The Division for Pedagogical Science of the University of Frankfurt has given courses on mass media since 1960 for its education curriculum. Its research concerns the educational courses of the Hessische Rundfunk, and the wider implications of education through the mass media.

The Institute for the Social Sciences (Institut für Sozialwissenschaften) at the University of Mannheim began giving regular courses on the mass media in 1966 for the Diploma in Sociology and Political Science, the Diploma in Political Economy and the teachers' training course. Of the twenty members on full-time appointments in this institute, four teach courses on mass media, and three are engaged in mass communication research.

The German Institute for Television Studies at the University of Tübingen produces courses for external students at university level, many of which include the use of radio and television. Its work, therefore, includes the instructional uses and effects of radio, television and books.

The Department of Agricultural Policy and Agricultural Communications in the College of Agriculture at the University of Bonn has given systematic instruction on mass media since 1953, for the Diploma in Agricultural Economics, and the Ph.D. in Agricultural Economics, while the Institut für Kommunikationsforschung und Phonetik (Institute of Communications Research and Phonetics) of the University of Bonn gives teaching on communication research, communication psychology and research techniques in communication research, as well as theory of spoken communication, and the sociology of communication.

The School of Agriculture at the University of Hohnheim offers some teaching on mass media for the diplomas in agriculture, agricultural economics and home economics, including the history, regulation and organization of radio and television; sociological and psychological studies of media in the Federal Republic of Germany and the United States, and research methodology.

Non-university institutions

Several non-university institutions, closely connected with universities are engaged in mass media studies.

The Hans-Bredow Institut für Rundfunk und Fernsehen (the Hans Bredow Institute for Radio and Television) is located at the University of Hamburg. It was established in 1950 as a foundation by the Nordwestdeutscher Rundfunk, and is financed by that broadcasting corporation, the Westdeutscher Rundfunk, and the City of Hamburg. These bodies, the federal government and the University of Hamburg, have representatives on its board of trustees. It is independent of the university, but its director must be a professor at the university, while its staff has lecturing appointments there. It undertakes interdisciplinary research on radio and television, and its staff also lectures on journalism and broadcasting. Its publications comprise *Rundfunk und Fernsehen* (Vol. 18, 1970), the *Internationales Handbuch für Rundfunk und Fernsehen* (Vol. 11, 1969/70), and *Studien zur Massenkommunikation* (five volumes so far published). Its field of research is communicator research in broadcasting corporations and other programme and transmission agencies; content analyses of radio and television programmes; and audience research.

The Institut für Zeitungsforschung der Stadt Dortmund (Institute for Press Research of the City of Dortmund) was founded in 1926. It collects and evaluates German newspapers and periodicals for study purposes in the fields of mass media studies, history, sociology, political science and education. It has two research staff. Its research centres on German press history from the sixteenth century onwards.

The Deutsche Presseforschung (German Press Research) was founded in 1957 as an independent department of the Bremen State Library. It locates, collects and evaluates the German-language press as a source of historical information. Its special fields are the German press of the seventeenth and eighteenth centuries, the press of the German Democratic Republic, German labour movement publications and the press of Bremen. It publishes a series, *Studien zur Publizistik,* and is compiling a list of German newspapers from 1609 to 1700.

In 1970, the ARD (Arbeitsgemeinschaft der Öffentlich-Rechtlichen Rundfunkanstalten Deutschlands or Standing Committee of Broadcasting Corporations in the Federal Republic of Germany) set up a working group to investigate competition between the different media; some of its findings have been published in a series of papers on *Rundfunkanstalten und Tageszeitungen* (Broadcasting Institutions and Daily Newspapers).

The Study Group for Broadcasting and History (Studienkreis Rundfunk und Geschichte EV) which held its foundation meeting in 1969 is closely connected with the broadcasting organizations. The Historical Commission of the Südwestfunk recently commissioned a survey of research into the history of broadcasting all over the world, which was presented at that meeting and published in 1970.

Television and film training in tertiary-level institutions

The Hochschule für Fernsehen und Film (Advanced School for Television and Film) in Munich was founded in 1967, as a joint venture of the Free State of Bavaria, the Bayerische Rundfunk, the City of Munich and the Zweites Deutsches Fernsehen (the second television station). It

> was intended neither as a traditional university nor a college of art, neither as a polytechnic for careers in television, nor as a mere field of experiment for film people with artistic ambitions, but rather as a mixture of [them] all ... better still a fusion of science and art, of theory and practice, of purposive professional higher training and not least a stimulus for general education.

At present it has the status of a college of art in the German educational system, but it is to be raised to the level of a university. Its staff consists of academics and media professionals. A three-year course is offered, leading to a final certificate. In 1970 it had about sixty students. There are departments for communication research and *studium generale*, films, information documentation and education on television and artistic production in television. The first two are arranged on academic lines, with lectures, seminars, colloquia and demonstrations, and the others conduct practical training. The school has at its disposal the studios and equipment of the Bayerische Rundfunk, the Munich studios of the Zweites Deutsches Fernsehen, and the services of the staff of a private film company. It appears to provide a bridge, hitherto lacking in the Federal Republic, between the theoretically oriented education provided by the universities, and purely vocational training.

The Deutsche Film und Fernsehakademie (German Film and Television Academy) in Berlin was founded in 1966. It trains directors, producers, cameramen and other professionals for film and television.

Journalism training

The German Journalists' School (Deutschen Journalistenschule) in Munich was founded in 1959, and is financed by various media organizations and professional associations, and the parties represented in the Bundestag. It trains future editors and journalists in fifteen-month courses followed by in-service training periods. The courses are practically oriented and cover the press and broadcasting.

The Deutsches Institut für Publizistische Bildungsarbeit (German Institute for Journalism Training) in Düsseldorf gives further training to editors, journalists and broadcasting personnel, and non-journalist staff in the publishing trade, and supplements in-service training with short courses.

A new Academy for Journalists was set up by the City of Hamburg in 1970, to give training and further training to apprentice journalists, editors, freelance journalists and managerial staff of publishing companies. The courses last from one week to a month.

Training by media institutions

The Zweites Deutsches Fernsehen has a training department which runs eighteen-month courses for its employees, to make them familiar with the practical work of the organization. The Norddeutscher Rundfunk runs a similar course. Deutsches Welle has a training department for radio journalists. Sudwestfunk also runs short courses for its staff.

The International Institute for Journalism in Berlin founded by a group of German publishers and journalists in 1962, provides advanced training in English and French in three-month courses to experienced journalists with at least four years' experience, employed by newspapers, radio and television companies in developing countries.

Learned societies and specialized periodicals

Finally it should be noted that there are many learned societies connected with mass communication research in the Federal Republic. The Deutsche Gesellschaft für Publizistik und Zeitungswissenschaft in Bonn was founded in 1963 to promote research and teaching in mass communication. The Deutsche Gesellschaft für Film and Fernsehforschung in Munich was founded in 1953 to promote research on films and television. The Deutsche Studiengesellschaft für Publizistik was founded in 1958 to study, *inter alia*, the effects of mass communication on children, teenagers, adults and the family, the proper working of internal and external freedom of the media, and the elimination of the expression of discriminatory views through the media. The

Studienkreis für Presserecht und Pressefreiheit (Study Group on Press Law and Press Freedom) founded in Stuttgart in 1956, studies legal questions related to the press. The Study Group for Broadcasting and History in Frankfurt founded in 1969 has already been mentioned. A special foundation, Stiftevereinigung der Presse e.v., in Bad Godesberg, was founded in 1966, by various publishers, journalists' associations and others, to support research and training in mass communications, and to finance research projects.

Finally, it should be noted that there is a quarterly journal for communication research, *Publizistik*, founded in 1956, published in co-operation with the German Association for Communication and Journalism Research (Deutsche Gesellschaft für Publizistik und Zeitungswissenschaft). It deals with the whole area of communication including the press, broadcasting, cinema, speech, public relations and advertising. Another quarterly journal, *Communicatio Socialis, Zeitschrift für Publizistik in Kirche und Welt*, deals with mass communication in the perspective of the church.

Hungary

Professional training

In Hungary universities do not cater for professional training for occupations in the mass media. There has been a shift in emphasis from the purely theoretical study of journalism, undertaken in the Faculty of Journalism at Budapest University between the two world wars (Desmond, 1949) to more practically oriented education since the Second World War. In the early 1950s, Eötvös Loránd University ran a four-year course for intending journalists comprising two years' study of academic subjects, a third year in which lecture attendance was combined with some practical training and a final year devoted to working in a press enterprise. But this system of education was found unsatisfactory in various ways and came to an end in 1956.

In the early 1960s the Hungarian Association of Journalists took over the formal training of beginning journalists. Since most entrants to the profession already had university degrees, the association ran a one-year professional course in Budapest, the successful completion of which was a compulsory prerequisite for permanent employment on the editorial staffs of Hungarian press enterprises. Lectures covered the theory and practice of print journalism including press history, law and ethics, stylistics, make-up, printing techniques, interviewing and other technical matters. But towards the end of the 1960s, when there was an acute shortage of would-be journalists with university degrees the system was modified to provide two parallel courses, a concentrated six-month course for graduates, equivalent to the original course, and a two-year course for non-graduates which included academic subjects (philosophy, political economy, Marxism-Leninism, history of labour movements) as well as the professional content of the other course. Since 1970 lectures on radio and television and on mass communication have been included in the training (Jakab, 1973).

The International Association of Journalists established an International Centre for the Training of Journalists in Budapest in 1962, and has run diploma courses for young journalists from Asia, Latin America and Africa since 1964, including courses in running a television network since 1969.

Professional training for occupations in the cinema is provided at the Academy for Theatre and Cinematic Art (Szinház és Filmmüvészeti Föiskola) in Budapest.

University teaching

There is no specialized teaching about mass media for degree purposes in Hungarian universities. But since 1965 international information has been a compulsory subject for the International Relations course of the Karl Marx University of Economic Science in Budapest, since the university considers that a thorough knowledge of the foreign press is indispensable for understanding international relations. The course considers the role and importance of the press, radio, television and film from the historical, psychological and sociological points of view (Nagy, 1970).

Mass media research

Mass communication research in Hungary began effectively in the 1960s. Before that time there had been occasional *ad hoc* surveys on radio listeners' tastes before the Second World War, some radio-audience research undertaken by the Public Opinion Service between 1946 and 1948, and some scattered attempts to gauge audience reactions in the late 1950s and early 1960s. Systematic, scientific audience research dates to the formation of the Public Opinion Research Group (later called the Public Opinion Research Department) of Hungarian Radio in 1963. In 1967 a small methodological research group to deal with such problems as content formulation and articulation, was founded within Hungarian Radio, and the two groups formed the basis of the foundation of the Mass Communication Research Centre of Hungarian Radio and Television in 1969. The centre comprises four main departments, the Mass Communication Research Department, the Social Psychological Laboratory, the Public Opinion Research Department, and a publication and documentation department. The Mass Communication Research Department has conducted regular audience surveys since 1965. It has also undertaken a variety of specific research projects on broader topics such as level of knowledge of the adult population on various topics, the effects of television on social contacts in villages; audience reactions to foreign radio broadcasts and to the pop song festival organized by Hungarian Radio and Television; political socialization of youth through mass media; a time budget study as the basis of research on the role of mass media in mass entertainment; the role of television and radio critics; the functions of local radio; the impact of television on book reading; and various other studies, including radio and newspaper content analyses. The Social Psychological Laboratory (founded in 1971) has conducted research on the characteristics of television screen personalities and their appeal, the influence of the Olympic Games on stereotypes of Germans and differences of perception of black and white and colour television (Jakab, 1973).

The Institute of Historical Sciences of the Hungarian Academy of Sciences and the Society of the Science of the Press are concerned with the history of the press and the research methodology involved, and are preparing a four-volume history of the Hungarian press (Markus, 1970).

The Institute of Sociology of the Hungarian Academy of Sciences was the first research organization in the field of sociology in Hungary. It was founded in 1963, when sociology emerged as an independent discipline in Hungary. Although its work has been mainly theoretical, concerned with social stratification and bureaucratic organizations, it has also done empirical work, some bordering on mass media studies. One of its major fields of interest has been the sociology of culture, especially the social function of literature and music, from the point of view of the individual's expectations, in reading or listening to music. Another has been leisure-time studies, including participation in the international time-budget co-ordinated by the Centre of Co-ordination and Documentation of Social Sciences in Vienna (Szelényi, 1970).

Recently a Hungarian Association for Mass Communication Research was founded, apparently under the aegis of the Association of Hungarian Journalists, which aims at organizing and co-ordinating research on mass communication undertaken in Hungary as well as following and documenting mass communication research carried out abroad.

Ireland

Specialized study of the mass media in academic institutions in Ireland is a matter of relatively recent date, and is undertaken only at St Patrick's College, Maynooth, a Pontifical University and a Recognized College of the National University of Ireland. It mainly trains students for the priesthood but it is also expanding its offerings in arts, science, education and theology. A spokesman for the College stated (Bennis, 1971):

> Recognising the importance of communications in priestly training and in the life of the Church the ... College established in June 1970, a School of Communications ... In the extensive expansion programme of Maynooth College now under way it was felt that priority should be given to areas of special relevance to the central purpose of the College not already catered for in existing University institutions in the country. The School of Communications at Maynooth is then a distinctive contribution by Maynooth to Higher Education in Ireland.

All students for the priesthood at the college take intensive short courses in television, radio and journalism

> designed to equip students for more effective impact as professional communicators ... [They] involve study of communication particular to each of the media as well as appreciation and criticism of the mass media in Ireland.

The only other academic institution concerned with mass media studies is the University College, Dublin, where an optional semester course in mass media is offered in the final year of the Bachelor of Social Science programme, from time to time since its inception in 1966.

The Catholic Communications Institute, a non-academic institution at Booterstown, founded in 1967, has a Communications Centre which gives brief training courses in press, radio, television, preaching and public speaking. About 1,000 students a year are catered for, including overseas students on occasional scholarships provided by the institute.

Italy

Mass media studies in Italy are concentrated in four main areas: journalism, mass communications, publicity and techniques of information, and cinematography. These activities are carried on both at university level and in a large number of independent centres and other institutions of various kinds.

Universities

The basic structural units in Italian universities are the faculties. Each degree and diploma course given by any particular faculty consists of a fixed number of fundamental subjects and a number of optional subjects. Optional subjects are divided into two types. The first group consists of options which apply generally to all faculties granting a particular degree. Each university containing the appropriate faculty may decide whether or not to include any of these optional subjects in the syllabus, and also may decide from year to year whether that option will actually be taught. The second group of options relates to particular individual universities which are entitled by law to include a particular subject in the syllabus for a degree, but are again free to decide whether or not that subject is taught in any year.

Table 12 indicates the range of mass media topics which individual universities are entitled to teach for the *laurea* (four-year undergraduate degree). It is clear that during the 1960s, and especially since 1965, the number of universities entitled to offer these topics has increased, and the range of topics has also broadened.

Journalism training and teaching

As far as journalism is concerned, although courses were given at the universities of Naples and Turin in the early twentieth century, and a systematic four-year course combining theoretical teaching and practical instruction was established in the Faculty of Political Science of the University of Perugia, in 1928, these courses were short-lived. The Unesco survey on the training of journalists published in 1958 could name only two systematic university-level courses in journalism. They were the three-year course instituted by the Press Association of Emilia at the Independent University of Urbino in 1949, and the three-year course run by the Institute of Journalism (set up in 1952) in conjunction with the University of Palermo, consisting of lectures in journalism history and public opinion given by the institute, and theoretical and practical instruction provided at the university. In addition to these systematic courses of journalism, there

TABLE 12. Optional subjects related to mass media studies in syllabuses for various degrees in Italian universities in 1971

	Undergraduate degree (laurea) in:							
Title of option	Political science	Letters	Philosophy	Modern foreign languages and literature	Education	Materie Letterarie	Economics and commerce	Sociology
Group 1 [1]								
History of Journalism	1968 [2]							— [3]
Sociology of Communication	1968 [2]							— [3]
Theory and Techniques of Mass Communication								
Group 2 [1]								
History and Technique of Journalism and Social Communication				Messina (1969)		Messina (1969)		
History and Technique of Information Media	Pavia (1969)							
History of Newspapers	Padua (1970)							
Sociology of Mass Communication	Padua (1970)							
Theory and Techniques of Mass Communication	Florence (1969)	Turin (1969)	Turin (1969)	Genoa (1969)	Genoa (1969) Aquila (1968) University Institute of Salerno (1967) Rome (1959) Lecce (1968)	Genoa (1969) University Institute of Salerno (1967)	Cagliari (1970)	
Pedagogy and Psychology of Mass Communication								
Psychology and Pedagogy of Information								
Methodology and Didactics of Instructional Media			Catholic University, Milan (1966)	Catholic University, Milan (1966)	Catholic University, Milan (1966)	Catholic University, Milan (1966)	Catholic University, Milan (1966)	

Europe

Course				
Methodology and Didactics of Audiovisuals	Genoa (1969)		Padua (1966) Genoa (1969) Parma (1964)	Padua (1966) Genoa (1969) Parma (1964)
Technique and Didactics of Cinematographic Language	Parma (1964)			
Filmology	Bologna (1970)	Bologna (1970)	Bologna (1970)	Bologna (1963)
History and Criticism of Cinema	Urbino (1969) Turin (1968) Catholic University, Milan (1961) Pisa (1961) Perugia (1967) Palermo (1968) Genoa (1970) Siena (1970)	Urbino (1969) Turin (1969) Catholic University, Milan (1969)	Urbino (1965) Turin (1968) Pisa (1961)	Urbino (1965) Turin (1969) Cagliari (1964) Padua (1966)	Urbino (1965) Turin (1969) Cagliari (1963) Padua (1966) Florence (1966) Trieste (1969)
History and Criticism of Film			Genoa (1967)	Genoa (1967)	Genoa (1967)
History of Cinema				Rome (1970)	
History of Cinema and Theatre	Padua (1970)		Florence (1969)	Florence (1969)	Florence (1969)
History of Entertainment (Theatre and Cinema)	Catania (1969)				

1. See above, page 117.
2. The *laurea* in political science is granted by the faculties of political science (at Bologna, Florence, Padua, Pavia, Perugia, Rome and the Catholic University of Milan) and by the faculties of law at Bari, Cagliari, Catania, Genoa, Messina, Naples, Palermo, Pisa, Siena, Turin and Trieste universities.
3. Date unknown.

Sources: Ministero dell' Pubblica Istruzione, Direzione Generale dell'Istruzione Universitaria, *Disposizioni sull' Ordinamento Didattico Universitario*, Rome, 1971.

was a Chair in the History of Journalism at Perugia University, and four other regular professors of journalism lectured on journalism history at the universities of Rome and Urbino (Unesco, 1958).

In 1970 there were still only two university schools of journalism: the Istituto Superiore di Giornalismo (Advanced Institute of Journalism) at Palermo University and the Scuola Superiore di Giornalismo (Advanced School of Journalism) at Urbino University. However, a survey conducted by the International Association for Mass Communication Research (IAMCR) in 1968 revealed that the institute at Palermo University was then giving a four-year course, with specialization in journalism and radio in the third year, while the Urbino course was still given over three years (IAMCR, 1968). Information was received in 1971 (RAI, 1971) that the Pro Deo University in Rome also had an Advanced Institute of Journalism (Istituto Superiore di Giornalismo). It has not been possible to obtain up-to-date details of these courses.

As far as the chairs for the history of journalism were concerned, the IAMCR survey revealed that there were then six chairs in that subject, at the universities of Cagliari, Florence, Messina, Rome, Perugia and Trieste. The National Institute for the History of Journalism (Istituto Nazionale per la Storia del Giornalismo) founded in 1962 to promote research and study in that subject, is also located at the University of Trieste. The Catholic University of Milan also has a Chair in the History of Journalism. A presidential decree (no. 1189) of 31 October 1968, modifying the ordinances regulating the faculties of political science included the history of journalism and the sociology of communication among the specialized options for the four-year *laurea* in political science. Bologna, Florence, Padua, Pavia, Perugia, Rome and the Catholic University of the Sacred Heart have faculties of political science. The faculties of law at Bari, Cagliari, Catania, Genoa, Messina, Naples, Palermo, Pisa, Siena, Turin and Trieste also grant the *laurea* in political science degree.

Mass communication

Teaching and research on mass communications takes place at a number of Italian universities. At the University of Rome, in 1967, the study of mass communications was being undertaken in three separate institutions. The Chair of Pedagogics and of the Psychology of Mass Communications in the Faculty of Law provided teaching on mass communications. The Centre of the Sociology of Mass Communications (founded in 1963 as the Centre of the Sociology of Cinematography by the Institute of Pedagogy at Rome University) was engaging in research and teaching on the relation between collective information and education. Finally, the Faculty of Statistical Sciences has a School of Techniques of Information (originally called the School of Publicity when it was founded in 1948 at the initiative of the Italian Institute of Publicity) which gives two types of course. One is the *corso propedeutico* or preliminary course for intending mass communication specialists, which deals with mass communication from the sociological and statistical points of view, thus permitting qualitative and quantitative assessments, and includes teaching on aspects like social techniques of mass communication and opinion theory. The second course involves the application of techniques of mass communication to professional practice. Successful completion of the curriculum is recognized by the title Expert in the Techniques of Information.

The Pro Deo International University of Social Studies (Libera Università Internazionale degli Studi Sociali Pro Deo), a private State-recognized school, has an advanced Institute of Mass Media and Public Opinion Techniques (Istituto Superiore di Scienze e Technique dell'Opinione Publica) which provides a two-year diploma course in mass media techniques. The first year consists of a general introduction to public-opinion techniques and the principles of public-opinion science, and the second of specialized options on public-opinion techniques in journalism, radio-television or the cinema.

The Catholic University of the Sacred Heart (Università Cattolica del Sacro Cuore) at Milan runs an Advanced School of Social Communications (Scuola Superiore delle Comunicazioni Sociali) originally founded at Bergamo and transferred to Milan in 1967. Its two-year post-graduate diploma course in mass communication is open to humanities graduates of the university. A general introductory year is followed by specialized options in criticism and techniques of the cinema, radio and television, or journalism and publicity.

This school, like the Advanced School of Social Communications at the University of Milan, is concerned, *inter alia*, with studies on psychological aspects of mass communications and the semiology of the signs in visual communications. Some psychology departments attached to medical faculties, including those at Milan and Bologna universities, are also engaged in the study of psychological and physiological aspects of the response to visual communication. The Advanced Institute for the Social Sciences at the University of Trento is concerned with mass media in relation to its wider interest in sociolinguistics and mass culture. The Gruppo di Studi Audivisivi (Group for Audio-visual Studies) of the Institute of Sociology in the Political Science Faculty of the University of Florence concentrates on the theory and techniques of the sociology of communication, and there is a Laboratory for the Study of Cinema and Television at the Institute of Education in the Faculty of Law. The Institute of Education in the law faculty of Padua University is also involved in study of the mass media. Since 1968, the Department of Philosophy of the Pontifical Gregorian University has given a course of lectures on mass communication.

Publicity

The IAMCR survey in 1968 showed that several Italian universities were giving teaching in commercial publicity and market research. The University of Turin gave commercial-publicity courses in the School of Industrial Administration, and there was a Chair in Market Research Techniques in the Faculty of Economics and Commerce. In the universities of Rome and Genoa, the Chair of Market Research Techniques gave training in both market research and commercial publicity, and the Bocconi University in Milan had a two-year course in commercial publicity.

The Bocconi University was the only institution in this field to submit detailed information on its activities in 1970. In its Institute of Commercial Techniques, teaching about mass communication is offered as part of a bachelor's level course in economics. Previous research by members of its staff has dealt with long-range planning, and the Italian distributive system, ant it is now surveying long-range planning practices in European business firms, marketing, finance and planning.

Cinematography

There is a Chair of the History and Theory of Cinematography in the Faculty of Education at the University of Genoa, and a Chair in the History and Criticism of Cinema in the Faculty of Education at the University of Urbino. The Catholic University of the Sacred Heart in Milan has a Chair in Film History. A survey of the film in university teaching undertaken in 1966 (Maddison, 1969) stated that the University of Cagliary also had a chair of film, and that 'there are, one gathers, courses in film at the Universities of Padua, Perugia, Trieste, Bologna, Milan and Siena, and other universities plan to offer courses', but no further information on these matters has been obtainable. The Salesian University in Rome has a Centre for Social Communication in its Faculty of Education which provides courses on mass communication for teachers. The course is focused on filmology and deals with the psychological, historical and aesthetic aspects of film. In 1970, courses on educational uses of audio-visual material were introduced.

Also in the field of cinematography, but in a more specialized direction, is the International Institute for Educational, Scientific and Social Cinematography (Istituto Internazionale per la Cinematografia Educativa, Scientifica e Sociale) at the University of Rome, founded in 1955 to foster the production and use of scientific and educational films.

Other institutions

Studies in mass communication or special aspects of it are also conducted at various non-university institutions.

The Academy of Fine Arts of Brera in Milan began lectures on mass media in 1968. It gives a systematic course on mass media for its four-year diploma students in the Sociology Department, concentrating on the sociology and psychology of mass communications, particularly in relation to mass culture, covering the United States, the developing countries, eastern Europe and Cuba. There is a Centre for the Study of the Third World at the academy, which is closely related to the Sociology Department, and which brings out a quarterly journal, *Terzo Mondo*. Its research is connected with cultural studies, and includes work on the mass media.

The Experimental Centre for Cinematography in Rome (Centro Sperimentale de Cinematografia) was founded in 1935 to provide professional training and practical instruction in artistic, technical and administrative aspects connected with film production for the cinema and television, and to stimulate study, research and practical work in cinematography. It offers two-year courses in direction, production, dramatic art and other aspects of professional cinematography, and a course in audio-visual techniques of information. It is administratively subject to the Ministry of Performing Arts, but is recognized by the Ministry of Public Instruction as a university middle school (*scuola media superiore*).

The Experimental Centre for Journalism (Centro Sperimentale di Giornalismo) in Milan is oriented towards practical aspects of journalism. Its programme in 1968 consisted of two years' professional orientation in journalism, two years of publicity journalism, a course in filmed journalism and photography, one in languages, and one in shorthand typing.

The Professional State Institute for Cinematography and Television in Rome was founded by the Ministry of Public Instruction to train high-level technicians for the cinema and television industries. The courses last three years, with one year's practical in-service training.

There are several independent institutes which conduct studies in mass communication.

The Centre for Documentation and the Study of Information (Centro di Documentazione e di Studi Sull'Informazione or CESDI) conducts no teaching but is engaged in research connected with mass communication and with documentation.

The Agostini Gemelli Institute for the Experimental Study of Social Problems of Visual Information (Istituto Agostini Gemelli per lo Studio Sperimentale di Problemi Sociali dell'Informazione Visiva) in Milan was founded in 1960 by the provincial administration of Milan and the National Centre of Prevention and Social Defence, and took its present name in 1960. The reason for its foundation was the feeling that visual techniques of communication and information greatly influence the individual psyche and especially the psycho-social equilibrium of children and young people, and the collective psychic climate, by inducing common sentiments, opinion and behaviour in social groups. It was felt that the widespread use of cinema and television for entertainment, education, information and propaganda raised practical and moral considerations which governments could not ignore, and which needed scientifically proved information in order to be tackled. It was thought that sociological methods of research had not yielded practical efficacious results, and in any case could not probe specific and deep realities including unconscious ones, which could only be investigated by experimental techniques.

The institute's work was divided into the following departments: the analysis of psychophysical reactions produced in the spectator by audio-visual techniques; the specific modalities of 'filmic' perception and its interference with various psychological processes; the specific influence of film on 'the dynamics of individual personality and the structures of the basic personality', its repercussions on social groups and interpersonal relations; the influence of visual information and its procedures in moulding the development of new generations; the 'factors of educational intervention revealed' by the new procedures of visual information, especially television, and the 'repercussions of new procedures on traditional modes of expression and communication; problems of the comparative study of modern and historic forms of visual communication'. In order to conduct these researches the institute made use of two laboratories equipped with closed-circuit television and cine-cameras. The institute works in close collaboration with universities, and is representative of one typical strand of research work on the mass media in Italy.

The Centre for Entertainment and Social Communication (Centro dello Spectacolo e della Comunicazione Sociale) was founded in Milan in 1950, and transferred to Rome in 1966. It is especially concerned with the sociological aspects of entertainment (particularly cinematography) and the language of social communication. Its studies are centred on the theory of imagination as a linguistic sign. It gives courses on these matters and conducts research.

The International Institute of Management and Communication, Paris, set up an Italian branch in January 1970. The purpose of the institute is, *inter alia*, to study and apply new informational and communication techniques on a social-economic level and to organize courses to form and train communication experts That section of its field related to the mass media is advertising, publicity and public relations. It publishes a monthly review, *Etocomunicazioni*, and is planning to start short courses in 1971/72.

Other institutions engaged in research on the mass media, according to a list issued by Unesco in January 1970 included the following bodies in Rome: the Italian Association for Public Relations, the Centro di Demodossalogia, the Centre of the Sociology of Mass Communication, the National Centre for the Study of Information, the National Centre for Audio-visual Media, the Centre for the Study of Cinematography, the Mass Communication Committee of the National Committee for Unesco, the Italian Institute of Publicity and the Roman Bureau of Social Communication. In addition, the Italian Institute for Public Relations in Milan was also apparently engaged in mass media research. A list issued by Radiotelevisione Italiana in 1971 also included among the most important centres of teaching and research in Italy: the Olivetti Cultural Centre in Turin; the Italian Centre for the Study of Mass Communication, Institute of Ethnology and Cultural Anthropology, Perugia; the Centre of Sociology and Social Research, Institute of Education, Rome; the Institute of Social Sciences and the International Institute of Communication in Genoa; the Italian Centre of Study and Research (CISER) Rome; and three institutions in Milan—the Italian Centre of Journalism; Demoskopea (Institute for Research on Publicity and Marketing); and Doxa (Institute for Statistical Research and the Analysis of Public Opinion).

Finally, it should be noted that Radiotelevisione Italiana (RAI), the Italian broadcasting organization, has two branches, the Servizio Opinioni and Servizio Documentazioni e Studi 'specially devoted to examining the characteristics of the radio and TV audience and studying the influence of radio and TV on Italian society under the various sociological, psychological and economical aspects'.

Netherlands

In principle, universities in the Netherlands are not concerned with professional training of any kind.[1] They therefore do not offer courses of professional training for occupations in the mass media, such training being provided in non-university institutions. In fact few university graduates of any kind are employed in the media. As Professor Rooy (1970) observed:

> In the Netherlands only 4% out of 2,000 journalists [on] ... daily papers have ... a university degree of ... [any] kind. This percentage is too low, in view of the knowledge required for leading editorial posts; the reason is that journalism as a profession has not ... a [very] high social status, and that the pay in competing jobs for graduates is better than the remuneration for journalists. This unfavourable difference is to be attributed to the fact that up till now newspaper enterprises ... were, as an average, middle size companies; only mergers, now appearing more and more, may create the broader strong financial basis also for better salaries in journalism. So there are two conflicting tendencies: on [the] one hand mergers are diminishing the variety of information; on the other merging is a pre-requisite for attracting better qualified journalists and for heightening the quality of journalism.

But although universities in the Netherlands do not provide professional training, a great deal of academic teaching on the mass media and mass communication is undertaken.

Academic teaching about mass media in Dutch universities

The Catholic University at Nijmegen is the institution where the study of mass communication is more extensively conducted than perhaps any other university in the Netherlands. Publisistics is one of the sections of the Faculty of Social Sciences at this university and three institutes of the university attached to the Faculty of Social Sciences are concerned with the mass media, the Institute for Mass Communication and the sociological and psychological institutes, each of which has a separate division, respectively concerned with the sociology and the psychology of mass communication.

J. G. Stappers of the Institute for Mass Communication at the Catholic University explained that a course on mass media was started there immediately after the Second World War in 1945. Around 1958 it became a specialization within the general field of social sciences, that is a specialized course lasting from three months to a year, and since 1967 it has been possible to take a free course *(vrije studierichting) doctoraal examen* in publisistics. This means that it is possible to study publisistics as a main subject for the *doctoraal examen* in social sciences, in a post-graduate course lasting from two and a half to three years, 'although it is not (yet) one of the main subjects officially mentioned in the law'.

Dr Stappers noted that the Catholic University at Nijmegen is the only Netherlands university to give a full course in publisistics (mass communication) 'comparable

---

1. Even in medical studies students must take an extra examination (which is not an academic degree) to qualify for general practice.

to the studies in Publizistikwissenschaft in Germany or communicatiewetenschap in Belgium (even though there are differences)'.

To be admitted to the free course *doctoraal examen* in publisistics students must already hold any of the *candidaats* degrees in the social sciences (psychology, anthropology, political science and education) conferred after a course of study lasting two to three years.

The course of publisistics contains four subjects: communication theory; research methods and techniques; descriptive publisistics (mass media); general publisistics. Other subjects required are philosophy and sociology and psychology of mass communication. The course is not intended to constitute professional training for journalism or any other profession in mass communication (press, broadcasting, public relations, advertising, etc.) but it does prepare for a research career, and most ex-students seem to get into research or into teaching jobs. Students from other departments who choose publisistics as an optional subject take only small parts of this course.

An introductory course in publisistics is taught in the Faculty of Social Science, and is followed by a large number of first- and second-year students mostly from sociology. In the Department of Sociology, the sociology of mass communication is one of the specializations students can take. The psychology of mass communication may be taken as an optional specialization for the doctoraal examination in psychology (Stappers, 1971).

In addition, from 1959 to 1966 there was an official Lecturer on Film as a means of cultural expression in the Faculty of Arts at Nijmegen University. This post no longer exists although lectures on film are still given.

The University of Amsterdam also gives a specialized course on the mass media, but instead of being a main subject, as at Nijmegen, mass communication is a specialization within another field (mostly political science) and therefore constitutes a smaller proportion of the students' total course of study.

The teaching offered in mass communication in the Faculty of Political and Social Sciences at the University of Amsterdam covers two years and deals with the mass media generally: newspapers, magazines, radio, television and advertising. Some work is also done on the cinema. These media are considered in relation to their historical development, regulation and censorship, economics and institutional structure in the Netherlands, and in Western, communist and developing countries. Professional ethics in the media, the aesthetics of content in the media generally and especially in newspapers and magazines, and methods of mass communication research, are also dealt with, as well as mass communication between countries through the media, and sociological and psychological media research. Two interesting and unusual aspects of the course are content analysis of the press in European communist countries, and governmental information and free access to government files, especially in the Scandinavian countries. The curriculum consists of an introductory core course, covering the main aspects of mass communications, followed by courses on specialized options.

The mass communications course is taken by students preparing for a degree in political and social sciences at a level equivalent to the master's degree. They are required to take two major subjects, one in a wide field—political science—(in which their degree is conferred) and the second in a more restricted field, which, in this case, is mass communications. The course is also taken by students in other departments, who may take mass communications as one of the two minor subjects which are required for the master's degree in the Netherlands.

Students who have taken mass communications as a second major course, and who do not intend to become professional journalists, have already done a specialized bachelor's-degree course in political science (including constitutional and civil law, sociology, contemporary history, economic principles and methods of social research, as well as political science) and then can find their way in the *policy making areas* (government, national and local authority) international organisations (intergovernmental like the EEC, UN and its daughters) national and international free organisations (employers' organisations, trade unions, secretariats and research institutes of political parties) as well as the scientific world (university, public opinion research and the like).

Just because at the present time any policymaker must take into account [the fact] that ... democratic decision processes [are becoming] ... more and more open and that giving information to the public, as an indispensable part of any policy, requires a fundamental knowledge of mass communication and of public opinion problems, our graduates, with mass media studies alongside their political science education, are better qualified for the policy making institutions than others. In this way our discipline is trying to contribute to the modern communication exigencies of society, also outside the journalistic world. This also applies to students from other departments (e.g. jurists, economists)

the Professor of Mass Communications wrote in July 1970 (Rooy, 1970).

Also in the Faculty of Political and Social Sciences of Amsterdam University lectures in film science are given on a part-time basis by one professor.

Teaching on the mass media has taken place in the Faculty of Letters of the State University of Utrecht since 1931, when the then secretary of the Netherlands Journalists' Association was invited to give a weekly lecture on newspapers and was appointed honorary lecturer in *publiciteitsleer* (publicity or communication science). When he retired in 1958, the present honorary lecturer in the subject took over, but widened the scope of the course to include communication theory in general (communicators, communications, media, recipients, and the effect of communications).

The Department of Theatre Research at the State University of Utrecht, has offered teaching on the mass media since 1966, as part of the master's-level course in drama. Teaching on the mass media also takes place in the Faculty of Social Sciences, on the application of photography and cinematography to the social sciences.

At the Vrije Universiteit (Free University) at Amsterdam, lectures on mass communications are given in the Faculty of Political and Social Sciences, particularly for students of the Department of Political Science after their bachelor's degree and before their doctorate degree.

Finally, some teaching about the mass media is given at the University of Groningen in the Faculty of Social Sciences; at the State University of Leiden in the Faculty of Law; and at the Agricultural University of Wageningen in the Department of Extension Education.

Professional training

The picture of mass media education in the Netherlands would be incomplete without some brief mention of the part played by non-university institutions, which provide professional training for careers in the mass media.

Professional training for journalism is provided in one institution only, the School of Journalism in Utrecht, a higher professional school of non-university level, established by the joint efforts of the newspaper industry of the Netherlands and the Journalists' Association, and financed by the State. The training period lasts three years, and includes practical work for three months, during the second and third year in newspaper offices. The school prepares students for careers in the print media as well as radio and television.

Training for broadcasters is provided to some extent by the School of Journalism and also by the Netherlands Broadcasting Corporation (Nederlands Omroep Stichting).

Two professional training schools provide professional training for would-be scenario writers, cameramen, sound technicians, directors and producers in the field of television and the cinema. They are the Netherlands Film Academy in Amsterdam, a department of the Netherlands Film Institute, and the St Joost Academy of Art in Breda. They offer a four-, and a five-year course respectively, with a good deal of practical training combined with academic teaching, and opportunities for specialization in various fields.

In 1969, *Wereldomroep*, a Dutch broadcasting organization, initiated a Radio and Television Training Centre for communicators from developing countries.

Research

A considerable amount of research on the social aspects of mass media and mass communication is being conducted by formally constituted research institutions placed in various Netherlands universities. One indication of the extent of interest in mass communication research in the Netherlands is the fact that a quarterly periodical, *Gazette* (founded in 1955), is published in the Netherlands, and although its editors come from all over the world, its editorial secretariat is located at the Institute of the Science of the Press associated with the University of Amsterdam. The World Association for Public Opinion Research, an international association for researchers and scholars in public opinion and communication, also has its headquarters in the Netherlands.

The Institute for Mass Communication at the Catholic University at Nijmegen has a full-time staff of five, engaged in teaching and research, while the Sociological Institute at Nijmegen has also undertaken research connected with the mass media.

The Institute of Applied Sociology (Instituut voor Toegepaste Sociologie) at the Catholic University at Nijemegen is allied to the Sociology Department, but is a purely research institution. It has a section of Mass Communication and Marketing with two full-time academic staff engaged on mass media studies.

The Institute of the Science of the Press at the University of Amsterdam has conducted research recently on forms of social participation and mass communication patterns (an analysis of a number of indicators of different forms of social participation and their relation to various reading, viewing and listening habits); on interest structure with regard to mass media (factor analyses of interest scores for various types of newspaper editorial, and a cross comparison of the various factors involved). A major ongoing project, expected to continue for four or five years is a study of the role of the mass media in the communication processes between the arts and literature, and the public at large.

Mass media research is also carried out at the Psychological and Sociological Institute of the University of Leiden, at the State University of Utrecht where there is an Educational Media Institute which does a considerable amount of work on, particularly, the educational use of film and television, and at the Department of Extension Education of the Agricultural University of Wageningen.

Outside these university institutes, mention should be made of the regular research conducted on radio and television programmes and their audiences by the Audience Research Department of the Netherlands Broadcasting Corporation. This department was founded in 1961, and has four full-time staff. Its present projects include a continuous, ongoing survey on the audiences for particular television programmes, and a similar survey of radio audiences. Both these surveys are financed largely out of licence fees, with a 10 per cent contribution, from advertising revenue, by the Advertising Foundation. A continuous telephone survey is also done between September and May each year, interviewing a random sample of about 400 people every Saturday on qualitative aspects of viewing and listening.

Norway

In Norway, as in many other European countries, training for journalism does not take place in universities.

Apart from correspondence courses given by the Norwegian Correspondence School since 1943, journalism training consisted of short courses provided by the Norwegian press organizations, until 1950, when a fact-finding committee recommended the establishment of a school of journalism. Consequently the Oslo School of Journalism was founded in 1951 by the Norwegian Association of Editors and Journalists and the National Federation of Norwegian Newspaper Publishers, and financed by contributions from press organizations and the State. It gave a ten-month course (Unesco, 1958).

This institution was superseded by the present school, the Norsk Journalistskole (Norwegian School of Journalism) in Oslo, founded in 1965, 'an independent State-financed educational institution'. It is not connected with any university but

> to afford essential quality in establishing a good professional standard of mass media studies and teaching the school . . . co-operates with research workers of relevant university departments, above all with the staff of the Institute for Press Research of the University of Oslo.

Until recently the school gave a one-year course, predominantly oriented to journalism, but in September 1971 the course will be extended to two years and all students will get professional training for journalism, for work in the press, radio and television (Dørsjø, 1970).

It is interesting to note that J. Dørsjø, the Director of the school, in submitting these details, added:

> I think that the main reason why education for journalism is organised in this way in our country is to be sought in the fact that the structure of higher education in Norway does not include any college institution.

The position has now changed. Regional colleges have been started which include mass communication in the scope of their activities.

The Norwegian Broadcasting Corporation (Norsk Rikskringkasting or NRK) provides courses for new employees in its programme service—an eight-week course for radio employees, two twelve-week courses for television journalists, and a sixteen-week course for television producers. Since new entrants usually have had university or other higher education, these courses are mainly concerned with practical and technical aspects of programme work, though ethical and artistic matters and questions of programme policy are also considered (Dahl, 1971).

Although it is of marginal interest to the terms of reference of this study, it is worth mentioning that courses in the use of audio-visual aids and closed-circuit television are given at the University of Trondheim, and also by the Norwegian Universities Press in co-operation with the University of Oslo for its own employees and for university lecturers (Dahl, 1971; Krohn, 1970).

Teaching in mass communication is provided for students of social science at the universities of Oslo and Bergen by the research staffs of the respective institutes, which conduct mass media research.

Research on the mass media in Norway takes place for the most part at the Institute for Press Research at the University of Oslo, and at the Sociological Institute at the University of Bergen. In the last few years the Institute for Press Research at Oslo University has carried out, among other projects, a study of leisure-time habits of schoolchildren before and after television (financed by the research committee of the Norwegian Broadcasting Corporation); a study of the 1965 election campaign on radio and television; a survey of the Norwegian journalistic profession; and a survey of mass communication research in Norway. Other Norwegian research includes analyses of journalistic news criteria.

The whole question of mass communication research in Norway is under official review and changes in structure and policy may well ensue (Nordenstreng, 1971*a*, 1971*b*).

Poland

There is a long history of specialized training courses for journalism in Poland. The first journalism department was opened in 1917 at the Academy of Political Sciences in Warsaw and several other courses were organized at the same time. In 1927 the Higher School of Journalism in Warsaw was established, and raised to academic rank in 1936.

University training and teaching

The oldest university-based institution concerned with journalism training is the present Institute of Journalism of Warsaw University, Studium dziennikarski VW. It was founded as a faculty in 1950, it became a school in 1952, and attained its present status in October 1971. It started with a four-year programme and in 1957 was offering a five-year course leading to a master's degree (Unesco, 1958). At present it runs a two-year full-time post-graduate diploma course. The number of graduates in recent years has been 80 in 1968, 95 in 1969 and 112 in 1970.

The diploma course covers the history of the press, radio and television, the operation and organization of media institutions, the economics of the mass media, practices and techniques in print, radio and television journalism, law of the media, sociology and the ethics of journalism. Teaching is also given on sociological and psychological studies of the media and on research methods.

T Kupis (1971) informed this survey that

>in addition to the two-year, postgraduate residence course, the Institute offers a two-year M.A. correspondence course for journalists who have

completed a professional higher education, as well as a three-year correspondence course in political science also meant for journalists. Some 120 journalists are now involved in the M.A. programme and some 200 in the political-science course. Warsaw University's Institute of Journalism conducts 4 doctoral seminars, one of which is devoted exclusively to the relay of information via satellites and to the social consequences of the worldwide TV satellite systems.

There are twenty-six academic staff teaching mass communication courses, fifteen of whom are on appointments of over one year, assisted by twenty part-time media professionals. Nine academic staff are engaged in research.

The Slaski University (Silesian University) in Katowice has been conducting a two-year post-graduate course in journalism since 1969. It expected that about eighty students would graduate in 1971. The course is run by twelve part-time academic staff and ten media professionals. As well as courses in modern history and literature, the curriculum comprises specialized aspects of journalism and mass communication, including the history of media in Poland and Europe, the ethics of journalism, legal regulation of the media, media institutions, practices and techniques of journalism, the educational role of media, sociological studies of media, and research methods.

The department does not conduct any research.

The University of Łódź offers teaching on mass culture in two faculties, the Faculty of Economic and Social Sciences, and the Faculty of Philology.

In the Faculty of Economic and Social Sciences there is a Chair (department) of Sociology and Social Doctrines, under the direction of the Professor of the History of Sociology and the Sociology of Culture. In the curriculum of the third and fourth year, about two-thirds of one term is devoted to sociological aspects of mass culture, stressing the press, radio, film and television, and a special course is taught by mass media specialists. In addition, students in other faculties taking a course on public instruction and mass culture in this department are presented with teaching on mass culture in relation to research, the popularization of culture, and so on.

In the Faculty of Philology at the University of Łódź the Chair of the Theory of Literature, Theatre and Film provides teaching to the level of a sub-specialization, with the accent on mass culture, especially in relation to the theatre, cinema and television. Individual courses are also offered for students specializing in philology, pedagogy or sociology who are prepared for professional careers allied to the theatre, the cinema, television and publishing houses (such as literary consultants to theatres, archivists specializing in theatre, film and television, editors, and so on). In particular, they are prepared for professions connected with the popularization of culture. Also, as future instructors, they may hope to transfer ideas about the popularization of culture, and the aesthetic education of the masses, to the secondary school.

The Institute of Pedagogy and Psychology of the University of Gdańsk includes some work on mass communication and practical exercises in the use of radio, television and cinema for teacher-training courses for high-school teachers. The complete curriculum lasts five years, during which about thirty hours in one half-year are designed for training in the use of mass media.

Non-university training

In Poland, professional training for the media also takes place outside the universities, in specialized schools and centres.

The Polish Centre of Journalism in Warsaw provides training in journalism. In Łódź, a higher school of film, Panstwowa Wyzsza Szkola Teatralna Filmova, trains film and television directors, and television producers. There is also a separate department for training film and television cameramen. The State School of Music in Warsaw, which provides advanced training in theoretical and practical education in music, is the only institution in Poland which prepares musicians for specialized work in radio, television and the cinema.

Research

A great deal of research on various fields of mass communications takes place in Poland, both in university-based institutions as well as in independent research centres.

Mass media research in universities

Nine members of the academic staff of the School of Journalism at Warsaw University are at present conducting research into ten main areas, all financed by university funds. They are methodology of press research; history of the Polish press; the organization of journalistic work; sociology of the press; professional organization of the press, radio and television; foreign press; history of the science of the press; legal problems of the press; economics of the press enterprise; and content analysis.

The Chair of the Sociology of Culture in the Faculty of Economic and Social Sciences at the University of Łódź has been conducting research into the mass media and their audiences since 1957. The main areas of concentration are content analysis of mass periodicals, press readership, and audiences for radio and television. Research is oriented towards the elaboration of appropriate methods of analysis of the deeper qualitative effects of communication in general, including mass communication, and of the intertwining of different levels of communication—primary, secondary and tertiary (mass media).

The Chair of the Theory of Literature, Theatre and Film in the Faculty of Philology at the University of Łódź, embraces the work of three centres, the Centre of the Theory of Literature, the Centre of Drama and Theatre, and the Centre of Film and Television These three specialized fields all have a common basis in linguistics and semiology, in the science of culture, and in sociology. Problems of mass culture enter into the domain of all three, though in different degrees. The Centre of the Theory of Literature deals only with literary *genres* (like the popular novel, the detective novel, science fiction, popular songs) and with the values transmitted through literature and literary works from the social point of view. The Centre of Drama and Theatre deals with mass culture from the point of view of the theatre and the public, forms of popular theatre, and the historic functions of the theatre. The research work of the Centre of Film and Television deals directly with problems of mass culture, both from the theoretical and the historical point of view.

Mass media research by non-university institutions

The Press Research Centre at Kraków was founded in 1956 by the biggest Polish press publishing institution, the Workers Press Publishing Co-operative Prasa, to undertake research into journalism and publishing. The work of the centre has brought about close co-operation between scientists and practitioners. Its work has been conducted in many disciplinary areas including economics, sociology, psycholinguistics, law, literacy research and documentary research. The centre comprises three main laboratories: the laboratory for analysis of press institutions, the laboratory for analysis of journalistic output, and the laboratory for analysis of press readership. It operates a specialized documentation centre on the press and press science, and publishes a quarterly review, a bibliographical series and two book series.

As far as broadcasting is concerned, audience research on radio and television, and public-opinion research are combined in the Centre for Public-opinion Research and Programming Studies associated with the Polish Broadcasting Company. In 1957 the government Committee on Radio and Television established a Centre for Public-opinion Research. In 1965 this centre merged with the Polish Broadcasting Company's Office for Programming Studies to form the Centre for Public-opinion Research and Programming Studies. The centre employs twenty-two academic staff and extensively co-operates with numerous associates outside the centre. The centre operates laboratories for analysis and evaluation of home radio and television programming; for analysis and evaluation of foreign publications; for analysis of experimental research; for analysis of atypical and experimental research; for research implementation; and for scholarly documentation and information.

Finally, mention should be made of several research institutes under the aegis of the Polish Academy of Sciences, which are concerned with mass communication and related fields. They include the Institute of Philosophy and Sociology (founded 1956) one of whose publications, *Badania nad Kultura Masowa*, deals with mass culture; the Institute of Literature Research Centre for the History of Polish Journalism in Warsaw (founded 1959) which deals with the history of journalism and public opinion in Poland, and publishes a quarterly yearbook on the history of Polish journalism, and a series of studies and documents; and the Research Centre for Polish Periodicals of the Nineteenth and Twentieth Centuries, which is concerned with the history of the press in Poland and of the Polish emigrant press in the nineteenth and twentieth centuries.

Portugal

Departments specializing in the professional training of journalists, broadcasters, directors, producers and other media practitioners have not yet been established in Portugal, either in universities or in other institutions of higher learning. Both the Secretariat of State for Information and Tourism and the National Syndicate of Journalists are at present making plans to establish schools of journalism, but not under the aegis of universities.

Nevertheless, teaching concerning the mass media is offered at university level. The Higher Institute of Social Sciences and Overseas Policy of the Technical University of Lisbon offers a one-year course on the sociology of information as part of its curriculum. The Institute for Art and Decoration, a State institution of tertiary education in Lisbon, offer an introductory course of studies on the aesthetics of the cinema.

Among privately run institutions, regular teaching on the mass media is offered only by the Institute of New Professions in Lisbon, which gives a course in public relations.

Other private bodies like the Syndicate of Journalists, the National Society for Fine Arts and the Portuguese Institute of Photography run occasional courses dealing with the mass media.

There is no specialized centre for mass media research in Portugal, although some research has been undertaken by two specialized centres attached to the Technical

University of Lisbon, the Higher Institute of Social Sciences and Overseas Policy, and the Centre of Social Studies belonging to the Higher Institute of Economics and Finance. Two government research centres have also engaged in some research connected with mass media. IMAVE, the Institute of Audio Visual Aids in Education, attached to the Ministry of Education, has conducted studies on the application of radio, television and film to education. The Bureau of Educational Research and Planning (GEPAE), also attached to the Ministry of Education, has done some research on the educational role of Portuguese daily newspapers.

Romania

The Faculty of Journalism and Language at Zdanov University, Bucarest, undertakes journalism training and research but no details of its present work are available. In 1967 its curricular system was said to be similar to that obtaining at Leipzig University, in the German Democratic Republic, one year's 'on-the-job' training, followed by two years' study at the university, a further period of work with a newspaper, radio or television enterprise, and a final year at the university.

The Institute for the History of Art in Bucarest has a separate department of Cinema History. It has published several studies dealing with the history of the cinema, but is also undertaking projects concerned with the psycho-physiological influence of film on spectators and with the sociological aspects of the film as a mass medium.

Spain

Professional training

Specialized training for journalism in Spain was first provided for by the Press Law of 1938, which established an Official Register of journalists; because of the shortage of journalists entered on this register, the Official School of Journalism was established in Madrid in 1941 to provide emergency training through specialized courses. It was controlled successively by the Falangist Party, the Ministry of Education and finally by the Ministry of Information and Tourism. Although in the period 1945–51, there was a possibility that it might be attached to the University of Madrid, this did not materialize, and it remains under the control of the Ministry of Information. It is the only institution entitled to award an official diploma in journalism to students who have undergone its four-year course.

Originally, the Official School of Journalism gave professional training in all the mass media, but in 1967 an Official School of Radio and Television was founded to give training in brodcasting, and there is an Official School of Cinematography which trains film personnel, including directors and producers (Alvarez, 1970; IAMCR, 1968; Unesco, 1958).

Apart from the Official School of Journalism, there are other schools which give journalism training. The main ones are that of the University of Navarra at Pamplona, and the tertiary-level School of the Church in Madrid.

Professor Vidal-Beneyto, of the University of Madrid, explained:
> The only institution entitled to give an official diploma in journalism is the Official School of Journalism in Madrid which depends on the Ministry of Information. The other existing schools ... give diplomas to their students which are 'socially' recognized by the newspaper publishing companies but have no official value. So that these diplomas [may] enjoy the same professional values as ... the official ones, a general examination takes place at the end of the last course; it is ratified by a board of examiners composed of one or various professors from the Official Schools who are appointed by the Ministry.

Recently, however, events have occurred which make it likely that the place of the official schools in training will be taken over by the universities. In September 1970, the Spanish State Official Bulletin published a statement making it possible for every university which requires it to create a faculty of information sciences, where three different cycles of study may be provided; the first cycle, of three years, corresponding to a bachelor's-level course, the second level of two years, corresponding to a master's course, and the third level of two years, to complete a doctorate. The faculty would be entitled to award diplomas at each of these three levels. Each faculty of information science would have three main sections 'corresponding to Journalism or written information, Radio or spoken information and TV/Cinema or visual information'. The faculty would also include schools for advertising and for public relations.

The Spanish State Official Bulletin has announced the opening of a Faculty of Information Sciences within the Madrid Complutense University and within the Universidad Autonoma of Barcelona. The Universities of Valencia, Sevilla and La Laguna (Canary Islands) have asked for a faculty of information sciences to be set up (Vidal-Beneyto, 1971).

In 1970, when this survey was undertaken, the Institute of Journalism at the University of Navarra, Pamplona, was the only university-based institution offering journalism training. Its four-year teaching programme culminates in the award of the title *periodista*. The course covers all the main media, the press, radio, television, cinema and advertising, and deals with history, ethics, regulation, the operation of media institutions, and practical techniques, as well as the aesthetics of media content, and research methods. In 1970 the institute had ten full-time and twenty-three part-time staff engaged in teaching.

Research

As far as research is concerned, until very recently, only the Public Opinion Institute (founded in 1963), attached to the Ministry of Information, and the Information Centre of the Ministry of Information, have actively promoted research, connected with the needs and interests of the ministry. The Public Opinion Institute has organized special training courses on research techniques in public-opinion polling, and has undertaken various researches, including public-opinion polls. It brings out a series of works on sociology and social psychology and a quarterly review, *Lo Revista Española de la Opinión Pública*.

In the last year or two, however, the School of Journalism of the Church and the Institute of Journalism of Navarra have also begun to undertake research. In 1970, there were twelve academic staff at the University of Navarra's institute engaged in research on journalism history, newspaper editing and studies of editors of Spanish dailies.

Sweden

Mass media studies in Sweden have been comparatively late in developing. Consequently 'there is a complete lack of organization in this field . . . a common theme at the sparse occasions when people interested in communications come together' (Ekecrantz, 1970). The newly formed Department of Theatre and Film Sciences at Stockholm University is the only specialized department for training mass media practitioners. Otherwise professional training takes place in schools and institutes of university level, but not in the universities themselves. Teaching about mass communication in universities, though increasing, is still limited, and is regarded as a subsidiary part of the subject-matter of other disciplines, especially sociology. As far as research is concerned, it is felt by many Swedish researchers that, as in other countries, there has been a preponderance of administrative rather than critical research so that many important areas of public as well as academic concern have been neglected. The present situation of Swedish mass media studies and the role of universities in that regard will be best illustrated by dealing in turn with training, teaching and research.

Training

Professional training for media practitioners is provided largely by institutions of higher education of comparable level with universities, but not in universities properly so-called.

Until 1945, the only journalism courses available to supplement in-service training were provided by a private college in Stockholm, Poppius' Journalism School. But in that year, the Press Club, the Union of Swedish Journalists and the Swedish Newspaper Publishers' Association took the initiative in arranging for occasional short courses given over the next ten years at Gothenburg and Stockholm universisites. But by 1957, on-the-job training was felt to be inadequate to impart the specialized skills demanded by modern journalism, and, on the basis of a report submitted by a committee representing the above-mentioned press organizations, they decided to set up a Journalism Institute in Stockholm.

At present journalism training is conducted by two specialized State-run professional schools of university-college level, the Journalisthögskolan in Stockholm (which apparently derives from the erstwhile Journalism Institute) and its counterpart in Gothenburg, founded in 1967. Both schools run on similar lines and their curricula are co-ordinated by a supervisory committee. They provide a two-year certificate course of four semesters. The first two semesters comprise basic instruction in sociology and psychology, language and composition, political science, economics, introduction to mass media, graphic techniques, press codes and ethics, and criticism of statistical sources. Then comes a semester of practical work, and finally, core courses in mass media, language and composition, political science, and research methods, with options in journalism or information. Students who pass the course are granted the title *journalist*, and those who have additional academic qualifications before they enter the schools may be granted an M.A. degree in journalism.

Until 1970, the Swedish Film Institute ran a school to train film and television professionals. It is now integrated into a new governmental training centre for film, theatre, radio and television, Dramatiska Institutet (Dramatic Institute), which opened in 1970. It has separate sections to train directors, production administrators, cameramen, sound engineers and set designers and makers. The courses last from two to three years. Teaching includes the history, ethics, legislation, censorship, economics and institutions in film and television, practical techniques, and the aesthetics, educational role and social and psychological studies of these media, as well as research techniques. Fifty students were admitted in 1971, all with previous experience in broadcasting, cinema or the theatre. The main part of the training comprises the creation of productions. Continuous audience research on these productions will determine the institute's future teaching.

Teaching

Teaching about mass media and mass communication is provided both by universities, mainly through departments of sociology, psychology, and political science, and by other educational institutions of similar status.

Swedish universities provide little specialized teaching about mass media. The only university department specifically dealing with mass media is the Department of Theatre and Film Sciences at Stockholm University which has a Chair of Film, inaugurated in 1970. Other departments at Stockholm University provide some scattered unit courses on mass communication. The Sociology Department gives one undergraduate course and one graduate course on the sociology of communication, the Political Science Department (where some master's theses, mainly communicator studies, have been submitted) gives an undergraduate course, and the Psychology Department teaches a master's-level course. Similar single courses are found in the departments of political science and of psychology at Gothenburg University, and the Sociology Department of Uppsala University has begun teaching a doctoral-level course on communication and communication theory.

Apart from these scattered unit courses, which lead to no qualification, a recent interesting innovation in Swedish universities is the introduction of a new programme of studies called *informationsteknik* (techniques of information) at the Universities of Uppsala, Lund, Gothenburg and Örebro since 1970. The courses are given through the sociology departments and are intended to give students who have completed their academic studies some preparation for mass media careers. At Uppsala University, the *informationsteknik* subdivision has two full-time academic staff and twenty-five media professionals. Sixty students graduated in 1970. The course aims at giving a broad perspective on the ideological, political, economic and social realities in which communication occurs, not specific training in techniques, though a little orientation in radio and television transmission, newspaper make-up and interviewing techniques is included (Bröström, 1971).

As far as other institutions of higher education are concerned, the Stockholm School of Economics has given a systematic course on mass communication in its Department of Economic Administration since 1964. The course lasts between six months and a year and is taken by bachelor- and master's-level degree students in business administration. The course includes the history of mass media in developing countries, the economics of advertising in Sweden, the educational role and uses of media in Sweden and the United States, sociological and psychological studies of mass communication and research methods.

Research

Until about the late 1960s, Swedish mass media research was largely dominated by market research, and studies of audience characteristics, consumption patterns and effects. Other types of research on recipient behaviour, such as uses and gratification studies, were rarely undertaken, as were investigations of communicator behaviour. In a detailed review of Swedish research Kjell Nowak (1968) concluded that only two institutions were concerned with systematic study of mass communication; although individual researchers were interested in mass media problems, the field remained heterogeneous because of difficulties of co-operation and co-ordination between institutions. He continued:

> As long as this situation remains, there will be no increase in ... systematic research and the heterogeneous character of the field will remain. Mass communication research is often very expensive, due to need for fieldwork as well as requirements of technical facilities, and therefore a certain homogeneity in research activities is desirable. It seems that a central institution for mass communication research, and of course for education in the communication field is highly desirable.

Although such a central institution does not yet exist there has been a recent perceptible change in Swedish mass communication research interest, 'a reorientation among many researchers towards "critical" research, mirrored in an increased interest in the structural restraints on the production side of mass communications' (Ekecrantz, 1971). This reorientation has taken place side by side with a general debate on the increasing concentration of power in the hands of central decision-makers vis-à-vis the ordinary citizen (Bröström, 1971).

One of the most active university departments in systematic mass communication research is the Political Science Department at Gothenburg University. Since the early 1950s it has undertaken a series of election studies partly concerned with opinion-formation, personal influence on voting behaviour and exposure to mass media propaganda, as well as content analysis, including measurements of the objectivity of controversial broadcasts of Sveriges Radio. The Political Science Department at Uppsala University has undertaken some research on professional communicators, and faculty members of the sociology departments at Uppsala and Lund universities have also conducted occasional mass media researches.

However, the research activities of these university departments is less extensive than that of the Stockholm School of Economics, a tertiary-level institution, where five full-time staff at the Economic Research Institute are engaged in mass media research. Its most important present research programme is on the functions and effects of information in the mass media, which aims at integrating effects research on information-seeking and information-giving (relating types of content to sociological and psychological variables) with uses and gratifications research (including experiments on the effects of varying source credibility with respect to the expected use of information by recipients) (Lundberg and Nowak, 1971).

Many non-academic institutions have taken an active and sustained interest in mass media studies. For example, in the mid-1960s, the research group of the Swedish Film Institute did a number of experimental studies on reactions to film content, and in 1968 was planning to initiate and finance research on the long-term influence of violent media content on forms and values, partly as a result of the expected abolition of film censorship (Nowak, 1968). The Board of Psychological Research at the Department of Defence has a long and impressive record of systematic media research. For some years, until about 1963, it undertook a series of field surveys on opinion leaders and the flow of personal influence in small groups in relation to political opinion-formation. Since 1965 it has had a section solely devoted to mass media research, and publishes regular reports on its work. But perhaps the most vigorous and sustained research is conducted by Sveriges Radio, the Swedish broadcasting organization, through its Audience and Programme Research Department (SR/PUB), one of the largest in Europe. SR/PUB was established to conduct applied research into mass communication, especially broadcasting 'to produce empirical evidence for taking decisions at different levels in the Corporation'. This aim has been interpreted very widely, particularly at the policy level where research is focused on the role of broadcasting in society and the objectives of programming. Policy-level decisions are considered to have the character of societal goals, therefore the corporation considers it needs information about the society in which radio and television operate and their role in society, and also about the media themselves and the way they have to carry out their societal missions. At planning level, research is concerned with audience determinants, including its size and reactions, so as to provide data on problems such as the interaction between broadcasting consumption, other media consumption and other activities, the development of viewing and listening habits, the role of radio and television in people's lives, and the needs satisfied by them. At production level, research is done on specific programmes, including studies of programme impact and the effects of variations in format.

SR/PUB has two sections, a field section of thirteen district organizations, which undertakes detailed audience measurements, and a research section of seven groups for radio research, television research, research for external clients, educational broadcasting, programme experiments, and long-term projects. In addition to general studies of media consumption, including listening and viewing patterns, audience size and reactions, SR/PUB has made many special studies of media consumption in relation to diverse types of programme and target groups including studies of radio, music and theatre audiences, and some large-scale investigations of children and young people in relation to broadcasting. SR/PUB also does research for the departments which produce educational programmes for children and adults, and for the Government Committee for Television and Radio in Education. Then there is a group of experimental studies including pre-testing alternative versions of programme content to test attractiveness, comprehensibility, changes of information levels and emotional effects of increased interest in the programmes, and more rigidly controlled experiments on readability of texts shown on television, and a recent series on perception and comprehensibility of information communicated by radio and television. The department has also done several effect studies including an analysis of the effects of the introduction of a second television channel in December 1969, a 'before-and-after' study of the effects of an information drive, and studies on children's television viewing including reactions to violent content. It also does research on subjects to be incorporated into programmes (Nordenstreng, 1971; Sveriges Radio, 1970).

Other media organizations also conduct some mass communication research. A special section of the Swedish Audit Bureau of Circulations called MAB (Media Research Limited) was for long concerned with readership research, although since 1970 it has been primarily concerned with media surveys, with research as a secondary function. Many of its recent studies have been concerned with media selection and the methodology of its measurement. The Swedish Newspaper Publishers' Association has a committee for mass communication research (MASSK) one of whose objectives is to initiate press research. One group of Swedish newspapers, Förenade Landsortstidningar, also recently set up a research committee, and sponsors mass media research.

Switzerland

Although the first attempt to set up a journalism course in Europe was one established at the University of Basle in 1884, and although the University of Bern and the University of Zurich introduced advanced instruction in journalism in 1903, there has never been a separate faculty or school of journalism at a Swiss university. As the Central Office of the Swiss Universities observed (Miller, 1970):

> For a training as journalist it is not necessary to study at a university; those who do usually study either law, economics, [or] arts and attend the courses offered in their field at a given university.

The most comprehensive teaching takes place at the Institute of Journalism in the Faculty of Law and Economic and Social Sciences at the University of Fribourg, which has two separate sections, a French- and German-language section. The institute has an academic staff of sixteen, with six part-time media professionals. It offers a two-year undergraduate course for intending media professionals, leading to the award of a certificate, and a two-year post-graduate diploma course for intending professionals and other students, which may be taken in cinema and television, or in journalism and broadcasting. Courses and exercises lasting five hours a week are given, and include courses on the cinema as a means of social communication, the ethics of mass communication, the Catholic press and Catholics in the press, printing techniques, editing in theory and practice, press history, professional organizations, introduction to television work, introduction to radio work, and the law of the press, radio and television. The main emphasis is on regulation, the structure and operation of media institutions and practices and techniques in professional work in the media. However, some attention is given to sociological and psychological aspects of mass communication, and to quantitative research methods. The Institute of Journalism undertakes some research.

At the University of Bern, in the Faculty of Law, there is an Extraordinary Chair of Press Science and Practical Journalism, held by the present incumbent for the last three years, so that at least some provision could be made for the academic treatment of this subject. But nothing further has yet been done in the way of assistants to the professor, or the setting up of a seminar in the subject, to make actual teaching in the subject possible (Dürrenmatt, 1970).

The University of Lausanne offers two lecture courses—one an introduction to the theory of journalism, the other on sociology of communications—and a seminar on sociology of communications in the School of Economic and Social Sciences. The Chair of Sociology for Mass Media was vacant when inquiries were made in connexion with this survey, and it is not known whether it has now been filled. There is an Institute of Mass Communication Research (founded in 1964) associated with this department but it has not been possible to obtain any information about its present activities.

At the University of Neuchâtel, two lecture courses are offered: an introduction to the theory of journalism, and an introduction to the practice of journalism.

The University of Zurich has a Section for Sociology and Newspaper Science in its Faculty of Philosophy I, where four lecture courses are given: on the history of the Swiss press in the twentieth century, on television and politics, on representative Swiss newspapers, and on new literature on *Publizistik*. There is also a seminar on journalism at this university (Miller, 1970).

The St. Gall Graduate School of Economics, Business and Public Administration also offers lectures on mass communication, including the modern mass media, the influence of the media, and seminars on *Publizistik*.

As far as non-university teaching on mass communication is concerned, the joint commission of the Union Romande de Journalistes and the Association de la Presse Suisse on professional training for journalists is concerned with journalism training. Professional training for advertising is catered for by the Swiss Centre for Education in Advertising and Mass Communication (Centre Suisse d'Enseignement pour la Publicité et l'Information) at Bienne, established in 1968 by the joint efforts of two Swiss professional advertising associations, and inaugurated in 1969.

There are several non-university bodies in Switzerland concerned with mass communication research. The International Association for Mass Communication Research (Association Internationale des Études et Recherches sur l'Information) has its headquarters in Lausanne, and its membership includes institutions and individuals interested in mass communication research from all over the world, especially Europe. It holds annual conferences, brings out a newsletter, and also engages in periodic research projects aimed at disseminating information on the activities of bodies undertaking mass communication research, all over the world.

The International Press Institute (founded in 1951), an association of publishers and editors of newspapers in non-communist countries, is another international body whose headquarters are in Zurich. Its aims are to safeguard the freedom of the press, facilitate the free exchange of news and aid in the improvement of journalistic techniques, and its research section has undertaken numerous studies on these subjects. It publishes a monthly journal, *Cahiers de l'IIP* (IPI News), in French, English, German and Japanese.

The Swiss Press Research Centre (Centre de Recherche et de Promotion de la Presse Suisse) was established at Lausanne in 1966, by the joint action of the Swiss publishers' and journalists' associations, to defend and promote the interests of the Swiss press. It has undertaken many investigations into mass communication in Switzerland, and the place and role of the various mass media. It publishes a monthly bulletin, *Presse Forum*.

The Society of Research and Studies on Publicity Media (Recherches et Études des Moyens Publicitaires) in Zurich was founded in 1964, by the Swiss association of newspaper publishers and various associations and bodies concerned with advertising and publicity. It produces regular analyses of audiences for the mass media in Switzerland, and also promotes basic advertising research.

Turkey

In Turkey, all professional training of media practitioners is performed by the media organizations themselves. Journalists receive 'on-the-job' training in newspaper offices, and the Turkish Press Institute and the Union of Journalists of Turkey also offer refresher courses. Turkish Radio and Television trains its own radio and television broadcasters, producers and directors.

Academic training in mass communication takes place at the Institute of Journalism in the Faculty of Economics of the University of Istanbul, and at the School of Journalism and Communications at Ankara University. The Institute of Journalism is the older of the two, and was founded in 1950. It offers a three-year course, mainly centred on newspaper journalism. The School of Journalism and Communications at Ankara University, founded with the assistance of Unesco in 1964, began its first academic year in 1965. The school offers a four-year undergraduate course leading to a *licence*, consisting of courses in political and social science and economics, and mass communications. The first two years consist of general courses, and the last two of more specialized courses. At this stage students may choose to specialize either in journalism and public relations or in radio and television. In the third year, courses are given in press history, mass communication and theory, public opinion, public relations and advertising, and documentation, as well as practically oriented courses like news gathering and writing, editing, broadcast programming and production. In the fourth year courses deal with law, management and production, as well as political sociology, adult education through mass media, civil rights and public relations (Abadan, 1971).

In addition, there are three independent schools of journalism, one in Ankara (Bashkent Gazetecilik Yüksek Okulu), one in Istanbul (Gazetecilik Yüksek Okulu, Aksaray) and the third in Izmir (Gazetecilik Yüksek Okulu). These schools were privately established, but the creation of private higher-level schools was considered to be contrary to the Constitution, and they were nationalized.

There has been recent research on the educational and cultural role of radio in developing countries and in broadcasting systems in Turkey and the Middle East by academic staff at the School of Journalism and Communications at Ankara University.

Union of Soviet Socialist Republics

Journalism training

Specialized training for journalism in the Soviet Union appeared almost immediately after the October Revolution, and coincided with the great expansion of printing and publishing that occurred at that time. Apart from short courses, like the one-month course instituted in 1919 for beginning journalists by Rosta, the predecessor of the Tass news agency, the first professional training programme was inaugurated at the State Institute of Journalism in Moscow, founded by the Soviet Government in 1921, and reorganized in 1923 to provide a three-year course. At about the same time other special schools of journalism were founded in other regions, and sections of journalism were established in two communist universities, now defunct, the Communist University of the Workers of the East, and the Communist University of the Peoples of the West.

In 1930, the Central Committee of the Communist Party completely reorganized journalism teaching. The State Institute of Journalism in Moscow was converted into the Communist Institute of Journalism, and similar institutes were created in other areas. Sections of journalism were created in various communist universities, such as the University of the Trade Union Movement.

At the same time efforts were made to make the teaching of journalism more profound. Sections of journalism were created at the university of Moscow and Leningrad and in the Advanced School of the Communist Party in Moscow where four- to five-year courses were provided to journalists with high-school education and several years' practical experience, who were given State scholarships, so that scientific and advanced studies could be undertaken in the field of the theory of journalism. The aim was to train lecturers for the professional journalism training schools.

During the Second World War, the system was modified, so that journalists could be quickly trained for fresh tasks, like war correspondents, and so that thousands of new reporters could be trained to fill the places of those who had gone to new duties. There was therefore a great upsurge of journalism training at this time. Special courses were provided by the Central Committee of the Communist Party, and accelerated courses were offered in the different republics of the Soviet Union and in the different regions of the largest republics.

But the present widely extended training for journalism through faculties and departments of journalism in universities dates to the period after the Second World War, and especially between 1956 and 1970, when both the number of faculties and the number of departments of journalism doubled.

Immediately after the war, a Section of Journalism was founded in the Advanced School of Political Studies of the Communist Party in Moscow. Afterwards other sections of journalism were created in the political schools of the Communist Party of the various Soviet republics and in the various regional schools of politics of the same type, also in the Central School of the Trades Unions and the Central School of Soviet Youth. In the Advanced School of the Communist Party, a specialized course of very high level was offered for directors of newspapers and chief editors.

In 1946, a Section of Journalism was opened in the Faculty of Philosophy of the University of Leningrad, and two years later another was founded in the Faculty of

Philosophy of the University of Moscow, which became a Faculty of Journalism in 1952. This was followed by the creation of other faculties, sections or departments of journalism in other universities elsewhere.

In 1956, there were faculties of journalism at three Soviet universities—Moscow, Kiev and Lvov, and nine others had departments or sections of journalism in their faculties of philology—Leningrad, Azerbaijan, Byelorussia, Sverdlovsk, Central Asia, Vilnius, Kazakhstan, Tiflis and Erivan (Klimes and Kafel, 1967; Unesco, 1958).

By 1970, there had been a great expansion of journalism education at university level, since twenty-four universities now had faculties or departments of journalism. Nine of these are in the Russian Soviet Federated Socialist Republic—the universities of Moscow, Leningrad and Sverdlovsk have journalism faculties, and those of Irkutsk, Kazan, Rostov, Vladivostock and Veronez have departments of journalism, as does the Patrice Lumumba University in Moscow (established in 1960), which caters mainly for students from developing countries. There are two faculties of journalism in the Ukrainian S.S.R., at the universities of Kiev and Lvov, and one in the Mordovian A.S.S.R. at Saransk University.

In many, though not all, of the other republics, there are journalism departments in a local university—in the university of Erevan in Armenia, in the university of Azerbaijan at Baku, in the Byelorussian University at Minsk, in the university of Tartu in Estonia, the Georgian University at Tiflis, the Kazakhstan University at Alma Ata, the Kirghiztan University at Frunze, the Moldavian University at Kishiniev, the Latvian University at Riga, the Vilnius University in Lithuania, the Tadzhikstan University at Dusanase and the Tashkent University in Uzbekistan.

The journalism curriculum in the Soviet Union lasts five years of full-time and six years of part-time study. A fairly recent article on the sections of journalism in Soviet universities stated that of the 2,100 students enrolled in courses of journalism in 1966–67, less than half attended courses, while the rest were studying through correspondence courses. The curriculum at all the journalism sections was stated to be essentially similar, resting essentially on the history of Soviet journalism and the study of foreign languages (comprising 550 hours of the course) and the history of journalism in the different republics of the Soviet Union (comprising 330 hours of the course). During the complete five-year training programme, students had to submit forty-three assignments and to pass thirty-two examinations (*Interstages*, 1969). In addition to general journalism training, the Soviet university schools of journalism specialize in one or two fields—television, radio, the written press and so on. At Kiev University, for instance, in the mid-60s, a special school for television training was set up, attached to the Journalism Faculty. Complete details of all the Soviet universities are not available, but the following will provide some examples of the types of activity of some of the leading Soviet journalism faculties.

The largest and most important Soviet faculty of journalism is that of the Lomonosov State University of Moscow. In 1947, a Section of Journalism was established in the Philological Faculty of this university which became an independent faculty of the university in 1952. In 1970 it had seventy-two full-time academic staff and thirteen part-time staff. There are eight chairs in the faculty: Theory and Practice of the Party Press in the U.S.S.R.; Radio and Television; Newspaper Editing and Book Publishing; Techniques of the Press and Mass Media; History of Journalism and of Russian Literature; History of the Party Press in the U.S.S.R.; Stylistics of Russian Language; History of the Press and of World Literature. There are three types of course: ordinary, evening and correspondence courses. The curriculum comprises twenty-nine compulsory subjects completed by specialization in one of the following fields: literary work in newspapers; book publishing; radio journalism; television journalism, photo journalism, international journalism. The faculty has a press, a newspaper run by students, radio and television studios, a typewriting and shorthand section as well as a photographic studio. At the end of the fourth semester, the syllabus envisages practical training in press, radio and television organizations, lasting one academic year. There are also special seminars and lecture courses, which prepare students for scientific work in journalism.

Another important journalism faculty is at the T. Sevcenko State University of Kiev, which has four chairs: History of Literature and of Journalism; Theory and Practice of the Soviet Press; Radio and Television; and Stylistics. The Zdanov State University of Leningrad has two specializations: the press and radio and television. It trains journalists and employees of publishing houses and newspaper offices. The Ivan Franko State University of Lvov's faculty of journalism, founded in 1954, has two chairs: History of Journalism and Theory and Practice of the Soviet Press. It trains students through full-time courses, and through correspondence. The A. M. Gorki State University of the Urals in Sverdlovsk, which originated as the Vladimir Majakovskogo Ural Communist Institute of Journalism in 1936 became a university faculty in 1941 and has three chairs: Theory and Practice of the Party Press in the U.S.S.R.; Press History; Language and Stylistics (Lisicka, 1973). In addition to specialized training imparted by the universities, there are also a large number of professional schools (estimated to number between forty and fifty in 1967) created by trade-union and other bodies, which are administered by the Ministry of Education.

Film training

In the U.S.S.R. considerable attention is devoted to cinematography and the training of personnel in all aspects of the arts and techniques of film. The most important institution in this regard is the All-Union State Institute for Cinematography in Moscow, founded in 1919. This institute gives training in drama and cinema, production, direction, shooting, screenplay and scriptwriting, and the economics of cinematography. It had 187 teachers and 1,500 students in 1970. Training in the arts and techniques of the cinema is also offered at the Byelorussian State Theatrical and Art Institute, Minsk; the Georgian S. Rustavelli State Institute of Dramatic Art, Tbilisi (Georgian S.S.R.); the Tashkent A. N. Ostrovsky State Theatrical and Art Institute, Tashkent, Uzbekistan; the V. Nemirovich-Danchenko Studio School attached to the Moscow Art Theatre in Moscow; the Kiev I. K. Karpenko-Kary State Theatrical Institute in Kiev (Ukrainian S.S.R.); the State A.V. Lunacharsky Institute of Dramatic Art, Moscow; and the Leningrad State Institute of Theatre, Music and Cinematography (which has a research department of fifty-two members). These institutions, though not universities proper, are of equivalent status. As far as can be ascertained, the Yakutsk State University is the only university which has a separate department of cinema.

Research in universities

All the Soviet faculties and sections of journalism apparently engage in research as well as teaching. Full details of their activities are not available. But a recent review of press research in socialist countries (Lisicka, 1973) indicated that at Moscow University eighteen faculty members were engaged in research in various fields including history of the press and the party in the Soviet Union; theory and practice of the party press in the Soviet Union; stylistics of the language of the press; the press and world literature; technology of the press and mass media; history of the Soviet party press; press theory;

language and style of the press; language of the press and television; organization of work in newspaper enterprises; and press history. At Kiev University the main research field is the history, theory and development of the Soviet-Ukrainian Press. The Journalism Faculty at Leningrad University does research on the history, theory and practice of Russian, Soviet and world journalism in press, radio and television. Lvov University has thirteen faculty members working in the field of the history and theory of journalism. At the Section of Journalism at the University of Tartu there were four members of staff engaged in the following fields: content analysis; structural linguistics and culture; journalistic *genres*, intelligibility and readability of text, typography, studio problems, sociology of mass media; and social psychology and mass communication. The University of Sverdlovsk is engaged in research on Leninist principles and traditions in the activity of the Party press in the U.S.S.R., the development of revolutionary and democratic journalism and press stylistics. In 1973, researchers in its Faculty of Journalism were engaged in work on the rules of development of the Soviet press; professional ethics and the psychology of journalism; the formation of public opinion; history of the press in socialist countries; theoretical concepts and social functions of the Party press in the U.S.S.R.; history of Russian journalism in the nineteenth century; theory of mass media and propaganda; history of the pre-Revolutionary Bolshevik press in the Urals; theory and practice of literary editing; history of the press in the Urals; scientific bases of the ideological activity of the press; and history of the press in socialist countries (Lisicka, 1973).

Research outside universities

Bodies outside the educational system conduct regular research on the mass media. They include the Division on Research on Mass Information of the Academy of Sciences in Moscow, the Scientific and Methodological Section of the Committee of Radio and Television in Moscow, and the Research Institute of Komsomolskaya Pravda, which specializes in public opinion and newspaper research, especially in relation to youth.

United Kingdom

Systematic education and research on mass media and mass communication in British universities has mostly developed in the 1960s despite a record of earlier initiatives going back to the inter-war period. Even today, although many universities are involved in various aspects of mass media study, activities tend to be split between various departments since there are comparatively few specialized units specifically designed for mass media studies, and these are more concerned with research than with teaching or training. One indication of the relative dearth of specialized teaching departments is that there is only one established chair in the field, the Chair of Film inaugurated in 1967 at London University, in the Film Department of the Slade School of Art at University College, London.[1] There is only one specialized university institution for professional training, the Centre for Journalism Studies founded in 1970 at University College, Cardiff, a constituent college of the University of Wales. By contrast, three specialized mass communication research centres were founded in the later 1960s. The Centre for Mass Communication Research at Leicester University and the Centre for Television Research at Leeds University, both founded in 1966, are university-based institutions unconnected with any department. The Unit for Communication and Attitude Change founded in the London School of Economics and Political Science (LSE) at London University is part of the Social Psychology Department. A fourth research centre, the Centre for Contemporary Cultural Studies, established in the English Department of Birmingham University in 1964 is largely, though not wholly, concerned with mass media studies. The Survey Research Centre founded at LSE in 1963 is also largely concerned with mass media. But in most British universities the study of mass communication is fragmented and fragmentary, and is pursued in many different departments, often in the same university, including drama, politics, sociology, psychology, English, education, liberal studies and others. On the whole when mass media are considered in British university teaching departments they are seen as an aspect of some other main concern, rather than constituting a distinct discipline or even a separable field of study.

It is only in the last decade or so that the concept of the study of mass communication as a single, total, social process taking place through various mass media separately or in conjunction, has emerged. As in most other countries, such studies as were undertaken tended to view each medium in isolation.

It is not surprising that there is little evidence of systematic specialized training or teaching in British universities before the 1960s. The one significant exception is the post-graduate diploma course in journalism set up by London University in 1919, at the suggestion of the Institute of Journalists, a trade and professional organization. The course was designed in the first place for ex-servicemen, and received the cordial co-operation of the newspaper industry. It continued until 1939, graduating about twenty students a year in the later 1930s. It was not resumed after 1945, partly because the university had no accommodation for it, but also because the newspaper industry was beginning to consider other methods of training for entrants, and eventually formed the National Council for the Training of Journalists which, since 1952, has run a training scheme for apprentice journalists in conjunction with local colleges of further education. Apart from London University's course, as far as can be ascertained the only continuing professional training course in journalism in the inter-war period was a privately run correspondence course operated since 1919 by the London School of Journalism, an institution which still exists. The Central Polytechnic at Regent Street, (the present Polytechnic of Central London) began its journalism course in 1949, partly to cater for colonial students. This course has been expanded to take in other information media besides the press, especially broadcasting.

As far as academically oriented teaching was concerned, there was no tradition of press studies as in Germany and other Continental countries. But the part played by the press in contemporary politics, or political or diplomatic history, or the freedom of the press as an aspect of constitutional history, or law, has long entered into the curricula of departments of politics, history and law, although only in a marginal way.

If there was little training or teaching about the press in British universities until recently, there was none at all about broadcasting or the cinema. The only educational effort in this direction was made by the British Film Institute which has disseminated

---

1. Leicester University awarded the Director of the Centre for Mass Communication Research a professorship in 1971, but this is a personal, not an established chair. In any case, the centre's main activity is research, not teaching.

information about the possibilities of using film in teaching, and has furthered understanding of the language of film through its Education Department since the late 1950s.

It has already been pointed out that before about the late 1950s, there was a fairly considerable body of research conducted in and out of academic circles on various aspects of the mass media, particularly the cinema and the press, but it could hardly be said that a tradition of systematic investigation had emerged. The cinema became a distinct field of study to psychologists, sociologists, educationists and others after it began to attract mass audiences in the late 1920s. Cinema research mirrored the duality of attitudes, rooted in hope or fear aroused in the public by the swift advent of the new mass medium. Research into various aspects of the press was a more scattered field, but valuable information has been built up by academic research and by the Press Commissions of 1948 and 1961. Broadcasting attracted scarcely any academic interest at all until the later 1950s. The BBC's Audience Research Department founded in 1936 played an important role in amassing basic data, mainly related to the size and composition of the British broadcasting audience. In so doing it created a model for future British empirical mass media research, especially in giving many researchers their original training there. But because its main purpose was to provide continuous up-to-date information on the size, composition and reactions of audiences to particular programmes, it had to eschew 'the study of the impact of broadcasting on society ... the field being so extensive that its research resources could not be committed for this purpose unless most other forms of research were abandoned' (Emmett, 1966).

The events leading to the formation of the Television Research Committee in 1963, the strategies it adopted, and its invigorating effects on British mass communication research have already been touched upon. It created the possibility of systematic empirical social research into the mass media and mass communication, and encouraged the formation of permanent specialized centres for mass communication research. In 1966 it established the Centre for Mass Communication Research at the University of Leicester to act as its 'institutionalized base', and encouraged the establishment of units for mass communication research at the London School of Economics, and the universities of Birmingham and Leeds. It also financed a variety of high-level empirical social research projects at these universities and at the University of Aberdeen. In all these ways it helped to create that 'critical mass' of research workers which is vital in bringing a new research field into being. The formation of a Mass Communication Study Group within the British Sociological Association in 1971 indicates that there is now a fairly large and permanent nucleus of research workers in this field in Britain. This may help to consolidate the hitherto largely fragmentary nature of university teaching in mass media studies in Britain, which remains a genuine gap in the range of studies available at British universities from several points of view.

In turning to current activities of universities in the United Kingdom, it seems appropriate to group them, not in accordance with whether they undertake training, teaching or research, but instead first to delineate the activities of those universities with specialized units for the study of mass media, and then to consider those universities whose activities are less highly organized.

Universities with specialized units for mass media studies

The largest centre for social scientific mass media research is the Centre for Mass Communication Research at Leicester University, established in 1966 by the Television Research Committee, from its own research unit. It was completely integrated into the university in 1972. In 1971 it had sixteen research staff, six of whom held established posts. Five post-graduate students were registered for higher degrees in mass communication, by thesis only. There is no formal teaching at the centre, but since its inception, members of its staff have provided specialized teaching for students at the schools of education and of social work of Leicester University. Since 1970, the centre has offered a full degree course jointly with the School of Education on the sociology of education and the sociology of mass communication leading to the degree of M.A. (Education). Teaching on the sociology of mass communication includes the sociology of communicators, communication organizations and audiences, and the social process of mass communication. Since 1967, the centre's staff have given courses on mass communication and on research methods for the post-graduate diploma course on the sociology and psychology of education, offered by the School of Education, and occasional courses on research methods to post-graduate students at the School of Social Work.

The centre's main activity is interdisciplinary mass communication research, and it has devoted much of its efforts to the effects of television and other media on young people, in accordance with the terms of reference of the Television Research Committee from which it springs. But it has also extended its field of interest beyond these limits since grants from other sources have enabled it to develop a more comprehensive approach to the study of mass communication as a social process, and of mass media as social institutions. It has received grants for commissioned research from the British Broadcasting Corporation, Independent Television Authority, European Broadcasting Union, Prix Jeunesse International, Council of Europe, Radio Telefís Éireann, the Nigerian Broadcasting Corporation, Swedish Radio, Bayerischer Rundfunk, Danmarks Radio, the World Association for Christian Communication, International Broadcast Institute and Unesco.

Projects undertaken by the centre have included a number of studies on such subjects as the role of the media in relation to crime, violence and aggression; the media and race relations; the part played by media in socialization and the structuring of values; as well as projects carried out in other countries, such as a comparative study of the production and content of televised news in Sweden, Ireland and Nigeria, the impact of television on Irish society, and the role and development of media in Zambia and Indonesia.

The Centre for Television Research established in 1966 at Leeds University is also wholly concerned with interdisciplinary, empirical research into mass communications. Its activities focus on the role of television (in conjunction with other sources of communication) in public affairs and in educational contexts. This combination of concerns largely reflects the way in which Leeds University extended its activities into various aspects of television as a mass medium and as an instrument for educational purposes, and illustrates the influence of finance in shaping institutional structures in mass media studies.

In 1959, Granada Television created a seven-year covenant which financed the Granada Television Research Fellowship in the Department of Social Studies at the University of Leeds, to investigate the impact of public-affairs broadcasting. In 1963 the university supplemented the Granada grant, mainly to enable an adequate level of research expenditure to be sustained. In addition, it received grants from the Department of Education and Science in 1963 and 1966 for research into schools television, and into the use of television in training teachers, and a special grant from the University Grants Committee enabled it to set up a closed-circuit television service in 1966. It then decided to merge the various research projects into a new Centre for Television Research with its own research director. The new centre was not attached to any faculty but was placed administratively within the television service, whose director was given over-all responsibility for both centre and service. In 1970, with the phasing out of the Granada funds, the university more than doubled its own contribution to the Centre for Television Research.

In 1971, the centre had six academic staff, two of whom held established posts. It undertakes no formal teaching, but it may, by arrangement, provide joint supervision for post-graduate students in other departments of the university.

Recent research projects have included gratification studies, the role of the media in the socialization of young children, the use of television in education, and a survey of young voters' responses to campaign communications during the General Election. It may also be noted that the University of Leeds Television Service, the largest in any Commonwealth university, provides training for closed-circuit television production and other audio-visual techniques and internally provides elements of courses for the M.A. degree in drama, the M.A. degree in the teaching of English as a second language for the Department of Linguistics, and for graduate students taking the Certificate of Education course. It also arranges courses in conjunction with the university's Institute of Education and the Department of Extra-Mural Studies.

The department of Social Psychology at the London School of Economics and Political Science has a long history of research related to mass media, and the only proposal accepted for funding by the Television Research Committee when it was first set up, emanated from this department. It has a continuing interest in children and mass media, especially in the formation of tastes and moral values, and in television and education. Since 1967 the department has offered a little teaching on mass media for the B.Sc., M.phil., M.Sc. and Ph.D. degrees in social psychology. There is also no specialized mass media teaching at post-graduate level, although communication and attitude change is one subject discussed in the post-graduate seminar.

The Survey Research Centre at the London School of Economics (soon to be an independent institution) is also partly concerned with quantitative research into mass communication. It conducts studies of the techniques of survey research with a view to assessing their over-all efficiency and to developing modifications and new procedures where necessary; provides training courses in survey research techniques; conducts social investigations, particularly those calling for special methodological preparation; and provides an information and advisory service on research techniques. It is financed from government, industry, university and other sources in the United Kingdom and abroad, and also runs a subscriber system based on annual donations from members. Its over-all purpose is 'to contribute to the development of professionalism in research methodology for business and social investigations'.

Since 1969 it has run a course in research methods, including those used in mass media investigations.

The Centre for Contemporary Cultural Studies in the Department of English at the University of Birmingham has a different orientation from the other research centres so far considered. Its activities are in many ways analogous to those of CECMAS at the École Pratique des Hautes Études in Paris. It was founded in 1964. Originally, it was entierely self-financing, and was able to start through a covenant made in its favour by Penguin Books Ltd, which has since been renewed, and which helps to meet its overhead expenses. It has also received grants from other funding bodies, including the Rowntree Trust, the Television Research Committee and others for particular research projects. It was formally taken over by the University of Birmingham in 1967.

In 1970, it had two academic staff doing teaching and research, one of whom teaches half-time at the centre and half-time in the English Department. The centre offers a course in contemporary cultural studies as an option for undergraduates in the English Department, and staff and students usually participate in a mass media lecture series for students taking the post-graduate Certificate of Education course at Birmingham University About twenty students are attached to the centre, mostly registered for M.A. or Ph.D. degrees, about half of whom are part-time students. There are also about five occasional students every year, from France, Italy, Latin America and the

United States. There is no formal teaching for students registered for higher degrees, but there are occasional seminars, often given by outside speakers. Students reading for higher degrees do so by thesis only.

Stuart Hall, the Acting Director, wrote in September 1971:
> Since its foundation the Centre has been concerned to develop a genuinely interdisciplinary approach in studying a wide range of cultural expressions. In the past, the main emphasis has been on the mass media but the intention in future ... is to widen the scope of work to include other contemporary cultural phenomena. We will continue ... simultaneously to look critically at leading theories of social expression and social change, and to construct and refine appropriate methods for particular close studies in the field. Due to this interdisciplinary approach, which includes the relationships between such fields as literary and linguistic studies, semiology, the sociology of culture, social theory etc., the range of our current research is wide.

The University of Birmingham also has a Television Service with four full-time academic staff engaged in teaching since 1969. Teaching lasting one year is offered for the bachelor's course in drama for an option in television techniques available to third-year majors. This includes the censorship, ethics, economics, organizational structure, and art and aesthetics of television and the cinema, the history and educational uses of television, and sociological studies of the cinema, as well as practical aspects of film direction. Teaching is also offered for a six-month unit course in programme learning, and for the post-graduate teacher-training certificate course in the School of Education, which consists of a six-month course on television, film and drama in education.

Activities of British university departments mainly concerned with teaching about mass media

University College, London, started its Film Department in 1960 in the Slade School of Art, as a result 'of successful persuasion on the part of the British Film Institute and other bodies'. It was financed for the first five years by the film industry, and consisted of only one member of staff, and one or two full-time students doing one-year research projects. When, in 1965, the department became an established part of the Slade School, another full-time member of staff was appointed. In 1970, it had two full-time and one part-time lecture.

In 1967, the Film Department started its two-year post-graduate diploma course. Students are expected to gain a sound understanding of the development of cinema all over the world and to pursue a research project of their own, on the results of which the diploma is awarded. The backbone of the course is the screening and discussion of a programme of films planned in different ways from year to year. Four films a week are shown and play the part that books play in most other university subjects. They include not only those considered aesthetically excellent, but also films which illuminate the social, political, economic and cultural context. Its full-time students may be registered for a post-graduate degree through another department, or may be taking the two-year Diploma in Film Studies. There are also students registered for one year who wish to pursue their own special interests, and some part-time students, who follow the history of cinema course as a subsidiary to another main subject, or for their own interest. Because the department has a small staff, the number of full-time students is limited—there were only ten in 1969.

All students follow a basic course on the history and development of cinema. Diploma students are also given simple training in the use of camera and other equipment, and they must present a research report at the end of two years. The approach of the film department is entirely academic. It gives some training in techniques only so that students may appreciate problems involved in film production, but professional training is decidedly not part of its aims.

A notable facet of the Film Department's work is its interest in film as a historical document. It has worked closely with the History Department at University College, London, and took a leading part in organizing conferences on 'Film and the Historian' in 1968 and 1969. In 1969 it received a grant from the Social Science Research Council for a pilot project for compiling an index of films useful for historians, comparable with the National Register of Archives.

The Department of Drama at the University College of North Wales in Bangor has run a course in television and film since 1965, originally designed for Part 1 undergraduate students and as an accessory subject to any honours degree in the Faculty of Arts. In 1970, an extended three-year course in film, television and radio was included for the joint honours course in drama.

The first year is concerned entierely with film, and includes the origins and development of the silent cinema, early sound pictures with special reference to the work of Eisenstein, and the beginnings of the documentary film. The course is conducted through lectures, tutorials, and the viewing of selected film material, and there are additional seminars conducted by visiting specialists from the industry, and experimental work. In the second and third year the study of film continues, alongside a course on the theory and practice of radio and television. There are lectures by practising professionals and practical work. The course aims to give students a reasonable grasp of the grammar of film and broadcasting.

Systematic study of film, radio and television takes place in the Drama Department of the University of Bristol and the Audio Visual Aids Unit associated with it. The Drama Department began offering teaching on the mass media for undergraduates in 1957, and started a systematic course in 1962. In 1967 a specialized one-year postgraduate course leading to a Certificate in Radio, Film and Television Studies was begun.

The undergraduate teaching is academically oriented, for students taking the three-year bachelor's course in drama. The course covers the practices and techniques, art and aesthetics, and educational role and uses of radio, television and the cinema; the structure and operation of radio institutions; the history of radio in Britain; and the history of cinema in France, Italy, the Soviet Union, Spain, and the United States.

Teaching for the post-graduate certificate is oriented towards intending media professionals; it concentrates on the history, aesthetics and educational use of broadcasting and film. All students have to prepare a work folder for a film and television programme, to demonstrate their ability to handle the creative, theoretical and practical aspects involved.

The Royal College of Art, a university level professional school, which since 1967 has been enabled to grant its own degrees, has a School of Film and Television founded in 1959. Initially the school was concerned with design, but in 1963 it initiated a three-year post graduate course in film and television leading to an MA/RCA. About fifteen students a year have graduated since 1968. Courses are taught by seven full-time academic staff, and four part-time professionals as well as visiting lecturers. The course covers practices and techniques of film; the history, economics, art and aesthetics, and educational uses of television and the cinema in Britain; and the history and art of world cinema.

The study of journalism was re-introduced into one British university in 1970, with the inauguration of the Centre for Journalism Studies at the University College, Cardiff. It provides a one-year post-graduate diploma course designed to give all-round professional training in all forms of journalism, especially newspaper journalism.

Other teaching and research in British universities

Many other British universities undertake mass media studies, but in a far less specialized way. To illustrate the diversity of interests, the activities of these universities are listed in Table 13. It will be noticed that teaching and research is centred in two main areas, education and social sciences, though other disciplines are also represented.

Tertiary-level institutions

Brief mention may now be made of courses dealing with mass media studies given in tertiary-level institutions, many of which have begun to offer professional training in film and television. In London, the Harrow Technical College and School of Art gives a three-year diploma course in photography specializing in cinematography, the London School of Film Techniques gives a two-year diploma course in film, the Polytechnic of Central London has a specialization in film production in its four-year Diploma in Photography, while the Ravensbourne College of Art has a three-year course in film production and direction. Two colleges of education, Bulmershe College in Reading, and the College of the Venerable Bede in Durham offer courses on film and television with reference to schools as a main subject in their three-year Certificate of Education courses, and the Hornsey College of Art offers a one-year course on film and television in education. Eastbourne College offers drama, film and television as a main subject in its three-year certificate course, while Kingston upon Hull College, and Trinity and All Saints College in Leeds give similar courses in drama and telecommunication, and communication arts and media respectively. The Lloyd Committee appointed in 1965 to consider the need for a National Film School, in 1967 reported in favour of an entirely separate professional school. It came into being in 1970 to run a three-year course for training directors, producers, writers and cameramen.

Several tertiary-level institutions offer diploma courses in communication studies, with a journalism orientation. The Polytechnic of Central London and the City of Birmingham Polytechnic both run a three-year course which includes journalism, advertising and public relations, while the Aberdeen College of Commerce has a two-year Diploma in Communication Studies including journalism. The Polytechnic of Central London and the Aberdeen College also deal with broadcasting in these courses. Sunderland Polytechnic has a three-year Diploma in Visual Communications, while Watford College of Technology has a one-year post-graduate Diploma in Advertising Administration, and a one-year Diploma in Advertising Writing.

Media organizations and other institutions

Professional training in journalism has been offered since the 1950s by the National Council for the Training of Journalists, which represents newspaper proprietors, editors and unions, radio and television, and academic interests. It provides a systematic national scheme of training for trainee journalists, which covers all provincial newspapers, where nearly all reporters begin. Trainee journalists must serve a three-year indenture with an employer (two years in the case of graduates). During this period, trainees attend block release, or day-release courses for instruction in newspaper law, English government, English usage, shorthand, current affairs, sociology, and news reporting and writing, and interviewing, and take a proficiency test leading to a

TABLE 13. Other teaching and research in British universities

University	Faculty, department or school	Concern with mass media
Aberdeen	Public Law	Elements on censorship, regulation of broadcasting, etc. included in courses on constitutional or international law
	Sociology	Research on media use by children
Bath University of Technology	Education	Course on communications in post-graduate certificate course in education
Cambridge	English	Occasional lectures on press history and sociology, and the aesthetics of cinema
Exeter	Education	Course on film and television for Master of Education by Advanced Study (Teaching of English) degree. Seminars on 'Communication in Relation to Education'
Glasgow	Television Service	Production staff participate in lectures and seminars in various departments including education, politics, extra-mural studies and Drama
Hull	Drama	Course on radio, television and cinema for undergraduate and post-graduate students
Kent	Social Science	Course in politics and mass media (option)
London	Chelsea College of Science and Technology	Full-time post-graduate course in modern social and cultural studies includes mass media
	Imperial College of Science and Technology	Communication Section within Department of Electrical Engineering. Teaching and research on influence of communication technology on human beings
	Institute of Education	Courses on educational radio and television. Teacher training in English and social studies includes television appreciation. Some research on media in education
Newcastle	Politics	Mass media touched upon in first-year course on British government and in third-year course on political behaviour
Open University	Social Science	Several research projects
Salford	Sociology	Communication course includes lectures on mass communication
Southampton	Education	Teaching on mass media for post-graduate certificate in education, Advanced Diploma in Education, and Master of Education degree
	Sociology and Social Administration	General teaching on mass media in B.Sc. (Social Science) degree. Some research projects
Surrey	General Studies	Option in film studies
Warwick	Business Studies	Ten-week seminar for senior executives in the newspaper industry. Industrial research into newspaper business

proficiency certificate. A similar one-year pre-entry course for school leavers is also held. Similar courses are given for trainee press photographers.

The Thomson Foundation in Cardiff runs three-month courses in journalistic techniques, newspaper management and press photography. The Thomson Television College in Glasgow provides two sixteen-week courses a year to students from developing countries and the Council for Educational Development Overseas (CEDO) gives two three-month courses in techniques of educational television production to overseas educationists and broadcasters nominated by their ministries or broadcasting authorities.

The BBC also supplies various courses in radio production, television production and film direction, radio for education, and broadcast management for its own employees and for members of overseas broadcast organizations.

Reference has already been made to the BBC's Audience Research Department, the largest in Europe. Its main activities consist of a continuous daily audience measurement, based on interviews with a large quota sample, the collecting and analysis of audience reactions to programmes by panels, and various *ad hoc* studies on particular programmes or programme types. It also does more general studies from time to time on audience tastes and reactions. There is also a small research unit attached to the Schools Broadcasting Council which is in charge of broadcasting to schools. The Independent Broadcasting Authority and most of the independent television companies have audience research departments though much of their routine research is done through specialized commercial companies on contract.

Yugoslavia

Specialized training for journalism was mooted in Yugoslavia at various times from the end of the nineteenth century onwards. But it was not until after the Second World War, when many ex-partisans were attracted to the professions, that on-the-job training was supplemented by short courses given by experienced journalists. In 1948, the Belgrade Academy of Journalism and Diplomacy was founded, which trained a number of well-known Yugoslav journalists by providing a theoretically oriented curriculum, while the Zagreb School of Journalism, active at about the same time, provided a two-year practically oriented course. But both these schools were short-lived, and until the foundation of the Institute of Journalism in 1960, the only training available was provided by the occasional seminars of the Yugoslav Journalists' Association and those in the Yugoslav republics. Then, in the early 1960s, the University of Ljubljana began to be involved in mass media studies, including professional training and research, and in 1970, both the universities of Zagreb and Sarajevo were considering entering this field. Thus in Yugoslavia mass media studies at university level is a comparatively new field.

Mass media studies in universities

The University of Ljubljana began giving courses on journalism in its School of Sociology and Political Science in 1961. In 1963 the first seperate university department of journalism and communication in Yugoslavia was founded within the school which became the Faculty of Sociology, Political Science and Journalism, and a four-year undergraduate degree course, at bachelor's level, was inaugurated. An average of eleven students a year have graduated since 1968. In 1966 a three-year post-graduate degree in journalism and political science at master's level was begun, and two students graduated in 1968. A Ph.D. programme, including teaching on the history and development of the media, their regulation, and the sociological study of mass communication, is also offered. In 1970, the department had seven full-time teaching staff, assisted by ten part-time media professionals.

In answer to an inquiry, France Vreg (1970), the Head of the department, explained that he felt it was imperative in the contemporary world that journalists possess 'a solid scientific knowledge and not only practice'. Therefore, although the undergraduate programme is intended for future media professionals, it includes a great deal of work on sociology, political science, economics, social psychology, history and so on. Only one-third of the total course work is devoted to the study of communications and journalism, but provision is also made for on-the-job practice during the four years of course work.

The department is oriented towards the study of mass communication, rather than journalism in the narrow sense. The course includes lectures on public opinion and mass communication, theory of mass communication, comparative history of world journalism and world literature, the sociology of the mass media and the political and philosophical history of public opinion, as well as covering aspects such as regulation and censorship, economics of the media, the structure, operation and organization of media institutions, the educational role of the media, and research methods in mass communication, and practices and techniques in journalism.

It appears that the University of Sarajevo has plans to establish a Chair of Journalism in its Faculty of Political Science.

The University of Zagreb too has recently turned its attention to the education of media professionals. In the summer of 1970, the Rector of the University of Zagreb wrote:

> My university chair and the Institute for Philosophy of Science of the Yugoslav Academy of Science and Art is preparing a two-year post-graduate study for philosophy and science and art especially for journalism. I feel that beside people working in the mass media who are trained in political sciences there have to be also people with a scientific background.

This very interesting aspect of teaching would appear to be unique to Yugoslavia at the present time.

The only university conducting research into mass communication and the mass media (as far as can be ascertained) is the University of Ljubljana, which has established a Centre for Public Opinion and Mass Communication Research, affiliated with the Journalism Department. Six academic staff members are engaged on research into the mass media.

The main areas of research interest recently have centred round the theory and history of journalism, the mass media in relation to self-administration in Yugoslavia, the study of public opinion, especially in its changing structural and functional aspects, and intercultural communication.

Non-university institutions involved in mass media studies

Two large independent research institutes, the Institute for Social Administration (founded in 1956) in Zagreb and the Institute of Social Sciences (founded in 1957) in Belgrade have also conducted mass media research as part of their wider programmes of research. The Institute for Social Administration specializes in problems of self-administration in production and enterprises, and members of its staff have investigated the mass media in relation to this. The Institute of Social Sciences in Belgrade has a separate Centre of Public Opinion Research within its structure, where mass communication research has been undertaken. Finally the Yugoslav Institute of Journalism (founded in 1960), an independent self-financing body, not only conducts short training programmes of different types for working journalists, but also engages in research, particularly on journalism, information, journalism training and the history of Yugoslav journalism.

Australasia

Overview

Mass media studies have not yet developed to any extent in the universities of Australia and New Zealand. At first sight this is somewhat surprising since in Australia, at any rate, journalism courses were provided from the early 1920s to the late 1960s. But these subgraduate courses were very narrowly geared to young trainee newspaper journalists, and they were inadequate both as a means of professional training for a range of media occupations, and as an avenue for establishing mass media studies as a valid field for academic education. There has been some intermittent academic research on the mass media and mass communication in Australia, but only recently has a permanent specialized research centre been established. In New Zealand, too, a university-based journalism course was started only in 1969, and comparatively little mass communication research has been undertaken. The relatively slight, and late development of this field in Australasia is at least partly attributable to a very limited conception of journalism education provided in the context of traditional attitudes towards the scope and function of universities. But the recent inauguration of more widely ranging university courses suggests that this situation may be changing.

Australia

Journalism training in universities

In 1917, the Australian Journalists' Association (AJA) passed a resolution calling for better training for journalists. Partly as a result, several Australian universities started courses. Sydney University and the West Australian University soon discontinued theirs, but the University of Queensland, which began a course in 1921, and the University of Melbourne, which did so about the same time, continued to provide education for journalists until the late 1960s.

At Queensland, the original course was limited to four arts subjects, supplemented after 1935 by two brief lecture segments with a journalism content; not until 1964 did these become two full course units: press history and law, and practical journalism techniques. The course covered two years' full-time study, but was normally taken part-time over a much longer period. Melbourne University's course had a similar pattern: five courses from the Faculty of Arts and the Faculty of Economics and Commerce, and two short courses on law, and on practical and ethical aspects of journalism (Townsville, 1970).

At both universities, the courses were tailored to fit in with the Industrial Awards regulating the employment of journalists on Australian newspapers. They stipulate that there should be a certain number of beginning journalists (cadets) to others employed, that these cadets must serve a four-year training period in which they receive practical training in newspaper reporting, and that employers must allow them up to four working hours a week to attend classes on the theory and practice of journalism (Unesco, 1958). Indeed, so closely were the courses specifically geared to the newspaper industry that they 'provided for something like a closed shop' (Townsville, 1970), since the diploma could not be granted to students who had successfully completed the course, unless they also had three years' practical experience in newspaper journalism. Yet the courses proved unsatisfactory to all parties—the universities, the Australian Journalists' Association, the employers and the cadets themselves.

As subgraduate courses, the diploma courses did not mesh well into the traditional pattern of studies at Australian universities. Not only the older universities, founded in the 1850s and modelled on the Scottish university system, but also those of later foundation were 'dedicated to the pursuit of excellence and sound learning in the traditional disciplines . . . and very much occupied with pure research especially in the natural sciences' (Elmore, 1971); only in the last decade or so have these traditional attitudes become somewhat modified, especially in arts faculties. Even at Queensland and Melbourne universities, the journalism content of the subgraduate courses could not be admitted for credit for degree purposes. The Australian Journalists' Association (which has long pressed for better education for journalism as a means to higher professional status and better pay) complained of 'the discouraging attitude of some academic authorities, which took the form either of an honestly admitted disregard for journalists at large . . . [or of] a dislike of part-time students'.

On the other hand, a Queensland University spokesman declared in 1968 that 'we have been disappointed, until recent years, about the minor place off-job studies have occupied in AJA policy', and also asserted that not all employers encouraged their cadets to take the course and finish it.

Employers in their turn found the courses expensive, difficult to fit into the ordinary routine of a newspaper office or broadcasting station, and interfered with essential training in subjects like shorthand.

As far as the cadets themselves were concerned, the courses fell between two stools. The less academically minded found it difficult to master the non-journalism subjects (which in any case seemed irrelevant to their future careers), especially since they were taken part-time over many years. Those who hoped for an academic education found that the journalism units did not count towards a full arts degree, and were therefore wasted effort from that point of view. Therefore most students lacked both professional and academic incentives to undertake the study involved to complete the course before their four-year cadetship period ended. Thereafter many students stopped attending lectures. Some feared they would have to bear the cost themselves. Others were offered jobs by new employers who did not insist on diplomas. Because only two universities ran such courses, it was impossible to insist that students complete them once they moved to other areas. Further, no system of bonding existed to force ex-cadets to remain with the employers who had originally paid their university fees.

Consequently, the results after some forty years were extremely meagre. Queensland University awarded forty-four diplomas between 1921 and 1968; Melbourne University fifty-four between 1924 and 1968 (Melbourne University, 1969; Townsville, 1970).

Nevertheless, despite all these short-comings, the subgraduate journalism courses might have continued, if only because of the difficulty of deciding what, if anything, should replace them. But the matter was settled when the Australian Universities Commission recommended in 1965 that universities should no longer be responsible for subgraduate courses but instead colleges of advanced education should be established to provide vocational courses equal in quality but different in scope and function from traditional academic courses.

This recommendation stimulated much controversy over several years on whether journalists required any special training, and of what kind, and whether it should be provided by universities or by tertiary-level institutions. The universities of Queensland and Melbourne, directly affected by the decision to abolish all subgraduate courses, had to make some decision about the future of journalism studies. Queensland University began to consider the possibility of a new degree-level course in journalism in 1964. Its Journalism Advisory Committee recommended in 1965 that a separate journalism degree, though advisable, was inopportune, and that a three-unit major course in journalism for a Bachelor of Arts degree be instituted, consisting of an expanded version of the erstwhile journalism segments (which would become Journalism I and II) and a third-year course on Communication and Public Opinion (Western, 1970). The latter course was begun in 1968, by the government department where a senior lecturer in journalism was appointed in 1970. The first students were enrolled for the three-course major in journalism within a ten-course B.A. degree in 1971.

In 1969, Melbourne University ceased enrolling students for the diploma course, partly for the reasons already mentioned and also because the Royal Melbourne Institute of Technology was starting a Diploma in Journalism in 1971. At the same time a 'widely representative' committee was established to discuss the possibilities of improving the existing facilities for the undergraduate education of those who intended entering journalism or the communications industry, by consultation with the AJA and proprietors of newpapers, radio stations and television channels. It was announced that the committee would

> explore ways of giving advice to students . . . [on] equipping themselves for future careers in journalism and related fields . . . advise the University on significant gaps in the range of courses now offered by the University . . . how

to fill these gaps and how to find the resources to fill them, and explore the possibilities of some form of scholarship or bursary scheme to encourage graduates to enter journalism. (Melbourne University, 1969.)

The present position, therefore, as far as Australian university-based professional training for the mass communication industries is concerned, is that only one university, Queensland, offers a major course in journalism. However, the Australian Government in 1972 accepted the recommendation of the Interim Council for a National Film and Television School (appointed in 1970) to set up a new training school, the Australian Film and Television School, on a site adjacent to Macquarie University. Pending legislative action, the Interim Council itself will undertake an interim scheme to train entrants to the film and television industries, and to provide advanced seminars for practising professionals. The twelve-month basic course will include about six months' practical training with the Australian Broadcasting Commission, the Commonwealth Film Unit, commercial film companies and television stations. The course will cater for scriptwriting for film and television as well as film and television production. The lecturers will be mainly practising professionals (Australia, 1971, 1972; Martin-Jones, 1970).

Academically oriented courses in communication in universities

Although only one university provides a full professionaly oriented degree course, some Australian universities have recently started courses on various aspects of communication, given under the aegis of other subject fields. The most comprehensive course, and the only one of its kind in Australia, is a three-year part-time post-graduate diploma course in human communication established in 1967 in the Division of Postgraduate Extension Studies of the University of New South Wales. The course focus is on linguistics and information theory, but the mass media are treated at several points including in relation to the effects of communication studied as a systems model within the social context. Scattered single courses are given in other units of the University of New South Wales, including a course on film history in the School of Drama, and a mass media course in the Department of Marketing in the Graduate School of Business. In 1970, La Trobe University established a research centre, the Centre for the Study of Educational Communication and Media, which provides undergraduate courses on screen education and on mass communication and society mainly for the Bachelor of Education degree. The Drama Department at Flinders University of South Australia pays considerable attention to television, cinema and radio in its undergraduate course, while a course on communication and cultural studies was begun in the School of Humanities in 1970. The School of English at Macquarie University started a half-year course on communication and the mass media in 1970. All these activities, though still somewhat limited, appear to indicate a growing interest in the wider aspects of mass communication in Australian universities since the late sixties.

Research in universities

Although individual Australian research workers have undertaken investigations into various aspects of mass communication, including the effects of violent mass media content on children, the first research centre in Australia is the Centre for the Study of

Educational Communication and Media at La Trobe University, founded in 1970. Its interests include

> The efficiency of the communication process in teaching, the effect of mass media on knowledge, attitudes and values in comparison with the schools; understanding media and technology; assisting teachers to use educational technology efficiently and to evaluate their effects. (La Trobe University, 1970.)

Its recent research includes a survey of audio-visual centres in universities in Australia, Canada, the United Kingdom and the United States, the effects of the introduction of television on the Darwin community, and some studies of audio-visual education.

Other research reported from Australia included several projects in the Political Science Department, Queensland University, on information media especially daily newspapers (content analyses, studies of new sources, career mobility in the press and broadcasting, controls over media content, and relations between parliament and the media); studies of British and Australian press history in the History Department, Newcastle University; work on mass media related to information theory at New South Wales University; and research in the Drama Department, Flinders University, on film history, and on the transmission of fictional and educational film material by the Australian Broadcasting Commission.

To sum up, the replies received in connexion with the Unesco survey indicate that despite the long history of university-based journalism training, only in recent years has a more widely ranging interest in mass communication become evident in Australian universities. However, it should be noted that universities are not the only institutions of higher education to undertake mass media studies. As in Canada, tertiary-level institutions have recently begun to provide vocationally oriented training for mass media occupations mainly in journalism, film appraisal and professional writing. The most extensive of these are the four-year Diploma in Journalism at the Royal Melbourne Institute of Technology, and the three-year Diploma in Film Appraisal at the Mitchell College of Advanced Education in Bathurst, N.S.W. But several other tertiary institutions offer qualifying courses dealing with the mass media, and many intend to increase their range and length of their offerings. It may well be that university-based mass media studies in Australia may benefit from the increase of vocational courses in tertiary-level institutions, which leave universities free to engage in more academically oriented teaching and in research—activities which harmonize with prevailing attitudes towards the scope and function of universities in Australia.

New Zealand

The only full qualifying university course on mass media is the professionally oriented one-year post-graduate Diploma in Journalism provided since 1969 by the University of Canterbury's English Department. It covers the history and regulation of the press and broadcasting and training in journalism techniques.

Apart from this, the only academic teaching in New Zealand comprises two unit courses on mass communications in the curriculum for the arts degree in political science at the Victoria University of Wellington, and some scattered teaching in the departments of education, anthropology, and political science at Otago University.

There is no specialized centre for mass communication research, but several projects on the New Zealand press (including content analyses, selection processes, and readership studies) are under way in the School of Political Science and Public Administration at the Victoria University of Wellington. A longitudinal before-and-after study on the effects of the introduction of television on children's activities, attainments and attitudes, begun in 1962 in the Education Department of Otago University is still incomplete.

Africa

Overview

The development of mass media studies in the universities of Africa is, on the whole a very recent phenomenon—largely a matter of the last five or ten years. This is a reflection of the fact that the greater part of Africa emerged from its nineteenth-century colonial status during the 1960s. Before national independence was achieved, Africa, like other developing regions, had few universities and a very undeveloped media system. In the colonial era both the universities and the media were modified versions of the institutions of the dominant colonial power and catered to the needs of Africa only in so far as they were consistent with its politically dependent condition. With the withdrawal of the colonial powers, the newly emergent independent African countries began to plan for the achievement of nationhood, and to develop national goals of economic and social amelioration. Because African statehood was achieved in the 1960s, at a time when all over the world the State was taking on more extensive functions, in Africa, too, these goals were articulated, planned and directed by the State, usually through the medium of the political party that had led the country from colonialism to independence. Consequently in Africa, in contrast to Europe or America, there is not only a tendency for both the universities and the mass media to be linked with plans that involve the wider purposes of the nation, but there is also a strong conviction that they should serve these purposes. The effective use of mass media is recognized as an important means of disseminating information about national goals, arousing enthusiasm to achieve them, and to some extent at least, providing the means of achieving them. Partly for this reason there has been a dramatic increase in mass media in Africa and a consequent pressing need to train those who will run them. In some countries, the mass media are very directly an arm of the State, and training takes place under the aegis of ministries of information. In others, tertiary-level institutions (technical colleges and the like) are undertaking basic training courses. But as the need grows for trained African professionals who can take into account the wider purposes and functions of mass communication in society, so the tendency will probably grow to place these training courses in universities where students may combine practical training in techniques with a wider theoretical education in the social sciences and the humanities. African universities are peculiarly well-fitted for this task. Since the Second World War, and particularly in the 1960s, the number of African universities has increased greatly, though some countries do not yet have a university. One of the main purposes in establishing these new universities was to provide a trained indigenous leadership for each African country in administration, science, education, business, industry and the professions. The concept of professional training is therefore central to the aims of most African universities. The relative newness of the mass media systems and of university systems will probably be of ultimate advantage in developing mass media studies in African universities. African education and research in mass communication will be able to build on the experience amassed in this field in other regions, and to bring about an integration of training, teaching and research about the mass media within the wider framework of the social role and function of mass communication in the context of African societies.

In 1950, there were only four independent countries in Africa—Egypt, Ethiopia, Liberia and South Africa. The rest of the continent had been carved between the main European colonial powers with little regard to its historical, geographical, linguistic or ethnic realities. But Africa, like Asia, experienced strong movements for national independence after the Second World War, which resulted in the emergence of thirty-five newly independent nations between 1956 and 1966.

In the early 1960s, the general level of media development was lower in Africa than in any other region of the world, although there were wide variations from country to country. Mass communication facilities were largely concentrated in urban areas, although the overwhelming mass of the population lived in rural areas. The spread of the media was severely hampered by the paucity of formal education facilities and by poverty. African populations suffered a very high over-all rate of adult illiteracy and a very low rate of purchasing power. Poorly developed and expensive telecommunication services, built up primarily to connect colonial administrative centres with metropolitan capitals in Europe rather than to link African countries with one another, greatly burdened the efficiency of media operations as did poor, slow and unevenly developed transport facilities.

On attaining independence, one of the first priorities of the new African States was to expand and improve their national media systems as an essential attribute of effective national sovereignty and as a means of solving their political and economic problems. They found themselves

> obliged to undertake campaigns of national reorientation and propaganda in order simultaneously to project and consolidate the new national identity, to destroy old antagonisms and build a new unity, and to promote urgent national development programmes involving agricultural reform, the establishment of new industries, educational expansion at every level, and vast investment in social and medical services. To both tasks a first essential is a developed system of communications, without which the state is like a body without a nervous system, unable to transmit the instructions of the brain to the members, or the needs of the members to the brain. (Ainslie, 1966.)

The pattern of media development in Africa in the early 1960s varied greatly from country to country. Where a literate indigenous middle class had emerged—as in Egypt and in the British West African colonies of Nigeria, Ghana, Sierra Leone and Gambia—African-owned newspapers, written by and for Africans, began to emerge in the nineteenth century. In Southern and East Africa, and in French North Africa, newspapers catering for white settlers predominated, though in French Africa a nationalist press, mostly in Arabic, also grew up.

> The policies of colonial governments towards the local press . . . generally permissive . . . in British West Africa, or repressive . . . in French-controlled Africa—determined the degree of freedom that indigenous papers were to enjoy. However, where the European contacts were the oldest and the closest—British West Africa, South and North Africa—indigenous journalism took hold most effectively . . . Primary education, especially in European languages, the development of urban cultures and modern elites with their

increasing political awareness and organisation were all by-products of colonialism that have contributed to the development of the media. (Hachten, 1971.)

After the Second World War, the growth of African national movements was accompanied by the growth of an African political and agitational press, which raised national consciousness, helped cement political organization and constituted a major means of achieving independence. Nevertheless, in spite of these developments in most countries the press is an urban phenomenon, which hardly reaches the rural areas where poverty and illiteracy prevail and where the majority of Africans live.

In Africa, as in other developing regions, radio is the mass medium *par excellence*, especially since the spread of the transistor radio in the 1960s. Radio broadcasting started in countries with large settler populations—South Africa (1920), Kenya (1927), Rhodesia (1932)—and was for long mainly oriented towards them, with Africans constituting an 'eavesdropping audience' (Hachten, 1971). In the mid-1930s, wired services began in Sierra Leone (1934), Ghana (1935) and Nigeria (1936). In British Africa, radio developed far more quickly than in French Africa. In 1936 Britain decided to develop radio as a public service in its colonies, and aimed at each territory having a separate administration modelled on the BBC. These eventually provided some indigenously produced vernacular programmes. French broadcasting policy, like its colonial policy, was highly centralized: transmitters in Dakar, Brazzaville and Paris long catered for all French West and Equatorial Africa, mostly in French-language programmes. The Second World War presaged the considerable expansion afterwards, mainly in British colonial territories, though French colonial radio development also made great strides. But the true radio explosion came with independence. Between 1955 and 1964, the number of transmitters grew from 151 to 370 and the number of receivers from 350,000 to nearly 12 million in 1965. Vernacular broadcasting also increased greatly, and several francophone countries began using radio for instructional and educational purposes.

Television was introduced mostly in the 1960s, since independence. By 1965, twenty-three countries already had television or were preparing to introduce it. But, with the exception of some North African countries, it is not yet a mass medium in Africa. The high costs of receivers and of maintenance, the necessity to use electricity for reception, and the expense and complexity of producing programmes without enough adequately trained staff are among the factors which have impeded its full expansion.

There has also been a striking increase in the number of national and regional news agencies in Africa since independence, a most necessary concomitant to a truly African news and information service, geared to African needs and interests. As in the case of other aspects of mass communication, the full development of African-controlled news agencies is impossible without local-born staff to run them.

Before 1960 very few regular courses for specialized training in journalism and mass communication for Africans had been set up in Africa. The only university training of long standing was in Egypt, where the two universities then existing in Cairo, the American University and Cairo University had established journalism training courses in the later 1930s. After some initial variations, both universities came to cater for Arab-language newspaper journalists, and many Middle Eastern journalists received their training through their courses. Elsewhere in Africa there were no opportunities for formal training, except for a two-year course provided by the School of Journalism at the Accra Technical Institute in Ghana. Most African journalists and broadcasters learnt their skills on the job. Few African newspapers could afford special training schemes, although the Argus newspaper group opened a training scheme for its (white) cadets in 1956 in Johannesburg, and the *Daily Times* in Nigeria employed a full-time training officer in the 1950s, and opened a special training centre in Lagos in

1962. A few English-speaking Africans had studied journalism abroad, at journalism schools in the United States, at the Regent Street Polytechnic in London or in short courses arranged by the National Union of Journalists in Great Britain. French-speaking African journalists attended the main centres of training in France, the École Supérieure de Journalisme at Lille or the Centre de Formation des Journalistes in Paris.

Although on-the-job training was the most common way of acquiring broadcasting skills, there were more formalized training schemes for broadcasters than for newspaper men. The BBC organized special courses for overseas students, including African broadcasting personnel, at its programme training school in Evesham, and helped the broadcasting organizations in Ghana and Nigeria to set up their own training schools in the later 1950s. The BBC also received experienced African producers on short-term attachments, and as time went on many other foreign broadcasting organizations, including the ORTF, the Canadian Broadcasting Corporation, the Australian Broadcasting Corporation, the Japan Broadcasting Organization, Radio Moscow and many American and German broadcasting organizations received personnel from African organizations for periods of attachment. Broadcasters from French colonial Africa were recruited by competitive examination by the Société de Radio-Diffusion de la France d'Outre Mer (SORAFOM) founded in 1956 to organize and control broadcasting in French colonies, and were trained at the Studio-École de Maisons-Laffitte near Paris. These arrangements continued when SORAFOM was replaced by OCORA (l'Office de Coopération Radiophonique) in 1962.

Thus in the early sixties, when national mass media systems were expanding rapidly, one of the greatest difficulties in achieving Africanization was the shortage of adequately trained personnel. In 1962, a meeting called by Unesco to consider the problems of developing information media in Africa 'strongly emphasized the paramount need and the urgency of mass communication training in Africa' and stressed that training was the 'indispensible first step in establishing new information media and services and developing existing media' (Unesco, 1962). That meeting may be said to constitute a landmark in training for journalism and mass communication for Africans. Since that time a number of initiatives of various kinds have been mounted to bridge the gap in professional training, both of a short-term and a more permanent kind, within and outside Africa.

The urgent need to train Africans for mass media occupations stimulated the development of several new training centres outside Africa to cater for their needs. Among the foremost of these are the Centre for Educational Television Overseas (CETO) established in London in 1962, which provides short courses in television production, including film production, make-up and graphics, and the Thomson Foundation, established in 1962, which runs a journalism training centre in Cardiff and a television college near Glasgow, where a television production course emphasizing news, current affairs and documentaries is provided. The International Organization of Journalists not only organized short courses and seminars in Africa, but established an international training school for journalists from developing countries in Budapest. Its members have also founded training centres in their countries, including the Czech Press Agency school in 1964. In Belgium, the Belgian Institute of Information and Documentation (INBEL) runs a permanent training centre for French-speaking African journalists. The Berlin Institute for Mass Communication in developing Countries also runs regular short courses. As Hachten (1971) observes, the proliferation of training courses partly resulted from Cold War competition. But their positive aspect was that African communicators have been provided with a variety of orientations, which other developing regions have sometimes lacked.

There is no doubt that these overseas training schemes have done much to help bridge the training gap, and have given Africans valuable opportunities for travel. But their greatest deficiency was that they were conducted outside the African setting. The need to provide training facilities for mass media personnel in Africa itself was stressed in a report by two Unesco experts who investigated the situation in regard to broadcasting in 1967:

> If broadcasting is to play its rightful role in the development of the continent, the African broadcaster cannot afford to be merely a print of his counterpart in the more advanced countries. His operations, outlook, and philosophy must be in harmony with the circumstances and aspirations of the continent. This can only be achieved with a training system which is alive to Africa's needs and takes into consideration the cultural texture and the responsibilities of the medium in the African society. (Quarmyne and Bebey, 1967).

Four years later, the All-West Africa Mass Media seminar comprising journalists, broadcasters, cinema and information workers, as well as university teachers from Dahomey, Gambia, Ghana, Liberia, Nigeria, Senegal, Sierra Leone, Upper Volta and Togo, which met in Ghana in 1971, observed that

> the shortage of qualified African mass media personnel compels most of our states to resort to foreign technical assistance to provide staff for our public information institutions. In an effort to remedy this state of affairs, a number of West African countries are ... sending prospective staff to training institutions abroad, or are attempting to provide make-shift training at home.

The meeting called the attention of West African governments to the existence of facilities for professional training in mass media techniques in certain West African universities and stressed the fact

> that the training provided in these institutions can be expected to have been designed in the light of African realities ... Such training centres within West Africa are undoubtedly the best way of guaranteeing high levels of competence and enhancing the sense of responsibility of our journalists and other mass media personnel.

It therefore urged all West African governments and media organizations to co-operate in developing and promoting these and similar institutions nationally as well as in co-operating among themselves inter-territorially for the wider purposes of West African unity. The conference also urged that 'special attention be given to enhancing the educational level and professional competence' of broadcasting personnel working primarily in the indigenous languages, since they reach the largest audiences of the mass media in Africa, and that 'as much as possible personnel involved in government Information Services should receive professional training'.

In the decade following on the 1962 Unesco meeting on the problems of developing information media in Africa, a great deal has been achieved in providing courses of communications training for Africans in Africa. These courses have been of two main types—temporary 'stop-gap' courses provided with the assistance of non-African organizations, and permanent, fully institutionalized courses provided by universities and other bodies.

In the early 1960s various types of 'crash' courses were held to provide interim training pending the establishment of permanent training institutions. The most sustained effort in this respect was made by the International Press Institute (IPI) through its Africa Training Scheme, which was financed by grants from the Ford Foundation. Through this scheme the IPI held nine sets of six-month courses for English-speaking beginning journalists, through which over 300 students from fifteen different African countries were given elementary journalism training. One series of courses was held in Nairobi from 1963 to 1968, and catered for prospective journalists from East and Central Africa. The other, geared to West Africa, was held in Lagos from 1964 to 1966. When these courses came to an end they were followed up by the establishment of permanent university training of a far more thorough and advanced kind, through the foundation of the Institute of Mass Communications at the University of Lagos in

1966, and of the School of Journalism at the University of Nairobi in 1970. No comparable programme of courses was available for francophone journalists. But Unesco organized regional courses in French on mass communication for economic and social development for African information personnel in Dakar in 1961 and 1964, and on educational broadcasting in Bamako in Mali in 1963. Similar courses were held in English at Kampala in 1964 and 1962 respectively.

These types of more or less *ad hoc* courses, though valuable in their own way, could never be an adequate substitute for permanently established regular specialized courses in journalism and mass communication. The most significant development in education for mass media occupations in Africa in the last decade has been the relatively rapid increase of institutions, many of which are in universities, to make permanent provision for advanced-level training.

In 1965, a Unesco report (Unesco, 1965) listed only three universities in Africa which were providing education for journalism and mass communications: the American University in Cairo, Cairo University and the University of Nigeria in Nsukka. At present seventeen universities in ten African countries—Algeria, Cameroon, Kenya, Malgasy Republic, Nigeria, Senegal, South Africa, Tunisia and Zaire—have set up specialized departments or institutes which offer full undergraduate degrees or diplomas in journalism and mass communication. (Five are in South Africa, three in Nigeria and two in Egypt.) The activities of these universities will be detailed below in separate entries under their country headings. But some of their main characteristics may be mentioned briefly here.

First, it should be noted how relatively recently these universities have come to include mass media studies in their curricula. With the outstanding exception of the two Egyptian universities, which have provided journalism training since the 1930s, the majority of African universities which grant mass media qualifications have become involved in this field only in the late 1960s and early 1970s.

Second, many of these universities have established regional training centres. Because of the urgent need of the emergent African nations to provide advanced-level training facilities as a matter of high priority, several of these new university-based institutions for mass media education were specifically designed to constitute regional training centres. It is interesting to note that in comparison with other regions there are far more regional centres for journalism and mass communication in Africa than elsewhere. By co-operating to establish regional, rather than national training centres, African countries have been able to pool their resources and (sometimes with the aid of financial assistance from external sources) have been able to provide the expensive technical equipment necessary for the whole gamut of the modern communications field, especially in relation to print and broadcast journalism. Thus, for example, Nairobi University's School of Journalism was set up with Unesco assistance in 1970 as a regional training centre for East, Central and Southern Africa. The ministries of information of Kenya, Tanzania and Uganda each have one representative on the school's Board of Governors. The school accepts students from Botswana, Ethiopia, Kenya, Lesotho, Malawi, Somalia, Sudan, Swaziland, Tanzania, Uganda and Zambia. The budget for the school's first four years is provided jointly by the governments of Austria, Denmark, Kenya and Norway. To take another example from francophone Africa, the École Supérieure Internationale de Journalisme de Yaoundé (ESIJY), within the Federal University of the Cameroon was founded by agreement between the governments of Cameroon, the Central African Republic, Chad, Gabon and Rwanda and accepts as students only nationals from these countries, which finance its operations. It has also received technical assistance from France and students spend their third year of study in France. The Institute of Mass Communication at Lagos University in Nigeria and the Centre d'Études de Sciences de l'Information (CESTI) at Dakar University in Senegal have also been designed as regional centres. It may be remarked in passing that partly because of the regional character of many of these African university departments and centres for mass media studies, partly because of the paucity of trained African educators in the field as well as the lack of African-language textbooks, the language of instruction in journalism and communications training at present is either English or French.

Another noteworthy feature that distinguishes many of these university-based programmes of training is that all of them to a greater or lesser extent not only provide purely technical subjects but also stress the general aspects of communication, the problems of economic and social development in Africa and other parts of the Third World, and the role of the mass media in the process of development. Thus, generally speaking, these new university courses in mass media studies have been designed from the beginning to make students aware of their role as communicators in the wide sense, rather than as journalists in a more narrow sense.

As we have seen, in ten African countries universities undertake specialized training for mass media professionals, and grant specialized mass media qualifications. In other countries universities do offer some education about mass media, but as an adjunct to some other main subject field, usually education or agriculture. Thus the Department of Audio-visual Education at Njala University College in Sierra Leone provides a one-year course in audio-visual education for students taking their education degrees, which includes some elementary audio-visual skills training and some communication theory. Likewise the University of Zambia's Education Department gives some instruction on basic radio techniques and the use of radio in the classroom, while the Mass Media Unit in the Adult Education Centre of Makerere University in Uganda gives short courses on mass media but does not attempt any comprehensive training. At the University of Khartoum in the Sudan the course in Agricultural Extension in the Faculty of Agriculture aims to give students an understanding of the communication process and of social change in relation to the rural population and some knowledge of communication skills, including mass media techniques.

In several African countries, it is not universities, but other types of institution which cater for professional education for journalists and mass communicators. In some countries, this function is undertaken by tertiary-level institutions. In Guinea, for example, where no university has yet been established, the Institut Polytechnique has recently begun to offer a *licence*-level course in journalism. In other situations, the urgent need for trained personnel has meant that courses must be designed to cater for students who have not completed their high-school education, and therefore a tertiary-level institution is a more appropriate locus than a university for such courses. This situation exists in Zambia, where a continuous adjustment has had to be made between the educational requirements of a sound communications education and the need to staff the country's media as quickly as possible with personnel who have had some training. A brief account of the changes which have occurred in the curriculum of the Evelyn Hone College of Applied Arts and Commerce in Lusaka (the main source of specialized training for mass media personnel) illustrates some of the problems involved.

Immediately prior to Zambian independence, the Evelyn Hone College established a Department of Communication which provided a twelve-month full-time course for government employees in the ministries of information, community development, education and agriculture as well as a two-year full-time course for private students which included photo-journalism, art and design. In 1964, a Unesco mission investigated Zambia's communication training needs in relation to national development, and, finding an acute shortage of trained African personnel, recommended that

> at the earliest possible moment training should be commenced which will ensure a flow of well-educated and basically trained personnel into the information services and the press, radio and television.

They suggested that the college provide a three-year course (for middle school-leavers) consisting of two years' general subjects, including English, and one year skills training in basic journalistic and broadcasting techniques. This was done, but by 1966, the manpower shortage had become so critical that on the government's instructions the two years' general subjects were abandoned, the entry requirements were raised somewhat, and the course was limited to one year's training in skills, aimed at producing journalism trainees with a basic knowledge of reporting, sub-editing, typing, broadcast journalism and photography. By 1971, after long negotiations with the government, the department was allowed to extend the course to eighteen months (Huxham, 1971) and by 1973 a twenty-three-month course was being provided (University of Lagos, 1973). But a proposal to mount a separate, university-level broadcast arts course at the college has not yet materialized. The experience of the Evelyn Hone College illustrates the possible difficulties that may arise in trying to arrive at a standard of instruction which meets academic educational requirements and at the same time allows the most rapid possible flow of urgently needed recruits with some basic training into the vital communications field.

In some countries, the solution has seemed to lie in the government itself undertaking the training of its communication specialists. One of the oldest permanent training institutions in Africa is the Institute of Journalism in Accra, established by Nkrumah in the late 1950s, which once accepted students from outside Ghana, but now only teaches Ghanaian citizens. The institute runs a twenty-four-month course which includes training in print and broadcast journalism. However, there has been a long-standing demand for university training in journalism in Ghana from practising journalists, and four successive governments since 1963 accepted this in principle and considered the problem from time to time. Finally, in 1968 the government opened negotiations with the University of Ghana in Legon, which finally resulted in the foundation of an Institute of Communication within the university which opened in 1973. To take another example, in Morocco, the Ministry of Information in 1971 concluded an agreement with the Friedrich Naumann Stiftung, a German foundation, by which the latter undertook to provide, at the Press Institute in Rabat, journalism courses lasting four years for *baccalauréat*-holders and sixteen months for students with bachelor's degrees in another subject. Successful candidates are awarded a State diploma equivalent to a university degree, and it is envisaged that after some years these courses will be incorporated into a specialized institute to be established at the Mohammed V University. The foundation has also undertaken to provide refresher courses for working media professionals, three-month courses for public relations specialists and training for documentalists.

Church organizations are another notable source of communications training in many parts of Africa. One of the most important institutions in this field is the Publicity Media Institute of the Nyegezi Social Training Centre in Mwanza, Tanzania, a Catholic institution founded in 1963, which provides an eighteen-month course in print and broadcast journalism. The Africa Literature Centre in the Mndola Ecumenical Foundation at Kitwe, Zambia runs regular short courses in writing. Very many other religious organizations, especially in East and Central Africa, provide basic techniques training. They include the Africa Evangelical Literature Office of the All-Africa Conference of Churches Training Centre, and the Office of Social Communication of the Association of the Episcopal Conferences in East Africa, both Nairobi, Kenya; the Literature and Radio Centre at Mukono, Uganda; the Literature and Christian Education Centre at Dodoma, Tanzania; CLAIM (Christian Literature Association in Malawi) at Nkhoma, and MEMA (Modern Evangelical Methods in Africa) at Lilonge, both in Malawi; Multimedia Zambia in Lusaka; the Rhodesia Protestant Episcopal Conference Radio and Television Production and Training Centre in Salisbury; and Radio Voice of the Gospel in Addis Ababa, Ethiopia, as well as others.

To sum up, in the last ten years or so, there has been a rapid increase in the number of institutions in Africa which provide regular formal courses of training for prospective media personnel in newpapers, radio and television broadcasting, ministries of information and other mass media occupations. Although a variety of different kinds of institutions exist which offer such training, African universities are taking a leading role in this field, and as time goes on, it may be expected that their importance will grow. Because of the pressure to provide trained cadres of Africans to operate the rapidly growing mass media of different countries, in this initial stage the emphasis of courses, whether in universities or in other institutions has been on professional training, rather than on research. So far there has been practically no research on the mass media and on mass communication undertaken by Africans in Africa. Such little research as has been done has been undertaken almost entirely by expatriate visitors. This is only to be expected in view of the relatively recent growth of mass media in Africa, and of the even more recent development of mass communication as a field of academic interest in African countries. Nevertheless, the university centres, institutes and departments that have been set up are making provision for research, and the first generation of prospective African researchers in this field is now being trained.

If the mass media are to fulfil their tasks in relation to economic and social change, it will become increasingly necessary that research becomes an indispensable concomitant to their operations. As Quarmyne and Bebey (1967) pointed out:

> If any radio or television programme is to serve any useful purpose, the aims and objectives of the programme must be clearly defined, and a system . . . set up for continually subjecting . . . [it] to rigorous testing and evaluation . . . The reason most commonly given for lack of activity in this field is the non-availability of qualified personnel. This is understandable when one considers Africa's general shortage of highly educated personnel and the fact that research of this nature requires the services of measurement specialists and others trained in the academics of research . . . The most desirable background for research assignments in broadcasting is a university education with some training in mass communication . . . University graduates with a background in mass communication will not only help in meeting the need for broadcast researchers, but will also provide desperately needed university graduates for other departments in broadcasting organisations.

Because African countries have set such a high priority on the development of their mass media systems and on utilizing them to the full for national objectives, it is very likely that in Africa in the coming period, new potentialities in the use of mass media and mass communication will come to light, and the media in the African context will reveal unexpected social possibilities. The beginnings of this process are already to be seen. One example comes from Zambia where the imaginative use of radio broadcasting to promote rural literacy has served as a model for similar schemes in other developing countries. A Unesco report on literacy broadcasting in Zambia (Natesh, 1972) observed:

> The staff requirements for the literacy broadcasting section . . . cannot conform to those in general broadcasting work. The programmes are not just straight talks or interviews. The literacy programme, of a duration of 30 minutes, is composite in character, consisting of drama, dialogues, studio lessons, questions and answers, comments etc. Many of the items are recorded in rural areas by the headquarters staff, with the participation of the local population. Moreover, there is the feedback from literacy listening groups which entails scrutiny of listening reports and other items of work . . . Literacy broadcasting is one of the most challenging experiments in adult education . . . It needs a thorough understanding of the principles of adult education, especially with reference to developing countries, and the application of

the techniques of radio broadcasting to suit the needs of adult illiterates in the respective countries. The adoption of the principles 'education through entertainment' and 'learning by doing', together with the utilization of the radio farm forum technique and feedback, as has been done in Zambia, involves great understanding and effort on the part of the organizers.

It may be expected that African universities will take up the challenges that this type of mass media service presents, both in their training courses and in their research. If this takes place, African universities may in future play a most significant role in helping to dissolve the compartmentalization that exists in many other regions between mass media content as entertainment or as information, between training and academic teaching, and between the day-to-day operations of mass media organizations and the conceptions and research results of mass media research specialists. In such an event they may be expected to play a vital part both in the operation of mass communication in society as well as in mass media studies as a field of academic concentration.

Algeria

In Algeria journalism training is provided within the University of Algiers, where a National Institute of Journalism (Institut National Supérieur de Journalisme) was established in 1964 to train the upper cadres of the national press and information media. Emphasis is on the written press, but the institute also intends to provide training in communication research.

The programme of studies covers three years, with a possible fourth year for further specialization, and is open to holders of the *baccalauréat* or an equivalent certificate, subject to a competitive entrance examination. Candidates already holding a bachelor's degree in letters or science, or who have successfully completed three years of study in law or economic sciences, may be admitted directly to the second year of the institute's programme. The course leads to a diploma which, since 1970, has been recognized as equivalent to a bachelor's degree *(licence)* with the title Graduate in Journalistic and Information Sciences.

There are two separate sections for instruction in Arabic and French. Subjects taught include general education, particularly in contemporary problems in the fields of political economy, sociology, law, information theory and the role of communication in national development; lectures and practical work on the grammatical and stylistic aspects of written and spoken journalism; and practical instruction in modern techniques of journalism complemented by working attachements in various national and foreign information enterprises.

The institute has its own photo laboratory and radio studio. In 1970 there were 160 students enrolled.

Cameroon

An International Advanced School of Journalism (Ecole Supérieure Internationale de Journalisme de Yaoundé or ESIJY) was established in November 1970 in Yaoundé within the framework of the Federal University of the Cameroon. It was founded on the basis of an agreement concluded between the governments of Cameroon, the Central African Republic, Chad, Gabon and Rwanda, and its budget is financed from contributions by the five countries. It has also received financial assistance under French technical co-operation, and its first director was seconded from the French Press Institute.

Entrance to the school, which is limited to nationals of the five sponsoring countries, is by competitive examination open to students having the *baccalauréat* or to media employees with at least two years' working experience. The school's programme aims to provide general education stressing contemporary African problems, the requirements of national development and an understanding of the modern world; professional training in press, radio, television and visual media; and an introduction to information science. In fact the syllabus is heavily accented on professional training: of 1,600 hours of study in the first two years nearly two-thirds are devoted to professional subjects. The third year of studies is carried out mostly in France and includes a seven-week internship in a media enterprise and two months of field work on the basis of which the student presents a report in order to obtain his diploma. The diploma of the school is equivalent to a bachelor's degree.

Egypt

Both the American University in Cairo, and Cairo University have long-standing departments of journalism in their arts faculties. The American University offered the first journalism course in the Middle East, when it established a Department of Journalism in 1937. Originally the course was given in English and Arabic and was focused exclusively on newspaper techniques, but as time went on, the liberal arts were combined with technical skills in a four-year course, and the language of instruction was confined to Arabic (Unesco, 1958).

Recently a proposal (Ragsdale, 1970) has been submitted that a two-year master's-degree course in mass communication be set up at the American University, with core training staff to be provided by the University of Wisconsin. It was proposed to teach this course in English, to meet the need in the Middle East for journalists with a good knowledge of English. The course will focus on research, since there is growing need for mass media research for governmental and for commercial purposes.

In 1940 the Egyptian University in Cairo established an Institute of Editing, Translation and Journalism which was affiliated to the Faculty of Arts. The duration of studies was two years, open to post-graduate students only. In 1948 an additional year was added, leading to a Diploma in Journalism. In 1954 a four-year bachelor's-degree course was inaugurated, and in 1958 the title of the institute was changed to Department of Journalism.

In 1969 Cairo University decided to establish an Institute of Communication, which opened in 1971, to provide teaching and undertake research in all fields of communication. It has three departments: journalism and publishing, radio-television, and public relations. Courses in the first and second years are common to the three departments, specialization beginning in the third year. A four-year course leads to a bachelor's degree, with further provision for studies leading to the master's degree and the doctorate.

The Higher Institute of Cinema in Cairo has the status of a college. It is a film school which provides training for producers, directors and other personnel for the film industry.

The Institute of National Guidance, run by the Ministry of Information, provides training in Arabic to graduates working at the ministry or its agencies, through a system of training periods, including general and more specialized instruction, on informative, political and national subjects, including journalism and techniques of information.

Kenya

The University of Nairobi has recently set up a School of Journalism to which the first students were admitted in April 1970, to follow a two-year course (involving 101 weeks of study) leading to a diploma.

The School of Journalism was established after the six-month training courses which had been given by the International Press Institute since 1963 came to an end in 1968. The then director of the IPI, Per Momsen, and the director of the courses in Nairobi, Frank Barton, made an agreement with the University College, Nairobi (as it was then) that the course should be taken over by the college. Unesco was approached for assistance, a planning committee was established, and plans for the new school and its syllabus were complete by July 1969. Austria, Norway and Sweden were approached for financial assistance, and agreed to contribute $120,000 each for the first three years, while the college itself contributed $150,000.

Twenty-eight students were admitted in the first year under scholarships provided by their employers. They came from Botswana, Ethiopia, Kenya, Somalia, Sudan, Tanzania, Uganda, and Zambia, and were sponsored by government information offices and media enterprises who undertook to pay the student a substantial part of his salary during his course. In return, the student undertook to return to the sponsoring body and work there for at least two years after completing the course.

The school has six full-time academic staff at present, and brings in a large number of part-time professionals. The course consists of lectures, largely in politics and contemporary world economics, with special reference to the developing countries, and practical training in writing and production. A great deal of time is spent in reading, discussing and comparing different newspapers, their style and the way they treat different news items.

It is hoped to attach a research unit to the school in the future to make a comprehensive study of the East and Central African situation in regard to mass communication.

Madagascar

In 1965 a Centre for the Training of Information Specialists (Centre de Formation des Spécialistes de l'Information) was established with the help of French technical cooperation within the National School for Social Promotion of the University of Madagascar. Intake is limited to twelve to fourteen students a year by competitive examination, open to holders of the *baccalauréat* or, upon nomination by their employers, to working journalists. In the first two years almost the totality of the entrants were from this second category but as of the third year the number of *baccalauréat*-holders began increasingly to outnumber them; this entailed a revision of the programme as regards both the level and proportion of general studies vis-à-vis technical subjects.

The course lasts two years, with a two-month internship in a media enterprise between the first and second years. The first year lays emphasis on socio-economic problems with particular reference to the country's development needs, and an introduction to the methods and techniques of the press and audio-visual aids, while the second year includes study of the contemporary world, community studies on the role of communication in development, and further training in communication techniques including radio and television.

Successful students are awarded a diploma, and have the possibility of obtaining a fellowship for further studies in France which would lead to a national diploma equivalent to a bachelor's degree.

Nigeria

There is a considerable degree of activity in university-level teaching on the mass media in Nigeria.

In 1961, the Jackson College of Journalism was set up at the University of Nigeria in Nsukka in the East Central State of Nigeria, to provide a three- to four-year undergraduate degree course. The university had to be closed down temporarily in 1967, due to the exigencies of the Nigerian civil war. When the civil war broke out, many students registered at Nsukka who came from the Lagos area returned there, and arrangements were made for them to continue their studies at the University of Lagos. Before this time, the only journalism training available in the Lagos area were short courses organized by the International Press Institute since 1963.

At first the University of Lagos ran a one-year Diploma in Journalism and Public Relations, a course which prepared individuals for immediate use in Nigeria's news and broadcasting media. Since 1968, planning for the establishment of an Institute of Mass Communications was put into motion, and an American professor spent two years as dean of the institute, helping to set up its programme.

The institute's courses are 'designed to prepare students for professional employment in the mass media—newspapers, magazines and broadcasting—and in positions involving public relations and information skills', and combine 'the academic background required for understanding social problems with the development of practical professional skills' (University of Lagos, 1970).

Two types of course are offered, a three-year programme leading to a B.A. degree in mass communications (open to candidates with university entrance level school-leaving qualifications), and a one-year diploma course (open to candidates with a lower level of school-leaving qualifications, and three years' practical experience working in communication media, who must also have an entrance examination).

Background courses consist of African cultural studies courses, history, social science courses and a modern (generally an African) language. Professional courses comprise functional English, communication techniques in print and broadcast media, communication theory, the mechanics and technology of print and broadcast media, communication law, research methods and media education and verbal communication skills.

The first nine degree students graduated in June 1971. Since 1966, ninety diplomas have been awarded. There were ninety-one degree students and twenty-four diploma students enrolled in 1972.

A $566,000 United Nations assistance programme for the institute was approved as of 1 January 1973. The three-year programme will provide fellowships for Nigerian staff, United Nations experts and equipment for print and broadcasting laboratories. A $300,000 Mass Communication Centre is already under construction, scheduled for completion by November 1973. Under the United Nations grant workshops and short courses are to be expanded.

The Department of Theatre Arts in the University of Ibadan has given some instruction on mass media since 1963 for students enrolled for its two-year undergraduate and one-year graduate Diploma in drama, and for its three-year bachelor's degree in drama. The department aims to carry out dramatic training, designed to develop the use of such media as theatre, film, radio and television in Nigeria and to train Nigerians for positions of responsibility there. Its teaching on the mass media includes a general review of the historical, legal and economic aspects of the media and a review of social and psychological studies of mass communication, and work on radio, television and advertising, with comparative examples from the United Kingdom and the United States. Research plans of the department include work on the effects of the media generally, and of radio and television, and research on the social consequences of the introduction of radio and television.

The Department of Adult Education in the University of Ibadan also undertakes research involving mass communication but precise details of this work have not been received.

The Ahmadu Bello University at Zaria in northern Nigeria has a Department of Administration with a communication section, which provides some courses in communication and training in broadcasting in connexion with the Adult Extension programme (University of Lagos, 1973).

Senegal

Senegal was the first country of French-speaking Africa to organize professional training in journalism and mass communication at university level. A short-term regional training course organized with the help of Unesco in 1961 was followed by a full academic year in 1963/1964, and in 1965 the Centre d'Études des Sciences et Techniques de l'Information (CESTI) was established within the Faculty of Letters of the University of Dakar. The courses were open to students from all the French-speaking countries of Africa and lead to a bachelor's degree.

Following the period of student unrest in 1968 the faculty was closed until 1970, when CESTI was re-opened. By that time the ESIJY at Yaoundé and the Centre of Information Sciences at Tananarive had been set up, so a common programme was agreed upon for the three institutes.

CESTI's principal objective is to provide professional training to meet the needs of African information media and communication services, with emphasis placed on the role of the information specialist in national development. In addition to its regular degree course, CESTI organizes, on an *ad hoc* basis, short refresher courses for working professionals on specialized aspects of communication (for example news agency operation, the rural press, sport journalism) and aims to promote mass communication research.

The three-year degree course leads to a diploma of the University of Dakar which is recognized as the equivalent of a *licence*. In addition to practical training in press, radio and television the programme covers the economic and social factors of development, contemporary African problems and world affairs. Between the first and second years students undertake working attachments in media enterprises of neighbouring countries, while the third year of studies is carried out partly in France and partly in Canada, by arrangement with these two countries which provide technical assistance to the centre. The final diploma is awarded after presentation to a jury of a survey report, in the form of a journalistic reportage, on an economic, social or cultural aspect of development.

The intake is fixed by agreement with the ministries of information and the media enterprises of the participating countries (Dahomey, Ivory Coast, Niger, Mali, Mauritania and Upper Volta in addition to Senegal itself) and admission is by competitive examination open to holders of the *baccalauréat* or equivalent diploma, and to working journalists having at least two years' professional experience. It is interesting to note that whereas in the early years the number of working journalists seeking further training made up a large proportion of the centre's enrolment, the number of secondary-school leavers has grown steadily and accounted for over 80 per cent of the latest intake.

The centre has a full-time teaching staff of nine and some thirty part-time lecturers and instructors.

South Africa

The first South African university to undertake systematic training of media professionals was the University of Potchefstroom, which has run a major course in communication and press since 1960, for degree purposes. The course includes special aspects of mass communications. Staff and post-graduate students do research.

Since 1960, the University of South Africa's Department of Business Economics has included teaching on mass media as part of its two-year post-graduate diploma course in market research and advertising, and there is also a course on advertising in the curriculum of the Bachelor of Commerce honours degree in business economics.

In 1968, a committee appointed by the Minister of Education, Arts and Science recommended that South African universities be requested to provide degree courses in communication and that the Human Sciences Research Council should establish a Communications Research Institute. The universities were approached accordingly, and several have since decided to introduce communications degrees or courses.

The University of South Africa established a Department of Communication in January 1969, and intends to deal with mass communication as an aspect of human communication, in a three-year undergraduate major course in communication and a one-year honours degree. In 1970, it had two members of staff, one of whom was doing a two-year study on the effects of suggestion in film persuasion.

In 1970, the Randes Afrikaanse Universiteit (Rand Afrikaans University) also set up a Department for Communication Studies emphasizing both human and mass communication.

In 1970, Rhodes University created a Sub-Department of Journalism within its English Department to provide a three-year major course for a Bachelor of Journalism degree. Thirty-six students enrolled in its first year. The Department of Fine Arts provides some teaching on visual communications for this degree and the two departments also combine in-teaching courses for a new Bachelor of Arts degree in visual communications started in 1970. The Department of Fine Arts also offers teaching for a one-year post-graduate diploma course in photography.

The syllabus for the degree in visual communications covers photography, communications and culture (pop art, advertising and the impact of the media on culture), the comic strip, the poster, lithography, commercial printing processes, layout and design, graphics and graphic art, fashion and visual communication, cinematography (history, aesthetics and techniques) and television.

In 1970 research on the interrelationship between photography and fine art; on photography and environment art; and on visual communications, was being undertaken in the Fine Arts Department. The Department of Sociology and Social Work was undertaking a sociological study of South African newspapers from 1967 to 1971 (partly funded by the National Council for Social Research). The Journalism Department also planned to do research on various aspects of newpapers.

Since 1971, a course on the sociology of mass communication has been offered for the Bachelor of Arts degree in sociology at the University of the Western Cape. The course emphasizes the role of mass media in education and social work. The university is planning to establish a Department of Communications.

The universities of Natal and Cape Town and Rhodes University give some radio training for their drama degree courses.

Finally it should be noted that the Human Sciences Research Council (the erstwhile National Council for Social Research), a government body in Pretoria, has a division for communication research. Its functions are to undertake research itself, to initiate and fund *ad hoc* research and to co-ordinate ongoing research in communication in South Africa.

Tunisia

In 1967 an Institute of the Press and Communication Sciences (Institut de Presse et des Sciences de l'Information) was created in the University of Tunis, to provide advanced education and training in problems and methods of mass communication. Previously journalism training of a less-advanced kind had been provided by the Institut Ali Bach Hamba, an institution jointly founded and supported by the Tunisian Government and a German foundation, the Friedrich-Naumann-Stiftung, to act as a centre of training and documentation in economic and social development, and to provide courses to train journalists, librarians and statisticians. With the foundation of the Institute of the Press in 1967, the Friedrich Naumann foundation signed an agreement with the Tunisian Government in which it pledged itself to support the work and the activities of the new, more advanced training centre.

The course is divided into two cycles of two years each. Successful completion of the first cycle is recognized by the award of a certificate, and of the second by a diploma. The course includes periods of internship in Tunisia and abroad (including Belgium, France, the Federal Republic of Germany, Romania, Sweden, the United States and Yugoslavia), amounting in all to about three months. In 1970/71 there were about 200 students enrolled, including about twenty scholarship students from French-speaking African territories. The course is open to professional journalists of five years' standing, or to students with a *baccalauréat*.

The course of studies consists of two types: general educational courses (on the history of the national movement, Tunisian history, economic problems and planning, and modern languages) and specialized training (on the technology of communication and journalism, press law and the development of information). In the second year of the second cycle, students may take one of four options: the press and press agencies, radio journalism, audio-visual journalism or public relations and publicity. Many overseas institutions, including CIESJ of Strasbourg, the International Press Institute, the Training Centre for Journalists in Paris, and the Belgian Institute of Information and Documentation, have provided visiting lecturers, and other assistance and advice to the Tunisian Institute of the Press.

Zaire

The National University of Zaire (formerly Université Lovanium) in Kinshasa, which had given instruction in journalism, leading to a certificate, since 1968, decided in 1970 to establish a Department of Social Communication in its Faculty of Economic and Social Sciences, to give undergraduate teaching up to the level of the *licence*. It intends to extend the scope of this department into an Interfaculty Institute of Social Communications.

The department (and later the projected institute) has three main functions envisaged for it: teaching, research and documentation. The scope of its activities includes mass communication generally, the use of the media in the service of development, and radio, cinema, television, the written press and public relations. It provides training for communicators and centres in these fields, especially teachers, educators, agents of cultural change and of community development.

The Department of Social Communication offers teaching up to the level of the *licence*. In future this will lead to a specialized degree of *licencié en communication sociale*, and, for those who successfully complete studies at the level of the third cycle, to that of *docteur en communication sociale*. Meanwhile, before this specialized degree is established, the teaching programme will lead to a diploma in advanced studies in communication. When the *licence* has been established, holders of this diploma will be able to convert it into a *licence* by passing a supplementary examination.

To receive the diploma, a student must hold a final diploma of the *licence* or *doctorat*, complete a two-year course of studies of 500 hours of lectures and seminars, and of practical work, and present a memoire. Certain courses of *candidat* level are a prerequisite for entering the course (including introduction to philosophy and psychology, general sociology, scientific method, techniques and social research, English, social psychology, political economy, statistics, study of African societies) but any deficiencies may be made up in the first year. The first year consists of 250 hours of courses, partly theoretical, partly practical—including introduction to mass communication, theory of information, radio, printed media, television, interpersonal and group communication and the cinema. The second year comprises more advanced courses, especially on social psychology, and on the practical application of theory, especially in information processing, economic development, public relations, cultural advancement and audio-visual education.

In 1971 a Department of Journalism was established at the Lubumbashi campus of the National University of Zaïre, to replace the courses for journalists and press attachés which had been given under the university extension programme. In 1972 the department took the title of Department of Information Sciences. It is attached to the Faculty of Social, Political and Administration Sciences, and aims to provide both theoretical and practical training in the mass media. It offers a diploma in information sciences.

Mass media education is also offered at a non-university institution, at the Institut Social Africain, at Bukavu, as an option in the course for *assistant social* which lasts four years. Mass media studies have been undertaken at this institution since 1967, and the first students graduated in 1970.

Zambia

In Zambia there is no university-level training for mass media professionals. As has been already seen, such training is provided by the Evelyn Hone College of Applied Arts and Commerce at Lusaka, a tertiary-level institution. The Commission for Technical Education held a meeting in Lusaka in 1971 including representatives of ZANA and the press to recommend areas of training in journalism, film and advertising, and public relations. The meeting agreed that training was most needed in news reporting, then in film, and lastly in advertising and public relations. Subcommittees were formed to examine the fields in depth and to draw up training programmes.

The University of Zambia gives some teaching on radio broadcasting techniques and the use of radio in schools in its one-year course in adult education provided by the Department of Extra-Mural Education. A full-time lecturer in radio was recently appointed to this department. Similar teaching is also given to students of education.

In 1970 Zambia Broadcasting Services set up a three-year fellowship in the Institute of African Studies at the University of Zambia so that a programme of audience research could be undertaken, more far-reaching than the traditional listener market research previously done by commercial organizations. The Zambian Government wishes to use radio as part of its wider plans for national unity and rural development, and to desseminate knowledge about the national philosophy of humanism. The central facet of the project relates to the language policy in broadcasting whereby seven of the seventy Zambian languages and dialects and English are used. The project is investigating the comprehension of these languages by listeners all over Zambia, and the attitudes of Zambians to the broadcasting language policy. In 1971, a twelve-month survey of 5,000 people in urban and rural Zambia was begun in order to investigate the audiences for radio, newspapers, magazines, television and films in relation to the language policy of Zambia Broadcaeting Services, to analyse the place of mass media and interpersonal channels in news dissemination of various kinds and the accuracy of news flow through these channels, and to evaluate educational broadcasting. Another purpose which this research will serve is to act as a form of 'feedback' information for broadcasters, and a regular viewer and listener panel is being established in 1972 to provide regular audience feedback.

Asia

Overview

Mass media studies have been taking place in Asian universities for over half a century. In that sense there is a long tradition of university activities in this field. Yet because in many countries mass media studies have been introduced only in the last few years it is equally true to say that in teaching, and above all in research, the field is still in its early stages of development in most Asian countries. The difficulties with which it is faced are many and various. Some derive from its comparatively recent appearance as a subject with which Asian universities are concerned. Others are connected with such matters as the relative development of the mass media industries in any particular country, the extent to which mass media occupations have become professionalized and the attitude of media practitioners towards formal training for beginners. Others again have to do with factors such as the academic traditions in different Asian countries, the availability of adequately qualified full-time teaching staff in universities and colleges, and the extent to which the social sciences in general, and empirically based social research in particular have developed as an academic field. Most of these difficulties are not unique to Asia. Some, especially those connected with the acceptance of the need for formal training for intending entrants to media occupations, are encountered to a greater or lesser extent all over the world. Others, especially the relatively new and weak social-science tradition, occur in many countries in Europe and the Third World. Yet despite these many difficulties, it is clear that in Asia as a whole the field of mass media studies exhibits considerable vitality, that there is a growing sense of community between educators and research workers from different Asian countries who are beginning to meet more frequently to exchange information on common problems and their solutions, and that in many ways a regional, rather than a purely national approach to the challenges of mass media studies is developing.

Although there is evidence of attempts to introduce journalism education in several Asian countries from about the beginning of the second decade of the twentieth century, there is a real sense in which the continuous history of mass media studies in Asian universities is a post-Second World War phenomenon. It is true that by the mid-thirties ten Chinese universities and colleges were offering courses of professional training modelled on those of the journalism schools of the United States (Unesco, 1958) and that in Japan, too, three universities had introduced courses showing the strong influence of *Zeitungswissenschaft* in the German and Swiss mode (Uchikawa, 1971*a*, 1971*b*). To these were added in the late 1930s the establishment of a university-based journalism course in Thailand and in the Philippines (East-West Center, 1971). Yet in China and Japan the forties were a period of disruption. In China, many of the erstwhile journalism courses were done away with. In Japan the State took over journalism education during the war, and immediately afterwards there was a brief (and largely unsuccessful) attempt to remould Japanese journalism education along American lines. Consequently even in these two countries, where the field had assumed more importance than elsewhere in Asia, the post-war period was as much a new beginning as the continuation of traditions already established in earlier years.

In many Asian countries, the forties and fifties saw the achievement of political independence and *pari passu* a great expansion of national press and broadcasting systems with a concomitant interest in advanced formal training for media practitioners in the fifties and sixties. In the last decade or so, more and more Asian countries have become committed to programmes of directed social change and economic development. They have hoped to be able to use mass media as essential tools in campaigns for literarcy, agricultural innovation, population control and other plans for social amelioration, and have recognized increasingly the need for special training in this regard. It is interesting to note that in many countries, including India, Indonesia, Thailand, the Philippines and several others, universities play an important role in providing such courses of formal training. This is in contrast to countries like Canada or Australia where tertiary-level colleges of advanced education predominate, many Latin American countries where separate journalism schools are much in evidence, or other countries like Hungary or Sweden where the journalism profession itself undertakes the preparation of new entrants. Although detailed research would be necessary to establish the full reasons why universities in any particular country have become concerned with mass media studies, some general factors may be mentioned. One of these is the growing recognition that journalists should be given a wider background education in conjunction with the imparting of purely technical skills, and that the teaching resources and library facilities of universities may be turned to good account in this respect. This consideration applies even more forcefully to the education of individuals who will use mass media to further plans of social betterment. It is becoming ever more apparent that in such circumstances the mass media are only one element in a complex social situation and that those who hope to use mass media effectively will be greatly benefited by some background knowledge of the social sciences. Here again, universities are usually the only institutions which can provide such an education. Conversely there is a growing feeling in most Asian countries that universities should make a positive contribution to national goals, and should not cut themselves off from the wider aspirations of the community as a whole by being élitist ivory-tower institutions which disdain technical or vocational training. It is interesting to note that many Asian universities which undertake journalism and mass communication courses are of recent foundation and their ethos and structure were specifically designed to cater for semi-academic education, while others are older institutions that have been reorganized to accommodate new multidisciplinary and interdisciplinary fields.

In any event, there is a perceptible increase of pace in the provision of formal courses of university education in journalism and mass communication in Asia during the 1950s and 1960s. By the late thirties there were probably fewer than twenty university and college journalism courses in the whole of Asia. By the early 1970s there are probably nearly four times as many. A fair number of these university courses and departments have come into being since about the mid-sixties. One or two examples will illustrate the pattern of this process. In the Philippines, for instance, the first attempt to introduce a full university journalism programme occurred in 1919, but it came to nothing. Thereafter scattered courses were provided by English departments and several universities and colleges tried to introduce journalism curricula but 'these programs came and went—and some came back again . . . journalism education . . .

countinued to be haphazard and half-hearted in the years immediately following World War II'. Although a few university departments may trace their history back to the 1950s or even to the 1930s, most of the important schools were founded, or reorganized, within the last decade. In India, the oldest existing university journalism department was founded in 1941. After Indian independence was achieved, five other universities started courses in the late 1940s and early 1950s, six others began in the 1960s, and at least four more universities were considering the introduction of curricula in the early 1970s. Again, in the Republic of Korea, although university journalism courses began to be offered from the early 1950s, seven of the eight universities which now provide mass media courses started to do so since 1960, and five of these began after 1965. (East-West Center, 1971). Hong Kong's two programmes have been founded since 1965; Afghanistan began a university course at about the same time, while the Malaysian university course started only in 1971.

What are the general patterns that are discernable in a broad survey of mass media education in Asia today? One of the most striking facts to emerge is the difference between Japan and other Asian countries, indeed in some respects between Japan and most other countries in the world. There are more universities and colleges in Japan—they were estimated at well over 800 in 1968 (Goto, 1970)—than in the whole of the rest of Asia. The Japanese population is more highly saturated with mass communication content than that of any country in Asia. Because the products of the mass media industries are highly evaluated, mass media studies are regarded as an important, even a necessary part of general culture. Consequently there is a great deal of general undergraduate teaching about mass communication which takes place under the aegis of many different disciplines in the humanities and the social sciences, apart from the specialized teaching that occurs in only a few universities. Moreover, these specialized courses in journalism and mass communication are academically oriented. They are not intended to constitute professional training, nor do they give students any special advantage in entering mass media occupations since the mass media industries conduct their own training schemes for new recruits who have passed a competitive examination. But, Japan apart, in most other Asian countries there is a much stronger emphasis on the strictly vocational aspects of courses, even where relatively little practical training in techniques takes place. The first broad pattern that emerges therefore is that, generally speaking, specialized courses in mass communication in Asian universities are intended to constitute formal preparation for careers mainly in journalism which in recent years usually includes broadcasting as well as the print media. Some Asian universities also prepare students for careers in writing and production in film and television. Specialized courses for information officers are rare, but there is some development of formal courses for training prospective agricultural extension officers in using mass media. However, when all is said and done it should not be forgotten that in Asia, as in other regions, there are many other routes to a career in the mass media besides successfully completing a university course.

There are great variations from country to country in the extent to which a university mass media qualification gives the holder a good opportunity of entering a mass media occupation. In Japan, as has been seen, no such advantage exists, nor is it intended, but the feeling has been voiced that there is something anomalous in this situation which needs serious reconsideration (Uchikawa, 1970). But even in other countries where the main aim of the courses is pre-professional training, students may not always derive visible benefits in the job market. 'In some cases hiring preference is not given to journalism graduates, in others salaries are not sufficient to make journalism a career providing adequate income for college graduates' (East-West Center, 1971). However, there are some signs that in some countries at least these conditions are beginning to change. For example, in India, where there has been a long and strong tradition (no doubt partly derived from the colonial British past) that journalists are born not made and that they require no more than on-the-job experience (Eapen, 1970) the need for training has come to be accepted by professional journalist organizations, while the Public Service Commissions are beginning to give due weight to trained applicants in selecting candidates for posts which need journalistic skills. In the Philippines, too, owners of mass media are coming to recognize the importance of journalism and mass communication education for their employees. But this is only one aspect of the problem. In Hong Kong, for example, although graduates find it easy to find jobs in the mass media industries, salaries are so low compared to teaching and the civil service that many leave mass media occupations altogether.

The attitude of mass media owners and executives to the question of journalism training does not only affect the student's future employment prospects: it may also affect the quality of the training he receives at the university. There are very few Asian university departments which can afford the necessary facilities for giving students adequate practical experience, especially in radio and television. Many Asian journalism departments run a laboratory journal, which gives students some practical preparation for newspaper journalism but few have the facilities of the University of the Philippines with its own radio and television studios. Therefore an internship programme which gives students some preliminary on-the-job experience is very necessary. Here again conditions vary greatly from country to country, even from university to university. In India, although the response from newspapers and news agencies varies from place to place, generally speaking 'the facilities for practical training available at present are hardly satisfactory' (East-West Center, 1971). The same situation appears to exist in Indonesia, in the Republic of Korea and in many other countries. But in Hong Kong and in Israel, for instance, cordial and co-operative relations between the mass communication departments and the local media have been built up.

Another serious problem which affects Asian university journalism and mass communication courses is a lack of trained staff. In several Asian countries, it has been customary to hire practising media professionals on a part-time basis, partly to have the benefit of their expertise, partly for reasons of economy. Good journalists do not always make good teachers, and part-time staff are sometimes less committed to their work than full-time teachers. A further problem is the shortage of local university teachers with an academic background in mass communication subjects or in relevant social science subjects. This runs hand in hand with a grave shortage of suitable textbooks, which is partly the result of the great multiplicity of languages in use in Asia, partly a reflection of the newness of mass media studies as an academic field. Although textbooks in English or other European languages may be used, they are expensive, they cannot be easily mastered by students with a different mother tongue and, most important, they are seldom written with the needs of the local situation in mind.

In most Asian countries mass communication research has been strongly influenced by concepts and methods originally developed in Europe and the United States. In Japan, for example, where there is a long vigorous research tradition, the first studies, in the twenties and thirties, were sociological, political and historical investigations influenced by German and other Continental conceptions of press studies. After the Second World War, Japanese research workers for the first time came into contact with the methods and concepts of American empirical mass communication research. There was a sort of 'golden age' in Japanese mass media research in the fifties and sixties, when these new ideas were enthusiastically taken up and carried through in many empirical studies mainly of uses and effects. By the later 1960s, however, there is some evidence of dissatisfaction with the limitations of this mode of research, of a feeling that the original impetus was being lost in a number of particular investigations which gave no answers to real and vital questions, and of a need to evolve a truly Japanese approach to problems (Eguchi and Ichinohe, 1971). In other Asian countries, too, the same search for an 'independent direction' is taking place, the realization that concepts, models and techniques evolved in other cultural settings must be adapted to local situations and problems and new concepts and techniques be developed to answer local research questions (East-West Center, 1971). These matters take on great urgency in Asia since many countries are planning to use mass media, especially audio-visual media, as essential vehicles for nation-building and for economic, social and cultural development. Therefore, it will presumably become ever more necessary to build in a research component as a necessary part of these plans, not only to test the effectiveness of particular programmes, but also to investigate wider social questions at the same time. In these circumstances it seems likely that in the fairly near future universities may become far more extensively involved in conducting fundamental research into mass communication, in training personnel to carry out these programmes of social change through mass media, as well as in training future university staff. These purposes are usually achieved through graduate degrees, which are already beginning to be provided in some countries, such as Japan, the Philippines and India.

Meanwhile, particularly in the last few years, efforts have been made to overcome the sense of isolation which affects many university teachers and research workers, and which is a real hindrance to the progress of advanced-level education and research. It should be emphasized that this problem is not unique to Asia, or to any Asian country. It exists to some extent in most regions and countries, and is a function of the relative youth of mass media studies, its multidisciplinary character, and the fact that it is both an academic and a vocational subject and one which has not yet been fully accepted from either point of view. But in Asia additional factors of distance, language and culture make the problem even more difficult. Most Asian university departments for mass media studies are small and inadequately financed, and their staffs are isolated from their colleagues in their own and in other countries. In some countries, there are sufficiently large numbers of individuals involved in teaching and research for specialized associations and journals to be founded, which provide a means for fruitful interaction. Japan is the outstanding case in point. There are five scholarly journals for mass communication research and a specialized society for studies in mass communication with a large membership, as well as subdivisions for the subject within the Japanese sociological, psychological and social-psychological associations. In India, there is an Association for Education in Journalism which provides links between the universities and the mass media industries and maintains standards in journalism education. In the Philippines, a journal for communication research has recently been founded. But recently the problem of isolation is beginning to be tackled on a regional as well as a national level. A few examples will illustrate the trend. Since 1970, the Hong Kong Baptist College Department of Communication has brought out a quarterly newsletter which provides details of teaching programmes and of research projects undertaken all over Asia. The East-West Communication Institute of the East West Center in Honolulu provides a bridge between communication experts in the United States, Asia and the Pacific *inter alia* by holding seminars and funding and organizing research. It has a Documentation Collection with special reference to Asian and Pacific communication research, and keeps a world-wide inventory of research on population and family planning communication. It also brings out a newsletter containing details of new developments in mass media studies in Asia and the Pacific. Another recently formed regional institution is the Asian Mass Communication and Information Centre (AMIC), Singapore, founded in 1971. One of its main tasks is to collect, abstract and store mass communication research material emanating from Asia, especially fugitive material, and to act as the Asian regional clearing-house in an international network for mass communication research. In this way a permanent repository of Asian research material will be maintained, and Asian scholars and others interested in mass media research will be able to have access to material in their own region and elsewhere. AMIC publishes regular lists of its holdings, as well as a bulletin containing information on Asian mass communication activities. Another interesting activity that AMIC has sponsored is to hold a series of travelling seminars, in which scholars from various Asian countries are given the opportunity to actually visit other institutions while discussing common problems in education and research. There is a strong possibility that one outcome of these activities will be the publication of a scholarly journal for Asian mass communication education and research. These regional initiatives will help to prevent not only the isolation of mass communication teachers and research workers, but a parochialism which might easily ensue if the search for independent direction were pursued too rigorously. The regional approach will allow broadly based initiatives to develop while still retaining a sense of the special circumstances which mass communication teaching and research in Asia must take into account.

Afghanistan

Kabul University established a four-year journalism course in its Faculty of Letters in 1963. Journalism subjects occupy approximately one-quarter of the programme (news writing and reporting, editing, make-up and typography, writing on public affairs, public opinion, radio and advertising) while others include the study of a foreign language, history, geography, literature, philosophy, sociology and psychology, and electives in economics, law, letters or science. The course leads to a B.A. degree. There were forty-five students enrolled in 1970.

China

China was one of the first Asian countries to set up university education for journalism. In 1918, the National Peking University offered courses in journalism, and the first university department of journalism was founded in 1920 at St John's University, Shanghai. In the next few years Fu Tan (Fu Dan) University in Shanghai and Yen Ching University in Peking also set up separate journalism departments. In the interwar period, ten Chinese universities offered courses in journalism. After the establishment of the Chinese People's Republic in 1949, some of the journalism departments were done away with. In 1957, three universities were known to offer journalism courses, the School of Journalism in the Department of Languages at Peking University, which offered a five-year course, the People's University at Peking which provided a three-year reorientation course for working journalists and a four-year course for would-be journalists, and Fu Tan University, which offered a five-year course (Unesco, 1958). The same information was repeated in the Unesco survey published in 1965 (Unesco, 1965), and is confirmed for 1968 in the 1969 *World List* of universities. [1]

The only other known institution to be engaged in mass media studies is the Chinese College of Cinematography in Peking, also referred to as the Peking Institute of Filmology, founded in 1959. It offers training for film directors and producers.

Hong Kong

Mass media studies have only been introduced into institutions of higher learning in Hong Kong since 1965. Nevertheless, both teaching and research have been energetically pursued by the two institutions with separate specialized departments in this field, the Chinese University of Hong Kong and the Hong Kong Baptist College.

Before the mid-1960s, when university-level training began, a course for training journalists was offered by the Evening School of Higher Chinese Studies operated by the Adult education Section of the Department of Education in Hong Kong.

In June 1965, the Vice-Chancellor of the Chinese University of Hong Kong announced the establishment of an undergraduate professional Department of Journalism in New Asia College, a constituent college of the university, and the creation of a Mass Communication Research Centre within the university's Institute of Social Studies and the Humanities. In the first two or three years after the establishment of the Department of Journalism and the Mass Communication Research Centre in September 1965, they were supported very largely by the Asia Foundation of San Francisco, and even after the Hong Kong Government took over the major financial burden in 1967, the foundation has continued to finance research projects and internship trips.

The organization of the department and the centre was based on a blueprint drawn up by Professor Frederick Yu of Columbia University, and since 1965 the Director of the Mass Communication Research Centre has always been a visiting professor from the United States, who teaches a course or two in the department, and conducts and co-ordinates research programmes and holds seminars at the centre. There have been six such appointments since 1965.

The Department of Journalism is in the Faculty of Commerce and Social Science. It has two full-time staff at lecturer level, and five part-time staff, all professional journalists. It has three basic aims: to train students for positions in the mass media, to prepare them for further study in their chosen fields, and to serve the profession.

The number of students admitted has been kept low deliberately, and they are chosen by selective tests from students of the Chinese University of Hong Kong who have completed their second year. About half the students have been humanities majors, a little less than half social science majors, and the rest studied pure science subjects before entering the Journalism Department. Students are encouraged to develop their previous fields of study as much as possible. There were nine graduates

---

1. No reply was received for 1969, so the information published relates to 1968.

on average between 1968 and 1970. The course is professionally oriented, with the emphasis on the practice of newspaper journalism. There is a compulsory ten-week internship period in English and Chinese language newspapers, the Government Information Services, Radio Hong Kong and commercial radio. Students publish a weekly experimental paper and other occasional publications. The successful completion of the course results in a bachelor's degree in social science. Instruction is in Chinese and English. It is intended that a one-year post-graduate programme may be offered in the Mass Communications Centre at some future time.

The Journalism Department of the Chinese University has very good relations with the local media. They support its internship programme, and interns receive about half the salary of local reporters. Two leading Chinese-language newspapers have financed eight scholarships a year since the foundation of the department, and an English-language daily has added another four since. Furthermore, local media professionals and entrepreneurs are represented on the Advisory Committee of the department and the centre.

The Mass Communications Centre is the research arm of the department. Its recent publications have included studies on communications patterns in Hong Kong, on the reading habits of Hong Kong college and middle-school students, and on freedom of information as an international problem.

A project under consideration is to establish a centre on Chinese journalism which will undertake projects on the history of modern Chinese journalism and on its technological and linguistic features, on legal and management aspects of the press, and also on broadcasting and film.

The other academic institution engaged in mass media studies is the Hong Kong Baptist College, a private college supported by religious institutions in the United States. It has a Department of Communication, founded in 1968, which offers a four-year diploma course recognized by the Hong Kong Department of Education. The programme is built more along the lines of American institutions than British or traditional Chinese. There were two full-time members of staff, and six media professionals engaged in teaching in 1971. The department is well equipped technically, having its own closed-circuit television studio, a teleprinter and monotype and offset machines.

The major course in communication includes minor options in journalism, radio-television, public relations and advertising, and cinema (since 1971). Practices and techniques of all the main media are covered as well as detailed study of the history, censorship, regulation, ethics and aesthetics of each medium, including the educational role of broadcasting. Nineteen students graduated in 1970, but because the department is new, the enrolment structure is pyramidical, and many more students are likely to graduate hereafter.

In 1970 the Department of Communication at Hong Kong Baptist College was conducting three major research projects. One, funded by the Asia Foundation, was a 'gatekeeper' study of newspapers in Hong Kong and Taipei to examine the translation sections and their impact on the selection and printing of wire-service copy. Another was a 'legibility' study, to determine the best column-widths for the Chinese-language press, also funded by the Asia Foundation. A third project, which has been under way for about five years, is a study of Chinese type composition, the aim of which is to discover ways of computerizing Chinese type-setting, which is still done manually. This study is funded by a number of interested institutions, including the Chinese Language Press Institute.

Finally, as far as non-academic institutions are concerned, it should be noted that the International Press Institute established a Chinese-Language Press Institute in Hong Kong in November 1968. Its aims are to protect the rights and privileges of the Chinese press and to uphold the freedom of the press; to hold seminars and training courses for journalists and technical staff, and arrange exchange programmes; to find ways of mechanizing Chinese newspaper type-setting; and to foster co-operation between the Chinese-language newspapers, and the development of the newpaper business through modern concepts of management.

India

India is officially committed to extensive plans of rapid social transformation covering agricultural improvement, birth control and literacy, and to the use of mass communication, including satellite communication, as a means to these ends, but an important limiting factor in this regard is seen by many informed observers to be the very limited role assigned to the training of competent professional media personnel to undertake new tasks.

Most of the education imparted in the departments of journalism that have been established in many Indian universities over the past thirty years, and more particularly in the 1960s, is almost entirely oriented to the print media, and even here the training given is not seen as being adequate.

The problems of professional training for the press and related fields reflect the influence of past traditions, and present difficulties, which affect both the media and the universities.

As far as the media are concerned poverty, illiteracy and a multitude of languages in a population of some 550 million (of whom about 80 per cent live in rural areas) spread over 1.2 million square miles, in densities varying from 1,127 persons per square mile in Kerala to 9 persons per square mile in Rajasthan, constitute the social setting in which they must operate. The press in India dates back to 1780, and newspapers equal to the best in the world have grown up. But, whether Indian newspapers supported the British Raj or espoused the cause of Indian nationalism and independence, they appealed to an élite, urban, readership, and still do and 'whether British owned or Indian owned held the mirror to Fleet Street' (Eapen, 1966).

Consequently, particularly before the Second World War, 'journalism education met with strong opposition from working journalists. Few thought that journalists needed training or that they could be trained' (Singh, 1971). This attitude is not dead today, and despite the recommendations of the Indian Press Commission of 1954 persons with a qualification in journalism do not yet have a preferential claim in the matter of employment or higher starting salaries on newspapers, although the public service commissions of the Union and state governments have been giving due weight to such candidates for jobs that require journalism skills.

But general recognition is hardly likely to come unless there is an all-round improvement in the training imparted. The Indian Press Commission recommended that a university journalism course should last three years, a general year devoted to history, sociology, economics and politics, followed by two specialized years including newspaper management and production techniques, printing and typography, press photography, radio journalism and so on. But these recommendations have not been generally followed. This has proved impossible for several reasons, including the lack of trained teachers; the fact that some departments are ill-equipped and neglected and cannot get government grants or private endowments to improve their situation; and the 'step-motherly treatment' accorded to them by professional journalists in refusing facilities for practical training. However, the founding of the Indian Association for Education in Journalism in 1956, *inter alia* to further the development of journalism training, to co-ordinate the efforts of journalism departments, and to provide a medium of contact between the profession and the training institutions, is a step in the right direction, as is the founding of the Press Institute of India in 1963.

Another development of great importance in training and research is the Indian Government's decision to establish at least one agricultural university in each state, whose courses will include agricultural communication. About a dozen of these universities have already been set up, and some, including U.P. Agricultural University at Pantnagar, Panjab Agricultural University at Ludhiana and the University of Agricultural Sciences at Bangalore have already embarked on agricultural communication activities.

University-based education in the mass media

The first attempt to provide formal training for journalism was undertaken by Annie Besant at the National University, Adyar, in Madras, in the 1920s, but it was soon discontinued as was the experimental programme set up by Aligarh University in 1938. The first department of journalism was established in 1941 at Panjab University in Lahore, which was transferred to Delhi in 1947 after partition, and finally to Chandigarh, the capital of Punjab in 1962. Madras University also established its Journalism Department in 1947, followed by the universities of Calcutta (1950), Mysore (1951), Nagpur (1952) and Osmania (1954). Although the Press Commission of 1954 strongly urged the need for trained personnel in newspapers and news agencies in India, it was only in the 1960s that more courses were inaugurated. The war with China in 1962 demonstrated the weaknesses of India's communication system, and of the Government's propaganda machinery. The Ford Foundation mass communication study team headed by Wilbur Schramm which undertook its inquiry in January and February 1963 also underlined the need for a centre for mass communications training and research (Schramm, 1963). This led to the formation in 1965 of the Indian Institute of Mass Communication in Delhi, under the Ministry of Information and Broadcasting to train government information specialists. Meanwhile Gujerat University had started a course in 1962 and Poona University in 1964. These were followed by the introduction of programmes at Gauhati, Jabalpur and Shivaji universities in 1968, and also at Ravishanker in the same period. Nagpur University which had started journalism diploma and certificate courses in 1954, and a bachelor's course in mass communication in 1964 had to close its department for financial reasons in 1966 but revived it in 1969.

Bombay University started a Bachelor in Journalism course in 1968; but the Registrar wrote in June 1970 that 'since there was no response from the students to the said course no instruction is being imparted'. Professor Singh of the Journalism Department at Panjab University reported in June 1971 that Agra University has included 'journalistic writing' as one subject for the master's degree in linguistics, that Aligarh University has drafted a scheme for a one-year Diploma in Journalism course, and that Delhi and Lucknow universities were 'toying with the idea of initiating journalism courses'.

Agricultural universities are beginning to take cognizance of mass media in their courses. Since June 1970, the Punjab Agricultural University has offered a two-year

TABLE 14. Journalism programmes in Indian universities, 1971

University	Level of instruction [1]	Duration (years)	Qualification	Practical training internship	Lab. journal	Research	Orientation
Panjab	PG	1	Bachelor of Journalism	Yes	Yes	Yes	Press, Advertising, Public relations
Madras	PG	1	Diploma	Yes	...	...	Newspapers
Calcutta	PG	2	Diploma	On own	No	No	Press
	PG	1	Master in Journalism	No	No	No	Press
Nagpur	PG	1	Bachelor of Journalism	Yes	...	Yes	Press, Public relation Advertising
Osmania	PG	1	Bachelor of Journalism	Yes	Yes	Yes	Press
Mysore	UG major		for B.A. degree	No	Yes	...	Non-professionel teaching
	PG	...	M.A. [2]	...	...	...	Newspapers
Gujerat	UG	2	Diploma	...	...	...	...
Poona	PG	1	Diploma [3]	Yes	Yes	...	Newspapers
Gauhati	PG?	1	Diploma	...	Yes	...	Newspapers
Ravishankar	PG?	1	Diploma	...	...	...	...
Shivaji	UG	1	Certificate [4]	...	...	...	Newspapers
Jabalpur [5]	PG	1	Diploma	Yes	Yes	...	Newspapers
Panjab Agricultural	PG	2	M.Sc.	...	...	Yes	Agricultural journalism and communication

1. PG = Post-graduate, UG = Undergraduate.
2. *Commonwealth Universities Handbook*, 1969.
3. Questionnaire.
4. Letter, Registrar, 6 July 1970.
5. University of Jabalpur, *Prospectus for the Examination for the Diploma in Journalism*, 1968.
Source: Singh (1971), with the exception of the above references.

programme for an M.Sc. degree in journalism. The University of Agricultural Sciences at Bangalore does not offer a programme in journalism, but the mass media are included in an undergraduate course in agricultural extension and in the M.Sc. in Agriculture course. It hopes to set up a Communication Centre for agricultural extension work which will also serve teaching and research functions. [1]

Table 14 gives a summary of journalism programmes being offered in Indian universities. It is evident that on the whole journalism departments are essentially

1. For detailed discussion on the problems of teaching and research in agricultural universities see Ward (1969).

geared to giving instruction in newspaper journalism, which usually includes practical training through a laboratory journal and a period of internship. The journalism content of the courses varies, from about 100 per cent at Panjab and Osmania universities to about 50 per cent at Madras, Calcutta, Gujerat, Poona, Gauhati and Ravishankar universities. Very little attention appears to be devoted to mass communication as such. Panjab University is the only one which demands specific knowledge—introduction to mass communications forms half of one examination paper out of eight—but Poona University combines mass communication with public relations in one examination paper out of five, and Jabalpur includes magazines, radio and television in its introduction to journalism paper. Most departments do not appear to adopt an integrated approach to mass communication as a whole, nor do they provide instruction in research methods.

One university which does so is Panjab Agricultural University, in its new M.Sc. course in journalism. Students must complete ninety credit hours, comprising fifty teaching, and forty research. The fifty teaching credits comprise twenty-five for the major discipline, journalism (including principles of journalism, editorial writing techniques, public relations, agricultural journalism, legal aspects of journalism and research methods), fifteen in a supporting discipline, English or Punjabi (including English grammar and usage, science writing, Punjabi literature, Punjabi prose, Punjabi culture) and ten credits in a minor discipline (mechanics of press, audio-visual aids, communication processes, photography). The University of Agricultural Sciences at Bangalore deals with communication and communication problems in an undergraduate and a post-graduate course given by the Department of Extension Education. The post-graduate course includes instruction on processing research information.

Non-university teaching in the mass media

The universities are not the only institutions to provide journalism training. Several private institutions offer diploma courses in journalism.

St Xavier's College, a Jesuit college in Bombay, has an Institute of Mass Communications which gives a two-year post-graduate diploma evening course in mass communications. The Bombay College of Journalism (founded 1960) run by the Hyderabad (Sind) National Collegiate Board, the Institute of Journalism, New Delhi, and the New Delhi Polytechnic for Women also run courses. The Bharatiya Vidya Bhavan Rajendra Prasad College of Mass Communication at Bombay apparently offered the first course in India on audio-visual communications (film, radio and television) in 1967. It also gives diplomas in advertising and public relations, journalism, marketing and printing. Its branches in New Delhi, Madras, Trivandrum, Bangalore, Guntur and Ahmadabad give similar courses. Several correspondence colleges also offer journalism courses.

Media organizations also provide training for journalism. The Press Institute of India in Delhi, founded in 1963, organizes in-service refresher courses, seminars and workshops. Some newspaper groups, including *The Times of India*, *The Hindustan Times*, *The Hindu* and the *United News of India*, run their own in-service training schemes.

Professional training is also conducted by government institutions. The Indian Institute of Mass Communication in New Delhi was established by the Indian Government in August 1965, the first of its kind in India. It organizes programmes for personnel in the Government of India and the states governments who are concerned with information, publicity and public relations, and also for industry. It has separate faculties for development communication, visual communication, printing and publications, radio and television, communication research, and advertising and campaign media. Since 1970 it has run a one-year post-graduate diploma course in journalism for developing countries, which covers mass communication and development, the history of journalism and its role in developing countries, news reporting and editing, radio and television journalism, press laws in developed and developing countries, and typing and stenography. It also runs other post-graduate training courses, lasting from ten days to fifteen months, oriented towards 'the problem of persuasive communication through the modern mass media of print, broadcast, film and all forms of visual communication, oral communication in its several forms and the traditional media of entertainment'. It also conducts seminars of specialists from various fields relevant to mass communications, which provide a forum for discussion and also serve to 'focus attention of the government as well as of the public on problems of national interest in which mass communication can play an effective role' (Kumar, 1970).

The Film Institute of India at Poona, the largest of its kind in Asia, was established by the Ministry of Information and Broadcasting in 1961, following on the recommendations of the Film Enquiry Committee in 1951. It offers three-year courses in screenplay writing, direction, motion-picture photography, sound recording and sound engineering, and two-year courses in film editing and film acting. All the courses involve a broad theoretical orientation as well as practical training. The institute has a full-time staff of twenty-seven and 'a few part-time teachers'. In 1968–69 there were 151 students enrolled, including 22 foreign students from Afghanistan, Ghana, Jordan, Nepal, Philippines, Singapore, Sri Lanka and Tanzania (Murari, 1969). The aim of the institute is

> that film makers should have sound technical training supplemented by cultivation of taste and a consciousness of the social responsibility of the artiste [and] of the potentialities of the film as an art-form and as a powerful means of mass communication. (India, 1970.)

There is also a separate film training centre in Madras, the Institute of Film Technology.

As far as broadcasting training is concerned All-India Radio trains its producers and staff artists at its own Staff Training School in New Delhi.

A recent development in training following on the recommendations of a group of experts from Unesco in November 1969 (Willings et al., 1969) is the setting up of a television training institute associated with the Film Institute at Poona, by the Indian Ministry of Information and Broadcasting, with the assistance of the United Nations Development Programme (UNDP), as part of a project to expand the use of the television media for adult education, family planning and intensified agricultural production. An agreement signed on 15 July 1971 between the Indian Government and UNDP lays down that UNDP will provide television equipment and experts at an estimated cost of $1.2 million, and fellowships for eighteen Indians to study abroad, while the Indian Government will provide about 11.7 million rupees (about $1.7 million) to establish the building. The project, which is being executed by Unesco, has been temporarily established in New Delhi where, up to the end of 1972, some 150 production and technical staff have undergone six-month training courses. The permanent institute in Poona will be ready by the end of 1973. Meanwhile personnel for the television centre opened in Bombay in October 1972 and for the one scheduled to open in Srinagar, are continuing to receive on-the-job training.

Mass communication research

That mass communication research is still a somewhat undeveloped field is not surprising when one considers the difficulties which exist in India. K. E. Eapen (1970) has called for the establishment of a Centre for Advanced Study in Communication which would help to identify and solve relevant communication problems in national development. In his view:

> Communication research findings on the Indian sub-continent are too meagre to make generalisations even about the major regions. Some of the existing data are based upon hurried attempts by foreigners with poor understanding of the Indian social system. Some others are replications of theory-testing, of theories developed in media saturated societies, which may have little relevance to India. Social science methodology is not among the strong weapons of the country's academic armoury, and, therefore, chunks of communication research have been poorly designed, executed and analysed.

Nevertheless, there is growing interest in various aspects of communication research in India both inside the universities and in non-university institutions. In a survey of Indian communication research, A. V. Shanmugam (1971) concluded that there had been 'an upward trend in the quantity and quality of communication research'. Although many studies were highly localized, even atomistic, some national and regional studies had been conducted. Among the most outstanding of these were the experimental study of radio farm forums (1960) sponsored by Unesco, which has inspired similar studies elsewhere, and a later study, also sponsored by Unesco on the impact of radio farm forums and other forms of social action on the diffusion of agricultural and health innovations.

At the time of this survey, the Department of Journalism at Poona University was undertaking four research projects. One member of the department was working on three two-year projects, all partly funded by the university—a readership survey of Poona newspaper readers, a content analysis of the leading articles in a Poona and a Bombay daily, and an investigation of the needs of newspaper proprietors in Maharashtra State. Another was preparing a doctoral dissertation on communication processes in Indian democracy with special reference to economic development in the Poona district. The Department of Extension Education at the University of Agricultural Sciences at Bangalore had three research projects under way: the contribution of radio and newspapers to farmers' knowledge of agricultural practices among the participants of the Farmers' Training Institute in Bangalore district, Mysore, the use of radio, newspapers, leaflets and posters in selected villages around Bangalore, and increase in knowledge due to radio listening among Farmers' Training Institute trainees. One of the members of the department of Economics and Sociology at the Panjab Agricultural University was planning to investigate the effects of the mass media.

Research is also undertaken outside the universities. The Indian Institute of Mass Communication undertakes research

> designed to fill the gaps in the present knowledge of how information reaches the people and has an impact on them. [It] has already completed several research projects and evaluation studies in this field. (Kumar, 1970.)

These include two major studies, on the flow of agricultural information at village level (1968) and on audience reactions to films screened in villages (1968). The Film Institute also undertakes research, very largely on historical and aesthetic aspects of the Indian cinema. The Press Institute of India also undertakes occasional studies on aspects of the Indian press and its quarterly publication *Vidura* provides a forum for discussion and research on the Indian mass media. The National Council of Educational

Research and Training, the National Council for Social Development, and the Division of Agricultural Extension of the Indian Agricultural Research Institute, all in New Delhi, have also done a great deal of mass communication research. The National Institute of Community Development at Hyderabad, the Central Family Planning Institute at New Delhi, the Indian Institute of Management at Ahmadabad, and the Indian Institute of Public Opinion at New Delhi have all conducted communication research. Various government departments have also actively engaged in research. They include the Department of Curricula and Evaluation, the Department of Audiovisual Education, the Department of Adult Education, various internal research units of the Ministry of Information and Broadcasting such as the Listener Research Unit of All-India Radio and the Research Cell of the Directorate of Advertising and Visual Publicity, and other bodies.

Indonesia

Journalism education in Indonesia dates back to the 1950s, the period immediately following Indonesian independence. In 1953, when a private school established in 1950 by a prominent Indonesian journalist closed down, another private institution was established in Jakarta and financed by the Indonesian Newspaper Publishers' Association and the Indonesian Journalists' Association. This graduate school, Perguruan Tinggi Publisistik, still exists, and its programmes will be discussed in more detail later. In the same year, 1953, two State universities—the University of Gadjah Mada (in Jogjakarta) and the University of Indonesia (in Jakarta) established chairs of press science. The University of Gadjah Mada began immediately to offer a three-year course leading to a bachelor's degree and a five-year master's degree course. The University of Indonesia, however, only filled its vacant chair and established a four-year major course in journalism in 1959. The late fifties and early sixties saw the establishment of other schools or departments of journalism in State and private universities including that at Padjadjaran University, Bandung (State), Hasanuddin University, Makassar (State), Ibnu Chaldun University, Jakarta (private), Alwashijah University at Jakarta and Berabai, South Kalimantan (private, now apparently defunct) and Universitas Muslimin Indonesia, Solo (private, now apparently defunct). The establishment of many of these schools in universities and other institutions was closely connected with national policy, and they were intended to promote the principles of Panjasila and Manipol/USDEK, the State ideology. They did not fully succeed, partly because of a lack of staff (Oey, 1971).

It has been extremely difficult to obtain information directly from Indonesian universities. It appears, however, that there are specialized departments of journalism or mass communications in many State and private universities. The Bambang Moertyoso Institute, a State university in Purwokerto, Central Java, has a Department of Journalistic and Publicity Studies. Diponegoro University in Semarang, Gadjah Mada University in Jogjakarta and Hasanuddin University in Makassar, are all State universities with journalism *(publisistik)* departments in their faculties of social and political science. The State University of Indonesia in Jakarta has a separate Institute for Mass

Communications, while the State University of Padjadjaran, Bandung, has a separate Faculty of Journalism and Communication Science. Three private universities, Ibnu Chaldun, and Professor Dr R. Moestopo, in Jakarta, and Sawerigading in Makassar, also have separate faculties of journalism *(publisistik)*. All these universities offer undergraduate teaching in mass media studies, and at least one, Universitas Padjadjaran, offers a post-graduate degree as well.

In a recent paper (Susanto, 1971), Astrid S. Susanto of the Faculty of Journalism and Communication Science, Padjadjaran University observed that since the media in Indonesia are not very widespread or influential, journalism schools are forced to put their stress on communication in general.

> The purpose of Indonesia's Journalism teaching programmes . . . [is] therefore to prepare people to become leaders (as journalists or opinion makers) Public Relations officers for private or government institutions, or just teachers. Communication teaching is more directed towards a co-operation between the decision makers and the decisive groups in the country on behalf of the development of the country itself.

But the history of each school also determined its teaching emphasis. For example, if the head of the department was a newspaper journalist, editorial writing and layout would be stressed, while an expert in public relations would have a different orientation. Dr Susanto also pointed out that the faculty within which the department was placed might alter its emphasis:

> when the School of Journalism at the Indonesia Universitas . . . Djakarta was part of the Faculty of Law, stress was put on law: now as a sub-division of the Faculty of Social Sciences, stress is put on Social Sciences. The adaptation to the country's conditions and needs therefore makes an inter-disciplinary approach necessary and the lack of experts and small number of teachers might in the long run lead to a re-orientation and reorganisation of the groups of faculties, changing at the same time the educational system into a major-minor relation system.

Dr Susanto illustrates the differences between different programmes by including the curricula of three universities which offer five-year undergraduate programmes—Gadjah Mada, Indonesia and Hasanuddin—and Padjadjaran, which offers a six-year programme. A study of these programmes reveals that, in contrast to other countries, like India for example, all offer some social science subjects, including social research techniques. But there are striking differences between them. Both Gadjah Mada and Hasanuddin universities have located their journalism sections within their respective department or faculty of social and political sciences. Judging from the course titles, at Gadjah Mada the course consists of twenty-one general background, and twenty-two specialized journalism courses. Half the background courses are in political subjects, the others are equally divided between social science, economics and humanities courses; while the specialized courses are strongly focused on journalism. At Hasanuddin there are eighteen background courses (one-third political, one-third social science, and one-sixth each economic and humanities) and twenty-three specialized courses, most of which relate to the media generally, and which include a strong emphasis on public opinion-related courses. At the University of Indonesia, journalism is a subdepartment within the Department of Social Sciences, and its curriculum includes twenty background compared to twelve specialized courses. Nearly three-quarters of the background courses are equally divided between social science and humanities courses, while the specialized courses apply to the mass media generally, and to a lesser extent to public opinion. Padjadjaran gives a six-year course in a separate Faculty of Journalism and Communication Science. The course comprises an almost equal number of background and specialized courses, largely humanities and politics courses, but with several social science and economics courses too, and a wide spread of specialized courses, concentrating on mass communication as a whole, but also including a good range of courses in individual media, including the press, radio, television and film.

Two State institutes of university standing, Institut Pertanian Bogor (Bogor University of Agricultural Sciences) and Institut Keguruan dan Ilmu Pendikan Sanata Dharma (Sanata Dharma Institute of Teacher Training and Education) include some teaching on the mass media, the former as part of the curricula of rural sociology and extension, the latter in the drama course and in the education curriculum.

As far as research by faculty members is concerned, those at Padjadjaran are studying changes in the Indonesian press since the 1965 revolt and plan to go on to a history of the press before 1966. The department is also co-operating with the Academy for Social Welfare in Bandung, in a survey of mass media use in Bandung, for family planning purposes. Members of the Diponegoro Department of Mass Communication are engaged on three projects—the relative effectiveness of newspapers and radio as information media in Central Java, the impact of radio in Central Java, and a survey of the Indonesian General Election campaign of 1971.

A number of tertiary-level institutions in Indonesia also provide mass media teaching. The most important is probably the Perguruan Tinggi Publisistik which is both a private teaching institution, giving instruction up to the master's-degree level in mass communications and journalism, as well as an institute for mass communication research. Students, since 1956, have been able to specialize in the study of journalism, communication arts (radio, television and film), public relations or advertising. The Sekolah Tinggi, a State institution in Bandung, Java, has separate faculties of journalism and of advertising. Two others, the Akademi Penerangan Djakarta and the Akademi Penerangan Bandung train personnel for the Ministry of Information.

Iran

Modern large-circulation newspapers developed in Iran only after the Second World War. This development posed the problem of training professional journalists. In 1955 the head of the Kayhan newspaper group who was also a professional neswpaperman and a professor of the Faculty of Law at the University of Tehran took the initiative in proposing the creation of a Faculty of Journalism at the university. The proposal was acceded to and a four-year programme was worked out with the aid of some American professors particularly interested in journalism training. But it could not be run entirely by foreigners, ignorant of the Iranian language, and Iranians competent to teach journalism could not be found, and so the scheme failed.

The Kayhan group decided to carry on itself. It provided funds for Iranians to study abroad, in France, the United Kingdom and the United States, and they, as trained professionals, took over the direction of the newspapers. It then established an Institute of Journalism in 1964 (now the Institute of Mass Communication) to run a two-year course oriented towards newspaper journalism, with the aid of the University of Tehran and visiting experts from all over the world.

Since 1966, the institute has provided a four-year course, and has been accredited by the Iranian Ministry of Education's Council of Universities, so that it may award degrees. It has four departments—journalism, cinematography and photography, public relations, and translation, and awards a bachelor's degree in each field. There are two years of general courses (social science and arts subjects) followed by a further two years in which students may specialize in journalism, radio and television; foreign languages for translation; public relations; or cinematography and photography. The emphasis is very strongly on acquiring proficiency in techniques, although there are also a few courses dealing with history, law, social impact and theory of mass media. The Journalism Department had a full-time staff of eighteen in 1970, while the translation, public relations and cinematography departments had teaching staffs of fourteen, eight and four respectively.

All the departments reported current research activity except the Cinematography and Photography Department. The projects included the history, content and use of foreign words in Iranian newspapers; techniques of translation and comparative etymology between English and Persian; and the techniques and policies of various Iranian public-relations organizations.

The Under-Secretary for Instruction and Research of the Ministry of Science and Higher Education in Iran informed this survey in November 1970 that the College of Television and Cinema, affiliated to the Organizations of National Television of Iran offered a two-year course including performing arts, directing, camera, scene scenery, organization and preparation of news reports, reporting, photography and film laboratory.

Iraq

In 1964, the University of Baghdad established the Department of Journalism in its Faculty of Arts. It offers a four-year undergraduate course for the Bachelor of Arts degree in journalism. It has six full-time teaching staff and employs two part-time media professionals. Fifty-four students graduated in 1968, the first year the qualification was offered, but the number dropped to fifteen in 1969, and sixteen in 1970.

The course is concerned mainly with aspects of the mass media in general, and the press in particular, offering comparative examples of press history from the Middle East, France, the United Kingdom, the United States and the U.S.S.R. Two members of the faculty are working for higher degrees at Moscow University, on theses concerned with the political party press in Iraq, and editing methods in the Arab press. Another presented a thesis on stylistic development in essay writing in the Iraqi press for a D.Litt. degree in Arabic language at Cairo University.

Future research is planned into the political role of the press in the U.S.S.R., research techniques in newspaper research in the U.S.S.R., and newspaper style in Egypt.

Israel

A first attempt to set up journalism training at university level in Israel was made in the mid-1950s, when a need began to be felt for specialized advanced-level training of newspaper journalists, which the short course initiated by various newspapers could not supply.

In 1954, three leading Israeli journalists took the initiative in inaugurating an undergraduate course in journalism at the School of Law and Economics at Tel Aviv. After the school was merged with the Hebrew University in 1959, the course was continued, but it is not clear whether at the Hebrew University's Tel Aviv branch or at Tel Aviv University. At first the course consisted of four years' study in the Department of Political Science as well as special courses in journalism. It was later altered to two years' study in political science, and a further two years' study in journalism (including courses on the layout of a newspaper, press and radio news, reporting, press history, economics and simple accountancy). Working journalists were given the option of taking a two-year course, leading to a certificate, instead of the four-year degree course. Nevertheless, by 1961 it was reported that 'the project got off to a slow start and six years after its beginning it appears to be foundering badly'. Courses did not always reach a uniformly high level, editors and publishers demonstrated little enthusiasm, few students took the course and even fewer completed it [1] (Isaak, 1961).

In 1956, the Department of Sociology at the Hebrew University also began introducing material on mass communications into its courses. Its orientation was academic rather than professional.

In 1965, the Communications Institute was founded in the School of Economics and Social Sciences of the Hebrew University as an interdisciplinary unit to conduct 'teaching, research and creative activities in selected fields of mass communications and interpersonal relations'. At present it has a teaching staff of thirteen full-time academic staff (most of whom hold joint appointments in other social science departments in the Hebrew University) and four part-time media professionals. There are also five full-time staff engaged in research.

The teaching emphasis of the Communications Institute is very different from the erstwhile school of journalism. The four-year undergraduate course has been replaced by a one-year post-graduate diploma, a two-year M.A. programme (sanctioned in 1970) which includes a thesis requirement, and a Ph.D. Instead of aiming at a programme of professional training, the institute rather attempts to 'give a perspective—from the vantage point of the several disciplines comprising it—on communications processes, and the various institutions in which they are embedded', but it is an integral part of this aim to give students some contact with actual professional activity. This is provided by workshops in journalism conducted by professional media practitioners, on topics like foreign correspondents, information services, public relations, radio, documentary photography and film-making. There is also a compulsory two- to three-months' internship for on-the-job training in various media organizations.

The institute's teaching curriculum consists of compulsory core courses, and specialized courses and seminars. The curriculum is organized around two main focal areas—mass communication (the processes of diffusion of information, education and entertainment from the social, psychological and aesthetic points of view) and public communication (problems of contact between bureaucracies and their publics). New

---

1. Between 1954 and 1961, about fifty students embarked on the course, and only fifteen graduated.

areas of specialization include communication in international relations and in education, and socio-linguistics.

The other universities in Israel do not offer comprehensive curricula in mass communications leading to a separate qualification, although teaching about mass media is included in other disciplinary courses. Bar Ilan University offers a course in educational television in the Department of Education, while its Department of Psychology considers the mass media in its courses on social psychology. At Tel Aviv University, two undergraduate courses on the history of journalism, and on mass media in modern society, are given in the Faculty of Social Sciences.

The American College in Jerusalem offers an introductory course in journalism as part of its English curriculum in the Humanities Division. A course in film-making was offered for the first time in 1970/71.

As far as research is concerned, the Communications Institute of the Hebrew University is the only university-based institution conducting research as part of its normal activities, some administered directly by the institute itself, and some administered through other departments of the university. Survey research is usually undertaken jointly with the Israel Institute of Applied Social Research, an independent body dating back to 1947 and chartered in 1955, specialized in field-work and data analysis in the social sciences.

In 1971, the institute had sixteen projects under way. They include two related projects concerned with assessing leisure-time activities and attitudes of a representative cross-section of the population. One project is the availability of various different cultural activities, and the construction of a 'time budget' for various activities, in connexion with the Ministry of Education's ten-year plan for culture and the arts, and on the other with studying the effects of the introduction of television on other media, on leisure activities and on values and attitudes. Another group of studies is concerned with the relations between officials and the public, including the part played by mass media. The Communications Institute and the Israel Institute of Applied Social Research also run a continuing quarterly survey of attitudes to current problems and indicators of social problems such as morals, intergroup relations, economic tensions and so on, which provides data for public agencies and for social research.

Japan

Mass media teaching in universities in Japan began in the years just before the First World War, when two private universities in Tokyo—Keio University and Waseda University—provided part-time lectures in journalism by professional journalists. In 1929 the Research Room (or Seminar) for Journalism was established in the Faculty of Letters at the University of Tokyo, a national university. Its essential function was research, but it also provided basic theoretical extra-curricular instruction to specially selected students who wished to become professional journalists. In 1932 the first department of journalism in Japan was set up at Jochi (Sophia) University in Tokyo, a private university, and modelled on that of the University of Zürich. Meiji University, also a private university in Tokyo, started a part-time journalism course soon afterwards. But the development of journalism education was halted during the Second World War, when the military government of Japan put journalism under strict control, suppressed university journalism teaching and established a vocational organization under the government Information Bureau to train journalists and to instil strictly prescribed ideas of *esprit de corps* and service to the State.

After the Second World War university teaching in journalism was much extended. This was partly due to the importance attached to journalism instruction by the Civil Information and Education Section (CIE) of the General Headquarters for the Allied Powers during the seven-year post-war occupation of Japan, which tried to encourage the American blend of practical and theoretical university level journalism training. Under the supervision of Professor Frank Luther Mott, Dean of the University of Missouri's School of Journalism, who acted as an adviser to the allied G.H.Q., several Japanese universities introduced journalism courses. Waseda University, Tokyo, inaugurated its department of journalism in 1946. In 1949 the Research Room for Journalism at the University of Tokyo was enlarged and reorganized as the Institute of Journalism with a permanent staff of three professors, three associate professors and three research assistants. In addition to its research functions, its staff, aided by prominent part-time media professionals, provided journalism instruction to fifty students a year, in a two-year course leading to a Certificate in Journalism. In the early 1950s, several Japanese universities set up departments of journalism, including Jihon (Nihon) University, Tokyo, and Kansai University, Osaka; courses in journalism were also set up at Doshisha University, Kyoto, Keio University, Tokyo, and others (Uchikawa, 1971a, 1971b). By 1958 a Unesco survey (Unesco, 1958) indicated that ten Japanese universities offered courses in journalism ranging from one to four years (Doshisha, Kansai, Keio Gijiku, Meiji, Nihon, Rikkyo (St Pauls'), Sophia, Tohoku, Tokyo and Waseda, and that nine others (Aoyama-Gakuin, Chuo, Hiroshima, Hosei, Kobe, Kyoiku, Kyoto, Nagoya and Tokoku-Gakuin) offered lectures on journalism.

Influences on university-based mass media teaching

Mass media teaching at university level in Japan has been affected by two main factors.

As several correspondents have pointed out, considerable attention is given in Japan to mass communication as a social process. All the mass media have undergone rapid progress in Japan, the technological and aesthetic standards of the media industries and their products are high, and a large amount of mass communication content is available to the population. The mass media are generally recognized as an important element contributing to the culture of the country, and it is generally accepted that university-level courses dealing with the mass media may not be inconsistent with a liberal undergraduate education. Thus many universities offer courses dealing with mass communication in various faculties and departments, including literature, education, economics and law (to name the most characteristic).

On the other hand, Japanese universities have generally not attempted to provide vocational or professional training to would-be aspirants to positions in the media, despite the attempt in the early post-war years to encourage training on the model of the American blend of courses which combine academic instruction with professional practice. Except in the natural sciences, there is no tradition in Japan of practical or technical training being offered in universities. It has therefore been difficult to introduce these aspects of education in mass media studies into the existing framework of Japanese universities. Furthermore, the system of recruitment followed by mass media enterprises has made it appear superfluous to attempt to provide practical training in the techniques of mass communication at university level.

Because there are a very large number of universities in Japan, and because the number of graduates is proportionately high, the media are able to select potential recruits for high-level positions by competitive examination. Most successful applicants are social science or literature graduates, but those with degrees in law, economics and even natural sciences are also welcomed. The media organizations on the whole prefer to train these new recruits themselves, and indeed, because of rapid technological change in media industries, are becoming increasingly concerned to provide retraining, in seminars and symposia, to experienced media professionals. The Japanese Broadcasting Corporation (NHK), the Japan Newspaper Publishers and Editors Association (NSK), and many of the large national newspapers and television networks run their own training programmes for new recruits, as do many professional associations; for example, the Association of Broadcasting Writers runs the Seminar for Scenario Writers and the Seminar for Copy Writers, the Association of Critics on Broadcasting in Japan runs the Documentary Seminar and the Advertising Creative Seminar, while the magazine *Senden Kaigi* (Propaganda Meeting) sponsors a Copy-Writing Seminar. These do not give any particular preference to university graduates [1] with academic qualifications in various aspects of mass media studies. Thus university education in journalism and broadcasting has remained theoretically oriented and has not attempted to provide practical experience for the would-be recruit to the mass media, even at the level of basic instruction.

At the same time, the number of specialized departments or full courses on the social aspects of the mass media and of mass communication is limited, and has not increased to any great extent since 1957.

Since the rate of recruitment of university graduates in journalism and mass communications to the mass media industries is not as high as might be expected, there is felt to be something ambiguous, even anomalous, in the present character of university education in journalism and mass communication, which constitutes a serious problem. The Japanese University Accreditation Association, which controls the accreditation of Japanese universities, and which has special sub-committees dealing with the accreditation of various subject areas, including journalism, has recently been partly revising the educational standards in this field. The whole problem is still under consideration and no concrete proposals have yet been made.

Extent of university-based teaching in Japan

According to the information provided by various individuals connected with university education or with media organizations in Japan, it would seem that a great many universities provide one or more courses in mass communication for undergraduates, notably in faculties or departments of sociology, literature, political science or economics. K. Goto of the NHK Theoretical Research Centre states that in 1968, 61 out of 166 public universities and colleges, and 67 out of 669 private universities and colleges, provided some courses in mass communication, including three public and twenty-two private universities which provided broadcasting courses. From the responses to this survey it appears that separate departments for mass media studies, or specialized major courses given under the aegis of other departments, are to be found in private, rather than in public universities. In fact the Institute of Journalism of the University of Tokyo is the only such specialized institution associated with a national university.

---

1. There are also a large number of so-called 'schools of miscellaneous sorts'—tertiary-level institutions which provide technical training courses lasting from one to three years in various fields including television schools and schools of photography.

Its position is in many ways unique in Japan, in that it is completely independent of the faculty structure of Tokyo University, and in that it is a large specialized research institute, whose teaching programme is, as it were, a by-product of its research activities. At the same time it offers an extremely comprehensive teaching programme to undergraduates, and is the only Japanese university institution which offers both the master's and the doctoral degree in mass communication.

The educational division of the institute provides a two-year course of extra-curricular, afternoon teaching to students who have completed their first two years of university education (known in Japan as the Course of General Arts and Sciences) at Tokyo University or elsewhere. In this respect the Tokyo University Institute of Journalism differs from most other institutions which give a specialized undergraduate course. Generally speaking, the course lasts four years with a concentration on journalism and communication subjects in the final two years. The institute admits fifty students a year by competitive examination. The thirty credits necessary for successful completion of the course are not added to the credits which its students amass in their regular course of study, which continues concurrently with their work at the Institute of Journalism. Therefore students at the institute have a double enrolment: at the institute and in other undergraduate programmes at Tokyo University or another Japanese university.

The course is intended to provide basic theoretical, not practical, instruction to students, many of whom intend to enter professions in the mass media industries. The subjects include theory of mass communication, history of mass communication, freedom of information, public opinion, comparative mass communication, international communication, survey methods, law of mass media, mass culture, industrial structure of the mass media, newspapers, broadcasting, magazines, motion pictures, publishing, news agencies, advertising and public relations.

The only other university institution which is formally constituted for research and teaching is the Institute of Mass Communication Research founded in 1958 at Keio University, a private university in Tokyo. In 1970 it had two full-time staff and employed eight part-time media professionals. It provides courses on theory and history of mass communication, social psychology, research methods and techniques, management of mass communication enterprises, introduction to broadcasting, broadcasting operation, broadcasting arts, cinema arts, comparative studies of newspapers, readings in foreign newspapers, advertising and magazine and book publishing.

In Japan, with one major exception, distinct, specialized university teaching departments for mass media studies are all departments of journalism or mass communications. The exception is Nihon (Nippon) University, a private university in Tokyo which has separate departments of cinema, and of broadcasting, in its College of Arts. The Department of Dramatics, also in the College of Arts, includes some courses on the mass media in its curriculum. Nihon University also has a specialized Department of Journalism, in the College of Law.

One of the oldest and most important of the specialized departments is the present Department of Communications (originally the Department of Journalism) in the Faculty of Literature at Sophia (Jochi) University which dates back to 1932. In 1971 it had six full-time and six part-time teaching staff, and two full-time staff on research appointments. Since 1945 it has offered a four-year programme for the Bachelor of Arts degree. There were forty-six graduates in 1970. In 1971 a master's programme lasting two years was started. Y. Kawanaka, the Chairman of the Department wrote:

> It might be as well to point out that this is the first of its kind in our country. Some other universities have offered a sort of interdisciplinary graduate program so far. But our department now can offer an independent graduate program in communications. (Kawanaka, 1971.)

Doshisha and Rikkyo (St Paul's) universities have Graduate Schools of Journalism, in which instruction for the master's degree is provided. They also provide undergraduate major courses.

Many private Japanese universities have departments of journalism or mass communications which offer undergraduate major courses only. They include the departments at Kansai University, Osaka (in the Faculty of Sociology) and at Seijo University, Tokyo (in the Faculty of Arts and Literature). The Journalism Department at Waseda University ceased registering students after April 1966, mainly due to the lack of trained staff, and its last students graduated in 1970. Henceforth its courses will be available as electives to students in the School of Political Science and Economics.

Many private universities offer full major courses in journalism or mass communications, though separate departments in these subjects have not been formally set up. They are given in the Faculty of Sociology at Kwansei Gakuin University, Nishinomiya, in the Applied Sociology Division of the Sociology Section of the Faculty of Literature at Ottemon Gakuin University, Ibaraki City, in the Department of Literature at Tokai University, Tokyo, and in the Department of Applied Sociology in the Faculty of Sociology at Toyo University, Tokyo.

Scattered individual mass media courses are compulsory or elective courses in many Japanese universities—public and private. They tend to fall within the framework of faculties or departments of education, political science, economics, sociology and arts.

International Christian University, a private university in Tokyo, includes many mass media topics in two interdisciplinary undergraduate major courses in its College of Liberal Arts: communication, and audio-visual education. The Graduate School of Education also provides a full course in audio-visual education, largely concerned with mass communication. Two national universities, Kyushu University, in Fukuoka, and Hokkaido University in Sapporo, also provide lectures and seminars on mass communication in their faculties of education.

Four universities indicated that they provided a fair amount of teaching on the mass media within the framework of political science or economics. At Gakushuin and Meiji, both private universities in Tokyo, this instruction takes place in the department of Political Science in the Faculty of Law, while the lectures and seminars at Takushoku University, also a private university in Tokyo, may be taken by undergraduates reading for degrees in politics, economics or commerce. At Kyoto University, Kyoto, a national university, lectures on journalism are given in the Economics Department.

Departments or faculties of sociology or social sciences also provide mass media courses, as for example within the School of Social Sciences of two Tokyo universities, Hosei (private) and Hitotsubachi (national). Kobe University, Kobe, a national institution, and Yahata University, Kitakyushu City, a private one, give teaching on journalism, and on mass communication respectively in their sociology departments.

University teaching on the mass media may also fall under the rubric of faculties of humanities, arts or literature. This is the case at several private universities including Atomi Gakuin Women's University, Ohtsuma Women's University, Seikei University, Senshu University and Tezukayama Gakuin University. All these institutions are located in Tokyo except the last, which is in Osaka-fu.

Mass communication research in Japan

The systematic study of mass communication in Japan dates back to the early twentieth century. The first Japanese scholars to turn their attention to the press did so under the influence of German sociologists of the Max Weber school like D'Ester,

Schone and Taub, and initiated socio-typological studies of the press, a tradition which continued to be prominent in the twenties and thirties. The second important tendency to appear before the First World War was the historical study of the press, which still remains an important aspect of mass communication research in Japan. Finally, also in the years before the First World War, as a concomitant to political opposition to the authoritarian control of the press in Japan, particularly by Marxist critics, publications appeared dealing with the political and legal aspects of press regulation, and the functions and effects of journalism in society.

After the First World War, mass communication in its modern sense took root in Japan: newspapers assumed a popular character and their circulations grew rapidly. Radio broadcasting, begun in 1925, soon attracted mass audiences, and motion pictures and popular magazines also became important communication media. In the late twenties, in addition to studies with a sociological and historical orientation, studies of the techniques of management of press enterprises, and of newspaper advertising as an aspect of management also began to appear in Japanese (Torii, 1971).

The first university institution for the systematic theoretical study of mass communication was the research office (or Research Room) for Journalism established in October 1929 as a university institute attached to the Faculty of Letters at Tokyo University. Its first director, Hideo Ono, had been a prominent Tokyo journalist and had come under the influence of German *Zeitungswissenschaft* studies. Under his direction, the Research Room provided a focus for Japanese studies of journalism on the German model, some German works on press science were used as textbooks of instruction for students, and there were lectures by visiting professors at German universities.

During the Second World War, journalism research declined, except for a few propaganda studies, but it received a great impetus in the fifties and sixties. Several reasons may be adduced to account for this. Foremost among these was the rapid extension of all the mass media—popular newspapers, magazines and comics, motion pictures, radio and, especially, television. Furthermore the guarantees of freedom of speech, of opinion and of the press, under the 1947 constitution focused renewed attention on the role of the media in the political process. Finally, in the 1950s and 1960s Japanese scholars for the first time came into contact with, and were greatly influenced by, recent American achievement in the behavioural sciences, and particularly by its empirical and statistical methods of inquiry.

Its impact on Japanese sociology was soon reflected in new approaches to the study of journalism, especially in the adoption of empirical and statistical techniques, which opened up new materials and revealed new types of findings. Empirical studies of audiences for the various media and the effects of media content have been undertaken both by academic scholars in universities as well as in the highly sophisticated investigations undertaken by research organizations attached to media institutions in Japan, notably the Radio and Television Culture Research Institute and the Public Opinion Research Institute of the Japanese Broadcasting Corporation, the Institute of Broadcasting of the National Association of Commercial Broadcasters in Japan, and the Japan Newspaper Publishers and Editors Association (NSK).[1]

Although historical study of the media still remains important, the dominant trend in contemporary Japanese mass media research is sociological or social-psychological. Professor Uchikawa (1971*a*), of the Institute of Journalism at Tokyo University, has estimated that over half the specialists in mass communication in Japanese are sociologists or social psychologists.

---

1. Detailed accounts, in English, of Japanese research on the Japanese broadcasting industry, on programming and production, on voting behaviour in relation to the mass media, and on television and the child may be found in Eguchi and Ichinohe (1971).

But perhaps the most far-reaching effect of the impact of American scholarship on Japanese research was the new conception of mass communication research as such. Before the Second World War, research on the mass media, in Japan, as elsewhere, had been almost entirely concerned with newspaper journalism. Although after the Second World War, with the rapid development of broadcasting, and especially television, motion pictures and popular magazines, these mass media began to be studied in their own right, each was studied separately, with little, if any, integrating point of view to link studies of different media. Furthermore, very many of these studies tended to be subjective and idealistic. The concept of mass communication research as the systematic, scientific and integrated study of all the mechanical media of mass communication was an enormously stimulating one and has become one of the outstanding currents in present-day Japanese research. It is partly a reaction to what is seen as the sterility of simple 'effects' studies.

The other important strand in Japanese mass media studies is the reappearance after the Second World War of a Marxist approach to journalism and mass communication. Marxist criticism of the contemporary mass communication system was one aspect of a more generalized interest in, and debate about, such issues as public opinion, and the freedom and responsibility of the press, which arose in the immediate post-war period, and which were also influenced by British political and constitutional theories. Recently Marxists have had an important influence on Japanese sociology, and this tendency has led to the critical analysis of the content and operation of the mass media and their economic and operational structure (Torii, 1971).

In general terms it may be said that in the last two decades, mass media studies in Japan have been characterized by two apparently opposing tendencies, which have, nevertheless, served to impart great vitality to the field. On the one hand, to the systematic study of newspapers has been added the study of other modern mass media, especially television, which was publicly transmitted from 1953. On the other hand, while each separate aspect of mass communication has received much more detailed and diversified study, there is also a powerful tendency to consider social communication in all its forms as a single whole. The possible tension between these two poles has had a most exhilarating intellectual effect, in serving to highlight both the differences and the similarities that may be discovered in the varied phenomena that make up the field. For example, in broadcasting research conducted by university-based institutions such as the Institute of Journalism of Tokyo University, the Institute of Human Science, Kyoto University, and the Social Psychological Centre of Hitotsubashi University, a variety of approaches have been used (including the history of broadcasting, the analysis of audiences, of programmes and of the effects of broadcasting, as well as the management and social responsibility of these media), many of which are applications to broadcasting of methods and techniques first developed in the study of newspapers, or of theories or findings of the social sciences relevant to social communication as a whole.

At the other pole, the integrated 'mass communication' approach has stimulated inquiries into theories of the process of communication both from the point of view of individual and social psychology as well as from the point of view of the social process as a whole. A further extension of this type of interest is to be seen in the appearance of a new trend of thought which emphasizes that mass communication is only an aspect of social communication as a whole, and that specialized methods designed to deal with present-day mechanical media may well be inadequate to study the processes of communication made possible by new technologies such as the computer, CATV, pocket television, video-tape cassettes, electronic newspapers, pocket telephones and other devices, which make it likely that the structure of future mass communication will be more plural, more polarized and more complicated than that of today. Therefore, to cope with these new phenomena, mass communication theories should concentrate on the effects of mass communication on the social process, rather than on the effects of mass media content on individuals.

On the other hand, the validity of a purely global approach is beginning to be challenged. Some Japanese researchers have begun to insist that theories of mass communication seen as the relationship between the stimuli provided by the mass media and their effectiveness in terms of audience response—which do not take into account differences in the content provided by entertainment, art or information—are inadequate. They feel that new theoretical principles must be formulated which can differentiate between the communication of news and other factual information—i.e. journalism—and other aspects of mass communication. The view is also expressed that

> the need has arisen to establish new principles of journalism for each branch of mass media, for example, for television and for newspapers—principles which would allow comparison of the special characteristics of each media instead of emphasising as heretofore only the general aspects of mass communication. (NSK, 1970.) [1]

It is evident from some of the discussions published in English, that mass communication research in Japan is engaged in lively controversy, and that its exponents are questioning both the theory and the methodology used in the past. Paradoxically, one evidence of the vitality of the field, is the reiteration of the feeling that Japanese studies have 'reached a sort of plateau', which is reminiscent of the mood of Bernard Berelson's famous 'obituary notice' of mass communication research in the United States in 1958. Many Japanese researchers feel that although a great many studies have been undertaken, especially in the post-war years, 'Japanese points of view have not been established in such studies, many of which were in the nature of introducing studies undertaken abroad' (Eguchi and Ichinohe, 1971). There seems to be a feeling that the 'stagnation' alluded to is partly due to the over-enthusiastic modelling of Japanese research on United States 'effects' research, and apparently there has been a re-examination of the German school of thought on journalism which dominated Japan's scholastic world prior to the Second World War, of Marxist mass communication principles, and of Japan's pre-war principles of journalism (NSK, 1970).

The extent of interest in mass media studies can be gauged from the number of specialized research periodicals and academic associations in this field in Japan. There are five specialized journals devoted to Japanese mass communications research, as well as the bulletins issued by the main universities and media organizations which publish the work of their own staffs. The Japanese Society for Studies in Journalism and Mass Communications, founded in 1951, now has a regular membership of over 500 and holds general meetings twice a year. Furthermore, the Japanese Sociological Association, the Japanese Psychological Association and the Japanese Social Psychological Association all have divisions for mass communications.

Current research

Though it is not possible to give a full picture of current research activities, information received from several institutions may give some idea of the range of research in mass communications in Japanese universities.

The Institute of Journalism at the University of Tokyo is the largest research institution of its kind in the country. In 1970 it had nineteen regular full-time staff (six

---

1. These matters were discussed at a symposium of the Japan Society for Studies in Journalism and Mass Communication on 'The Re-examination of the Principles of Journalism', held at Kansai University, Osaka, in June 1969.

full professors, seven associate professors and six research assistants). The Research Division of the institute has separate sections for theory of mass communication, history of mass communication, process of communication, media of mass communication, public opinion and propaganda, and broadcasting. Recent research has included a survey on educational and cultural programmes in broadcasting (1970), including their history and the images held of them, the policies and systems of producing and broadcasting them, attitudes of producers towards them and audience perceptions of them; two surveys undertaken in 1967 and 1968 in the Okinawa Islands before and after the introduction of television, to test its cultural effects, and a survey of communicators of community papers (1968).

The Institute of Mass Communication Research at Keio University, founded in 1958, has seven full-time staff. In 1969 an article on the agreement between Japanese and American aesthetic evaluations was published by members of its staff. Research projects planned include work on the aesthetics of the mass media, the legal regulation, content and effects of newspapers, and the history and effects of radio, in Japan.

At the Graduate School of Journalism of Doshisha University, Kyoto, six faculty members are engaged on mass media research. Recent publications include works on informational behaviour (1970) on the 'mass' era, a study of anti-war resistance in Japan, the control of freedom of speech in the Okinawa Islands, and a critique of the morality underlying entertainment programmes (1969). Present ongoing projects are concerned with the history and development of Japanese newspapers, and a study of protests during the Second World War.

At Sophia University, several members of the Department of Communications were undertaking research. Recent publications included books and articles on modern communications; the science of communication in the information age; communications theory in America; freedom of mass media in modern America; journalism education in the United States; trends in the content of the Japanese newspaper; journalism and its inherent functions; the impact of journalism on culture in America, and anti-capitalist criticism of the press. Current research in 1971 included projects on the Japanese press—past and present; international news communication through news agencies in Japan; the Japanese press and government; a socio-psychological approach to reporting, editorial policy of the newspaper in the Toisho period; the reporting of urban problems; survey of Japanese press clubs; the influence of television on the Japanese elections of December 1969; motivation appealed to in Japanese advertisement; the backgrounds for international disputes; and data process.

Current or recently concluded research reported from other universities include studies on desirable methods of regulating broadcasting in Japan and on the social functions of media-moulded information (Takushoku University); the psychological effects of the media from the viewpoint of group dynamics (Kijushu University, Fukuoka); economic aspects of news and newspapers including problems of news industrialization and the site of interpretative news (Kyoto University); the effects of a televised national election campaign measured by the semantic differential method (Gakushuin University); audio-visual and radio-television education (International Christian University) and teaching methods used in educational television and the effects of educational television programmes (Tezukayama Gakuin University, Osaka-fu).

Republic of Korea

Although some pioneer scholars in Korea began to undertake research into newspapers well before the Second World War, it was only in the mid-1950s that departments of journalism, broadcasting and newspapers, and broadcasting, were set up in colleges and universities, after the establishment of the Seoul Journalism Institute in 1947, and the introduction of journalism courses in the College of Liberal Arts and Sciences of Seoul National University in 1950 and at Yonhi University in 1953. However, most of the now existing departments concerned with mass media education and training were established in the 1960s, many of them after 1965 (Lim, 1971), as Table 15 shows.

All these universities and college departments run four-year undergraduate degree programmes. Seoul National University has a Graduate School of Mass Communication established in 1968, a professional school which provides an M.A. course and a research course. Chungang and Hanyang universities have Departments of Journalism in their graduate schools, and Ewha Women's University offers mass communication as a course of the Department of Sociology in its Graduate School.

Keun Soo Lim of the Graduate School of Mass Communication at Seoul National University points out in a paper (Lim, 1971) that the content of journalism education has much in common with that in United States journalism schools, but that some institutions teach newspaper and broadcasting subjects only, while others teach publication, communication, film, advertising and speaking techniques as well. Sogang University specializes in communications and in film. Its offerings include eight courses in mass communication (including courses in culture, the psychology of mass media, mass communication theory and practice, research methodology and audio-visual communication) and fifteen in drama and cinema, including theoretical and practical courses. Kyonghi and Sungkyunkwan universities both offer five courses in mass communications, including theory and research methodology. Chungang, Korea and Ewha Women's universities offer courses in publication, while Sungkyunkwan and Hanyang both give two courses in advertising.

Dr Lim calculated that each of the seven universities and colleges turns out about thirty graduates a year, while about 170 new reporters are annually taken on by the Seoul media (more if financial and provincial newspapers are included). But very few

TABLE 15. Date of establishment of departments of mass media studies in Korean universities and colleges

Before 1960	Between 1960 and 1964	1965 and after
Hongik College (1954) (abolished 1962)	Ewha Women's University (1960)	Korea University (1965)
		Kyonghi University (1965)
Chungang University (1957)	Hanyang University (1963)	Sungkyunkwan University (1967)
	Sorabul Arts College (1964) (abolished)	Sogang University (1968)
	Seoul National University (1963)	Pusan Hansong College (1970)
		Seoul National University Graduate School (1968)

graduates can get jobs and only after passing a separate examination, as in Japan (HKBC, 1971*b*).

It is possible that this problem may be related to some extent to the conditions of teaching in the journalism departments. Dr Lim emphasizes the shortage of books and data in Korea in relation to research, but this is also relevant to teaching. He also refers to the lack of professors who have academic training in journalism. Only three or four of the thirty-seven journalism professors originally majored in journalism, although three-quarters have working experience on newspapers or broadcasting stations. The majority majored in politics, English or Korean literature, psychology or sociology. Each professor usually teaches four subjects and a special subject including practical ones. Therefore 'it is very difficult for students to be trained as professional journalists' (Lim, 1971).

As far as research is concerned, before the Second World War, Korean scholars interested in the mass media were influenced, like those in Japan, by German *Zeitungswissenschaft*, and concentrated only on newspapers, focusing 'their concern on the historical study of mass communications, press freedom and social responsibility or the functional relationship between political power and the press'. Only in the late 1950s (several years later than in Japan) was the concept of mass communication first introduced to Korea, through the introduction of sociological approaches, such as 'the theory of functions and disfunctions of mass communications'. However, before 1963, this type of research was confined to sociologists who conducted studies on the exposure of the rural population to the mass media, and changes in their attitudes and values. In 1963, the Seoul National University established its Journalism Research Institute, and its staff 'began to conduct positive studies on mass communication in Korean society and brought about some valuable accomplishments on content analysis', using the methods of Lasswell and Berelson. Other universities at this time 'conducted audience surveys of Seoul dailies and broadcasting stations, marking great progress in the study of mass communication'.

But it was only in the later 1960s that Korean translations of American works appeared which dealt with mass communication as an integrated social process, involving the mutual relationship between communicator and recipient and 'positive effect analysis' (like Emery's *Introduction to Mass Communications*, and Wright's *Mass Communication*, both translated in 1966, and Schramm's *Mass Communication* translated in 1970).

During the 1960s, several university journalism departments introduced lectures on mass communication and some periodicals began to carry articles on the field. There are now more than ten Korean mass communication researchers who received their training in the United States who are teaching in Korean university schools of journalism and broadcasting. Although not all were trained in mass communication as a social science all use the approach of viewing mass communications as a comprehensive social process (Lim, 1971).

In addition to the eight university and college journalism departments, there are now four journalism research institutes—at Seoul National University (1963), Chungang University (1968), Korea University (1970) and the Newspaper Research Institute of the Korean Newspaper Editors' Association (1964). Many journalism students have taken their M.A. degree in mass communication, many books have been published, and many seminars held in this field in the last few years.

But Dr Lim feels that mass communication studies in Korea confront several important problems. The field is new in Korea, and one problem for Korean researchers is to choose between the different methodological traditions that have been developed, the two major ones being the

> theoretical method ... a speculative or cultural scientific method developed in German academic circles and the social survey approach ... favoured

by U.S. scholars. It is not easy to judge which is the more suitable method for journalism studies or which method is more objective. And it is a very dangerous way of thinking to cling to only one method, insisting that only that method is right.

Mass communication research in Korea is 'still at a stage of search for independent direction by adopting and digesting various advanced methods and assumptions of other countries'. Therefore the 'latest books and research [results]of advanced countries should be introduced as fast as possible' not so that Korean scholars should follow them blindly, but so that they may be in a better position to evaluate them and to find their own direction in the light of 'numerous materials from inquiring into Korean society' which are also needed. All these materials must be collected and collated, a large-scale programme which can be carried out effectively only by 'public organisations such as schools, research institutes and libraries'. Another requirement is to broaden the field from mere newspaper science to mass communication in the broadest sense, including all mass communications and personal communications, and to break down the 'invisible walls between the different sciences in Korea' which hinder the development of interdisciplinary research based on 'economics, politics history, anthropology, sociology, psychology, law, demography or folk-lore'. There is also a lag between the development of the media and the number of specialist teachers and researchers in mass communication. Finally, the problem of distribution of relevant books and data (often held in private hands, rather than made available in university departments and research institutes) and raising research funds needs to be solved.

To turn to the research of individual universities, it is known that three universities—Seoul National University, Chungang University and Korea University—have press research institutes, and that the journalism departments of Sogang, Hanyang and Ewha Women's universities also undertake research. The Readership Research Center of the Institute of Mass Communication Research at Seoul National University has published an annual survey of the Asian press since 1967. The institute regularly publishes a research bulletin, mostly in Korean, with English-language summaries. It was reported that a recent issue contained articles, mostly written by its faculty, on the history of English journalism in Korea, relative distance concept of word free association and the associative meaning; communication patterns in a Korean rural village; and human communication model and its problems. Hanyang University also has a research institute of mass communications which has been carrying out mass media audience studies since 1967. Currently it is 'concentrating on the diffusion of science news and science policy in regard to national development'. Current research at Sogang University is focused on the production and effects of educational television (HKBC 1971a, 1971b).

Lebanon

In 1969, an Institute of Journalism and Mass Communications was established in the University of Lebanon, Beirut, with the assistance of Unesco, to provide a programme of training for Arab journalists. Unfortunately no details are available at present on its activities.

The Middle East College in Beirut provides small segments of teaching in journalism and in speech.

A Department of Mass Communications is being established at the American University of Beirut. Paul B. Snyder, the Professor of Mass Communications, wrote in January 1971:

> We are anticipating . . . the establishment of such a department soon; the matter is before various committees for final action. We have our own budget and faculty but certain administrative details have to be approved before formal establishment.

Two members of staff have been appointed to the department, which intends to offer a three-year course leading to a B.A. in mass communications, to deal generally with all the mass media. The department also plans to engage in research (Snyder, 1971).

Malaysia

University-level mass media studies have only just begun in Malaysia. The new University Sains Malaysia, founded in 1969, began journalism and communication courses in June 1971 based in its School of Humanities, the first department of this kind in Malaysia. The two-year full-time programme includes courses in communication and culture, mass media and society, international communication, comparative media systems, mass communication theory, communications research techniques, developmental journalism, and courses in writing, editing, production and direction. 'The curriculum emphasises team teaching, interdisciplinary courses, generalist and specialist possibilities to students'. There are two full-time and five part-time staff, but it is intended to increase the faculty to six full-time personnel in 1973/74, when an M.A. degree programme will be offered. New facilities to include broadcasting studios and newsrooms are being planned (Lent, 1972).

The University of Malaya is also considering starting courses in this field, but at present work is restricted to the post-graduate level.

A feasibility study of the establishment of a communication programme at the MARA Institute of Technology, a tertiary-level institution, was conducted in 1971/72 by a professor of communication from Ohio University. The institute began communication courses with special reference to journalism in July 1972.

The South-East Asia Press Centre, a professional institution in Kuala Lumpur, which has connexions with the Press Foundation of Asia, runs short seminars and workshops for journalists from time to time, in which university staff and government officials participate. It was closed from May 1969 to March 1970, due to political disturbances, but since then it has conducted several training programmes for Malaysian and South-East Asian journalists. It has recently completed separate reports on the print and broadcasting media in Malaysia and Singapore.

As a result of a joint survey by Unesco and the Asian Broadcasting Union of training requirements for broadcasters in Asia, it has been proposed to set up an Asian Broadcasting Training Institute in Kuala Lumpur, as an extension of the Malaysian National Broadcasting Training Centre, which began giving short training courses

Pakistan[1]

late in 1971. The first regional courses of this centre were held in 1972, but it has been proposed that full regional operation should begin by 1975, and that it should offer a more substantial training in broadcast engineering, production, design and graphics, film, broadcast news and current affairs, and administration and management.

Mass media studies at university level in Pakistan date back to 1941, when the University of the Panjab, at Lahore, set up an evening course for a one-year diploma in journalism. In 1954, the number of lectures was increased, and the course was expanded to include courses on radio, journalism and aspects of specialized journalism. Karachi University began a one-year diploma course in 1955, with the emphasis on practical training upgraded to a two-year master's degree in 1962, and in 1955 Sind University in Hyderabad also established a department of journalism which offered a two-year course leading to an M.A. in journalism, and a one-year post-graduate diploma course (HKBC, 1971*b*; Unesco, 1958).

By 1965, a Unesco survey showed that Panjab, Karachi and Dacca universities all had departments of journalism which offered post-graduate instruction, an M.A. degree, and a one-year diploma respectively. Sind University's department had apparently been abandoned (Unesco, 1965).

As far as the content of teaching is concerned, details are available only for the Karachi M.A. course, which is given in Urdu or English.

> Courses include theory of journalism and mass media, advertising and public relations, radio and television, feature article writing and research methods also . . . editorial techniques courses.

A ten-week internship on a newspaper, news agency or radio station and a research report are both required for successful completion of the course. Sixty students in all were enrolled in 1971 (HKBC, 1971*b*).

All three university journalism departments in Pakistan (at Panjab, Karachi and Dacca universities) conduct research as well as teaching. In 1969 the Department of Journalism at Panjab University started a new journal, *Journalism*, dealing with film, radio, television and the press, and containing professional articles, journalism research reports, and abstracts of M.A. theses (*ICB*, 1969). The head of the Karachi Journalism Department has recently published an article based on a content analysis of news about Pakistan in three American news magazines, and has also written on mass communication in Pakistan. The department for the last eight years has been conducting preliminary studies on communication patterns, mainly in Karachi, and content analyses of Pakistani newspapers, and hope to publish a book on their research results soon (Richstad, 1971).

As far as other institutions are concerned, the Pakistan Press Institute, established by the Pakistan Press Foundation in 1967, has established the first School of Press

---

1. This survey was conducted in 1970 before the separation of Bangladesh.

Photography in Pakistan. A School of Practical Journalism will be set up soon and a School in Printing is planned (HKBC, 1971a).

Probationers of the Central Information Service receive professional and technical training at the State Information Services Academy at Rawalpindi. The professional part of the syllabus includes science of communication (the 'circuit' in mass communication, public opinion; effectiveness of mass communication; social responsibilities of mass media; importance of interpersonal communication in Pakistan; and propaganda), as well as social-science subjects. The technical part includes government public relations (press, publications, radio, film, television and research). Field studies and research projects are undertaken by students (Siddiqui, 1969).

Philippines

In a recent paper on journalism education in the Philippines in 1971 (East-West Center, 1971), Crispin Maslog, Director of the School of Journalism and Communications at Silliman University commented:

> Communication and journalism education in the Philippines is still in its infant stage, although the first journalism school was set up by the University of the Philippines in 1919. One reason for the slow development of journalism education . . . is the traditional disdain, indifference and suspicion that the practising journalists have had for journalism schools and their products.

The first initiative in journalism education came in 1919 when the State University of the Philippines in Quezon City invited an American professor to develop a curriculum, but the necessary budget was not finally made available. Thereafter isolated courses were given by English departments until 1936 when the University of Santo Tomas inaugurated a journalism major in the Faculty of Philosophy and Letters, leading to the degree of Bachelor of Literature in journalism. This is the oldest surviving Philippine journalism programme. [1]

In the next ten or fifteen years the Far Eastern University, Philippine Christian College, Philippine Women's University, and De La Salle College all made sporadic attempts to provide journalism courses, and the English Department of the University of the Philippines began a journalism major leading to a Bachelor of Arts or a Bachelor of Philosophy degree.

But even after the Second World War journalism education was still 'haphazard and half-hearted'. The schools were 'mostly staffed by full-time newspapermen who came to class unprepared to lecture [and] usually ended up talking about their work in the newspaper'. Also, few graduates found media employment. Most of the Manila newspapermen were not journalism graduates and lacked 'the necessary general technical background to be qualified journalists by European or American standards' (East-West Center, 1971).

The situation began to change in the 1960s. The number of universities and

---

1. Since 1964, when the university was reorganized, it has been replaced by a Bachelor of Arts in journalism and a Bachelor of Communication Arts, both offered in the new Faculty of Arts and Letters.

colleges offering mass media education increased, and the curricular emphasis began to shift from journalism to the broader field of communication. The number of full-time faculty increased too, especially in the University of the Philippines (which set up a large Institute of Mass Communications in 1965 with the assistance of Unesco) and in the Ateneo de Manila and Silliman universities which established programmes in 1966. At the same time, the Philippine Press Institute, founded in 1962,

> contributed greatly to the upgrading of the journalism profession . . . and to the refurbishing of the journalism educator's image [by] conducting seminars and institutes for working journalists and sending them abroad on various training programs, [so making] the words journalism education respectable in the eyes of the hard-nosed working newspapermen.

Mass media owners are now beginning to recognize the importance of formal training and to employ more graduates in journalism and communication.

Despite these changes, journalism and communications education in the Philippines still suffers many disadvantages. One is the lack of interest in the subject. Dr Maslog remarks that

> very little has been done or written about communication and journalism education in the Philippines . . . First of all, we don't know exactly how many communication or journalism schools there are in this country. Most communication educators themselves haven't heard about other schools outside of four or five.

Only seven of the twelve schools listed in the Philippine Press Institute directory could supply him with programme catalogues. The rest said they were still revising their curricula.

This lethargy may be partly a function of other difficulties. Only one institution, the Institute of Mass Communication at the University of the Philippines, is free from financial pressure, because it is a State university. All the others are private universities 'and must live within their limited resources'. Thus the Lyceum School of Journalism, which relies mainly on tuition fees for income, cannot afford the expensive equipment needed for technical training. Likewise, the University of Santo Tomas has only a small radio studio, and newspapers and other mass media are reluctant to accept student interns for fear of accidents. Even the Ateneo de Manila school, which gets grants from the Ford Foundation and other agencies, has insufficient facilities for radio, television and film students. It has made training arrangements for its students with commercial television stations and the State-owned National Mass Media Production Center, but this means that 'the department has to adjust to the schedules offered by the outside agencies'.

Another difficulty is lack of locally produced textbooks. The only relevant, available textbooks are American. They are expensive and must be paid for in dollars. Ateneo de Manila University attracts mainly upper-class students who could afford these textbooks, but the university lacks dollars to buy them. Silliman University has dollars, as it receives American Church support in dollars, but its students cannot afford to buy the imported textbooks. In any case, the Silliman faculty feels most American textbooks are irrelevant to the Filipino situation and what is needed is communication and journalism textbooks written 'by and for Filipinos'.

Most Philippine journalism programmes also have problems connected with teaching staff. While the Institute of Mass Communication has a large full-time trained staff, most of the other schools do not. The Lyceum of the Philippines and Santo Tomas University

> cannot afford, or do not want to hire full time faculty just to teach communication courses. Because the enrolment is relatively small [as are the number of communication courses] a faculty member might end up teaching all the subjects to all the students, which is not an ideal thing.

TABLE 16. Universities and colleges in the Philippines offering degree programmes in mass media studies, 1971

University	Unit	Degrees	Duration (years)	Emphasis
University of the Philippines (State)	(a) Institute of Mass Communication, Diliman, Quezon City Undergraduate 1965 Graduate, 1970	A.B. journalism	4	Metropolitan journalism, mass communication
		A.B. in broadcast communication	4	Theory, research, public service
		M.A. in journalism	2	Non-degree, research course
		M.A. in broadcast communication	2	Non-degree, public service
		M.A. in communication (Proposed: Family Planning Communication)	2	Course for media practitioners
	(b) College of Agriculture, Los Baños, Department of Agricultural Communication	B.S. in agricultural communication M.S. in agricultural communication		Agricultural communication
Ateneo de Manila University, Manila, (private)	Department of Communication	A.B. in communication M.A. in communication Concentration: Radio-television-film, theatre arts, journalism and advertising, public relations	1	Developmental communication, Theatre arts and mass communication — theory and practice
University of Santo Tomas Manila, (private)	Institute of Journalism and Communication Arts, Faculty of Arts and Letters. Undergraduate, 1964	B.A. in journalism	4	Metropolitan journalism, advertising and public relations
		B.A. in communication arts	4	
Silliman University Dumaguete City, Negros Oriental (private)	School of Journalism and Communication, 1966	B.J.	4	Community journalism (newspaper and radio)
		A.B. in creative writing — journalism (Minor in Journalism for B.S.E. and M.A.)	4	
Lyceum of the Philippines, Manila	School of Journalism, 1952	B.S. in journalism A.B. in journalism	4	Metropolitan, nationalistic journalism

219
Asia

Far Eastern University, Manila	Institute of Arts, 1934	A.B. in communication Major in theatre arts, speech arts, mass communication Speech and theatre arts
Central Escolar University	College of Liberal Arts	
Mary Knoll College, Quezon City	Department of Communication Arts	
Philippine Women's University, Manila	College of Liberal Arts	
St Paul's College	College of Liberal Arts	
St Theresa's College	School of Journalism and Communication Arts	
San Beda College	Department of Communication Arts	
Siena College Quezon City (private)	Journalism Department	Major in Journalism 4
University of San Agustin, Iloilo City (private)	College of Liberal Arts, Journalism Department	
University of Manila, Manila (private)	College of Liberal Arts, Journalism Department	

Sources: East-West Center, Communication/Journalism Education in Asia, Background and Status in Seven Asian Areas; Background Papers prepared for Communication/Journalism Teachers' Seminar, June 13-26, 1971, Honolulu, East-West Center, East-West Communication Institute, 1971. (Mimeo.)
Minerva, 1969; Unesco, Schools of Journalism and Communications Research Centres, January 1970, Paris, Unesco, 1970. (Com/WS/134). (Mimeo.); World of Learning, 1970.

They also find it hard to attract working professionals as full-time academic staff.

Finally, both the University of Santo Tomas and Silliman University have cause for concern in the poor quality of journalism students. Their command of English has grown poorer, since the teaching of English has been de-emphasized in the elementary and high schools. But English is still the language of journalism. This problem relates to the larger problem of what the national language of the Philippines should be.

The University of the Philippines does not have any of these problems. It has excellent facilities, a large full-time academic staff, a well-stocked library and it attracts the best students. But it has a problem ot its own,

> the problem of affluence . . . the problem of attitudes. [Its] students are rejecting the traditional concepts of journalism, which are Western in origin. For example [they] are rejecting the concept of objective journalism for the concept of committed journalism. (East-West Center, 1971.)

Table 16 indicates the universities and colleges in the Philippines which, as far as can be ascertained, offer degrees in mass media studies.

The most important of these is the Institute of Mass Communication at the University of the Philippines. Dr Maslog calls it 'the giant in almost all aspects—enrolment, faculty, facilities, resources and quality'. Its 1-million-peso building has 'spanking new facilities—air-conditioned faculty offices, library, radio and television studios and lounging areas'. It has twenty-one full-time faculty members 'led by two PhD's in mass communication who teach one or two subjects a semester, and spend the rest of the time in research and writing'. Its programmes emphasize mass communication research, theory and public service, and it concentrates on turning out journalism and broadcast-communication graduates for the metropolitan mass media. In 1970, 190 students were enrolled in its undergraduate, and fifty in its graduate programmes. The undergraduate curricula in journalism or in broadcasting comprise 146 units, fourteen of which are in required communication subjects, and six in language electives. Journalism-degree candidates must also complete eighteen required journalism units, six mass communication electives and thirty social science or humanities electives. The broadcast curriculum includes twenty-seven units in broadcast communication, nine in mass communication electives, and twenty-one in social science or humanities electives. The first two years of the programmes are taken in the College of Arts and Sciences, and the last two in the Institute of Mass Communication. There are also graduate studies in communication research, journalism, broadcast communication and film, leading to the Master of Arts degree in journalism, broadcast communication or communication.

The institute conducts a

> continuing three-pronged research program. Staff and students build up basic communication data for teaching, research and public service, and the staff conducts short-term projects geared to the needs of practitioners and policy-makers, and long-term projects tied in with national development in collaboration with governmental and private agencies. Its research programme calls for studies on the history or development of various mass communication media, [their] availability and use . . . in government information and other offices, and on the communication process [including] . . . cross disciplinary studies on communicators, messages, audiences, media and media effects. (University of the Philippines, 1971.)

The institute has six full-time research staff. It has recently begun to publish a journal for communication research.

The other unit of the Universtiy of the Philippines engaged in mass media studies is the College of Agriculture at Los Baños, Laguna. It has a specialized department of agricultural communication, and gives an undergraduate degree in this subject.

Ateneo de Manila University, like the Institute of Mass Communication, also offers an undergraduate and a graduate programme in its Department of Communication in the College of Arts and Sciences. It emphasizes 'the cultivation of critical and creative insights necessary for leadership in the areas of theater arts and mass communication in a developing Philippine society', and concentrates on theatre and film arts. It is reputed to be one of the quality communication schools. In 1970 there were two full-time and six part-time teachers, and an enrolment of sixty-five undergraduates and forty graduates in its programmes. The Bachelor of Arts programme in communications comprises twenty-four units of required communication courses (introduction to communication arts; introduction to communication research studies and techniques; survey of theater; film principles with particular reference to the Philippines; radio principles; television principles; critical writing; and independent study in communication arts) and fifteen units of elective courses, either communication or humanities and social science subjects. In addition to lectures, the department presents a film series integrated with its film courses, and periodically holds colloquia on problems and issues in theatre arts and mass communication in which students, the faculty and professionals participate. For its production courses it uses the facilities of the university's Center for Educational Television (an instructional television centre which trains teachers and school administrators) and a major commercial television station.

The Institute of Philippine Culture at the Ateneo de Manila University undertook a major research project in 1966 on communication effectiveness in the Philippines, involving a review of previous research on innovation, diffusion and credibility, and a field study on rates of exposure to various media and the credibility of various interpersonal communication services. Although later studies have included mass media exposure as one variable, the institute has not conducted another major study oriented to the mass media as such.

Silliman University is also reputed to be a quality journalism school. It is the first, and only, journalism school outside the Manila metropolitan area. It

> sees its mission as the improvement of community journalism in the Philippines ... [and] tries to produce journalism graduates oriented to working with the community press, cooperates with the Philippine Press Institute in conducting seminars and workshops for community newspapermen, and conducts research in the community press.

It has two full-time and four part-time staff, and had forty students enrolled for its bachelor's course in 1970. Its programme demands 24 compulsory and 15 optional units in communication, and 110 general units including 39 social science subjects. One of its recent research projects has been a detailed economic study of ten local newspapers.

The University of Santo Tomas has a very high enrolment in its bachelor's degree courses in journalism and in communication arts. There were 230 students enrolled in 1970. It trains its students for the metropolitan mass media. It has a staff of nine, all part-timers.

The Lyceum of the Philippines is 'wed[ded] to the goal of nationalism, in line with the nationalistic sentiments of the founders and owners of the school', the family of a late Philippine president. Their aim 'is to produce nationalistic journalists' and it has included a course in Tagalog journalism among its offerings since 1952, about one-third of its required courses in its B.J. degree are journalism, and about a quarter social science courses.

In 1970 the University of San Carlos in Sebu City was offering four graduate courses in audio-visual communication for a master's degree in education in its International Media Center. It began a systematic course in this field in 1967. Its courses focus on the instructional use of audio-visual materials, but included in a proposed new Master of Science degree in audio-visual communications are a practical course in motion-picture, radio and television production, and a theoretical course on communication media. The centre hopes its new course will qualify the graduate for a career as audio-visual communications specialist in administration of Radio-TV production, training for mass communications research in college and university media programs, communications specialist for government agencies, business, industry and military.

The centre also offers one undergraduate course in audio-visual communications in the Teachers' Training College. Previous and current research has concentrated on technical problems of introducing media systems into rural schools for large group instruction (Lasola, 1970).

The Department of Education at Central Luzon State University at Munoz, Nueva Ecija, at present offers two one-semester courses in mass communications in the agricultural education and elementary education *baccalauréat* programmes. It hopes to expand its courses as well as to undertake research in the future.

Several private Philippine universities reported that elementary journalism courses were provided by their English departments, including Foundation University in Dumaguete City; the University of Negros Occidental—Recoletos in Bacalod City; Central Philippines University in Iloilo City; and Xavier University in Cagayan de Oro City. All these institutions had contemplated expanding these limited offerings, but were hampered by lack of finance. Xavier University, for instance, operated a radio station from 1964 to 1968 and hoped to use it to train students, but was forced to close it down for financial reasons. The Central Philippines University had been prevented by lack of finance and trained staff from expanding its courses in journalism and announcing, given by the English Department, into a fully mass communications department. The University of Mindanao in Davao City also reported that the lack of professionally trained instructors in the region had hitherto prevented it from offering mass media courses, but that from 1970/71 broadcast communication subjects would be taught in the College of Liberal Arts. If these proved sufficently popular, the university plans to establish an Institute of Mass Communications in 1973.

Singapore

In 1970 Nanyang University was considering the possibility of setting up a one-year post-graduate diploma in journalism for arts graduates, or a department of journalism offering instruction for a bachelor's degree. Meanwhile, one elective general survey course on fundamentals of journalism for second- and third-year arts students, was started by the Department of Government and Administration in 1970. It covered historical, legal and ethical aspects of journalism in the press, radio and television, public relations and advertising. Another elective course on news writing was also introduced in 1970.

In February 1971, a new independent non-profit educational institution, the Asian Mass Communication Research and Information Centre (AMIC) was established in Singapore under the joint sponsorship of the Singapore Government and a German foundation, the Friedrich-Ebert-Stiftung which agreed to finance AMIC in its initial stages until it could become financially self-sufficient. The establishment of AMIC followed a meeting of Asian mass communication specialists and representatives of national and mass media organizations held in Tokyo under the auspices of the Friedrich-Ebert-Stiftung in 1967. They called for the establishment of a regional clearinghouse in mass communication in Asia to collect and disseminate basic information about mass communication in Asia, about the activities of organizations working in this field and about research findings concerning mass communication in Asia. They recommended also that group visits of journalists, broadcasters, scholars, information officers and other mass communication specialists should be organized within Asia so that they could gain first-hand knowledge of relevant activities in neighbouring countries and exchange information and experience, that research and training on a regional basis be promoted in Asia and that books and other publications on Asian problems in the field of mass communication be encouraged. These recommendations were the basis of AMIC's objectives and activities. Its primary role is to collect material pertinent to its activities from institutions and individuals in Asia and elsewhere, including published works and unpublished 'fugitive' material. AMIC has been named one of six regional centres constituting an international network for the storage, abstraction and dissemination of mass communication research material, and brings out regular lists of its holdings. It will shortly bring out a comprehensive bibliography on Asian mass communication research. It has organized travelling seminars of educators in journalism and mass communication and other conferences and symposia. It publishes a regular newsletter and a series of occasional papers on mass media, and plans to bring out a journal for Asian mass media studies.

Thailand

Mass media studies in Thailand date back to 1939, when a one-year diploma course in journalism was set up in the Faculty of Arts and Science at Chulalongkorn University, Bangkok. This course was designed for students who had successfully completed their second year in the Faculty of Arts. This full-time course was replaced by a three-year part-time course in 1940, but it had to be abandoned altogether because of the exigencies of war in 1941. It was resumed in 1948 and lasted until 1951. In 1965 an evening course in mass communications and publications, directed by a specially appointed committee, was initiated, open to students who had either successfully completed their high-school studies, or to those with a lower level of high-school education but with three years' experience in the media. The course was originally designed as a diploma course, but was then expanded into a degree course open to full-time and part-time students. Since the programme in mass communications and public relations could not be fitted into any existing department, the university, with the support of the government, decided to set up a separate department in this field in 1966, 'to promote the academic status of mass communications and public relations in Thailand, and to signify its recognition of a profession in this field in modern times'. The aims of the department are to produce effective and responsible mass communications and public relations personnel for Thailand, to contribute to a knowledge of this field among government officials and the public at large, to encourage higher standards and greater stability in the professions of mass communications and public relations, to provide research in the theory and techniques of the field, and to encourage a more extensive role for mass communications and public relations as an aid to national development. The status of the department was to be raised to that of a full Faculty of Communication Arts in 1971. Between 1971 and 1975 the faculty will be extended to include eight departments: journalism, radio and television broadcasting, cinematography, advertising, public relations, speech communication, drama, and theory and research in communication.

The course lasts four years and leads to a bachelor's degree. In the first two years the curriculum covers general subjects in the arts and social sciences as well as theoretical and technical courses in journalism, public relations and mass communication. In the last two years students can specialize in four professionally oriented fields of journalism, radio broadcasting and television (at present combined to form the mass communication section), public relations, and speech and drama. Something like 20 per cent of the total number of units of the whole course is taken up by the specialized mass communication and public relations subject courses (Bumrongsook, 1970, 1971).

When Chulalongkorn University ceased giving journalism teaching in 1951, the Thai Government opened a separate Department of Journalism in the Faculty of Social Administration of Thammasat University, Bangkok, in 1954, which began by offering an evening course in journalism, but soon set up a full-time four-year programme (Unesco, 1958). In 1966 evening classes for media professionals were also begun, leading to a certificate in journalism, which were upgraded to a diploma in 1967. In 1970 the department became an independent Department of Journalism and Mass Communications. In 1971 there were 20 full-time teachers in the department, with a total enrolment of about 350 students (Bumrongsook, 1971).

Chiengmai University, Chiengmai, also offers a four-year major course leading to a bachelor's degree in mass communication in the Mass Communication Division of its Faculty of Humanities. The course started in 1964. Over one-third of the curriculum is devoted to mass communication courses, with the emphasis on imparting training in mass media techniques, particularly in broadcasting. There are eleven full-time and five part-time faculty members in the department. An average of thirteen students have graduated between 1968 and 1970.

The social aspects of the mass media and of mass communication are touched on in the courses on audio-visual aids and on instructional media offered in the Faculty of Agriculture and the Faculty of Education at Khon Kaen University, Khon Kaen. The College of Education Prasarmit in Bangkok, and the College of Education at Pisnuloke also offer limited aspects of mass communication education in their audio-visual education courses, the former at master's, the latter at bachelor's level.

Republic of Viet-Nam

Journalism teaching is offered in the universities of Dalat and Van Hanh.

Dalat University has a School of Journalism which forms part of its Politics and Business School. The curriculum is divided into two sections: four introductory courses offered to students in their third year of the bachelor's programme in the

Politics and Business School at Dalat, and twelve professional elective courses taught in Saigon, open to research students in their fourth year at Dalat University, and to graduates of other universities. The department awards the Diploma of Bachelor in Politics and Business Management with a major in journalism, and the Certificate in Journalism to graduates of other universities. The programme is oriented towards practices and techniques of news media, especially the press, but includes courses on public relations, advertising, broadcasting and television-cinematography. The department has fourteen members of staff. There were eighteen graduates in 1968/69.

There is a Vietnam Research Centre at the university, the director of which is on the teaching staff of the Journalism Department.

The Department of Journalism at Van Hanh University in Saigon (established in 1968) has twenty-seven teaching staff and is part of the Faculty of Letters and Human Sciences. Van Hanh University offers a four-year programme leading to a Bachelor of Arts in Journalism degree. Half the courses offered are arts and social science subjects. The journalism courses are all concerned with newspaper journalism except for one on advertising and public relations. The students publish their own newspaper (HKBC, 1971a; Huyn-Dinh-Té, 1970).

Latin America

Overview

The dominant activity in mass media studies in Latin America, whether in universities or in other educational institutions, is journalism training. Haiti is the only country in the Latin American region where some attempt has not been made in the last thirty-five years or so to institute formal courses of training for journalists. Today almost every country has at least one institution which provides such education. With about a hundred schools of journalism or mass communications in 1971, most of which are associated with universities, the Latin American region taken as a whole is in the forefront of the Third World in relation to the involvement of its universities in mass media studies.

This situation is related to the fact that there is a strong concentration of the media in private ownership and a strongly partisan political press, as well as a multiplicity of universities—public and private, religious and secular, old and new. These circumstances have created demands from a number of particular interest groups (rival political newspapers, political parties, journalist associations and religious groups) for special training for journalists, while the variety of different universities that exist in the region have helped to meet these different needs. In many cases

> the provision of training for journalists [has been] the fruit of private initiative supported by action on the part of the local universities, the former consistently affording the impetus and looking to the latter to supplement or complete its efforts. (Unesco, 1958.)

Latin American universities were able to undertake the task of professional training for journalism without many difficulties in principle, unlike many universities in other regions, because their activities in all fields are geared to professionalism and vocational training rather than general education and research, and as they are organized as a loose collection of virtually autonomous faculties, institutes and schools, the introduction of a new area of professional training also posed fewer administrative problems than elsewhere. The example of the United States, where journalism training has long been undertaken by universities, has also had a strong influence in Latin America.

It is true that the idea of journalism training is still resisted as being unnecessary in certain quarters and that in some countries 'there does not exist in our mass media the journalist typical of the United States, the product of university training' (Nixon, 1970). But since the mid-thirties, the rise of an informative newspaper press and the trend towards specialization in journalistic work in Latin America has increasingly created the necessity for specialized formal training for journalism, a necessity increased by the establishment of public television enterprises in some countries and the provision in others that commercial stations devote a proportion of their time to cultural programming. After the establishment of schools of journalism in Argentina and Brazil in the mid-thirties, other countries followed with quickening speed. Colombia, Ecuador, Mexico, Peru and Venezuela all started their first schools in the 1940s, Chile, the Dominican Republic, El Salvador, Guatemala and Uruguay in the 1950s, and Bolivia, Costa Rica, Cuba, Honduras, Nicaragua, Panama and Paraguay during the 1960s. Of eighty-one schools in existence at the end of 1969, twelve were established before 1950: twenty-five were founded during the 1950s and forty-four were started in the 1960s. These facts point to an increasing, and more widespread recognition of the need for specialized training for journalism. Indeed in Brazil and Chile, legislation has already been passed 'requiring all new entrants into a wide range of journalistic occupations to have a bachelor's degree from an approved school of journalism', and there is strong pressure for similar measures to be taken in other countries including Mexico and Peru (Nixon, 1970).

In Latin America, therefore, there is undoubtedly a growing trend towards the institution of specialized pre-professional training for journalists in universities.

Nevertheless, as might be expected, there are considerable differences from country to country. At one end of the scale are Brazil and Argentina, where there is a long history of journalism training, and where a large number of institutions have been established to provide it. In Brazil alone there are now something like forty schools of journalism, while Argentina has just short of twenty. Together these two countries have well over half the total number of institutions in the whole region. At the other end of the scale are countries like Cuba, whose one journalism school, at the Universidad de la Habana, is of comparatively recent foundation, being established in 1962; the Universidad Central de Las Villas at Santa Clara was contemplating starting a school in 1971 but had not yet reached a firm decision on the point when this survey was undertaken. In Bolivia there is only one school, established in 1968: the Instituto Superior de Ciencias y Técnicas de la Opinión Pública at the Universidad Católica Boliviana in La Paz. In the Dominican Republic, for many years only one institution provided journalism training, the School of Journalism at the Universidad Autónoma de Santo Domingo, founded in 1953; the second school, a private, tertiary-level institution, the Instituto Dominicano de Periodismo in Santo Domingo, began only in 1968. Uruguay has no formal training at present. Sporadic attempts to form private schools in the 1950s failed, while the University of Montevideo's School of Journalism established in 1964 was short-lived.

The difficulty is that in the conditions prevailing in Latin America, the market for those with journalism training is rather limited, and is easily overstocked. Although as Professor Nixon notes

> not surprisingly, in some of the smaller countries and the smaller cities where journalism training is most recent . . . one finds the most cordial relations between the schools and the media [because] newspaper editors often discover that even inadequate training is better than no training at all

yet, in these very conditions, a point of saturation may soon be reached. In Paraguay, for example, where the National University's establishment of an Institute of Journalism in 1965 was followed in 1966 by the setting up of a Department of Communication Sciences at the Catholic University, there are now two journalism schools in Asunción, and fears have been voiced that new graduates will soon be unable to find employment. To counter such an eventuality, in some countries, Venezuela and Colombia, for instance, the existing schools have co-operated to prevent the proliferation of new schools and courses (Nixon, 1970). The dangers of over-expansion are particularly evident in Argentina, for example, where fully half the schools are in or near Buenos Aires, and where a large number of courses are below university level.

One reason for the tendency towards over-expansion is that journalism as a career offers opportunities for upward social mobility in an otherwise rigidly classbound society. This is achieved through the enhanced status derived from a white-collar occupation with paid holidays and annual bonuses. A study of journalists in Argentina, Bolivia and Mexico in 1965 (Day, 1968) showed that while 26 per cent reported that their fathers were working-class, only 8 per cent considered themselves as such. But an academic qualification from a journalism school does not necessarily mean a better chance of obtaining a position in the media. A survey in Brazil in 1967 revealed that less than three out of ten graduates of Brazilian journalism schools jound employment in the media. Professor Nixon concluded in 1969 that 'family and friendship ties are far more important in gaining employment in journalism than professional qualifications alone'.

This situation is partly a reflection of the conditions that obtain in the media, particularly the press, partly a function of deficiencies in the education provided by many schools. As far as the media are concerned, the level of salaries is so low that the vast majority of working journalists have to hold two or more jobs, or leave journalism for better paid work in advertising, public relations or in unrelated fields in business. Thus the professional standards in the Latin American media remain low, even in radio and television where salaries are higher than in newpapers, but where the information content is generally extremely low.

As far as the journalism schools are concerned, they share many of the same difficulties that exist in other parts of the Third World. Some of their weaknesses

> are inherent in the characteristics of higher education in Latin America . . . the predominance of both part-time teachers and students, limited funds and facilities, political disruptions, little or no opportunity for research, and lack of a broad general education as a pre-requisite for admission to professional schools.

But journalism education faces special difficulties, whether it is conceived in comparatively narrow terms of technical training for journalistic work on newspapers, or, all the more so if it is oriented towards education about mass communication as a social process within the context of the social sciences in general. These difficulties are particularly great where journalism training takes place in tertiary institutions which are either run by journalist associations or are privately owned. These schools do not require completion of a secondary-school education for entry, and their courses of study tend to be shorter than those schools which have university-level requirements. In Latin America, although some university-level schools run three-year courses, the majority now have four-year courses, and some few universities require five years' education for journalism. By contrast, tertiary-level schools usually provide courses lasting three years. In 1969, there were eight such schools in Argentina, three in Peru and two in Brazil, all giving three-year courses. One school, the Instituto Dominicano de Periodismo in the Dominican Republic, gave a two-year course. In such institutions, normally poor and badly equipped, it is very difficult to provide students with the technical and theoretical education which is most appropriate for modern mass media practitioners.

Even the education imparted by universities in Latin America has been strongly criticized by mass media owners, by students and by teachers as being deficient in many respects. One major criticism is that courses are overloaded with lectures and lack opportunities for practical experience. Most Latin American schools of journalism are very poorly equipped, especially to provide technical training for broadcasting; indeed many of them lack even such rudimentary equipment as typewriters and specialized reference books. The main reason is that most Latin American universities are very inadequately financed in any case. But journalism schools seem often to suffer more deprivation than other professional schools. One Brazilian teacher of journalism felt that one reason why journalism schools had been allowed to proliferate was that many university administrators did not even recognize that special equipment was needed, and schools were set up without taking into account this essential need. In such circumstances, the support of local media owners in helping to provide students with practical pre-professional experience is of paramount importance, and this is not always forthcoming. Another reason for inadequate instruction is that the great majority of university teachers in Latin America are part-timers—indeed Professor Nixon reported that 'not more than half a dozen schools, to my knowledge, have even one teacher who is classified as "full time" '. They therefore do not have the necessary time to devote to their students. Furthermore, very few indeed have had graduate experience in the field of mass communication, or in empirical social science research, which is a rather new and undeveloped area in Latin American universities. Consequently most curricula in journalism and mass communication lack the fructifying effect which ongoing research into the mass media in the Latin American context could have on undergraduate courses. In addition to these difficulties, in some countries there is concern that the best students are not being attracted to journalism, not only because of limited job opportunities and low pay, but because the entrance requirements for journalism are lower than those for other professional schools.

Despite these strong criticisms there is no doubt that there have been considerable advances in education for journalism and mass communication in Latin America in the past decade. A major reason has been activities of CIESPAL, the Centro Internacional de Estudios Superiores de Periodismo para América Latina (International Centre for Higher Studies in Journalism for Latin America) one of the regional centres established with the help of Unesco to improve education in journalism and mass communication. The decision to found CIESPAL arose from the resolutions of a Unesco meeting of Latin American journalists at Quito, Ecuador, in 1958, which led to a formal agreement by the Government of Ecuador and the Central University in Quito, that a regional centre be established on the university campus.

CIESPAL's work falls into three main categories: education, documentation and research. Its educational activities are directed towards improving education in mass communication by giving intensive training to the teachers in that field, through annual ten-week seminars of further training. From 1960 to 1969, these seminars brought together 61 lecturers (professors from 18 countries in North America, Europe, Latin America and Asia) and 624 students, including journalists, and directors and professors of university journalism schools from 21 Latin American countries. More than half the students have had scholarships to enable them to attend. These advanced-level courses have been concerned with the analysis of fundamental problems of mass communication, particularly in connexion with social and economic phenomena which affect the development of Latin American countries. The CIESPAL seminars have been crucial in broadening and deepening the previously simple conceptions which underlay the training provided in journalism schools. Through CIESPAL's influence new communication-oriented subjects previously unknown in Latin America, including the sociology of communication, the psychology of collective information, public opinion, and especially the scientific investigation of mass communication, have been introduced into many educational institutions, particularly universities, and have promoted a new conception of the role of the journalist, and of the mass media generally, within the functioning of society as a whole.

Its other activities have made its influence more decisive. One of its first endeavours consisted in a thorough examination of Latin American journalism education—its academic level, the types of training offered and the teaching techniques used. A seminar at Quito in 1963 considered basic principles in journalism education and its detailed recommendations have served as guidelines since. In 1966 the first Central American Round Table Conference (Mesa Redonda) adopted *in toto* CIESPAL's study plan, largely based on these recommendations. In 1965 CIESPAL organized a series of regional seminars on education for journalism and mass communication in Argentina, Brazil, Colombia and Mexico, which included representatives of the schools, media professionals in the press, radio and television, and professional organizations. The aim was to harmonize academic and educational criteria of the schools and to create cordial contacts between teachers and media practitioners. The results were collected and published, and circulated throughout Latin America.

CIESPAL maintains contact with eighty-one Latin American journalism schools. In 1969 it reported that seventy-one had introduced fundamental changes in organization and curricula based on CIESPAL's basic study plan. Changes included the adoption of the title 'information science' instead of 'journalism' by the schools, their conversion into independent faculties and institutes, the introduction of new subjects especially sociology, and psychology of mass communication, and communication research methods, and the raising of entry qualifications for students.

It has also sent itinerant experts to give courses in the journalism schools. The first, a one-mounth course on survey methods, was given in Brasilia, Lima, Buenos Aires, Medellín, Guayaquil, Mexico City, São Paulo and Porto Alegre in 1969. Its aims were to train future professors of mass communication research, to establish groups of researchers who could proceed to investigate fundamental problems of mass communication in those areas, and to clarify the methodology involved in survey methods and laboratory investigations.

It has done much to combat the obstacle to improved education in mass communication constituted by the lack of scientific texts in Spanish. It has translated and published existing texts from other languages and published new texts in Spanish on the theory, methodology and problems of mass communication. Between 1960 and 1969, fifty-four different texts (some 30,000 books) were distributed free to journalism schools, and sold at cost to interested parties in Latin America and Europe. One effect of this vigorous publication policy has been to create and standardize a Spanish-language technical and scientific vocabulary in the field of mass communication.

CIESPAL has also assembled a comprehensive collection of documentation on journalism and mass communication including works in Spanish, English and French, which is unique in the region. Since 1969 it has distributed bibliographical *fiches* including bibliographical data and abstracts of the content of the most important of these works to journalism schools in the region. This has served to systematize documentation and bibliography in a rapidly growing field. CIESPAL is one of six regional documentation centres on mass communication all over the world which co-operate to establish an international network for storing, abstracting and disseminating information about mass communication research within and between each region.

In regard to research, because, until recently, there have been few attempts at systematic, scientific research on the mass media and mass communication in Latin America, CIESPAL's role is most important. It serves two main purposes: to assemble scientific information on the mass media and mass communication, and also to provide conceptual and methodological models of research which may be used as a basis for other investigations by the schools of mass communication in particular. The course on survey methods held in 1969 was used to promote field studies in the areas where the course was held (CIESPAL, 1969).

Other institutions are also working to improve standards in mass communication education and research. One of the most important of these is the Instituto Interamericano de Ciencias Agrícolas (Interamerican Institute of Agricultural Sciences or IICA) of the Organization of American States, established in 1942 with headquarters in San José, Costa Rica, to promote the agricultural development of its member nations. One of its main tasks is to provide training in methods and techniques of agricultural communication. From 1949 to 1965 the IICA concentrated on providing middle-level training through short courses organized by its Service of Scientific Exchange in various parts of Latin America. But by 1965 it was felt that the time had come to organize a permanent post-graduate programme at a Latin American university with a strong nucleus of professors in the social sciences. The National Agrarian University of La Molina in Peru was chosen to receive this specialized course since it had a flexible administrative and curricular structure, and a number of lecturers in the social sciences. It also already had some experience in running post-graduate programmes. Therefore in 1967, with the aid of the IICA and the Consortium of Universities of the Middle West of North America (Illinois, Indiana, Michigan and Wisconsin) La Molina inaugurated the first Master of Science programme in communications. In 1969, another post-graduate programme in agricultural information began at Chapingo, in Mexico. These courses 'opened new perspectives for graduate level training to Latin American professionals interested in the theory and technique of rural communication' (Fonseca, 1970) because they were offered in Spanish and in the local context in which these future agricultural communicators would operate.

The programme at La Molina is oriented towards the interdisciplinary study of communication as a social process. It was felt that a graduate programme should solve problems as well as collect information. Therefore the main focus is on the communication process, as a basic ingredient, and an indispensable instrument, for Latin American rural development plans which are limited by the nature and quantity of information diffused within national boundaries. To achieve more efficient diffusion of information a broader conception of the communication process adapted to Latin American conditions and based on empirical, quantitative data is needed. The programme therefore emphasizes study of the processes of decision, diffusion and adoption, including the psycho-social and sociolinguistic bases of exposure, comprehension and action in countries with different subcultures, and the structural variables which limit the use of information by individuals and social groups. The courses aims at forming a 'strategic' communicator—a professional capable of analysing situations of social change, clarifying the proposed objectives for change, planning the use of media and messages, supervising its execution and evaluating its effects—a key element in high-level decision-making for development programmes. The course integrates communication, social science and agricultural subjects. The master's programme in communication and agricultural development at the National School of Agriculture at Chapingo, Mexico, has a similar orientation. Both programmes have attracted students from all over Latin America.

As might be expected, these new specialized post-graduate, interdisciplinary programmes, which place the problems of agricultural information within the total context of the communication process, have encountered some difficulties. One critical factor was the number and quality of teachers available. At La Molina, for example, only two or three professors had adequate training to teach social communications, and budgetary and institutional factors made it impossible for more to be recruited, so that a very heavy teaching load was imposed on them. Another difficulty was that five out of the six professors with doctorates had been trained at the universities of Michigan and Wisconsin 'which resulted in too one-sided and uniform an orientation in a field which would benefit from a more ample and varied theoretical focus'. Luiz Fonseca, the visiting IICA expert in charge of the La Molina programme, was led to comment in 1970 that in the light of La Molina's experience, a university should not start a postgraduate programme which involves a demanding degree of teaching and thesis supervision until it has an adequate number of permanent staff with the highest academic qualifications, preferably with a diversified academic background. To some extent La Molina's staffing difficulties reflected the lack of adequate financing, which also affected other essential prerequisites for establishing a new programme—the provision of imported textbooks and other library facilities, laboratories for practical work and research resources. In La Molina's case, the inadequate finances characteristic of all Latin American universities, and the low priority usually accorded to social-science subjects in contrast to biological subjects in agricultural universities, were compounded further by the budgetary difficulties of all universities in Peru in the late 1960s. Recently La Molina has had to fall back on financial aid from external sources interested in promoting agricultural information in Latin America. In spite of these difficulties, however, these specialized programmes in agricultural communication are attracting students from all over Latin America, and are thus helping to diffuse a more far-reaching conception of communication throughout the region, which may help to reinforce a broader, more widely based education in the schools of journalism and mass communication. Furthermore, because, as graduate programmes, they involve research into local conditions as an integral part of graduate training, they are helping to provide the necessary data for teaching and research. The research activities which are an integral part of these graduate programmes are helping to provide much needed data on communication in Latin America, which will be of value to educators and to researchers in the general field of mass media studies.

In addition to the activities of CIESPAL and IICA, other Latin American organizations are attempting to improve the standard of mass media studies. One of the most active of these groups is the Latin American Federation of Catholic Schools of Journalism which has been trying to improve the standard of education in its member schools, especially in Peru. The Latin American Union of the Catholic Press (UCLAP) in Montevideo has channelled funds from religious organizations, especially in the Federal Republic of Germany and Spain, to Catholic schools. Other organizations, including the Inter American Press Association (IAPA), the United States Information Agency, and the Thomson Foundation of Great Britain, by organizing seminars in Latin America or abroad, providing scholarships for Latin American journalists or students, and publishing material which can be used as textbooks have also helped directly or indirectly in raising the standards of mass media education in Latin America.

Despite the many sources of dissatisfaction that still exist, there can be no doubt that in the past five or ten years mass media studies in Latin America have shown great progress. Most university schools now provide a four-year course in journalism or mass communication, and a few schools even offer a five-year course. Some of the larger schools in prosperous cities, such as the Universidad de São Paulo in Brazil or the Universidad Autónoma de México in Mexico City, to name two outstanding examples, have recently revised their curricula and now offer a wide range of training in all aspects of mass communications which includes both theoretical and technical training, and which stresses the social and social-psychological aspects of communication, and research methods. Another indication of a broader outlook towards the field is that universities, especially in Brazil and Mexico, are beginning to be involved in research. It may well be that these beginnings will become signposts towards a more securely founded and broadly based conception of mass media studies in the region as a whole.

Argentina

Mass media studies in Argentina exhibit several distinctive features compared with many other Latin American countries. There is a long tradition of systematic training in journalism—Argentina was the first Latin American country to start a journalism training course. Over the years a large number of institutions have provided such training, ranging from universities to sub-university-schools both public and private. The length of the programmes offered in these different institutions varies considerably, more so than in any other Latin American country. Most of them are concentrated in or around Buenos Aires. Another distinctive feature of Argentinian journalism education is that on the whole journalism is taught in separate schools, institutes or faculties. Finally, several universities in Argentina have a special interest in cinematography, and in publicity, and offer degrees or professional titles in the subject.

As early as 1901 the first Argentinian National Press Congress agreed to a resolution proposed by the editors of the two leading Buenos Aires newspapers, *La Prensa* and *La Nación*, that a Free University and School of Journalism should be set up in Argentina. When the decision to establish the first course in journalism was taken in 1933, the initiative came from a group of journalists on *La Prensa*, working with professors belonging to the National University of La Plata, the capital of the province of Buenos Aires, situated about thirty-four miles from Buenos Aires city. A series of preparatory and advanced courses and lectures for journalists began in 1934, and in 1935, a School of Journalism affiliated to the National University of La Plata was established. The founding of the school was apparently strongly influenced by the example of the Pulitzer School of Journalism at Columbia University whose dean was one of its earliest guest lecturers.

Meanwhile another school, the Instituto Grafotécnico, had been set up in Buenos Aires city by a group of leading Catholics, including journalists on the rival Buenos Aires daily newspaper *La Nación*. It began operating in 1934. Originally it aimed mainly at training illustrators, translators and proof-readers, and later it expanded to include an Advanced School of Journalism, and other schools to train writers, cinematographers, décor artists and so on.

By 1957 there were six journalism schools in Argentina, three in Buenos Aires, one in La Plata near by, and two in the provinces, in Mar del Plata (Buenos Aires province) and San Juan (San Juan province) respectively. In addition two other provincial university schools, one in Tucumán and the other in Mendoza, had been established in 1947 and 1954 respectively, but had failed (Unesco, 1958). By 1965 there were twelve schools of journalism in Argentina, five in Buenos Aires City, three in the province of Buenos Aires (at La Plata, Mar del Plata and Martinez) and four others in Córdoba, Mendoza, San Juan and Rosario (Santa Fé province) respectively (Unesco, 1965). By January 1970, there were sixteen schools of journalism, including seven in Buenos Aires, one each in La Plata and Mar del Plata, two in Concordia, two in Rosario (Santa Fé province), and one each in Mendoza, San Juan and Salta respectively. In addition, three more university-based schools were scheduled to open in 1970, two in Buenos Aires (associated with the John F. Kennedy University and the Universidad Popular) and one in Córdoba, at the National University there (Nixon, 1970). This means that nine out of nineteen schools in Argentina are centred in Buenos Aires.

Table 17 below illustrates the age of the various schools in Argentina in 1970 and the type of institution to which they were attached. It is interesting to note that although journalism training has been carried on for nearly forty years, over one-third of

TABLE 17. Date of establishment of institutions providing journalism training in Argentina in 1970

Type of institution	Date of establishment				Total
	Before 1950	1951–60	1961–65	1966–70	
University					
Public	1	1	0	1 [1]	3 [1]
Private	0	1	0	4 [2]	5 [2]
University level					
Public	0	1	1	0	2
Private	1	0	0	0	1
Below university level					
Journalism association	0	1	0	1	2
Private	0	2	3	1	6
TOTAL	2	6	4	7	19

1. Including one to be established during 1970.
2. Including two to be established during 1970.
Source: R.B. Nixon, *Education for Journalism in Latin America*, New York, N.Y., Council on Higher Education in the American Republics, 1970.

the nineteen schools were five years old or less, and over half were ten years old or less. The table also demonstrates the variety in the types of institution which provide journalism training—universities (public and private), tertiary-level institutions (public and private) with similar entrance qualifications to universities, two schools run by professional associations, and six privately run sub-university schools. The variety of parent organizations is no doubt partly responsible for the fact that programmes offered vary between three and five years.

Until fairly recently, most journalism programmes in Latin America lasted for three years or less. Partly as a result of the efforts of the International Centre for Higher Studies in Journalism for Latin America (CIESPAL) in Quito, Ecuador, which has been pressing for higher standards in journalism education, there has been a general tendency for three-year programmes to be extended to four years. This tendency has been less marked in Argentina than elsewhere. According to Professor Nixon's survey, in January 1970, while about one-fifth of the total number of Latin American journalism schools were in Argentina (sixteen out of eighty-one) these included ten of the twenty schools with three-year programmes and eight of the thirteen schools with sub-university entrance requirements. Two of these schools, one privately run and the other belonging to a journalism association, were founded in Buenos Aires in 1969.

The Escuela Superior de Periodismo at the National University of La Plata and the Instituto Superior de Ciencias de la Comunicación (Advanced Institute of Communication Sciences) at the Domingo F. Sarmiento University in San Juan (both public universities) offer a basic programme of three years and two additional years leading to an advanced degree. They appear to be unique in Latin America in so doing.[1] The three other university-based courses are in Catholic universities, and offer

1. Only three Latin American universities offer a five-year programme: two in Mexico (the National Autonomous University of Mexico and the Iberoamerican University) and the National University of El Salvador (Nixon, 1970).

four-year programmes: in the Facultad de Ciencias de la Información, Facultad Católica de Humanidades in Rosario, Santa Fé, and the Escuela Superior de Periodismo y Ciencias de la Información at the Instituto Católico de Estudias Sociales in Buenos Aires (in process of becoming a university). It is to be expected that the three new university-based schools (at the Centre of Studies in the Sciences of Information at the Popular University, in Buenos Aires, the school to be formed at the John F. Kennedy University in Buenos Aires, and the one at the National University in Córdoba) will also have four-year programmes. There are three other journalism schools, which demand university-level entrance qualifications. One run by the Department of Schools in Mendoza gives a four-year programme. The others—at the Instituto Grafotécnico in Buenos Aires and at the Instituto de Profesiones Tecnicas in Rosario, Santa Fé, provide three-year courses.

If the change of title from 'journalism' to 'communication' or 'information' can be taken as an indication of a broadened curriculum (in line with one of CIESPAL's recommendations in 1963) it may be significant that only five of the sixteen Argentine institutions offering training programmes (including four universities) had incorporated these terms in the titles of their schools or faculties in 1970.

Three national universities and one private university offer courses in other aspects of mass media studies. The Universidad Nacional del Litoral in Santa Fé has an Institute of Cinematography and awards a professional title—*fotoreportero* (photo reporter)—after three years' study and a degree in photographic direction and production after four years. The Universidad Nacional de Córdoba has two centres concerned with cinematography: the Centre of Cinematographic Production and the Centre of Cultural Diffusion of Cinematography. Cinematographic study takes place in its School of Arts, and a four-year degree in cinematography (cinematographic technique and cinematographic direction) is offered. This university has run a biennial festival of experimental and documentary film (the fourth occasion being in 1970) which has attracted participants from all over the world. The Universidad Nacional de Cuyo in Mendoza publishes a review, *Cuadernos Cinematográficos*, and offers a programme in the subject. The private Universidad del Salvador in Buenos Aires has separate schools of television, and of arts and techniques of publicity (advertising and public relations). It awards a professional title in television, and one in advertising and public relations after three years' study and a degree (*licenciado*) in advertising and public relations after five years' study. The Catholic Institute of Social Studies (Instituto Católico de Estudios Sociales) in Buenos Aires has an Advanced School of Human Relations and Public Relations in addition to its Advanced School of Journalism and Sciences of Information.

Brazil

Brazil has the distinction of being the second Latin American country after Argentina to establish a university chair in journalism. In 1935, the Director of Education for the Federal District established a professorship in journalism in the Faculty of Philosophy and Letters at the new Federal University of Rio de Janeiro, to study journalism as a social and literary phenomenon rather than to train journalists (Nixon, 1970). But the course came to an end when the university was abolished in 1939 and replaced by the University of Brazil. In the late thirties the Brazilian Government by decree granted certain facilities to the Brazilian Press Association and obliged it in return to set up and maintain a school of journalism. After numerous discussions between the government and the association a journalism course was established in the Faculty of Philosophy at the University of Brazil in 1943, modified by further subsequent decrees to a form established by legislative decree in 1950, upon which other later journalism courses were modelled. Meanwhile, in 1947, the first school for professional training in journalism, the Caspér Líbero School of Journalism, had been established in the Faculty of Philosophy, Science and Letters at the Catholic University of São Paulo, with governmental recognition. By 1956, there were eight courses in journalism in Brazil, all at universities (Unesco, 1958).

According to a survey undertaken by R. B. Nixon in January 1970, Brazil then had twenty-four courses or schools of journalism or mass communications, twenty-two of which were at universities, or were of university level. All of these provided a four-year course. Table 18 below shows the pattern of the establishment of these courses and schools over time: it can be seen that there has been a very rapid development of mass media studies of this type since 1960, particularly in public universities.

With twenty-four schools of journalism, of which nineteen are in universities, and three more of university level (i.e. requiring a secondary-school education for admission to the diploma course), Brazil has the largest number of institutions offering training in journalism, and one-third of the fifty-eight university schools of journalism in the whole of Latin America, according to Professor Nixon's survey in January 1970. In addition, he notes that at least seven new schools were then being planned, and observes that:

> One factor pointing to a prospective further increase in the number of Brazilian schools is the Federal law decree of October 17, 1969, requiring all new entrants into a wide range of journalistic occupations to have a bachelor's degree from an approved school of journalism,

including journalism *per se* and public relations.

However, there appear to be an even larger number of institutions offering courses in communications or journalism than Professor Nixon's survey suggests. A list drawn up by CIESPAL, sent to this survey in May 1970 includes two courses, one in communications and the other in journalism, not included in Professor Nixon's list, and

TABLE 18. Number and types of university in Brazil which established mass media programmes between 1943 and 1969

Date course established	Type of university		
	Public	Private [1]	Total
1943–49	1	1	2
1950–59	2	4	6
1960–64	2	4	6
1965–67	2	1	3
1968–69	4	1	5
TOTAL (in 1970)	11	11	22

1. Including three schools not belonging to a university, but with university-level requirements.
Source: Nixon, op. cit.

another list of journalism schools in Brazil, issued by Unesco in January 1970, includes three more institutions. Assuming that all the entries in these compilations are correct there were about thirty institutions offering full programmes in journalism or mass communications at the beginning of 1970, and there are probably close on forty by now.

It is also interesting to note that in Brazil there are a considerable number of universities in which specialized units for mass media education have been formed. In most cases these specialized units are concerned with communication rather than with journalism, a possible indication of a broader orientation towards the field. Also the Brazilian Ministry of Education and Culture has recently approved the minimum curricula for communication courses (Diégues Júnior, 1970) which should help to raise standards.

In nine of the educational institutions concerned with mass media studies on Professor Nixon's list, there is a *curso* (programme) of journalism, offered in their respective faculties of philosophy, of philosophy, science and letters, or of social sciences and philosophy. They are the federal universities of Paraná, Ceará, Goiás, Juiz de Fora, Rio Grande do Sul. the Catholic University of Rio de Janeiro (Pernambuco) and the Pontifical Catholic University of Paraná. The Faculdade de Filosofia Epitacio Pessoa, a private institution, also offers a four-year programme in journalism, with sub-university entrance requirements. A university-level course in public relations is taught at the private Faculdade de Economia e Administração (Faculty of Economics and Administration), Mogí das Cruzes (São Paulo state). CIESPAL's list includes a course in communications at the Centro Universitario de Brasília (CEUB) and a journalism course in the Faculty of Philosophy, Sciences and Letters of the University of Pará in Belem do Pará. The Unesco list includes journalism courses at the Faculty of Philosophy, Sciences and Letters of the Instituto Nuestra Señora de Lourdes at João Pessoa, Paraíba, and at the Tribunal de Contas do Estado, Macció, Alagôas.

But in the remaining institutions, mass media studies are conducted in separate administrative units. The Pontifical University of Rio de Janeiro (Guanabara state) has a Department of Social Communication. The Federal University of Fluminense has an Institute of Arts and Social Communication, and the Federal University of Santa Maria at Pôrto Alegre (Rio Grande do Sul state) has an Institute of Social Communication. Several universities have attached schools for mass media studies: the Catholic University of Pelotas (journalism), the University of São Paulo (communication and arts), the Federal University of Rio de Janeiro (communication), the Federal University of Minas Gerais (communication) and the Federal University of Bahia (library science and communication). There is also a private, sub-university level School of Public Relations in Recife. There is a Centre of Human Communication in the Advanced School of Administration at the Federal University of Pernambuco, and in 1971 a Center of Studies on Information was founded at the Universitária Gama Filho, a private institution in Rio. The other universities have variously named faculties of mass media studies: the Caspér Líbero Faculty of Journalism at the Pontifical University of São Paulo, faculties of communication at the University of Brasília and the Catholic University of Santos, the Faculty of Social Communication Media at the Pontifical Catholic University of Pôrto Alegre, and the Faculty of Humanities and Communication at the Fundação Alvares Penteado in São Paulo (a private institution in process of becoming a university).

In 1963, CIESPAL recommended that schools of journalism should seek to become an 'autonomous faculty' within the university. Professor Nixon's survey found eight such units in Latin America, including five in Brazil. CIESPAL also recommended that as schools broadened their curricula they should adopt the designation of 'Sciences of Information'. In Brazil, many of the universities have adopted a variation of this term. Although titles as such are not particularly good indicators of the type and standard of course given, there would appear to be some significance, at least, in the fact that Brazilian universities have been flexible enough to implement CIESPAL's recommendations to this degree.

Nevertheless Brazil shares, with other Latin American countries, many handicaps and deficiencies in its training for journalism. A 1967 survey showed that less than three in ten graduates of Brazilian journalism schools had obtained journalistic employment. Employers interviewed in this survey stated that they did not 'object to journalism schools in principle' but only to their 'poor quality'. Newspaper editors specified that there was little relationship between the output of the schools and the job market (a complaint which Professor Nixon deemed valid, particularly in some of the larger cities, and which must surely become more deeply felt with the increasing number of schools, unless entrance requirements are raised, and the number of students limited). They also criticized the students' lack of practical experience and the 'theoretical' nature of much of the instruction, attributable to the lack of intensive training of most teachers and the lack of facilities in most journalism schools (Nixon, 1970). In view of this criticism, it is interesting to note that the University of São Paulo, which now has a very comprehensive programme, was able to place the large majority of its students in 1970. Sixteen out of twenty-one students who graduated in 1970 from the Department of Journalism and Editing in the School of Communications and Arts found work in the media of São Paulo, as did fifteen out of twenty-one third-year, and eighteen out of forty-five second-year students. The department is intending to create a placement agency for its students in 1971.

While it would not be possible to give the details of the work of all individual universities, three examples may be given to illustrate the scope of the programmes.

The most ambitious and comprehensive programme of studies takes place in the School of Communications and Arts at the University of São Paulo, which revised its structure and curriculum in 1970. All students in the school must take a basic one-semester cycle of seven courses. There are then two main teaching streams—communications (journalism, editing and publishing, public relations, publicity and propaganda, radio and television, library science and documentation) and arts (cinema, theatre, music and plastic arts), each of which has two semesters of common courses.

The various professional cycles now diverge. The communications stream has four semesters of specialized courses for journalism, editing and publishing, public relations and propaganda, and five semesters for radio and television and library science. All the arts-stream specializations last five semesters.

Judging from the printed curriculum, each of the specialities is at once diversified and broadly based, as well as comprehensive in relation to the range of techniques and theoretical knowledge necessary to its performance. For example, the journalism option includes courses in news, graphic arts, photography and various types of specialized journalism in press, radio, television and cinema, as well as law and ethics, while the editing and publishing option (in process of being developed) emphasizes printing processes, record production, translation, distribution and administration. Public relations has courses in economics, administration, human relations, public-opinion research, governmental and business public relations, tourism, and techniques of persuasive communication, while the publicity and propaganda course has more courses related to the theory and technique of advertising in all media, and so on.

The Jackson de Figueiredo School of Journalism in Santos has, since 1970, become an autonomous university school, the Faculty of Communication of the University of Santos which was then in the process of organization. The school was founded in 1955 and gave a three-year course leading to a bachelor's degree. From now on it will give a four-year professional course leading to a bachelor's degree in communication. The school employs a part-time teaching staff of thirty. It has departments of journalism, advertising and public relations and a centre of communication research.

At the beginning of 1971, 241 students were enrolled in the faculty including 130 in the first year.

The faculty's programme consists of a basic two-year cycle to provide a 'humanistic-sociological' formation followed by a two-year professional cycle which allows for specialization in journalism, advertising or public relations. All students take courses in theory of public opinion and communication, verbal expression (Portuguese and English), photography, audio-visuals and design, and social psychology. Journalism specialists have courses in printed, radio, television and movie journalism, introduction to radio and television broadcasting, and to theatre and cinema, and teaching in techniques. The advertising and public relations specialists have very similar courses, including courses on general psychology and law, and separate courses on advertising and propaganda, and advertising practices on the one hand, and on public relations, principles of administration and organization and administration of enterprises on the other. All students must complete a research project in communication to obtain the final degree.

The Pontifical Catholic University of Rio Grande do Sul in Pôrto Alegre has had a journalism course since 1952, a course in propaganda and publicity since 1965, and one in public relations since 1968, in its Faculty of Social Communication Media. Since 1968 journalism students have received practical training on the school journal as well as in training periods with newspapers, and in radio news departments. The teaching of mass communications includes journalism, television, radio and the cinema, and there are separate departments in these subjects in the specialized institute of Communications attached to the Faculty of Social Communication Media.

Mass communication research[1]

There is a comparatively weak tradition of mass media research in Brazil. Audience research for commercial purposes has been developed only comparatively recently, no doubt partly because

> the quality newspapers have been aimed at a small but educated segment of the public. Radio ... is aimed largely at a non-educated rural public, and television at the non-educated urban population.

In Brazil, research into communication media and processes started for all practical purposes in the 1940s when the Brazilian Institute of Public Opinion (IBOPE) a private market-research agency, was started. It undertakes regular audience studies, especially in relation to radio and television audiences, which it sells to propaganda agencies, communication media organizations and advertisers. Afterwards other similar firms were founded—the Institute for Opinion and Market Research (IPOM) the Institute for Social and Economic Studies (INESE) and Market Research and Planning (Marplan). The use of research for making commercial decisions is becoming more general in Brazil, which has led to the creation of market-research departments which mainly hire sociologists for their research tasks. But as the Director of the Latin American Center for Research in the Social Sciences wrote in July 1970:

---

1. This section is based very largely on a report furnished by Manuel Diégues Júnior, Director of the Latin American Center for Research in the Social Sciences (Centro Latinoamericano de Investigaciones en Ciências Sociales), Rio de Janeiro on 16 July 1970. Unless otherwise stated the quotations are from this source. Mr Diégues Júnior has largely drawn upon the account of mass communication research contained in José Marques de Melo, *Comunicação Social, Teoria e Pesquisa*, 2nd edition, Petropolis, 1971. This work contains detailed accounts of several research projects on mass communication undertaken in recent years, and a bibliography of Brazilian communication research. Cf. 'Pesquisa', p. 127–285.

> In reference to the communication media—newspapers, publishers, radio and TV stations—we find no tradition of research in our country. The few researches... performed have the objective of researching [into] decreases in circulation, [reasons for the] greater success of competitors, advertisers' forecasts etc. (Diégues Júnior, 1970.)

In the 1960s, however, some of the Brazilian universities began to form specialized research institutes for mass communication, and to give research oriented courses. Manuel Diégues Júnior writes:

> The first attempt at forming the mentality for research into communication took place in Recife, Pernambuco, with the creation of the ICINFORM (Institute of Information Sciences) at the Catholic University of Pernambuco, which has already performed a few studies in the field of journalism. [This University]... was also the pioneer institution in teaching methods and techniques of communication research, with the promotion of a course for journalism students, in 1966.
>
> The University of Brasília, with the creation of its School of Communication, integrated... research on information media with its activities, by establishing experimental organisms and offering specific courses for the training of researchers.
>
> In São Paulo [regular communication research began] at the 'Caspér Líbero' School of Journalism of the Catholic University of São Paulo [when] a Center for Research of Social Communication was created [which has] already performed several projects with the participation of the students.
>
> Also the School of Cultural Communication of the University of São Paulo is already performing field and laboratory research under the orientation of specialists in Journalism, Linguistics, Cinema, Radio and Television, as well as under the direction of teachers of Sociology, Psychology, Theory of Communication etc. This School is now preparing, to be implemented [in 1970] its Center for Research of Comparative Journalism, and the Press Museum, thus giving new incentives to the initiatives of scientific research in the area of communication nowadays.
>
> The School of Communication of the Federal University of Rio de Janeiro is now beginning to promote a few [research] activities [on an exploratory basis]. The Catholic University of Rio de Janeiro recently created its laboratory of Social Communication and Public Relations with the purpose of performing experimental projects.

Manuel Diégues Júnior also mentioned that in 1966 the Instituto Universitário de Pesquisas do Rio de Janeiro attached to Candido Mendes schools undertook a preliminary study of patterns of mass media exposure in Rio de Janeiro in collaboration with CAPES (Organ of Improvement of University Graduates) attached to the Ministry of Education and Culture.

In his recent work on *Social Communication, Theory and Research* (1971), Marques de Melo, Director of the Department of Journalism at the School of Cultural Communications of the University of São Paulo, stresses that all these research efforts by Brazilian universities have come about as a direct result of the continuous efforts of CIESPAL to diffuse a mentality of scientific research into mass communication throughout Latin America.

According to CIESPAL, two other research centres in Recife are involved in mass media research: the Centre of Human Communication in the Faculty of Administration at the Federal University of Pernambuco, and the Centro Educativo de Comunicação Social at the Faculdade de Filosofía do Recife. The Unesco list published in January 1970 states that the Faculty of Social Communication Media at the Pontifical University of Rio Grande do Sul and the Journalism Department at the Pontifical

University of Rio de Janeiro were engaged in research, which was also being undertaken in connexion with the journalism programmes at the Federal University of Rio Grande do Sul and at the Epitacio Pessoa Faculty of Philosophy in Brasília. The National Centre of Human Resources of the Institute of Social and Economic Planning (IPEA) informed this survey (Soifer, 1970) that the Centro de Communicaçoes Sociais do Nordeste (Centre for Social Communications of the North-East or CECOSNE) in Recife, was also engaged in mass communication research, and that the Fundação Alvares Penteado in São Paulo and the Instituto Nacional de Estudios Pedagogicos (National Institute of Educational Studies or INEP) was involved in mass media research to a limited degree. Furthermore members of the Instituto Universitário de Pesquisas de Rio de Janeiro (University Research Institute) and the Instituto de Estudos e Pesquisas (Institute of Study and Research) of the Federal University of Rio Grande do Sul, as well as the Ford Foundation, had recently been, or were then engaged in research involving the mass media.

Research on agricultural communications has apparently been undertaken by the Associação Brasileira de Informação Rural (ABIR) in Rio de Janeiro. At university level, research into agricultural communication has been undertaken by the Schools of Agronomy (*escolas de agronomia*) of Piracicaba (São Paulo state) and Viçosa (Minas Gerais state), as well as at the Centre of Rural Communication (Centro de Comunicação Rural) of Campinas (São Paulo state).

Finally, it should be noted that there is apparently a considerable interest in popular culture and mass culture in Brazil. A pioneer investigator and theorist in this field was Luis Beltrão at the Instituto de Ciências da Informação (Institute of Mass Communication) at the Catholic University of Pernambuco.

Central America

Journalism training in universities

University involvement in education for journalism in Central America began just after the Second World War. In 1947 the Universidad de San Carlos in Guatemala recognized the need to form a school of journalism in the area and began to organize a plan of studies with the Guatemalan Journalists Association. The first Central American Congress of Universities in 1948 and the Central American Congress of Journalists in 1951 both urged that this new proposed school should be regarded as a Central American venture, based in Guatemala. The university and the Guatemalan Journalists Association agreed to this and in 1952 the Central American School of Journalism (Escuela Centro-americana de Periodismo) was established accordingly.

But it was not long before universities in other Central American countries began to set up their own journalism schools. The first to do so was the Universidad Nacional

Autonoma de El Salvador, in 1954, followed by the Universidad Nacional Autonoma de Nicaragua in 1959, the Universidad de Panama in 1961, the Universidad Autonoma de Honduras in 1966 and the Universidad de Costa Rica in 1968. All these schools exist today, except that in Honduras which was closed in 1969 through lack of interest by students. In 1970, therefore, five Central American countries provided a systematic qualifying course in journalism.

These courses are mainly oriented towards newspaper journalism. Three of them—in Costa Rica, Nicaragua and Panama—are four-year courses. The Central American School of Journalism offers a basic three-year diploma course, leading to the professional title *perodista*, which may be converted to a *licentiatura* (equivalent to a bachelor's degree) after one year's additional study in humanities and social-science subjects, as well as a post-graduate course for practising journalists similar to the basic diploma course. The journalism course in the University of El Salvador lasts five years (Nixon, 1970; Unesco, 1958, 1965, 1970*b*).

Other mass media courses in universities

Recently two other Central American universities have begun to offer other courses in mass media. The Universidad José Simeon Cañas, a new university in El Salvador, began a two-year course in the media of social communication in 1969, dealing with journalism and mass communication, and including detailed study of the cinema. In 1970, the Universidad Rafael Landivar in Guatemala began a three-year course in publicity and advertising, leading to a professional title in co-operation with the University of San José in Philadelphia.

Other institutions

Other institutions besides universities have provided courses in journalism in Central America. Among these may be mentioned the United States Information Agency which has held short courses for practising journalists and broadcasters in El Salvador, Honduras, Nicaragua and Panama (Nixon, 1970) and the Interamerican Institute of Agricultural Sciences (IICA) of the Organization of American States, whose headquarters are in Costa Rica, and which has organized short courses in communication and technical writing related to agricultural information in Guatemala and other Central American countries (Becerra, 1970).

Chile

Chilean universities began to include journalism among their courses of training in the early 1950s. At present five universities give degrees in journalism and mass communication, two in Santiago and one each in Concepción, Valparaíso and Antofagasta. All these universities provide four-year bachelor's-level courses. In contrast to countries like Argentina, Brazil and others, where tertiary-level schools also provide journalism education, in Chile universities are the only institutions to do so. A further impetus to the concentration of mass media studies in universities, and the possible maintenance of some equivalence between their curricula is a recent law which lays down that only holders of a bachelor's degree from an approved school of journalism may enter a wide range of journalistic occupations.

The first two schools of journalism were founded round about the same time in 1953, in Santiago and Concepción, at the Universidad de Chile in Santiago, a public university, and at the private Universidad de Concepción. There was further expansion of journalism training in the early sixties. The founding of a School of Journalism by the Universidad Católica de Chile in Santiago in 1961 was followed in 1963 by the establishment of the School of Collective Communication Sciences at the Universidad de Chile de Valparaíso. The most recent school is the School of Social Communication at the Universidad del Norte in Antofagasta.

The School of Journalism at the University of Concepción undertakes research, while the Department of Political Science at the Catholic University of Chile in Santiago has been investigating the political role of mass media and intends to expand its activities in this field.

Colombia

At the beginning of 1970 five Colombian universities provided training programmes in mass communications, three in Bogotá, and two in Medellín. The earliest school to be founded, in 1949, was the School of Journalism at the Javeriana Pontifical University at Bogotá, which assumed its present designation, School of Social Communication Sciences, in 1965. It gives a four-year programme. This was followed by the establishment of another school of journalism and advertising at the private University of America in Bogotá in 1952, which has also recently assumed the title School of Communication Sciences. Its course lasts three years. There is a third school, the School of Journalism at the Jorge Trades Lozano University in Bogotá. Its date of foundation is not known, nor how long its course lasts.

The two Medellín university schools were founded in close succession, the present School of Humanities and Social Communication Sciences in the Faculty of Humanities at the Bolivariana Pontifical University in 1958, and the School of Communication Sciences in the Faculty of Education at the University of Antiquoia (a public university) in 1960. Both schools run four-year courses.

R. B. Nixon (1970) observed that

> in Medellín .. the co-operation of booming local industries and the newspaper *El Colombiano* with the two local schools of journalism has resulted in improved instruction, and facilities, especially in the growing field of public relations. The journalism facilities of the two universities, one public and the other Catholic, also have co-operated to hold the danger of overexpansion to a minimum. Although the students are predominantly women, most of them appear to find employment with business firms.

The Rector Encargo at the University del Valle, in Cali (Tono, 1970), informed this survey that there was a proposal to establish a four year *licenciatura* (bachelor's-level degree) in journalism there, by setting up either a department or a school of journalism in the Division of Humanities. Since then, a School of Journalism has been founded, attached to the Faculty of Philosophy and History. In 1971, the Universidad Autónoma del Caribe in Barranquilla also established a School of Social Communication Sciences.

As far as can be ascertained, the only institution to engage in mass media research is the School of Communication Sciences at the University of America, but no details of its activities are available.

Several non-university institutions concerned with agricultural development touch on mass media in the course of their activities. The Social Science Department of the Instituto Colombiano Agropecuario (Colombian Institute of Agriculture or ICA) has been concerned with the mass media since 1969, and planned to give an eighteen-month course on communication to start in 1971 as a minor for the Master of Agricultural Science degree. The mass communication content of the course would cover newspapers, periodicals, radio, television, the cinema, and the media generally, and would include professional ethics, structure and organization of media institutions, practices and techniques, educational role, and research methods in relation to these media. The department had ten research projects under way, concerned with the content of newspapers and radio, and the audiences for the press, radio, television and the cinema, in relation to the diffusion of agricultural innovations. The Director of the IICA-CIRA (Inter-American Institute of Agricultural Sciences of the OAS and the Inter-American Centre of Rural Development and Agrarian Reform) wrote in October 1970 that although the centre did not itself undertake training and research in communication, it planned to co-operate with the Colombian Institute of Agriculture's proposed master's programme in agricultural communication. The International Centre of Tropical Agriculture (CIAT) is also partly concerned with the mass media in its studies of innovation and diffusion.

The Sociological Research Section of the Acción Cultural Popular in Bogotá, a radio school, is undertaking three projects concerned with radio audiences in rural communities, the effectiveness of the multi-media approach in development programmes, and the influence of radio schools in the adoption of innovations.

Ecuador

There are two old established schools of information science in Ecuador: one at the Central University in Quito, the other at the University of Guayaquil (both public universities). Journalism teaching started at the Central University in 1941 as an extension course, and at the University of Guayaquil in 1945. The schools at these universities now both give a four-year course leading to a *licenciado* (bachelor's) degree. The school at the Central University is not attached to any faculty, that at Guayaquil is in the Faculty of Philosophy, Letters and Education Sciences.

No details are known about the syllabus at the Central University. In 1969 Guayaquil University's curriculum consisted of thirty-one courses over the four years, seven or eight each year. There were four courses (one in each year). These included general background courses, mostly concentrated in the first two years in Spanish, English, the organization and function of the State, and the history of political, social, economic and cultural development in Ecuador. In addition there were specialized mass media courses: introduction to information sciences and world journalism history in the first year, journalism history in Ecuador, news journalism, and graphic arts in the second year, interpretative journalism, publicity and propaganda, radio and audio-visual techniques, and Ecuadorian law in the third year, and editorial work, organization of press and broadcasting institutions, public relations, the history, organization and functioning of Latin American and international organizations, the contemporary world situation, sociology and psychology of mass communication, and press ethics and press legislation in the fourth year. In 1970 all the State universities of Ecuador were closed by the new government because of terrorism, and a new organization of courses may follow re-opening.

Ecuador is, of course, the seat of the Centro Internacional de Estudios Superiores de Periodismo para América Latina (the International Centre for Advanced Studies in Journalism for Latin America) better known as CIESPAL, one of the regional centres set up with the help of Unesco to improve education in journalism and mass communication. Its aims and activities have already been briefly outlined in the Latin American overview section.

Mexico

Mexico was one of the three Latin American countries to initiate university-level training for journalism before the Second World War, with the establishment of a journalism school at the private Universidad Feminina de México in Mexico City whose work opened up the journalistic profession to numbers of trained women graduates.

There are now about a dozen institutions in Mexico which offer courses of professional training in journalism and mass communications. The majority of these are either in universities, or else demand university-level entrance qualifications, and the training offered is in 'sciences of information' rather than 'journalism', indicating that professional education in Mexico is, generally speaking, of advanced level and broadly based, in accordance with the recommendations of CIESPAL. (It is interesting to note, however, that only three universities have established autonomous faculties of journalism or mass communications, the others still preferring to place their schools or courses within traditional academic disciplinary faculties.)

University courses in journalism and mass communication

Two universities in Mexico City now offer a five-year programme in communication: the Universidad Nacional Autónoma de México (a public university) and the Universidad Iberoamericana (a Catholic-supported university). The National University originally set up a three-year course in journalism, in its Faculty of Political Science, in 1951, which concentrated entirely on newspaper journalism. By 1965 this had become a School of Journalism within the School of Social and Economic Sciences, with a five-year course. It is now a *'carrera de ciencias de la información'* (career in information sciences) in the Faculty of Political and Social Sciences.

Its programme is a broadly based one, in which both theoretical and practical aspects of journalism are set into a communication context. Courses cover a wide field including theoretical and technical aspects of journalism, public relations, publicity and propaganda, radio, television, the cinema and press agencies, the psychology of information, sociological aspects of mass communication, journalism history and ethics, law in relation to journalism, research techniques (including historical and social research, content analysis, and the use of documentary material), style and language, printing and graphic techniques (their uses and effects), reporting, editing and administration of media enterprises. A variety of teaching techniques are used including lectures, audio-visual material, seminars, practical work, visits to media enterprises and a thesis.

The Iberoamericana University has a separate School of Sciences and Techniques of Information (Escuela de Ciencias y Técnicas de la Información) founded in 1960, that trains students for the whole broad field of mass communication: newspapers, magazines, radio, television, cinema, advertising and public relations. It has received support from local foundations and business firms, as well as from religious [Catholic] organisations; most of its graduates are finding jobs [and it] enjoys very good relations with the press. (Nixon, 1970.) In 1968 the school had two full-time and forty-eight part-time staff.

Another institution with very good relations with the press, is the Faculty of Journalism established in 1954 at the public University of Veracruz. Its facilities are also good, since the Government of the state of Veracruz in 1967 completed the construction of a new building designed especially for the Faculty of Journalism. It gives a four-year course.

Three other universities offer programmes in journalism. A three-year course is offered by the public University of Chihuahua, whose School of Journalism (founded in 1963) is attached to the Faculty of Philosophy, Letters and Journalism. The Women's University of Mexico, mentioned above, a private university, also has a *carrera* in journalism, lasting three years, as well as a School of Publicity, both attached to the Faculty of Law and Social Sciences. Another private university, the University of the Americas, in Mexico City, has a Department of Journalism which belongs to the American Association of Schools and Departments of Journalism (AASDJ). But, according to CIESPAL (1970), it merely offers various courses without conferring any title or degree in journalism.

Information was received that the School of Communication Sciences of the Universidad Autónoma de Guadalajara (consisting of a director and five other academic staff) would begin to offer two courses related to journalism from September 1970. The plans of study are based on those of the Universidad Nacional Autónoma de México, since the two universities are associated institutions. The two programmes are the *licendiado en periodismo*, an undergraduate degree course, and a shorter programme leading to the professional title of *redactor* (journalist). The *licenciado* (bachelor's degree) course covers ten semesters amounting to 300 credits (228 compulsory course credits and 72 optional course credits). The courses include background courses in politics, economics and statistics; courses on practical techniques especially in newspaper journalism and publishing but also in radio, cinema and television; public opinion; publicity and propaganda; psychology, and sociology of information; press regulation; and content analysis. From the fifth semester onwards, students take their optional courses. A wide range of choice is allowed mainly of courses dealing with contemporary politics, economics, social conditions and ideologies in Mexico and the rest of the world. A more restricted course is also offered leading to the title of *redactor* consisting of 172 compulsory course credits and 16 options, but covering essentially the same grounds. Among the future plans of the University of Guadalajara (which is in process of reorganization) is the creation of a Centre of Information (Centro de Información), including the establishment of a studio for educational film material.

Non-university courses

There are also four other non-university institutions which offer journalism programmes with university-level entrance requirements. Three private, Catholic-supported schools give four-year programmes: the Escuela de Periodismo Carlos Septien García in Mexico City, founded in 1949, its affiliate, the Institute Social Femino in Puebla (founded in 1952) and the Escuela de Ciencias y Técnicas de la Información belonging to the Instituto Humanidades Pío XII in Guadalajara (founded in 1962).

The Instituto Tecnológico y de Estudios Superiores de Monterrey, a professional educational institution, will start a six- or seven-semester course after junior college leading to a *licenciado* in communication in September 1971. The course will consist of general courses on Spanish language, foreign languages, history of culture, literary theory, sociology, psychology, social psychology, economics, social economics, accounting, cost accounting, history of culture in Mexico, law, personnel administration, as well as specialized courses in journalism, journalism techniques, radio, television, radio and television techniques, advertising and publicity media, techniques of social investigation, psychology of advertising production, professional ethics, public relations, radio and television journalism, market and advertising research, economics of an advertising institution and marketing techniques.

Finally, there is also a correspondence college, the Instituto de Capacitación de Periodistas (Institute for the Training of Journalists) founded in 1958 in Mexico City, which offers a journalism course.

Programmes in applied communications

The National School of Agriculture at Chapingo, a post-graduate college, has a Department of Agricultural Communications (Rama de Divulgación Agrícola) which started a new master's programme in communications and agricultural development in February 1969 with eight students from Colombia, Honduras, Mexico and Peru. The following year another eight entered—from Brazil, Chile, Mexico and Uruguay.

The course has practical and theoretical lectures and seminars on subjects like social psychology, the decision-making process in agricultural development, general and rural sociology, rural leadership, agricultural methods, the use of media in development programmes, the process and effects of communication, the production and use of audio-visual aids, editing in agricultural communication and so on. In seminars students examine and criticize programmes and strategies of technological change and agricultural development. The students are field officers and government information officers on leave. They get practical training by working in ongoing development programmes in the area. Each student prepares a thesis as part of the requirements for the degree. The programme has a permanent director, and has had two full-time staff on leave from the Department of Agricultural Journalism of the University of Wisconsin.

The Instituto Latinoamericano de la Comunicación Educativa (Latin American Institute of Educational Communication in Mexico City or ILCEMEX), has a School of Educational Communication (Escuela de Comunicación) attached to it, which provides courses in this field.

The following institutions are involved in mass media research: the Universidad Nacional Autónoma de México through its Institute of Social Investigation and its course on sciences of information, the School of Sciences and Techniques of Information of the Universidad Iberoamericana, the Faculty of Journalism of the Universidad Veracruzana, the Carlos Septien García School of Journalism, and the National School of Agriculture at Chapingo.

Peru

In January 1970 Peru had eight schools of journalism, four of which were in Lima (Nixon, 1970). As in many other Latin American countries, the majority of these schools (five in all) were established in the 1960s, four since 1964, indicating an increased demand for this type of training in recent years. All the schools, except two affiliated institutions run by the National Association of Journalists, are in universities, three in Catholic and three in public universities.

The first school of journalism was established at the Pontifical Catholic University of Peru in Lima in 1945. The two other Catholic university schools of journalism are of much more recent date. The Santa Maria Catholic University at Arequipa founded a school of Journalism and Public Relations in 1964, which became the Faculty of Social Communication Sciences in 1969. The San Martin de Porres Catholic University at Lima founded its School of Journalism in 1968.

Interestingly, the pattern of establishment of schools of journalism in the public universities of Peru is similar. One school, at the National University of San Marcos in Lima, was founded in 1947; the other two were founded in the 1960s—the School of Journalism at the National University of Trujillo in 1962, and the School of Journalism and Public Relations at the National University of San Antonio Abad in Cuzco in 1964. However, while the Catholic university schools are all separate administrative units, those in the public universities are connected with faculties of letters (the Faculty of Letters and Human Sciences at San Marcos National University, the Faculty of Letters and Education at Trujillo University and the Faculty of Letters and Sciences of Humanities at Cuzco National University).

The schools run by the Federation of Journalists of Peru are all called the Jaime Bausate y Mesa Institute of Journalism. The oldest one at Lima was established in

1958, an affiliated institution at Iquitos was started in 1967, and a third school was set up at Huancayo in 1970. The Instituto de Ciencias de la Comunicación (Institute of Communication Sciences) at Lima also belongs to the Federation of Journalists.

All the university schools offer four-year programmes except the Pontifical Catholic University of Peru in Lima, which runs a three-year course. The journalism association schools run three-year, sub-university entrance level courses.

As far as it has been possible to ascertain, only the Journalism School at the Pontifical Catholic University of Peru undertakes research, but no details of its work are available.

None of the university schools of journalism provide post-graduate teaching or training. The only instance of this kind in Peru at present is the post-graduate course in communication provided at the La Molina National Agrarian University, in collaboration with the Inter-American Institute of Agricultural Sciences (IICA) of the Organization of American States. This programme was the first of its kind in Latin America, and was inaugurated in 1967. It has attracted students from all over Latin America. Despite the many difficulties it has had to face, some of which have been briefly alluded to in the Latin American overview, it has made a genuine contribution to university education in mass media studies not only in Peru, but in the Latin American region as a whole.

Enrolment in the communication programme at La Molina is open to all students with previous knowledge of social psychology, sociology, social science methodology and statistics. The curriculum includes courses up to graduate level chosen from a complementary field: agricultural economics, sociology, phytopathology, genetic amelioration, nutrition, soils, agricultural engineering, entymology or animal production. Students take eight courses in the main field of communication: communication theory, mass media (particularly in relation to development programmes), communication in formal organizations, (especially in relation to decision-making), communication and persuasion, intercultural communication in relation to modernization programmes, psycholinguistics, communication of innovations in social transformation, (theory and strategies) and advanced rural sociology (applied to socio-economic development in rural Latin America). There are also seminars on special communication problems which influence programmes of social action, and on new projects in communication research, related to students' theses.

In order to test communication theories in an actual communication situation, the university has decided to establish a Centre of Communication. This will serve both as an instrument of university extension to diffuse the results of biological and social investigation, and as an instrument for research projects in communication related to the diffusion of technological information in the rural areas of Peru, which are at present passing through a period of profound social transformation caused by the process of agrarian reform, which is modifying the whole rural structure (Fonseca, 1970).

Venezuela

Journalism training began in Venezuela in 1947, when a School of Journalism was established at the Central University of Caracas, on the advice of the Dean of the Columbia School of Journalism. At first the school operated as an independent unit but in 1954 it was reorganized, and placed in the Faculty of Humanities and Education so that the teaching could combine cultural background studies with technical training, including the publication of an experimental periodical, the university bulletin. The course lasts four years and leads to a *licenciado* in journalism. Since 1957 it has included courses in radio and television, journalism and newspaper illustration, as well as several modern languages. In May 1970, the curriculum of the school was changed, and it was renamed the School of Social Communication, but no details are available on its offerings.

Two years later, the Andrés Bello Catholic University in Caracas established a School of Journalism and Sciences of Social Communication in the Faculty of Humanities and Education. In 1969 its staff included two professors and one associate teaching radio-television, two professors and one associate teaching journalism, the same number teaching publicity, two professors of graphic techniques, as well as others teaching public relations, news journalism in Latin America, ethics and public opinion, public-opinion research, cinematography, photography, press legislation, Venezuelan history and journalism, and editing. In his survey of Latin American journalism, R. B. Nixon (1970) commented on the 'broad programme of courses' given at the Andrés Bello school, and noted that it had 'been particularly successful in placing its graduates'.

It appears from Professor Nixon's account that Venezuela is one of the few Latin American countries where the training of journalists in the schools has not exceeded the demand, partly because the existing schools have co-operated to prevent new schools being founded.

Both the Central University at Caracas and the Andrés Bello University have separate research institutions concerned with mass media research. No details are available for the work of the Institute of Press Research at the Central University, but in 1970 two full-time staff at the Centre for Studies of the Future (Centro de Estudios del Futuro de Venezuela) at Andrés Bello University were engaged in a privately funded project lasting one and a half years, entitled 'Media in Venezuela, a Prospective Approach (Diagnosis, Projections, Desirable Future)'. The School of Journalism at the University of Zulia also undertakes research but no details are available about its activities.

Conclusion

It now remains to draw together some of the threads that have appeared in the discussions on the development of mass media studies in the different regions of the world. The main body of the report has attempted to show the diversity of forces which have shaped this field in different times and places, and to illustrate the evident fact that there may be considerable variations even between institutions in the same country, quite apart from differences between different countries in a particular region. Enough has been said to make it clear that any generalizations are likely to have important exceptions. Nevertheless, it may be useful to attempt some broad, though necessarily tentative conclusions covering the development of mass media studies in the world as a whole, first by drawing on the evidence derived from the survey questionnaires, and then by discussing some facets of the present state of mass media studies as a field of academic activity that this investigation has revealed.

The responses received from the survey questionnaire provide the possibility of making some global generalizations in quantitative form about the patterns of activity in mass media studies at the present time. Naturally these generalizations must be treated as very rough approximations to reality as they derive from a relatively small, self-selected sample of respondents. Many institutions did not respond to the inquiry at all. Others preferred to send catalogues and other similar material, or to provide written statements about their work. The range and variety of these materials made it impossible to attempt to code them in accordance with the questionnaire categories, although they proved invaluable sources of information for the main body of the report. Thus the quantitative data discussed in this section is derived only from survey questionnaires completed by the respondents themselves and returned in time for them to be processed by computer. A detailed note on the survey methods used and their limitations will be found in the Appendix.

The postal survey yielded 350 completed questionnaires, received from 250 university departments, 77 tertiary-level institutions and 23 other institutions including media organizations. Thus 71 per cent of the sample derived from the survey is based in universities, 22 per cent in tertiary institutions and 7 per cent in media organizations and other non-educational bodies. As far as the global spread of the whole range of activities related to mass media is concerned, this distribution is somewhat skewed in the direction of universities, since it does not reflect accurately the great amount of professional training undertaken by private schools, especially in Latin America, and by broadcasting organizations.

Nevertheless, as the main body of the report has demonstrated, in some countries universities have always played a predominant part in training, teaching and research related to mass communication, and in others they are becoming increasingly active in this field, although the extent of their involvement varies considerably from country to country. The reasons are not far to seek. Universities on the whole have better facilities for conducting teaching and research in the mass media field. They are usually in a better financial position to provide premises, specialized teaching staff in the humanities and the behavioural sciences, general and specialized library facilities, and specialized and costly equipment for practical work. They are also usually better able to attract grants for research than other institutions. Even as far as training is concerned, as the general educational level of audiences for the media has risen, employers all over the world are becoming less hostile to the idea of university-based training, and in some cases actively promote it. Furthermore, with the growth of many new media-based occupations, public relations, advertising, and audio-visual, educational and social advertising careers in information ministries and departments, agricultural extension, cultural promotion and so on, there is growing recognition of the need for a broadly based, general, media-oriented education so that future media professionals can adapt to a variety of careers. This tendency is clearly evident in the United States. But, whereas in France, for example, vocational training for middle-range tertiary occupations is provided by university institutes of technology, in other countries, including Australia and Canada, it is provided by tertiary-level institutions, and in most countries film schools and academies of dramatic art are not part of the university system.

Global and regional patterns in mass media studies in 1970

Analysis of the questionnaire returns provides quantitative data on the regional distribution of institutions which conducted mass media studies in 1970, the length of their involvement in this field, the extent to which their teaching leads to specialized mass media degrees, and the characteristic orientations and the range of subject-matter of the courses they provide.

The regional distribution of responding institutions and the date when they commenced mass media studies is indicated in Table 19. As might be expected, the majority of responses came from North America, because of the very great extension of mass media studies in the United States, where more institutions are involved in this field than in any other country. The long-standing interest of these institutions in education and research related to mass communication is also reflected in Table 19, although it is also very evident that many institutions in this region have become active in this field only since 1965. Indeed, the most striking conclusion to emerge from the

TABLE 19. Date of commencement of mass media studies in responding institutions in different regions

Region	Date of commencement				Total responses
	Before 1944	1945–64	1965–71	Not known	
United States and Canada	38	81	60	17	196
Europe and Australasia	7	31	56	17	111
Africa, Asia and Latin America	1	16	21	5	43
TOTAL	46	128	137	39	350

Conclusion

table is the very rapid growth of mass media studies all over the world since 1965. During the short period since this date, more institutions became involved in this field than at any other time before. Indeed, of the 311 institutions which could give the date when they began teaching or research about the mass media, nearly half (44 per cent) did so since 1965, as compared with 41 per cent between 1945 and 1964, and 15 per cent before 1944. Despite its long history, mass media studies is a relatively youthful field especially outside North America. In Europe, Australasia and the developing countries, the growth of mass media studies, in terms of the number of institutions commencing activities in this field, is related to the great extension of mass communication since the Second World War, the increased need for trained media professionals, and the growth of interest in mass media and mass communication as an academic field. The coming of national independence in Asian countries from the late 1940s to the early 1950s, and in African countries after 1960, and the consequent establishment of national media, has highlighted the need for trained professionals to run the media and to use them for national goals of social and economic advancement. It is very likely, therefore, that the coming period will see an increasing number of institutions in the Third World turning to training, teaching and research in mass communication, as a concomitant, as well as a means of social change and development.

Since mass media studies have expanded so greatly in recent years in every region, have they become accepted as a distinct field of academic interest, or are they regarded as an appendage to traditional disciplines? One measure of the answer to this question is to discover the relative proportion of courses which lead to specialized degrees in journalism, mass communication, broadcasting, and so on, provided by institutions in the different regions, as in Table 20.

Since mass media studies have been embarked upon relatively recently in many institutions all over the world, it would be interesting to assess how far the field has become regarded as a distinct specialized area of academic concentration in different regions. Table 20 sets out the proportion of teaching programmes which result in a full degree or subgraduate qualification awarded in a mass media field (journalism, broadcasting, mass communication and so on) compared with those which result in a degree awarded in a traditional discipline (sociology, social science, English and so on). Globally speaking some two-thirds of these courses resulted in a specialized mass media degree or qualification. In Europe and Australasia the proportion of specialized degrees or qualifications is far lower than in North America or the Third World, which suggests that mass media studies are less readily accepted as a valid area of academic concentration than in the other regions. Since the structure of the university systems of many developing countries, especially in Africa and Asia, are based on European

TABLE 20. Proportion of teaching programmes offered for specialized degrees or subgraduate qualifications in mass media studies in institutions in different regions in 1971

	United States and Canada		Europe and Australasia		Africa, Asia Latin America		Global	
	Number	%	Number	%	Number	%	Number	%
For mass media degree or subgraduate qualification	326	70.4	52	40.3	36	63.2	414	63.8
For degree in traditional discipline	137	29.6	77	59.7	21	36.8	235	36.2
TOTAL	463	100.0	129	100.0	57	100.0	649	100.0

TABLE 21. Orientation of specialized mass media degree courses in different regions in 1971

Orientation	United States and Canada		Europe and Australasia		Africa, Asia Latin America		Global	
	Number	%	Number	%	Number	%	Number	%
Professional	182	56.2	17	42.5	20	60.6	219	55.2
Other	142	43.8	23	57.5	13	39.4	178	44.8
TOTAL	324	100.0	40	100.0	33	100.0	397	100.0

models, it is significant that the proportion of specialized degrees and qualifications should be so much higher than in Europe. The explanation lies largely in the fact that the developing countries have had to concentrate on providing professional training courses for new media personnel as a matter of high social priority and have therefore tended to set up specialized institutes or departments for this purpose, which are often located in new universities specifically designed to cater for interdisciplinary courses with a vocational aspect. Table 21 indicates the high proportion of professionally oriented programmes leading to degrees in mass media studies in the developing countries, as in North America, compared with Europe and Australasia.

The extent to which universities have been able to adapt themselves to mass media studies is also reflected in the proportion of teaching programmes for specialized undergraduate as against post-graduate degrees. As Table 22 shows, in North America and the developing countries some two-thirds of the teaching programmes for specialized mass media degrees are at undergraduate level, while in Europe and Australasia the proportion is slightly less than half the total. Since it is generally more difficult to introduce new, interdisciplinary fields at undergraduate level, it may be concluded that in general mass media studies have been less readily accepted as university subjects in European universities than in those of other regions, although there are clearly great differences from country to country and university to university in this respect.

The aspects of mass media studies so far considered have revealed many similarities between institutions in North America and the developing countries. However, when a regional comparison is made of the different types of specialized mass media degrees offered by institutions which responded to this survey, interesting differences emerge between North America and the other two regions. As Table 23 shows, in the United States and Canada, the most common degree titles are mass communication, journalism, and broadcasting. Few specialized broadcasting degrees were reported to be offered by responding institutions in Europe and Australasia, and none at all by

TABLE 22. Level of teaching programmes for specialized mass media degrees in different regions in 1971

Level	United States and Canada		Europe and Australasia		Africa, Asia Latin America		Global	
	Number	%	Number	%	Number	%	Number	%
Undergraduate	202	62.3	18	45.0	23	69.7	243	61.2
Post-graduate	122	37.7	22	55.0	10	30.3	154	38.8
TOTAL	324	100.0	40	100.0	33	100.0	397	100.0

Conclusion

TABLE 23. Types of specialized degrees in mass media studies offered by institutions in different regions in 1971

Degree title	United States and Canada		Europe and Australasia		Africa, Asia Latin America		Global	
	Number	%	Number	%	Number	%	Number	%
Mass Communication [1]	81	25.0	22	55.0	17	51.5	120	30.2
Journalism	106	32.7	11	27.5	14	42.5	131	33.0
Broadcasting	88	27.2	3	7.5	0	0.0	91	22.9
Film	16	4.9	2	5.0	1	3.0	19	4.8
Other [2]	33	10.2	2	5.0	1	3.0	36	9.1
TOTAL	324	100.0	40	100.0	33	100.0	397	100.0

1. Including Communication, Communication Arts, Sciences of Information, etc.
2. Including Advertising and Public Relations.

those in Africa, Asia and Latin America. The significantly higher percentage of North American broadcasting degrees compared to other regions is, of course, attributable to the multitude of commercial and educational radio and television stations which provide important career outlets for those with specialized professional qualifications in this field. In the rest of the world just over half the degrees offered are in mass communication, with journalism also being an important degree type. The popularity of the mass communication designation in these regions may partly reflect the influence of modern conceptions of mass communication as a total process which Unesco-sponsored regional centres such as CIESPAL have helped to spread.

Through the data derived from the responses to this survey, some evidence in quantitative form has been presented to demonstrate that, notwithstanding variations due to differing local conditions, in all the regional areas the social aspects of mass media and mass communication are increasingly the subject of study in universities.

It is now proposed to elaborate on some of the points which have come up in the course of this report.

The problem of finance

One theme which appears again and again in different countries is the often crucial difference which financial factors can make in either hindering or promoting training, teaching or research. The question of finance has become more acute than ever now, when so many countries are going through a period of sharp economic restriction. Even in the United States, where universities are better endowed than in most other countries, financial pressures are becoming painful. One well-informed correspondent from the United States wrote recently (Woodliff, 1971):

> I note in conversations with colleagues a new panic. The problem in the U.S. now is not like other budget crises where one might get a small increase or maintain the status quo. Now it is really big and it seems universal. One school that I know had to cut its broadcasting staff (not teaching primarily although many of them did some teaching) from 43 positions to 30. A large number of institutions ... are not being allowed to fill vacancies. The position is just eliminated. At any rate these pressures will have just as big an

impact on mass media studies as upon other areas. I personally believe that over the long term it will be good for every institution to go through this. It is true that in some United States universities, historical circumstances have fostered fragmentation of mass media studies, especially in broadcasting education which is still often split between journalism and speech departments in the same university, resulting in inconvenient duplication sustained by interdepartmental rivalries. In such cases the spur of financial stringency may promote more efficiency through consolidation. Other universities may have a great deal of capital tied up in expensive technical facilities which are no longer used to best advantage because of changing conditions in the media industries. The present financial crisis may force such universities to tailor their equipment to their needs and to rethink the content and orientation of their courses. But straitened circumstances may also induce a more conservative frame of mind, especially as improvements are usually expensive to carry out.

Economic factors come into play in research also. Survey research is extremely expensive to undertake. Furthermore university staff on research appointments are rarely given permanent tenure and may be the first to go when the pinch is felt. Many research centres in universities can undertake large-scale research only because a small core of established staff supported by the university budget is supplemented by additional researchers who are paid by grants from other sources. The availability of these grants may be drastically diminished at a time of general economic difficulty.

In this connexion one may recall that developments in mass media studies have often depended on non-university sources of finance. The most obvious example is the support derived from the media by universities in the United States, starting with Pulitzer's gift to Columbia University. The Annenberg School of Communications at the University of Pennsylvania and the Newhouse Communications Center at the University of Syracuse bear witness to donations made by publishers, and these are only two of many examples of munificence, which have included the endowment of many chairs of mass media studies in American universities (Jones, 1968). In the United Kingdom, a large grant by the Independent Television Authority brought into being the Television Research Committee which has done much to foster and finance mass communication research. In Finland and Sweden, the active role of the broadcasting organizations has been a major factor in the increase and development of broadcasting research in universities. Government agencies, such as the National Institute of Mental Health in the United States, or the Swedish Board of Psychological Defence have also played an important role in financing mass media research. Finally, Unesco, by sponsoring the establishment of regional centres for the advancement of education in journalism and mass communication, by organizing a multitude of conferences on mass media, and by commissioning large numbers of research projects, has stimulated the growth of the field, as have other international, regional and national organizations.

The continued expansion of mass media studies on the scale witnessed in the last decade or so, must depend more than ever on its practitioners being able to demonstrate that it is worth while for investments in this field to be continued or extended. The growing tendency for cost-benefit analyses to be applied to universities can only reinforce this necessity.

Nevertheless, it is worth stressing that availability of finance is only one factor in determining whether or not mass media studies continue to expand, and to break new ground—for expansion *per se* need not necessarily be desirable. Perhaps as a result of the large-scale institutionalization of mass media studies in universities during the later 1950s and 1960s—a boom period almost everywhere—the crucial role of finance tends sometimes to be exaggerated. As far as teaching is concerned, it is worth recalling the precarious finances of institutions such as the Bauhaus, for example, whose achievements and influence were out of all proportion to the money invested in them. In any

Conclusion

case, whatever the current financial situation, funds for innovation will always tend to be relatively scarce. As one American broadcasting educator commented (Woodliff, 1971):

> The very existence of many programs is due to the presence of strong personalities at the various schools . . . The newer broadcasting curricula are very expensive. Yet private universities which can afford it least have been leaders in broadcasting education. In several cases it has been due to the powerful influence of one person. Examples that come to mind are Bartlett at Syracuse, Donner at Stanford, Porter at Denver. The plain fact is that new curricula or expansion of the old has to take place fundamentally in an atmosphere which does not welcome new ways of getting into the common pie.

In research, too, as is well known, there has not always been a direct correlation between the availability of funds and the importance of the work produced. In experimental physics, which today attracts generous funds in most countries, fundamental progress in the past was made on what would now seem ludicrously small budgets. Leo Szilard, a central figure in the discoveries that resulted in the nuclear chain reaction and the atomic bomb, financed a crucial series of experiments in the early 1940s by borrowing $2,000 and finally getting a $6,000 grant from the United States Government (Fleming and Bailyn, 1969). The availability of finance does not, in itself, guarantee imaginative and fruitful approaches. It is worth recalling the fate of the several million dollars distributed between more than a thousand projects under Title VII of the United States National Defense Education Act of 1958 (Public Law 85-864) which authorized 'the expenditure of funds to support research, experimentation and dissemination' about the uses of mass media in education. The result was a mass of trivial reports, with no central purpose behind them, which did little to solve problems of communication and education. Malcolm S. Maclean, reviewing some of the results of Title VII commented that 'a project which seemed to hold such great promise now looks like a straggly old dog', and concluded that

> frequently, the best designed, most carefully thought out and conducted, the most useful research seems to be that done by one investigator, possibly with help from a graduate student, on a budget of $500 to $1000. There seem to be some things about the research team and the $50,000 or $500,000 budget that stifle common research sense. (Kitross, 1967.)

A great deal of investigation would be necessary to determine whether or not the research team, the large budget, or both in combination, stifle sound research; but certainly funds, in themselves, are not enough to foster original, stimulating and meaningful research. The crucial point is how funds are used, and this does not entirely depend on the research worker, though he must bear a major share of the responsibility when the final research product is assessed. But he may not necessarily be very influential at an earlier stage, when priorities are allocated in the distribution of scarce resources—and resources for certain activities are always relatively scarce.

J. D. Halloran, speaking at a seminar on broadcaster-researcher co-operation held in 1970 commented that

> there are few indications, past or present, . . . that the mass media are prepared to face up to their responsibilities as far as research is concerned. Moreover, this failure is not mainly a question of shortage of funds . . . Millions of pounds are spent every year on the essentially utilitarian tasks of head-counting and appreciation research, but very little is spent on impact, influence and effects studies, and practically nothing on systematic and independent enquiries into the production process, the nature of decision-making, and the organisation structures, general policies and operations of the media institutions. Apparently money is available to serve the research

needs of the media as defined by those working in the media and as built into the operations of the media institutions. But I would argue that such research is not only of very little use to society, but is not always the most appropriate way (even in terms of their own declared and limited objective) of serving the media. (Halloran, 1970.)

He pointed out also that in some cases where funds had been provided, the necessary access and facilities had been denied. The whole problem of the relationship between research sponsors, research workers and the final product is one that affects social research in general, and has been the subject of much discussion, particularly by American sociologists.

Professional training versus academic studies

Another point which has emerged from this survey is the increasing tendency all over the world for mass media studies to approach some blend of technical and academic instruction. In the United States, journalism, which was once taught very largely through a number of 'frighteningly narrow technical courses' (T. Peterson, 1960) has become far more academically oriented, while in Germany, where *Publizistik* was once a highly abstract theoretical subject, many universities now give at least a modicum of practical training. In very many countries the tendency is growing to combine training, teaching and research in mass media studies in universities. At the same time, there is some evidence that with the proliferation of new technology, and the prospect that established skills will soon become obsolete, a much wider view is being taken of what mass media teaching should aim at. In the United States, for instance, it seems that many educators now feel that their teaching should aim not so much at meeting the immediate employment requirements of newspapers or commercial broadcasting organizations, but should rather focus on the needs and demands of the students.

In many countries, the 'student revolt' has focused renewed attention on what the role of universities should be. Because mass media teaching is so often undertaken for purposes of professional training, and because media reflect, and often reinforce, the prevailing power structure, and seem also to reflect the dehumanizing effect of living in advanced industrial societies, educators are beginning to join students in insisting that education should not merely provide trained people to 'service the machine'. In many American institutions an important purpose of mass media courses is to promote 'visual literacy', so that trained judgement applied to television may raise the standards of consumers and producers alike.

There are, of course, many forces working against the attempt to innovate. Not least among them is the tendency 'to go on doing what we know how to do, and not to attempt what we know should be done but do not know how to do', as Gerhart Wiebe (1970) of the School of Public Communications at Boston University put it. Another major force working against innovation is the often justified fear that media proprietors may become alienated by the introduction of more imaginative approaches (Rooy, 1970). When governments are directly concerned in the question of mass media education, through the immediate and pressing need to increase the number of professionals working in the media, as in many developing countries, teaching staff may face great difficulties in trying to broaden their courses.

Universities in the Third World have a double task to perform in undertaking mass media studies. Especially in newly independent African and Asian countries, the rapid growth of mass media has created, or will soon create, a critical shortage of trained media professionals, particularly in broadcasting. This poses difficult problems in devising methods of imparting technical skills quickly and effectively to as many students as possible. At the same time, if national mass media systems are to meet national needs and become the effective instruments of social change that they are expected to be, future media professionals must be given more than technical training. They must be fired with a sense of mission in terms of the wider purposes of their countries and a sense of respect for the audiences whom they will serve. But they must be able to translate ideals into practice. Their education should ideally provide them with administrative, managerial and financial skills and, above all, with the ability to assess critically the limitations and advantages of mass communication, in conjunction with other social forces, in setting and in implementing societal goals. These tasks underly sound education in mass media studies all over the world, but they are particularly urgent in developing countries where mass media are expected to play a vital role in implementing national plans for increased literacy, population control, agricultural improvement and so on. But it is precisely in these countries that such tasks are most difficult to achieve. Students often lack the necessary educational background to successfully complete advanced level courses. There are few teachers with the necessary training in social sciences, research methods and specialized mass media subjects to provide adequate instruction; and in many countries universities are too poor to recruit full-time teachers. Local-language textbooks relevant to local conditions are virtually non-existent; imported textbooks are expensive, written in foreign languages which may be difficult for students to master, and, in any case, are generally not slanted to the needs of developing countries. Even elementary training facilities which are taken for granted in North America or Europe may not be provided.

The problem of isolation

It is not easy for educators in the Third World to overcome these problems, especially in countries where media industries still doubt the utility of specialized university courses and are reluctant to co-operate with universities in establishing internships for students, or in countries where there is great pressure from governments to make courses as short and simple as possible so that staff with even a modicum of training may be recruited to media institutions. Until recently these problems were compounded by the fact that educators in developing countries were isolated from one another and from the mainstream of teaching and research in mass communications, concentrated as it was in the United States and Europe. But there are signs that the position is beginning to change. Several universities in the Third World, such as the University of São Paulo in Brazil, or the University of the Philippines, to name only two examples, are now sufficiently well financed to be able to instal excellent facilities and to recruit full-time staff. Regional centres such as CIESPAL are helping to train university lecturers in research methods, to disseminate a wider outlook towards mass media studies, and to produce textbooks for local use. In the past few years conferences, symposia and travelling seminars have helped educators in developing countries to meet their colleagues from all over the world. These meetings are very important in replacing a sense of isolation and demoralization by a feeling of community and confidence. Above all they make it possible for the particular difficulties of individual institutions to be formulated in a more general way, and for solutions to common problems to be worked out.

One of the most important ways in which progress in a new academic field can be extended and consolidated is in creating a sense of solidarity, a sense of belonging to an intellectual specialism that transcends national and regional differences, and that brings together its practitioners through the common bond of working in that field, however different individual approaches and orientations may be. It is not only in developing countries that those who teach mass media courses have a sense of isolation. In Australia, Canada, Denmark, New Zealand, the United Kingdom and many other countries there is still a considerable amount of fragmentation of mass media courses. The point made by Whannel (1969) in relation to film, that it will not establish 'its own body of knowledge and expertise, if its use in education is confined to being a secondary element within some other course' applies equally to the whole field of mass communication. To the extent that mass communication lacks, or appears to lack this body of knowledge and expertise which can be directed to further coherent growth as a teaching and research field, it will not become separately institutionalized in universities and for that reason alone will remain disorganized and fragmentary. This self-perpetuating circular process is difficult to break, especially when it affects vested interests which are particularly strong in undergraduate teaching. Denis McQuail (1970) commented that in Britain

> there seems room for a general improvement in the amount and quality of teaching in this field in higher education. This would be of advantage for those who later take up work in mass communications or related fields—publishing, research, advertising, information services—and strengthen general education. It would help, for instance, to provide a bridge between some arts and social science teaching. I would not advocate a large investment in vocational training for intending media professionals, but the facilities seem notably lacking and the intellectual resources to make even a modest start in this direction seem absent. In universities there is a general lack of opportunities for interdisciplinary co-operation in teaching and research in this field, although this stems from the prevailing departmental structure and the lack of a clear allocation of mass media studies to an existing academic discipline. Divisions between disciplines are often arbitrary and there is little doubt that progress in mass media studies has been hampered by the way in which intellectual resources are organised and allocated.

One very important aspect of this situation in Britain is

> a very serious weakness in library and bibliographical support facilities . . . There is no centralised and accessible collection of material, [or] up to date and comprehensive bibliography, and much important foreign work seems almost unobtainable through normal channels. This must be a bar to development in the future if it is not remedied. It is already a stumbling block.

As a new field, practised through many academic disciplines and perspectives, mass media studies is peculiarly prone to difficulties of information storage, retrieval and dissemination, which affect most academic fields to some extent today. The importance of efficient mechanism for tracing developments in mass media studies has been emphasized at several Unesco conferences, and the recent establishment of an international network of documentation centres for mass communication research sponsored by Unesco, will help to remove this difficulty.

New avenues for research

The mention of bibliographical weaknesses in mass media studies underlines the conexion between training and teaching on the one hand and research on the other. In many ways it seems true to say that, especially at university level, improvements in the content and quality of training and teaching ultimately depend to a very large extent on research, and on the perspectives which new knowledge derived from research can supply. As more universities all over the world take up mass media studies at under-

Conclusion

graduate and post-graduate level so the connexions between education and research must become closer, and education about mass media will become ever more dependent on research for its substantive content and its orientations.

The investigations undertaken in the course of this survey have revealed that in mass communication research, as in education, there is a strong desire to broaden perspectives, to break out of the mould of stereotyped approaches and problems, and to develop new methods of studying the mass media. In the past ten or fifteen years mass communication research has expanded rapidly, and has now reached a point where researchers all over the world have begun to take stock of what has been achieved, and to undertake a critical reassessment of the field and its problems. In recent years mass communication researchers from many countries have criticized the narrow specificity of much mass media research, the paucity of efforts put into raising and trying to solve fundamental theoretical problems, the concentration of effects studies *per se* (Brown, 1970; Burgelin, 1966; Halloran, 1970; Nordenstreng, 1968; Tunstall, 1970). These reassessments seem to indicate that mass communication research has passed the first stage of hopeful enthusiasm and has entered a period of sober maturity and self-conscious awareness. As Eguchi and Ichinohe (1971) put it:

> With the appearance of a new mass communication medium [which is expected] ... to exert social influence, a critical appraisal and the study of such a medium are conspicuously active in any culture or nation ... However, even a new medium begins to show social establishment in a few years. Meanwhile, research does not progress as smoothly as the researchers had initially anticipated. It becomes evident that, instead of widening comprehensive aspects, the incomprehensive aspects expand and deepen like an abysmal swamp. And the researcher gradually realises that the abysmal swamp might lie beyond the overall understanding.

In a thoughtful and insightful review of broadcasing research in Japan these two members of the NHK Radio and Television Culture Research Institute in Tokyo point out several fundamental ways in which mass media research in general has failed to live up to its earlier expectations. There is first of all a gap between broadcasting research and broadcasting practice. On the one hand researchers tend to take day-to-day programming for granted, and seldom attempt to control the variables involved in the actual conditions of broadcasting. On the other hand, although research has concentrated on the social function and impact of broadcasting, and problems of the free flow of information, neither the day-to-day practice of broadcasting institutions nor legislation regulating broadcasting has taken any note of broadcasting research. Although researchers might find this situation undesirable, Eguchi and Ichinohe consider that in most countries

> researchers are in no position to give form to measures designed to solve such a question ... We have not been able to obtain sufficient knowledge to grasp and explain comprehensively [the] daily expanding activities of mass media, neither is it certain whether ... in ... future [we will] be able to come into possession of such knowledge.

There is also an ever-widening gap in outlook between social critics and mass communication research. Researchers no longer posit a direct impact on individuals by the media, but consider that media content takes effect through the mediation of the individual's primary group and other sociological and psychological factors, or through factors in the individual's own make-up, related to information-processing and the like.

> Thus the ultimate form of the impact [is conceived as taking place] independently of the intentions of the sending party ... Researchers have focussed attention exclusively on the analysis of the receiver's side [and such analysis] is following a tendency [to] branch ... out into further details.

Meanwhile, social phenomena, such as violence, undesirable behaviour and manners etc. which are popularly considered attributable directly to the mass media, are spreading wider, and the social critics are expanding their utterances in the [opposite] direction to that taken by research. Though efforts have been made to rectify such an unfortunate situation [including] the concentration of knowledge in an interdisciplinary manner by limiting the attention to individual social problems . . . there are not many instances of such attempts having . . . adequately solv[ed] the problems.

Furthermore, they point out, while the evolution of new technology presents the possibility of changing fundamental aspects of present-day concepts of broadcasting, research continues in the same way, without developing new concepts or techniques, so that researchers are in no position to advise society how this new technology may be institutionalized.

In Japan future developments preceded by [new] technology such as CATV, EVR, . . . home video players, [or] 'wired city' . . . are not mere topics [of discussion] . . . Means of establishing such systems institutionally in our society are already being studied in a concrete manner . . . Materialisation of such techniques as . . . the pseudo-individualised communications systems through consolidation of terminal devices for home use, viewing of programs unrelated to broadcasting through dissemination of video tape recorders for home use etc. . . . is likely to bring about the breakdown of today's concept of broadcasting or [its] broad revision . . . [Meanwhile] researchers who are studying broadcasting . . . by traditional sociological, socio-psychological and psychological disciplines . . . are working on a level practically unrelated to [the] social realisation of such technological innovations . . . Researchers . . . are not committed as to how such technological innovations will be institutionalised in future . . . they do not seem to be in possession of a methodology effective enough to make commitments. A new medium is not significant [because] . . . it is new; its significance lies in the manner in which it is utilised, i.e. for what new purposes it is designed . . . Under the circumstances, new technological means will probably attain social realisation merely as technical intentions. Would not this gap come to require too great a sacrifice to be left untouched?

Taken together, the formulation of these major gaps in research amounts to a massive indictment of the ultimate social irrelevance of a good deal of mass communication research, not only in Japan, but elsewhere.

How far are these criticisms valid? Some large broadcasting organizations do, in fact, conduct operational research in connexion with particular programmes, or even for programme policy in general. This applies particularly to those, for example in Sweden and Finland, which are explicitly committed to the idea that broadcasting should broaden the horizons of the public, constitute a forum for discussion of important public issues, and contribute to the public good. The ORTF has also undertaken operational research through its audience research department. Other broadcasting organizations including the BBC, Radio Telefís Éireann, the Danish Broadcasting Corporation and others have allowed researchers to undertake participant observation studies of their methods; so too have many newspapers. However this type of research is usually, though not always, focused on news and gatekeeping processes in the selection and presentation of news, and it seldom involves more than the 'middle-level' communicator. For obvious reasons, it is difficult for university researchers to penetrate to the upper levels of policy-making, and this may be equally true of media-based research organizations. The question of how to extend the range of communicator research is complex. It involves not only problems inherent in the client relationship, but also the reconciliation of the differing orientations and aims of researchers and

Conclusion

media (Halloran, 1970). Partly because of these problems, research into the production side of mass communication is less often undertaken than research on content, audiences and effects.

The high concentration on effects studies is, of course, partly a reaction by researchers against simplistic notions of the deleterious influence of film and television on young people. As investigations proceeded on how attitude changes occur in connexion with the media, so the real-life situation was shown to be more complex, both in mechanism and in effect, than at first appeared. But in concentrating on isolating intervening variables between stimulus and possible effect researchers appear to make the sender's role less important than that of the recipient. This research focus has therefore helped to deflect attention away from the role and responsibility of the media. This may partly account for the meagre influence which regulation studies have had on legislation.

If mass communication research merely studies the media and the mass communication process in isolation from the total social context in which the media operate, researchers cannot but take broadcasting practices for granted or make vague references to the social context which is taken as given. It then becomes highly unlikely that research will lead to significant changes in policy or in legislation concerning the mass media, since such changes can only come about through social pressure. But, of course, researchers, like evreyone else are affected by the climate of opinion of their own time in their own country. Unless forces are operating which make the investigation of certain problems imperative so that action may be taken to solve them, tradition and natural inertia are likely to combine to keep things going in the usual way. There are always strong vested interests operating against change. As Gunnar Myrdal (1970) points out there is a social function to ignorance as well as knowledge, so that

> we almost never face a random lack of knowledge. Ignorance like knowledge is purposefully directed. An emotional load of valuation conflicts presses for rationalization, creating blindness at some spots, stimulating an urge for knowledge at others, and, in general, causing conceptions of reality to deviate from truth in determined directions.

This may be one reason why there are, comparatively speaking, so few economic studies of mass media, particularly studies of interlocking ownership nationally and internationally. It must certainly be one reason for the gap between research and the evolution of new technology.

In this report several instances have been mentioned in which social concern has stimulated the development of certain aspects of mass media studies. In many countries, including Japan, the United Kingdom, the United States, and others, concern over social problems, particularly violence and delinquency, has encouraged the growth of research into the effects of violent content in film and television on children's attitudes, values and behaviour. In the United States, the Cold War and the general circumstances of American foreign policy particularly in its economic and political aspects have helped to stimulate research into international communication, while a growing body of research into mass communication in relation to disadvantaged groups in the United States, or into environmental problems shows the clear imprint of contemporary public anxiety in these fields. In Sweden, a growing concern over the gap between a small group of decision-makers in government, and a general public which lacks information on vital questions, has stimulated research into news production and the possibility of objectivity in news. In many developing countries, there is a focus on the interplay of interpersonal and traditional channels of opinion formation and information diffusion with mass communication so that the media may be used effectively for national goals. All these are examples of how current social problems have left their imprint on the course of mass media research.

In this connexion the problem raised by Eguchi and Ichinohe of the limitations of behavioural research methodology and its underlying concepts of mass audiences in relation to the very different forms of communication that new technological advances may bring about is extremely interesting. Even today, the methods and orientations applied to the cinema, which are almost always historical and aesthetic studies focusing on the individual creator and the product in relation to genre and style, rather than on audience preferences and reactions, stand in sharp contrast to the focus of research into other mass media, where quantitative methodologies tend to be applied to sociological and psychological problems. In some ways these differing approaches are associated with two differing views of the media, as providers of culture and entertainment on the one hand, and as providers of information on the other, approaches which are seldom brought together in concrete instances of research. It is possible that the establishment of new forms of communication brought about by technological innovations may lead to audience-centred research being superseded by other forms, and that new methodologies will be developed in consequence.

In the past few years there has been much uneasiness, particularly in sociology, about the assumptions underlying the idea of 'value-free' social research and the limitations of the strict quantitative methodology associated with it. In mass communication research also there is a noticeable search for new methodologies which will combine the rigorousness and precision of quantitative research methods without their limitations. The use of open-ended interviews, participant observation and other qualitative or quasi-qualitative methods as instruments of mass communication research is growing. As mass communication research is conducted into new problems in new areas, so the search for new methodologies and orientations which will reduce the gap between the results of academic research and real life problems must intensify. There is already some evidence that researchers are realizing that what may appear to be the one valid method for all times and places, may be time-bound and culture-bound, and not necessarily appropriate for all types of mass media study. In the Republic of Korea, doubts have been cast on the efficacy of the survey as an instrument for mass media research in societies with very different traditions, attitudes and values from those Western countries in which survey methodology was first developed (Lim, 1971). In Japan, some researchers have felt that each mass medium has its own specific character and problems and that these should be taken into account in research (NSK, 1970). In many countries, including the Federal Republic of Germany and Japan, attempts are being made to combine the older critically oriented political and ethical aspects of *Publizistik* and Marxist approaches, with the rigour of American behavioural research methods.

Thus although there are certain broad similarities to be discerned in education and research on mass media which cut across regional differences, nevertheless it would be quite mistaken to conclude that the field of mass media studies suffers from a dull uniformity. The sections on individual countries have revealed the existence of several distinctive traditions of great vitality, including *Publizistik*, filmology, and structuralism, as well as the dominant tradition of quantitatively based social science research. Furthermore, even in the same country, several different approaches and orientations may exist together. There has been evidence from many countries that new approaches are being developed as new interests arise, and in many countries those concerned with mass media studies are consciously searching for better ways of comprehending the mass media as social institutions and mass communication as a social process. It is to be hoped that this survey will make some small contribution to this field, in demonstrating the extent to which it has developed, particularly in the last few years, and the variety which it exhibits.

Appendix: a note on the survey methods employed

The procedure adopted was first to locate the actual or potential institutions in which mass media studies were undertaken. For the reasons outlined in the Introduction it was decided to include other institutions and organizations besides universities, although the main emphasis was nevertheless placed on university-based activities. Consequently, letters of inquiry were addressed to the chief administrative officer of every institution in the world which could reasonably be classified as a university, omitting only those which were exclusively confined to medicine or engineering. Agricultural universities were included in the survey because of their involvement in training for agricultural extension work, and because of the particular relevance of mass media studies, especially in developing countries, to schemes of agricultural improvement.

The preliminary letter, addressed to the chief administrative officer,[1] inquired whether any form of mass media study was undertaken by the university or was planned for the future, and he was asked to provide the names and addresses of the individuals concerned. Questionnaires were then sent to the appropriate individuals or departments, and a covering letter was enclosed explaining the aims and scope of the survey and asking for comments on their own work and on the development of mass media studies in their country. In cases where such studies were known to be in progress, questionnaire forms were enclosed with the preliminary letter and the university was asked to confirm the accuracy, and the completeness, of the survey in this respect.

The survey also canvassed other institutions of higher learning, particularly tertiary-level educational institutions (technical colleges, polytechnics, and so on), film schools, and academies of art, drama or music, where there was reason to suppose that mass media studies already took place or might do so in the immediate future.

Letters of inquiry were also addressed to international and national organizations which might reasonably be expected to have information on the subject. These included bodies directly involved in mass media studies such as the International Association for Mass Communication Research, the American Council for Education in Journalism and so on, as well as organizations such as the International Sociological Association. Educational associations, including national or regional university associations like the Association of Commonwealth Universities, and government depart-

---

1. The Rector, Vice-Chancellor, President, Secretary, and so on.

Appendix: a note on the survey methods employed

ments or councils concerned with higher education and university-based research, were also consulted for their help and advice.

In framing the questionnaire forms certain basic decisions were taken. Because of the great number of inquiries to be undertaken, the survey took the department to be the basic unit for mass media studies. Most recipients seemed to agree that this was a reasonable decision, though one American academic commented:

> The questionnaire assumes that all research in this area, as well as learning, is institutional, and that is actually not the case. Though I have in the past accepted grants to finance research, I no longer do so, and though I am still connected with a university and teach I do not regard this as the most effective means of acquiring and transmitting new data.
>
> My most recent book on mass media ... is to be serialized in various magazines ... and newspapers ... A forthcoming book ... will first be delivered as a series of lectures ... A forthcoming film ... is designed for network television.
>
> These works were independently undertaken and financed. I think the problem of investigating mass media via institutional means is self-contradictory, though clearly you think otherwise.

Although useful and interesting data has no doubt thereby been eliminated, particularly in regard to research, the initial inquiries, and the final assessment of them in this report, have, as far as possible, focused on institutions rather than individuals, very largely because any other procedure might have invidious consequences and because it would add to the difficultues of handling and comparing the information received.

The departments to which the questionnaire was addressed were asked to supply details of the size of their present academic staff, the date mass media studies began, the degrees offered in mass media studies, the length, orientation and academic level of their programme(s), the annual numbers of graduates since 1969, the subject-matter taught, and any recent research activities.

The information called for represents a compromise between the information ideally required and the amount of time and trouble respondents might reasonably be expected to take in filling it in.

Although the framing of the questionnaire made it possible to tap the activities of departments like English, sociology, drama and so on, where mass media studies were taught as part of the curriculum for a degree in some other subject, the survey did not attempt systematically to canvass any criticism of media content that might take place, since in practice it was impossible to locate beforehand all the possible departments in any university where this might occur. Nor were any questions included about the technical equipment to which the department had access, although this is obviously very important for training purposes, nor whether any in-service training was provided for. The main emphasis of the questionnaire is on academic teaching and research. Even from this point of view the questionnaire did not attempt to be fully comprehensive. It made no attempt to discover whether or not the department had access to specialized collections of documents, films and so on, although, as one respondent observed, the availability of such teaching and research resources is obviously very germane to the inquiry. Here again, it was felt that such questions would greatly add to the difficulty of filling in the questionnaire.

As it was, the questionnaire involved a great deal of time and trouble to complete, particularly for respondents in very large and active university departments. When a great deal of work is being undertaken apparently simple facts about ongoing activities can be very difficult to acquire. One candid correspondent from a large United States university said it 'made his blood run cold to see so many precise questions' and he felt the questionnaire could be filled in only by 'clerks or liars'. At the Department of Speech and Journalism in the University of Kansas, the questionnaire passed

Appendix: a note on the survey methods employed

through six different hands before it was sent back, and Laurence Day noted in June 1971:

> I thought it would be instructive for you to see the process by which your survey was completed at K.U. I would venture a guess that you get low response . . . As you can see anyone in the 'chain' could have stopped the survey cold. Note it took 9 hours of work.

The difficulties involved can become overwhelming, particularly in the United States, where so much survey research is undertaken. One administrator in a middle-sized college in the United States said that he had received twenty-one questionnaires within the past three months, and that therefore he could not find the time to answer this one.

No doubt partly for this reason some of the largest United States universities did not fill in the questionnaire at all, or only filled in certain parts, often leaving out the details of current and future research. But, since many sent catalogues and reports, it has been possible to fill this gap to some extent in the text, although it remains a limitation in the quantitative aspect of the data collected.

The organization of the questionnaire form and its covering letter also affected the response rate. Certain institutions indicated in their answers by letter either that they were not universities, or that they undertook no teaching, and that the questionnaire was therefore not applicable to them. In such cases, particularly when the type and scale of their activities seemed to warrant it, questionnaires were sent to them with covering letters explaining that some record of their activities would nevertheless be valuable. Some of these were returned, but some were not. It is very likely that many institutions which did not reply at all felt it was not worth doing so for this reason.

Other decisions were taken which might have affected the response rate and the answers provided. It was decided to send out all letters and questionnaires in English. The main reason was not only that it was difficult to find translators who could translate both the original inquiries and the answers to them, but also because, on balance, more errors might have resulted through multiple translation than in using English throughout. In the event many respondents replied in their own languages, and many documents were received which had to be translated into English. Furthermore, in framing the questionnaire it was decided to use categories of Anglo-American usage, particularly in regard to academic matters, in order to try to build some common standard into the questionnaire itself. Most respondents translated their own situation into Anglo-American terms, or explained its divergencies, but this might have constituted an insuperable difficulty for others, particularly those who were not fluent in English.

On the other hand, there seems to be no doubt that the response rate was increased, because so many respondents felt the inquiry to be worth while and wanted to see a copy of the final report. The fact that it was an international survey sponsored by Unesco was generally felt to be one of its advantages. Many busy people spent a great deal of time and trouble not only in filling in the questionnaires, but also in writing additional details about the activities of their institutions and their views on mass media studies. These letters constitute the most valuable kernel of the information received.

Considering that the inquiry was conducted by means of a postal survey (with the intervention of a long postal strike which made all communication impossible) the results were gratifying. Completed usable questionnaires were received from 350 units around the world. They comprised 250 university departments (including United States colleges with graduate schools), 37 liberal arts colleges, 40 polytechnics, technical colleges and other tertiary-level institutions, 8 research institutions not attached to universities and 15 other institutions (including media organizations, journalist associations and so on). About 100 questionnaires were not considered applicable by the respondents, mainly because their activities were too marginal to the study to be described as systematic. In addition, another fifty or so were returned too late to be handled by the computer, including several from the United States and the United Kingdom, but this information has been incorporated into the reports on individual countries. However, between 3,000 and 4,000 letters were received giving information of some kind. It is these letters, in conjunction with the completed questionnaires, supplemented by secondary source material, which form the basis for this report. In the case of certain countries where no responses at all were received the accounts in the text had perforce to derive entirely from secondary source material, often out of date.

Other limitations, apart from the response rate, must be kept in mind when interpreting the results provided in the report.

Inevitably, the questions asked reflect certain presuppositions on the part of the author, as well as on the part of the respondents. From the author's point of view, the range of questions asked reflect certain built-in biases—for example, in the questions asked about the subject-matter provided in the courses, and in the research fields specified. Although room was provided for other information to be inserted, the existence of certain set categories provides an arbitrary division of the field, as well as of its range, which may not be acceptable in all cases to those actively engaged in mass media studies. Generally speaking, the built-in bias is perforce an Anglo-American one. Conversely, in translating the details of their activities into the set categories provided by the questionnaire, the respondents may not have been able to do justice to their activities. Indeed, the way the questionnaire was filled in, particularly the section on teaching field and future research plans, inevitably depended on who filled it in, and a different response might have been obtained even from another member of the same department. To that extent, it is illusory to expect genuine comparability of information of this kind, except at a very crude level. Furthermore, the report can say nothing about the quality of the teaching or research undertaken at any institution; it can only speak in terms of size, volume and range. It can provide no insight into depth, nor does it pretend to do so. However, in order to try to present as far as possible the differences between one situation and another, quotations from letters received have been used as far as possible, although many interesting comments could not be included because of limitations of space in an already long report.

Finally, it should be remembered that letters of inquiry and questionnaires were mostly sent out between June and September 1970 (although some were sent later due to delays in replying to the preliminary inquiries). On the whole the responses refer to the situation from about the middle to the end of 1970. But in the case of late responses (which were not analysed by computer) more recent information has been obtained, which is incorporated in the body of the report.

References

ABADAN, N. 1971. Letter, School of Journalism and Communications, University of Ankara, 31 March 1971.
ACEJ. 1970. *ACEJ 1970 accredited programs in journalism*. American Council on Education for Journalism.
ACU. 1969. *Tenth congress of the universities of the Commonwealth, 1968, report of proceedings, Sydney, August 17–23,* London, Association of Commonwealth Universities.
AINSLIE, R. 1966. *The press in Africa, communications past and present.* London, Gollancz.
ALFVEGREN, L. 1966. Journalist training in Nordic countries. *Gazette*, vol. 12, no. 1, p. 53–54.
ÁLVAREZ, A. 1970. Letter, Consejo Superior de Investigaciones Científicas, Madrid, 30 June 1970.
AMES, W. E. 1970. The AEJ presidential address. *Journalism quarterly*, vol. 47, no. 4 (winter), p. 812–17.
APBE. 1968. *Radio-television-film composite course outlines.* Washington, D.C., Association for Professional Broadcasting Education. Vol. II, February 1970.
AUCC. 1971. *University affairs*, 5 May 1971. Ottawa, Association of Universities and Colleges of Canada.
AUSTRALIA. 1971. *Parliamentary debates. 27th Parliament, 2nd session (fourth period), 8 September, 26 October 1971 and 2nd session 1972, 19 April 1972.* Canberra, Government Printer.
BACHY, V. 1973. Letter, Centre de Techniques de Diffusion, Université Catholique de Louvain, 4 April 1973.
BECERRA, J. 1970. Letter, Training and Research Center of Interamerican Institute of Agricultural Sciences (IICA), Turrialba, Costa Rica, 22 September 1970.
BELANGER, D. 1970. Letter, Université Montréal, Montréal, 18 June 1970.
BENNIS, P. 1971. Letter, Department of Education, Dublin, Ireland, 23 September 1971.
BLUM, Eleanor. 1969. *Communications research in US universities, a directory.* Urbana, Ill., University of Illinois.
BOCKSTAEL, E.; FEINSTEIN, O. 1970. *Higher education in the European Community: reform and economics.* Lexington, Mass., Heath (Studies in social and economic process.)
BRÖSTRÖM, A. 1971. Letter, Sociology Department, Uppsala University, Sweden, 19 January 1971.
BROWN, Roger L. 1970. Approaches to the historical development of mass media studies In: J. Tunstall, *Media sociology, a reader.* London, Constable.
BUMRONGSOOK SIHA-UMPHAI. 1970. Letter, Department of Mass Communications and Public Relations, Chulalongkorn University, 6 October 1970.
——. 1971. *Communication/journalism education in Thailand.* Paper delivered to Journalism/Communication Teachers' Seminar, June 1971. Honolulu, East-West Center. (Mimeo.)
BURGELIN, O. 1966. Structural analysis and mass communication research in France. Reprinted in: H. Eguchi and H. Ichinohe (eds.), *International studies of broadcasting with special reference to the Japanese studies,* p. 219–44. Tokyo, NHK Radio and Television Culture Research Institute, 1971.

CARTER, R. F.; PORTER, W. E.; JENSON, J. W.; PETERSON, T. 1963. Journalism, communications and the future of the discipline, a symposium. *Journalism quarterly*, vol. 40, no. 4. (autumn), p. 580–93.
CIESPAL. 1969. Informe de diez años de labores, 1959–1969. Quito, CIESPAL.
——. 1970. List of Latin American journalism and communication courses enclosed in letter, Dr G. Córdova, CIESPAL, Quito, Ecuador, 8 May 1970.
CLARK, T. N. 1968. The structure and functions of a research institute: The Année Sociologique, *Archives européennes de sociologie*, vol. 9, no. 1, p. 72–91.
CLOUTIER, J. 1970. Letter, Audiovisual Center, Montreal University, Montreal, 13 August 1970.
DAHL, O. O. 1971. Letter, Royal Ministry of Church and Education, Oslo, 29 July 1971.
DANIELSON, W. A.; WILHOIT, G. C. jun. 1967. *A computerized bibliography of mass communication research 1944–1964*. New York, N.Y., Magazine Publishers Association.
DANISH RESEARCH SECRETARIAT. 1971. Statens Humanistiske og Samfundsvidenskabelige Forskingsråds symposium, 10 og 11 maj 1971, på Den Internationale Højskole i Helsingør om Massekommunikationsforskning. (Mimeo.)
DAY, J. Lawrence. 1968. The Latin American journalist: a tentative profile, *Journalism quarterly*, vol. 45, no. 3 (autumn), p. 509–15.
DE FLEUR, M. L. 1966. *Theories of mass communication*. New York, N.Y., McKay.
DE SANTO, J. 1970. Letter, Bemidji State College, Bemidji, Minn., 20 November 1970.
DESMOND, R. W. 1949. *Professional training of journalists*. Paris, Unesco.
DEXTER, L. A.; WHITE, D. (eds.). 1964. *People, society and mass communications*. New York, N.Y., Free Press of Glencoe.
DIÉGUES JÚNIOR, M. 1970. Letter, Latin American Center for Research in the Social Sciences, Rio de Janeiro, 16 July 1970.
DØRSJØ, J. 1970. Letter, Norsk Journalistskole, Oslo, 19 October 1970.
DUNCAN, Charles T. 1961. Some basic realities in journalism education today. *Journalism quarterly*, vol. 38, autumn, p. 520–6.
——. 1971. Letter, 23 September 1971.
DÜRRENMATT, P. 1970. Letter, University of Bern, 25 August 1970.
EAPEN, K. E. 1966. A quarter century of university education. *Gazette*, vol. 12, no. 4, p. 302–16.
——. 1970. *Some thoughts for a centre for advanced study in communication*. (Mimeo.)
EAST-WEST CENTER. 1971. *Communication/journalism education in Asia, background and status in seven Asian areas; background papers prepared for Communication/journalism Teachers' Seminar, June 13–26, 1971*. Honolulu, East-West Center, East West Communication Institute. (Mimeo.)
EGUCHI, H.; ICHINOHE, H. (eds.). 1971. *International studies of broadcasting with special reference to the Japanese studies*. Tokyo, NHK Radio and Television Culture Research Institute.
EKECRANTZ, J. 1970. Letter, Sociological Institute, Uppsala University, February 1970.
——. 1971. Letter, Sociological Institute, Stockholm University, 26 August 1971.
ELMORE, H. L. 1971. Letter, Royal Melbourne Institute of Technology, Melbourne, 4 May 1971.
EMERY, E.; AULT, Philip H.; AGEE, Warren K. 1965. *Introduction to mass communications*. 2nd ed. New York and Toronto, Dodd, Mead & Co.
EMMETT, Brian P. 1966. A brief history of broadcasting research in the United Kingdom, 1936–1965. Reprinted in: H. Eguchi and H. Ichinohe (eds.), *International studies of broadcasting with special reference to the Japanese studies*, p. 267–90. Tokyo, NHK Radio and Television Culture Research Institute, 1971.
FENSCH, T. 1970. *Films on the campus*. South Brunswick, New York and London, A. S. Barnes.
FERNANDEZ, J. 1966. Problems related to the training of journalists in Latin America. *Gazette*, vol. 12, no. 1, p. 45–51.
FIDDLE, S. 1948. *The Bureau of Applied Social Research*. (M.A. thesis, Columbia University, New York (microfilm).)
FLEMING, Donald; BAILYN, Bernard. 1969. *The intellectual migration, Europe and America, 1930–1960*. Cambridge, Mass., Harvard University Press.
FONSECA, Luiz. 1970. *Estudos de post-graduacao em comunicacao na America Latina: a experiencia de La Molina*. Paper given in Primer Seminario Brasileiro de Informacao Rural, 4–8 May 1970, Brasilia, Brazil. (Mimeo.)

References

GORDON, D. R. 1970. Letter, Department of Political Science, University of Waterloo, Ontario, Canada, 2 September 1970.
GOTO, K. 1970. Letter, NHK Theoretical Research Center, Radio & Television Culture Research Institute, Tokyo, 23 January 1970.
GREENSFELDER, L. B. 1970. *The American Film Institute's guide to college film courses*. 2nd ed. Chicago, Ill., The American Library Association for the American Film Institute.
HACHTEN, W. A. 1971. *Muffled drums, the news media in Africa*. Ames, Iowa, University of Iowa Press.
HALL, S. 1971. Letter, Centre for Contemporary Cultural Studies, University of Birmingham, 23 September 1971.
HALLORAN, J. D. 1970. *The effects of television*. London, Panther.
HALME, V. 1970. Letter, Turku School of Economics, Finland, November 1970.
HANCOCK, G. 1970. Letter, University of King's College, Halifax, Nova Scotia, 1 September 1970.
HARTING, W. L. 1971. *Dimensions of public communication: publizistik, the system of Emil Dovifat*. Manila, Regal Printing Co.
HEAD, S. W.; MARTIN, L. A. 1956–57. Broadcasting and higher education: a new era. *Journal of broadcasting*, (winter) p. 39–46.
HEGENER, K. C. 1970. *Peterson's guide to postgraduate study in the United States*. Vol. 5: *Mass communications*. Princeton, N.J., Peterson's Guides.
——. (ed.). 1971. [*Peterson's*] *Annual Guide to Graduate Study*. Book 5: *Communication, including Journalism and Speech and Hearing Sciences, . . . 1970 Directory*. Princeton, N.J. (Graphical summary.)
HEW news, 9 September 1970. Washington, D.C., United States Government Department of Health, Education and Welfare, National Institute of Mental Health.
HIEBERT, R. E. 1965. Backgrounds and positions of public relations teachers. *Journalism quarterly*, vol. 42 (summer), p. 470–1.
HIRSCH, K. W. 1970. *The program in broadcasting: an analysis, with recommendations and a suggested integrated program in communication*. Sacramento, Calif., Sacramento State College. (Mimeo.)
HKBC. 1971a. *Newsletter*, no. 1, March 1971. Hong Kong, Communications Department, Hong Kong Baptist College.
——. 1971b. *Newsletter*, no. 2, June 1971. Hong Kong, Communications Department, Hong Kong Baptist College.
HUXHAM, N. 1971. Letter, Evelyn Hone College of Further Education, Lusaka, Zambia, 9 September 1971.
HUYN-DINH-TE. 1970. Letter, Vietnamese National Commission for Unesco, Saigon, 18 February 1970.
IAMCR. 1968. *Association Internationale des Etudes et Recherches sur l'information*. I: *Répertoire européen des organismes de recherche et des chercheurs dans le domaine de l'information*; II: *Répertoire européen des ouvrages publiés depuis 1966 et des recherches en cours concernant l'information*. Lausanne, IAMCR. (Mimeo.)
ICB/International Communications Bulletin, July 1969 and January 1973.
INBEL. 1970. *Les possibilités de formation aux carrières de la communication en Belgique*. Brussels, Service des Stages, Institut Belge d'Information et de Documentation.
INDIA. FILM INSTITUTE. 1970. *Film Institute of India, Poona, prospectus 1970–1971*. New Delhi, Ministry of Information and Broadcasting.
Interstages, no. 54, 15 February 1969. Brussels, Service des Stages, Institut Belge d'Information et de Documentation.
ISAAK, C. 1961. The training and recruiting of journalists in Israel. *Gazette*, vol. 7, p. 123–7.
JAKAB, Z. 1973. Personal communication, March 1973.
JANOWITZ, Morris. 1968. The study of mass communication. In: David L. Sills (ed.), *International encyclopedia of the social sciences*, no. 3, p. 41–55.
JENSEN, J. W.; PORTER, W. E.; CARTER, R. F.; PETERSON, T. 1963. Journalism, communications and the future of the discipline, a symposium. *Journalism quarterly*, vol. 40, no. 4 (autumn), p. 580–93.
JONES, R. L. 1968. Journalism education in the joyful sixties. *Journalism quarterly*, vol. 45, winter, p. 547–9.
KAWANAKA, Y. 1971. Letter, Sophia University, Tokyo, May 1971.

References

Kitross, J. M. 1967. Meaningful research in ETV. In: A. E. Koenig and R. B. Hill (eds.), *The farther vision, educational television today*. Madison, Milwaukee and London, University of Wisconsin Press.

Klapper, J. 1960. *The effects of mass communication*. New York, N.Y., Free Press.

Klimes, V.; Kafel, M. 1967. La ensenanza del periodismo en los países socialistas. *Cuadernos de trabajo, 1*. Pamplona, Ediciones Universidad de Navarra. Reprinted in: *Cuadernos de jornalismo e editoração*, 1, p. 14–25. São Paulo, Escola de Comunicações e Artes, Universidade de São Paulo, September 1970.

Kline, F. G.; Tichenor, P. J. (eds.). 1972. *Current perspectives in mass communication research*. Beverly Hills, Calif. and London, Sage Publications (Sage annual reviews of communication research, 1.)

Kosyk, K. 1971. Letter, Sektion für Publizistik und Kommunikation, Ruhr-Universität Bochum, 26 October 1971.

Krohn, C. 1970. Letter, Trondheim University, Trondheim, Norway, 23 September 1971.

Kuiper, J. B. 1972. Letter, Library of Congress, Washington, D.C., 10 February 1972.

Kuiper, J. B.; Wilson, G.; Tyo, J. 1966. *Information on film studies in American colleges and universities, prepared by the Curriculum Committee of the University Film Producers' Association*. Autumn 1966. (Mimeo.)

Kumar, A. 1970. Letter, Inter-University Board of India and Ceylon, New Delhi, 8 June 1970.

Kupis, T. 1971. Letter enclosed in letter, K. Duchowski, Polish Cultural Institute, London, 5 November 1971.

Labbens, J. 1969. The role of the sociologist and the growth of sociology in Latin America. *International social science journal*, vol. 21, no. 3, p. 428–32.

Larsen, Otto N. 1964. Social effects of mass communication. In: R. E. L. Faris, *Handbook of modern sociology*. Chicago, Ill., Rand McNally.

Lasola, B. 1970. Letter, International Media Center, University of San Carlos, Cebu City, Philippines, 9 July 1970.

La Trobe University. 1970. *Centre for the Study of Educational Communication, La Trobe University, Melbourne*. (Leaflet.)

Lazarsfeld, P. F. 1962. The sociology of empirical social research. *American sociological review*, no. 27, p. 757–67.

——. 1963. Trends in broadcasting research in the United States. Reprinted in: H. Eguchi and H. Ichinohe (eds.), *International studies of broadcasting with special reference to the Japanese studies*, p. 183–99. Tokyo, NHK Radio and Television Culture Research Institute, 1971.

——. 1969. An episode in the history of social research: a memoir. In: Donald Fleming and Bernard Bailyn, *The intellectual migration, Europe and America, 1930–1960*. Cambridge, Mass., Harvard University Press.

Lazarsfeld, P. F.; Thielens, W. jun. 1958. *The academic mind; social scientists in a time of crisis*. Glencoe, Ill., Free Press.

Lent, J. 1972. Letter, University Sains Malaysia, Malaysia, 10 March 1972.

Lim, K. S. 1971. Paper on journalism education and research in Korea read at Journalism/Communication Teachers' Seminar, East-West Center, Honolulu, Hawaii, June 1971.

Lisicka, T. 1973. *Informateur sur les centres de recherches sur la presse de certains pays socialistes*. Kraków, Section de Documentation et d'Information Scientifique, Centre de Recherches sur la Presse ‚Prasa-Ksiazka-Ruch', RSW.

Lodman, M. 1970. Letter, Svenska Handelshögskolan, Helsinki, 30 September 1970.

Lundberg, D.; Nowak, K. 1971. Statement enclosed in letter, F. Olander, Stockholm School of Economics, 23 September 1971.

Lyons, G. M. 1969. *The uneasy partnership: social science and the federal government in the twentieth century*. New York, N.Y., Russell Sage Foundation.

Maclean, M. S. jun.; Danbury, T.; McNally, J. T. 1965. AEJ members and their attitudes to journalism issues. *Journalism quarterly*, vol. 42, winter, p. 98–107.

McQuail, D. 1970. Letter, Department of Sociology and Social Administration, University of Southampton, 6 April 1971.

Maddison, John. 1969. *The film in university teaching, a study*. [Strasbourg], Council of Europe. (Mimeo.)

Mamet, H. H. 1971. Letter, University of Alberta, Edmonton, Alberta, Canada, 20 January 1971.

MARKHAM, James W. (ed.). 1970. *International communication as a field of study: reports and papers from the Wingspread Symposium on education and research on international and comparative communication.* Iowa City, Iowa, International Communications Division, Association for Education in Journalism.
MARKUS, L. 1970. Letter, Institute of Historical Sciences of the Hungarian Academy, Budapest, 7 August 1970.
MARQUES DE MELO, J. 1971. *Comunicação social theoria e pesquisa.* 2nd ed. Petropolis, Brazil.
MARTIN, L. A. 1952. *Brief history of the University Association for Professional Radio Education prepared by Leo A. Martin, November 1952.* (Mimeo.)
MARTIN-JONES, J. 1970. Letter, Interim Council for a National Film and Television Training School, North Sydney, Australia, 22 June 1970.
MERTON, R. K. 1968. *Social theory and social structure.* Rev. and enl. ed., 9th imp. London, Collier-Macmillan.
MILLER, A. 1970. Letter, Schweizerische Zentralstelle für Hochschulwesen, Zürich, 23 June 1970.
MILLS, C. W. 1959. *The sociological imagination.* New York, N.Y., Oxford University Press.
MOELLER, Leslie. 1968. Journalism and the new industrial state. *Journalism quarterly*, vol. 45, autumn, p. 496–508.
MURARI, J. 1969. *Film Institute of India.* Poona, Film Institute of India.
MYRDAL, G. 1970. *Objectivity in social research.* London, Duckworth.
NAFZIGER, R. O. 1969. Official report of the 1969 convention, Association for Education in Journalism. *Journalism quarterly*, vol. 46, no. 4 (winter), p. 872–3.
——. 1970. Letter, University of Wisconsin, Madison, Wis., 5 August 1970.
NAGY, L. 1970. Letter, Eötvös Loránd University, Budapest, 20 July 1970.
NATESH, A. M. 1972. *Zambia, rural broadcasting (literacy), December 1969–December 1972.* Paris, Unesco.
NIVEN, Harold. 1959. Fourth annual survey of colleges and universities offering course work in radio and television, 1958–59. *Journal of broadcasting*, no. 3 (autumn), p. 353–7.
——. 1961. The development of broadcasting education in institutions of higher education. *Journal of broadcasting*, summer, p. 241–50.
——. 1972. *Broadcast education 1972, thirteenth report: radio-television programs in American colleges and universities 1971–1972.* Washington, D.C., National Association of Broadcasters.
NIXON, R. B. 1970. *Education for journalism in Latin America.* New York, N.Y., Council on Higher Education in the American Republics (CHEAR).
NOELLE-NEUMANN, E. 1971. Letter, Institut für Publizistik, Johannes Gutenberg-Universität Mainz, 21 September 1971.
NOELLE-NEUMANN, E.; HAUSER, J. D. 1970. *Dokumentation 1970: Publizistik-Zeitungswissenschaft—communication research-journalism.* Herausgegeben von der Deutschen Gesellschaft für Publizistik und Zeitungswissenschaft. Konstanz, Druckerei und Verlagsanstalt Konstanz Univ.
NOELLE-NEUMANN, E.; SCHULZ, W. (eds.). 1971. *Publizistik.* Frankfurt am Main, Fischer Taschenbuch Verlag. (Das Fischer Lexikon.)
NORDENSTRENG, K. 1968. Communication research in the United States, a critical perspective. *Gazette*, vol. 14, no. 3, p. 207–16.
——. 1971. Broadcasting research in Scandinavian countries. In: H. Eguchi and H. Ichinohe (eds.), *International studies of broadcasting with special reference to the Japanese studies*, p. 245–65, Tokyo, NHK Radio and Television Culture Research Institute, 1971.
——. 1971. Letter, Institute of Journalism and Mass Communications, Tampere University, Finland, September 1971.
NOWAK, K. 1968. *Mass communication research in Sweden.* Stockholm, Sveriges Radio Audience Research Department.
NSK. 1970. *The Japanese press 1970.* Tokyo, Nihon Shinbun Kyokai.
O'BRIEN, J. E. 1970, 1971. Letters, Communication Arts Department, Loyola College, Montreal, Canada, 18 December 1970 and 6 October 1971.
OEY, H. L. 1971. *Indonesian government and press during guided democracy.* Zug (Switzerland), International Documentation Centre (IDC). (Hull monograph series.)
ORLIK, P. B. 1970. Letters, Speech Department, Central Michigan University, Mount Pleasant, Mich., 26 May and 3 June 1970.

References

PAUPIE, K. 1970. Letter, Institut für Publizistik der Universität Wien, 17 September 1970.
PETERSON, P. V. 1970a. *Journalism education-1970: a list of all known college journalism courses and programs*. Princeton, N.J., Ohio State University, The Newspaper Fund.
——. 1970b. Journalism majors offered by 212 colleges survey shows, *Journalism quarterly*, vol. 47, no. 1 (spring), p. 160–2.
PETERSON, T. 1960. The changing role of journalism schools, *Journalism quarterly*, vol. 37, autumn, p. 579–85.
PETERSON, T.; PORTER, W. E.; CARTER, R. F.; JENSEN, J. W. 1963. Journalism, communications and the future of the discipline, a symposium. *Journalism quarterly*, vol. 40, no. 4 autumn, p. 580–93.
QUARMYNE, A. T.; BEBEY, F. 1967. *Training for radio and television in Africa*. Paris, Unesco. (Mimeo.)
RAGSDALE, W. 1970. *Draft proposal for a master's degree program in mass communications at AUC* [American University, Cairo]. (Mimeo.)
RAI. 1971. Letter, Radiotelevisione Italiana RAI, Rome, 27 September 1971.
RICHSTAD, J. A. 1971. Letter, East West Communication Institute, East-West Center, Honolulu, Hawaii, 27 December 1971.
ROEVER, J. E. 1970. Letter; Speech Association of America, New York, N.Y., 19 June 1970.
ROOY, M. 1970. Letter, Instituut voor Perswetenschap, University of Amsterdam, 13 July 1970.
SCHRAMM, W. 1957. Twenty years of journalism research. *Public opinion quarterly*, vol. 21, spring, p. 91–107.
——. 1959. Comment on B. Berelson, 'The state of communication research'. *Public opinion quarterly*, vol. 23, spring, p. 6–17. Reprinted in L. A. Dexter and D. White (eds.), *People society and mass communications*. New York, N.Y., Free Press of Glencoe.
——. 1962. Mass communication. *Annual Review of Psychology*, vol. 13, p. 251–84.
——. 1963. *Report of the mass communication study team sponsored by the Ford Foundation*. Faridabad, Ministry of Information and Broadcasting, Government of India.
SELBY, S. A. 1970. Letter, Department of Communication Arts, University of Windsor, Windsor, Ontario, 23 September 1970.
SHANMUGAM, A. V. 1971. Communication research in Asia: the Indian situation. *Philippine journal of communication studies*, vol. 1, no. 1 (September), p. 97–106.
SHAW, D. L. (ed.). 1969, 1970. Journalism abstracts, M. A., M. S. and Ph. D. theses in journalism and mass communication published by the Association for Education in Journalism, vol. 7, 1969 and vol. 8, 1970.
SIDDIQUI, A. 1969. *Information Services Academy, Rawalpindi, Pakistan*. (Mimeo.)
SIEBERT, F. 1956. Journalism. *Higher education in the United States*. Washington, D.C., American Council on Education.
SINGER, B. 1970. Letter, Sociology Department, University of Western Ontario, London, Ontario, 29 July 1970.
SINGH, P. P. 1971. Journalism education in India. In: East-West Center, *Communication/journalism education in Asia, background and status in seven Asian areas; background papers prepared for Communication/journalism Teachers' Seminar, June 13–26, 1971*. Honolulu, East-West Center, East West Communication Institute. (Mimeo.)
SLOAN, T. 1969. Evidence, Senate of Canada, *Proceedings of the Special Senate Committee on Mass Media*, no. 3, 11 December 1969, p. 70–1.
SMYTHE, D. W. 1970. Letter, University of Saskatchewan (Regina Campus), Regina, Saskatchewan, Canada, 17 July 1970.
SNYDER, P. B. 1971. Letter, American University of Beirut, 4 January 1971.
SOIFER, J. 1970. Letter, Centro Nacional de Recursos Humanos, Instituto de Planejamento Economico e Social (IPEA), Rio de Janeiro, 14 July 1970.
SPARKS, K. R. 1971. *A bibliography of doctoral dissertations in television and radio*. 3rd ed. New York, N.Y., School of Journalism, Syracuse University.
STAPPERS, J. G. 1971. Letter, Institut voor Massacommunicatie, Katholicke Universiteit, Nijmegen, Netherlands, 20 August 1971.
STEHR, N.; LARSEN, L. E. 1972. The rise and decline of areas of specialization. *The American sociologist*, vol. 7, no. 3 (August), p. 5–6.
SUSANTO, A. S. 1971. *Communication problems and journalism teaching purpose in Indonesia*. Paper given at Journalism/Communication Teachers' Seminar, East-West Center, Honolulu, Hawaii, June 1971. (Mimeo.)

References

SVERIGES RADIO. 1970. *A presentation of the Audience and Programme Research Department of the Swedish Broadcasting Corporation*. Stockholm, Sveriges Radio.

SZELÉNYI, I. 1970. Letter, Institute of Sociology, Hungarian Academy of Sciences, 27 July 1970.

TANNENBAUM, P.; GREENBERG. B. H. 1968. Mass communication. *Annual Review of Psychology*, vol. 19, p. 351–86.

TELECOMMISSION. 1971. *Multidisciplinary manpower study, December 1970*. Ottawa, Department of Communications. (Study 7e.)

TONO, H. T. 1970. Letter, Universidad del Valle, Cali, Colombia, 22 July 1970.

TORII, H. 1971. Letter, Takushoku University, Tokyo, 3 March 1971.

TOWNSVILLE. 1970. *The education and training of journalists, being the report of the proceedings of a seminar . . . held at the University College of Townsville 11–12 May 1968*. Townsville, James Cook University of Northern Queensland.

TUNSTALL, J. 1970. *Media sociology, a reader*. London, Constable.

TVRC. 1966. *Problems of television research, a progress report of the Television Research Committee*. Leicester, Leicester University Press.

UCHIKAWA, Y. 1971a. Letter, Institute of Journalism, Tokyo University, 2 February 1971.

——. 1971b. Study and education on mass communication in Japan. Unpublished lecture delivered to Institut für Publizistik, Freie Universität, Berlin, 18 January 1971.

UNDERWOOD, P. S. 1970. Letter, School of Journalism, Ohio State University, Columbus, Ohio, 9 September 1970.

UNESCO. 1958. *The training of journalists: a world-wide survey on the training of personnel for the mass media*. Paris, Unesco.

——. 1962. *Developing information media in Africa, press, radio, film, television*. Paris, Unesco. (Reports and papers on mass communication, 37.)

——. 1965. *Professional training for mass communication*. Paris, Unesco. (Reports and papers on mass communication, 45.)

——. 1970a. *Mass media in society: the need of research*. Paris, Unesco. (Reports and papers on mass communication, 59.)

——. 1970b. *Schools of journalism and communications research centres, January 1970*. Paris, Unesco. (COM/WS/134.) (Mimeo.)

——. 1972. *Intergovernmental conference on cultural policies in Europe, Helsinki, 19–28 June 1972, final report*. Paris, Unesco.

UNITED STATES. SURGEON-GENERAL'S ADVISORY COMMITTEE ON TELEVISION AND SOCIAL BEHAVIOR. 1972. *Television and growing up: the impact of television violence; report to the Surgeon-General United States Public Health Service from the Surgeon-General's Advisory Committee on Television and Social Behavior*. Rockville, Md, National Institute of Mental Health.

UNIVERSITY OF LAGOS. 1970. *Institute of Mass Communication, University of Lagos*. 30 June 1970. (Mimeo.)

——. 1973. *A preliminary survey of communication training in Africa*. Institute of Mass Communication, University of Lagos. (Mimeo.)

UNIVERSITY OF MELBOURNE. 1969. Press release, Vice-Chancellor, Melbourne University, 4 October 1969.

UNIVERSITY OF OREGON. 1970. *Report and recommendations of the ad hoc committee to review broadcasting at the University of Oregon, April 21, 1970*. (Mimeo.)

UNIVERSITY OF THE PHILIPPINES. 1971. Manila, Institute of Mass Communication, University of the Philippines.

VAN PARIJS, G. 1969. La situation actuelle de l'étude des communications de masse en Belgique. *Techniques de diffusion collective*, no. 16, p. 38–48.

VAN WINKLE, H. 1970. Letter, School of Journalism, Kent State University, Kent, Ohio, 30 November 1970.

VIDAL-BENEYTO, J. 1971. Letter, Ann Arbor, Mich., 21 October 1971.

VREG, F. 1970. Letter, Faculty of Sociology, Political Sciences and Journalism, University of Ljubljana, 1 September 1970.

WALLACE, W. H. 1971. Letter, Department of Radio, Television and Motion Pictures, University of North Carolina, Chapel Hill, N.C., 21 January 1971.

WALSH, E. A. 1968. *Criteria for the selection of journalism faculty in the United States*. Paper presented to annual meeting of International Association for Mass Communication Research, Navarra, Pamplona. April 1968. (Mimeo.)

References

WARD, W. B. 1969. *Communication and the agricultural universities in India, rationale and guidelines for establishing a center of strength in the field of agricultural communication.* New Delhi, Ford Foundation. (Mimeo.)

WEBB, J. W. 1970. Letter, University of Minnesota, Minneapolis, Minn., 4 September 1970.

WESTERN, J. 1970. Letter, Government Department, University of Queensland, St Lucia, Queensland, Australia, 5 June 1970.

WHANNEL, P. 1969. Film education and film culture. *Screen*, vol. 10, no. 3 (May/June).

WHITE, D. M. 1964. Mass communication research: a view in perspective. In L. A. Dexter and D. White (eds.), *People, society and mass communications*. New York, N.Y. Free Press of Glencoe.

WIEBE, G. 1970. Letter, School of Public Communications, Boston University, 21 October 1970.

WILD, J. L. 1970. Letter, Department of Journalism, University of Western Ontario, London, Ontario, Canada, 11 June 1970.

WILLINGS, J.; CLEE, D.; SCHWASS, R.; KAHNERT, F.; SEVERN, G.; RAMAKRISHNA, V. 1969. *India: television development and training*. 1st ed. Paris, Unesco. (Mimeo.)

WOODLIFF, C. 1971. Letter, Western Michigan University, Kalamazoo, Mich., 23 September 1971.

YLEISRADIO. 1967. *Policy of Yleisradio the Finnish broadcasting company, tasks and aims of broadcasting by the working group.* Helsinki, Yleisradio.

YOUNG, C. 1971. Letter, National Film School, London, 17 December 1971.